3-D art/techné

THE NEW MEXICO
ARTIST SERIES

ALINE BRANDAUER
CURATOR

JON CARVER
ARTIST PROFILES

Fresco Fine Art Publications, llc
9812 Nimitz NE, Suite 100
Albuquerque, NM 87111
505 822-0062
fresco@newmexico.com

Aline Brandauer, Curator, Essay
Jon Carver, Artist Profiles
Nancy Stem, Design

Color by Mankus Studios, Santa Fe

Printed by Areagroup Media
Milan, Italy

ISBN 0-9741023-5-0
Library of Congress Control Number: 2004113100

THREE-DIMENSIONAL ART IN NEW MEXICO

THE ARTISTS

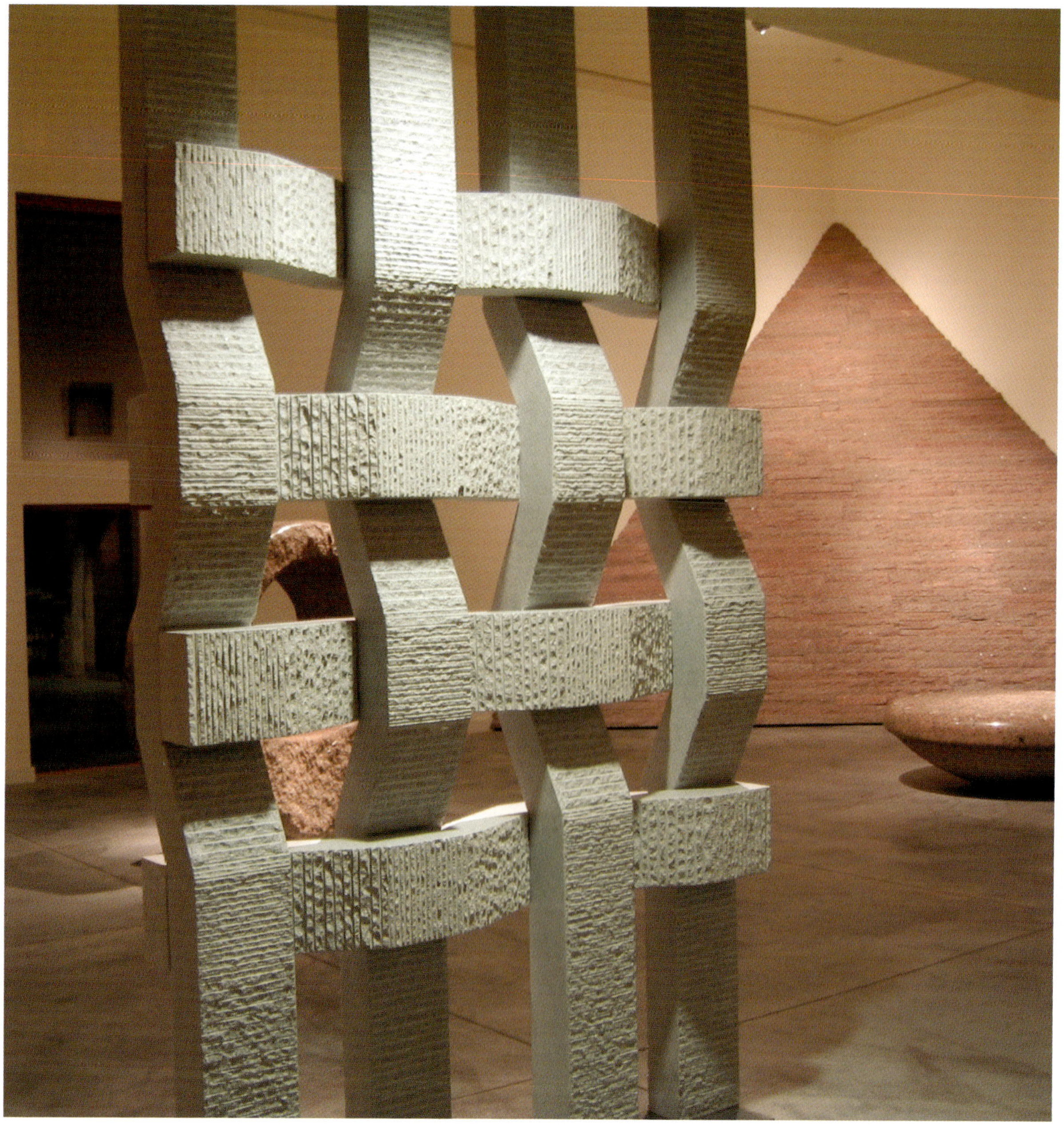

JESÚS MOROLES
Granite Weaving
Gray granite
108 x 60 x 10 Inches
Courtesy LewAllen Contemporary

TRANSMUTATION, CONCATENATION AND BODIES: COMMENTS ON THREE-DIMENSIONAL ART IN NEW MEXICO

In 1910, Wilhelm Worringer wrote a book about sculpture called *Abstraction and Empathy: A Contribution to the Psychology of Style*. His argument was based in the nascent branch of psychology known as gestalt psychology although it drew heavily from Kant. The gist of his rather longwinded argument was that when people look at three-dimensional objects they first respond to them in terms of their whole body; is it bigger or smaller than I am; does it look like me; does it threaten me? In other words there is a sort of naturalistic response to the object. This was the Empathy in his scheme. Abstraction, on the other hand, is another sort of instinctive response designed to alienate the viewer from the visual and sensual cacophony of the world. By operating in a different visual register, art, especially three-dimensional art, would inspire a response that was unrelated to "natural" experience and thus gives rise to a transcendental, or at least other worldly, experience. For Worringer, this strategy was associated with what was then called primitive art. Primitive art included most art from non-European cultures, but also much medieval art and folk art. His thesis was to defend and explain the abstract as a powerful, necessary and, ultimately, transcendent form. As people attempted to understand their world and stand in awe of it, their response was not the mastery of naturalism but the isolation of abstraction. His book was a smash hit and was cited and recited for the next thirty years as an explanation for and defense of modern art. This argument was reformulated during the 1960s in the positively vituperative discussions of minimalist versus modernist painting and sculpture. Despite the radically different perspectives on the role and worth of art espoused by different theorists, the field was clearly delineated as phenomenological. The minimalist aesthetic was devoted to experiencing real objects in actual time and space whereas the modernist perspective maintained that true art invoked transcendental responses from the viewer. Much of the initial minimalist art was deliberately anti-aesthetic. The sculpture resisted visual resolution from a single viewpoint, the performances were often painfully dull and long. Whereas defenders and practitioners of modernism were concerned with the 'aha!' of instantaneous apprehension, those devotees of minimalism preferred the immersion in the quotidian. Eventually, this rift provided a fertile space for artists to think about looking for art in everyday things and places, but being willing to give in to the glamour of the visual experience.

In contemporary New Mexico, these two streams play out and complicate themselves in a different way. On the one hand, there are those who take materials in their simplest state and transmute them into pure objects, narrative schemes or series. These are artists like blacksmith Tom Joyce, glassworker Stacey Neff, wire weaver Tracy Krumm, metalsmiths Tom Waldron and Amy Westphal, and stoneworkers Jesús Moroles and Doug Gray. The work of the work of art is done by pushing the formal capacities of the material.

Tom Joyce has the ability to make the inorganic seem organic. In the work, *Untitled*, cast iron resembles sea creatures or seed pods. It is not, however, like a replication of an animal or a plant,

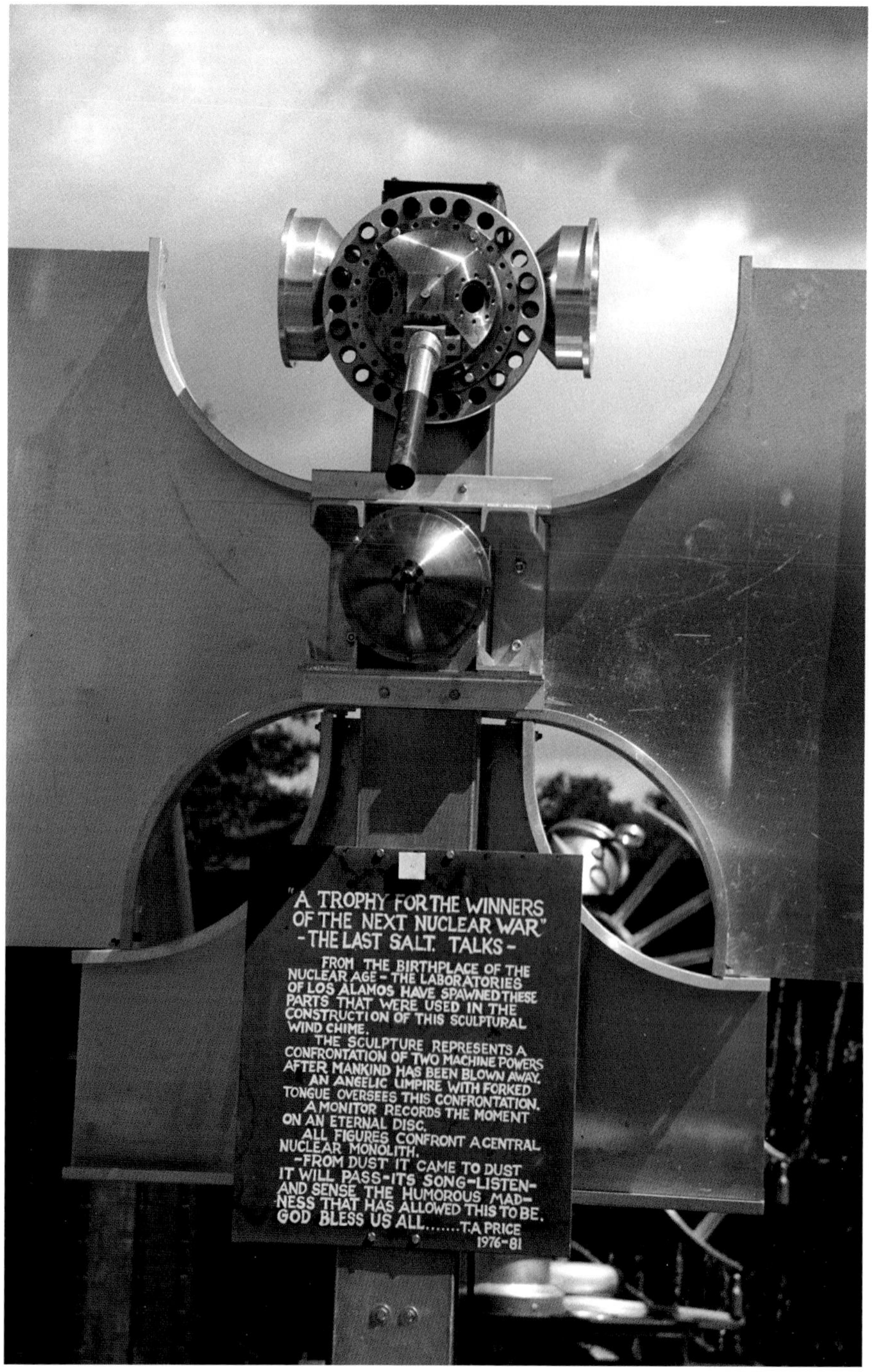

TONY PRICE
Prize of the Last Salt Talks
©Lisa Law

but an evocation of texture and movement that leads us to believe in its life. Joyce can take iron shaped like old-fashioned bread paddles and refashion them into a gate: utilitarian yet elegant, lifted from the mundane and returned to it. Blacksmithing is an alchemical art. Joyce has maintained his fascination with fire as the purifier and transformer. Many of his works retain the signs of forging even as they are perfectly transmuted.

In glass, Stacey Neff deals with many of the same issues. Emphasizing the fluidity of molten glass, Neff creates fields of biomorphic forms. Biomythology is her term for the moments of parthenogenesis that she evokes in her drooping globular objects, objects that are often supported by seemingly impossible stalks. Tom Waldron has the ability to activate space with his volumetric metal sculptures that makes one love the idea of corners pushing back. Amy Westphal, on the other hand, eschews closed volumes by inventing and invoking the narratives of women encased in her over-sized hoop skirt. Feminist narratives are also an integral part of Tracy Krumm's work. By crocheting with wire and found industrial materials, Krumm returns to women's work with a post-modern twist.

Stone becomes sinuous, defying its crystalline tendencies in the monumental work of Jesús Moroles. Moroles' work harks back to the pre-Columbian—to Mayan ball courts and Aztec temples. Granite is woven into open walls, leading the viewer to question its weight and function. Doug Gray also evokes our association with the weight of stone and its apparent solidity. By carefully constructing nests and webs of solid rock, he draws us into a kind of material faith—the piece can be solid yet make us sense the precarious.

On the other hand, there is a large group of artists who use materials in a far different way. Gail and Zachariah Rieke, the late Tony Price, Erika Wanenmacher, Colette Hosmer, Franky Kong, Andrea Senutovitch, Mary Bennett and James Westwater all use objects, found or made, with a respect for the objects' own history. In the case of Tony Price and Erika Wanenmacher, the detritus of nuclear experimentation and production in New Mexico is transmuted. In Wanenmacher's *Trinity Site Flea Market*, that transmutation is accomplished by magic. In Price's work, it is achieved through reference to Native American rituals and forms. (*Prize of the Last Salt Talks*). By exposing and recomposing the objects (which often do still have a literal charge) and the sites, these two artists attempt to heal what they perceive as the collective psychic wound of the atomic age. Colette Hosmer uses animals and resin to create still life sculptures and installations. In *Pipeline* minnows are frozen into place as water in the corner rather than being fish in the water. Hosmer's witty renderings include twenty-first century *vanitas* constructions. The artist's commentaries center on the flow of life and consumerism in such works as *Neon Globes with Bullfrog, White Rat, Minnows, Bobcat Skull & Snake*.

Several of these artists use found objects and juxtapose them with each other to create narratives that are somewhat real, somewhat fictional, yet always possible. Gail and Zachariah Rieke have

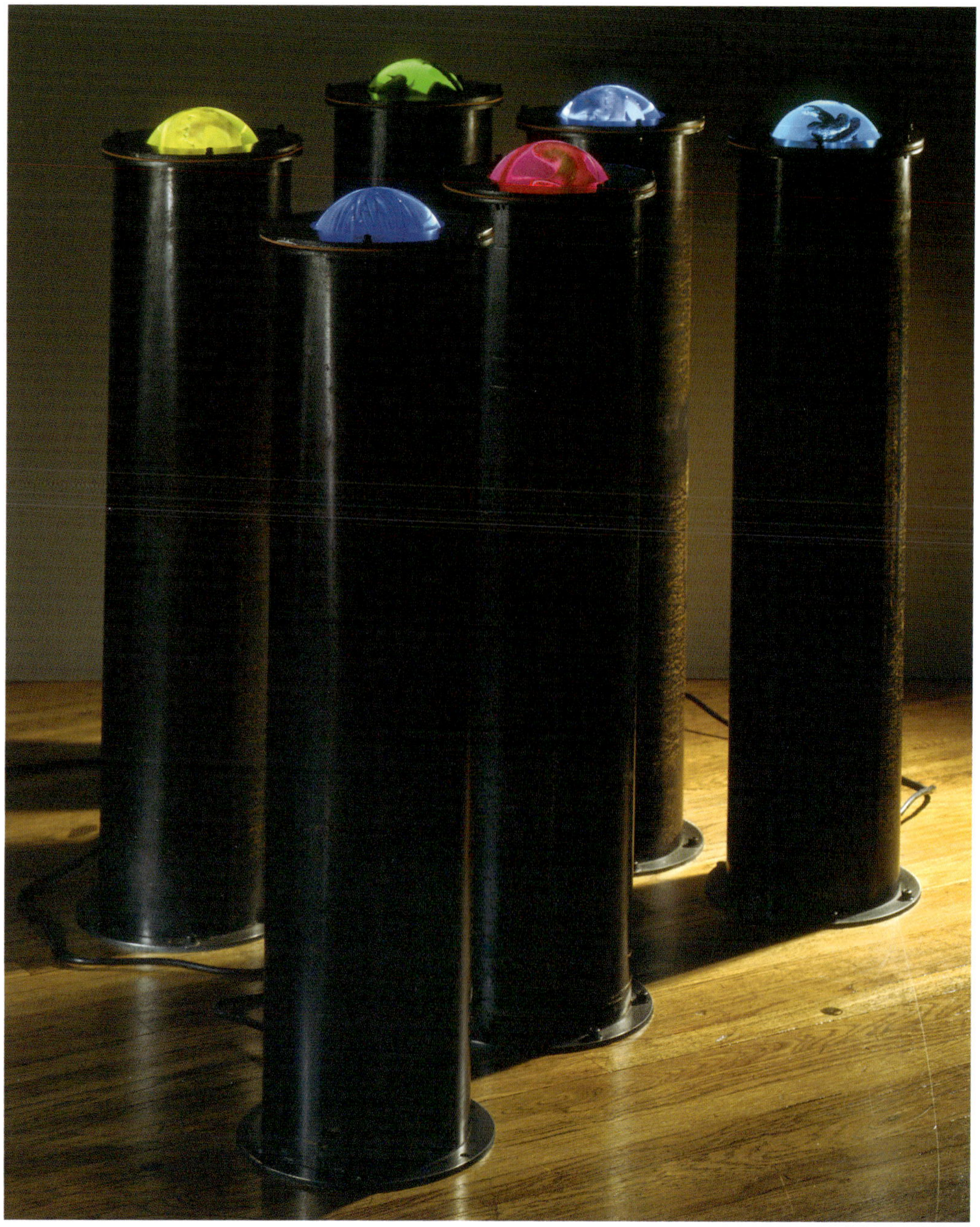

COLETTE HOSMER
Installation
Neon Globes with Bullfrog, White Rat,
Minnows, Bobcat Skull, & Snake
Glass and steel
39 x 10.5 Inches

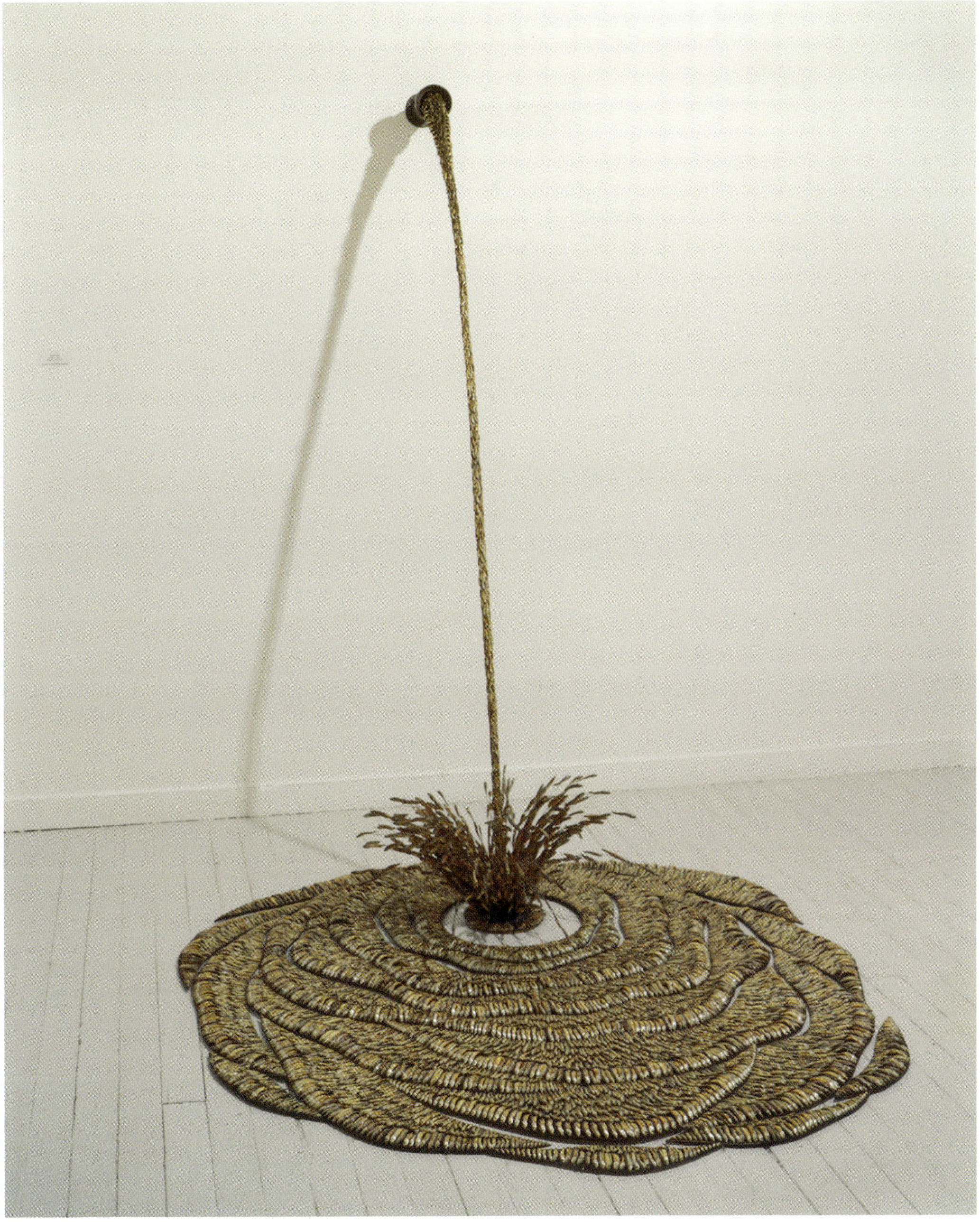

COLETTE HOSMER
Pipeline
Dried minnows and steel
9 x 6 Feet

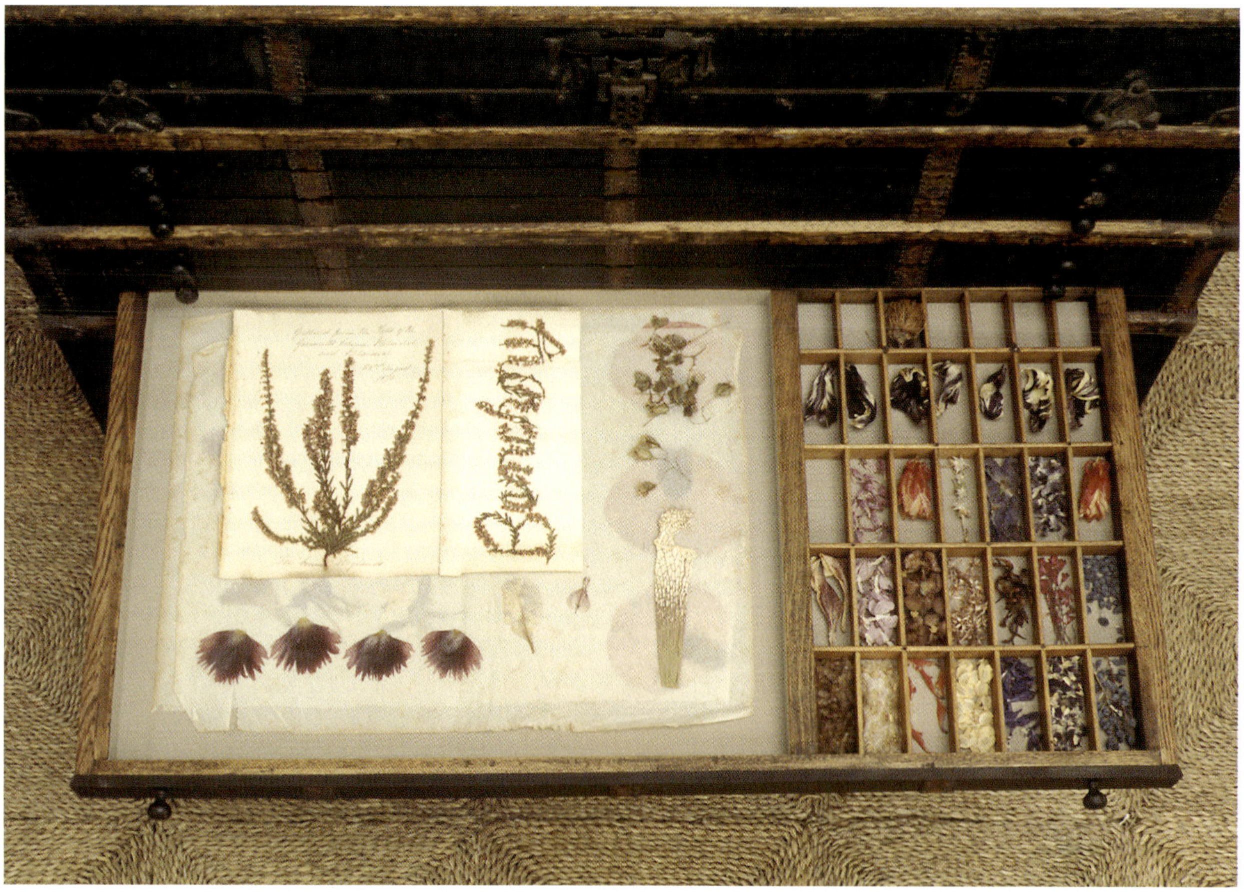

GAIL RIEKE
Steamer Trunk, 1995
Mixed media assemblage
Box: 29 x 38 x 23 inches

created a series of boxes over thirty years that combine found objects to create open-ended stories. In *Steamer Trunk, 1995,* a Victorian woman's diary provided the impetus to create a trunk full of treasures that allows the viewer to take a voyage with her. Andrea Senutovitch uses old objects and reconfigures them with a Surrealist touch, often using fetishism that reminds one more of Hans Bellmer than Joseph Cornell or Marcel Jean. Her special touch comes from the use of things that have a very close connection to the body, but are often mechanical. Horse teeth are suspended from a nineteenth-century IV stand. This grisly projection of what it feels like to have liquid of uncertain cleanliness dripped directly into your body from this crude stand makes you want to grit your teeth—and sense the feel of the horse teeth extracted equally crudely from the beasts' mouths. This ineluctable affect is what makes the piece work. Senutovitch has a perfect feel for the Surrealist projection of nostalgia and repression embedded in the body.

Mary Bennett has been working in another way with found objects. Taking books whose life as such has ended, Bennett has made them into delectable objects. They expose the aesthetic pleasure in the physicality of books but, like Hosmer's work, there is always a message about the frailty of mediums of knowledge.

In *Aunt Mackey's Seduction Omelet*, Madelin Coit touches on frailty too—the frailty of remembered experience mitigated through words. She tells the story of Mackey and her eggs. The first part is about definitions of eggs—eggs 'out there.' The last three parts are of the eggs enchanting Mackey as a child, then Mackey using the eggs to seduce. Coit flirts with us as well as with Surrealism in her invitation to read and recollect.

A hipper sentiment towards things informs Franky Kong's art. Kong calls himself a Conceptual Opportunist. Going fifty years beyond the situationists, Kong intervenes in everyday life with works such as *A Little Bit of Fire is Good for the Soul* in which images of his contorted face are put on matchheads. In another work, *History of Art*, the artist creates a post-conceptual take-off of Yves Klein's money exchanges and variable painting prices by not destroying the cash-register paper and pencil. Westwater, like Kong is a mind-tripper. Through altering found objects, be they paintings or "made" assemblages, the artist can quickly turn one's thoughts to post-structuralism through his ability to interweave kitsch, Deleuze and neo-pseudo-geometric painting. When one feels so caught in the cleverness of the cycle is when one gets it: what does terminally, endlessly intellectually cute imply? Is there no way out?

Tim Jag and James Westwater play with symbols and things with a post-modern pop sensibility. Jag's palm fronds remind one of nothing so much as *Beach Blanket Bingo*. Plastic and neon work together to make us think that we're in a lounge from the 1960s, but the simulacrum is too cute. The scene succeeds in seducing us so that we cannot help but project warmth and "realism" into the scene. Westwater's ubiquitous pink lozenges are literal ciphers, open signifiers that can and do hold any

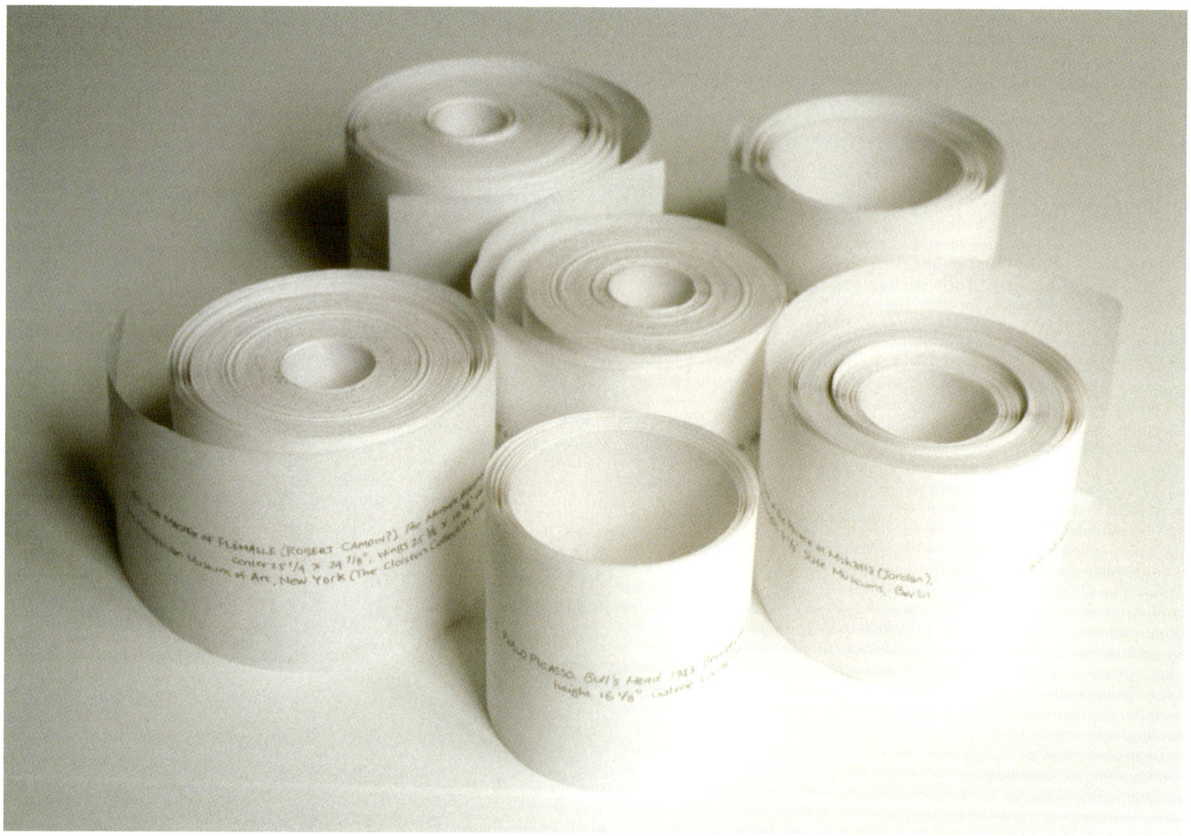

FRANKY KONG
History of Art, 2001
Pencil on cash register paper
Variable dimensions

meaning we want while they function as the artist's signature. Westwater knows that desire will fill the space with an endless assortment of meanings, so he picks the least likely receptacle for our semantic meanderings.

The human body, lyrical yet with its inscription into fields of power, informs yet another group of three-dimensional art in New Mexico. Worringer claimed that naturalistic sculpture of the human figure was the embodiment of the empathetic response. Here, close to a century later, sculpture of the human figure holds empathetic responses across the spectrum. Some of this work is designed to comfort the viewer with its depiction of charming scenes from everyday life; children playing, women whispering together and so on. Appealing to many who are not usually fond of art, it recalls the painted genre scenes of earlier centuries. Other artists use realistic or slightly abstracted bodily forms for different reasons. Malcolm Alexander's nudes recall the torsion and voluptuousness of an Aristide Maillol. These pieces turn from us in a way that makes us feel them as solid and forever out of reach. Shirley Klinghoffer has turned away from the precise frozen beauty of her earlier nudes toward commentary by repetition and the literal depiction of our guts and brains. She addresses the roles that female anatomy plays in its placement in society and the occasional auto-betrayal that happens in grave illnesses like cancer. Recent research by cognitive psychologists has revealed that the brain reacts to posture and gesture at least as strongly as it does to facial reactions. This might lead one to conclude that Empathy as a simple aesthetic category goes beyond mere delectation to a kind of hardwiring that is almost impossible to avoid. Worringer may have known intuitively what many have decried; that a viewer will be tied to a limited set of responses by the overwhelming cognitive reaction to particular human postures. This necessary reduction of possible affective responses was perceived by Worringer (and has been implied by many others) to be counterproductive. The full range of human experience must, he and they claimed, go beyond the emotional reactions to Abstraction or to those responses that were (often interchangeably) described as intellectual or spiritual. Klinghoffer, like other so-called Realist artists in two or three dimensions, plays on our expectations of comfort from the figure to create unease.

There are also spaces for those bodies to inhabit, with or without ease. Sydney Hamburger and Sabra Moore create structures and boats that one can't really live in, but that imply a past and a refuge. Hamburger's sculptures combine sacred objects with which to focus one's energy—a created safe haven in the mind with frames of steel or wood where one might actually go to remove oneself from the hurly-burly of the contemporary world. Moore, who has written books and stitched quilts as narrative art for years, gives us a boat made of materials that are destroyed in water and loosely stitched. They will carry our histories and expectations down the rivers of life, but they will only carry bodies in our minds.

Webs of steel and wood map out location in Linda Fleming's sculpture. Like wedges and globes of alternative worlds, these structures imply that the map precedes the territory. Similar to Westwater's

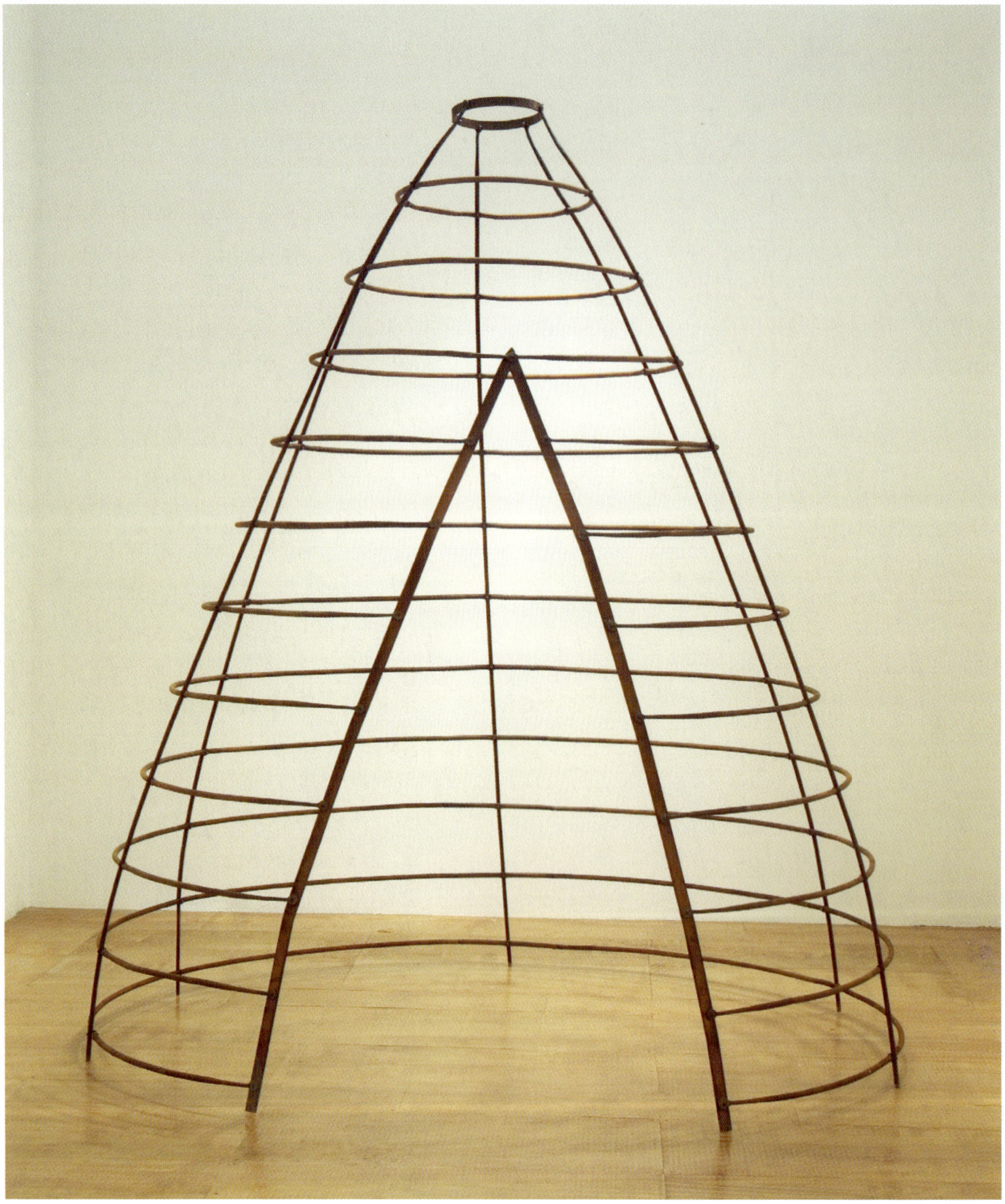

AMY WESTPHAL
Hoop Skirt
Steel with rust patina
11 x 9.5 Feet

enigmatic pink lozenges, Fleming's empty spaces can receive many desires and interpretations. Her references to the natural world point to another shared trait among three-dimensional artists; evocation of patterns found or at least played off of in nature. Barbara Zusman's tightly wound forms often allude to female anatomy, but echo shells and plants. Stacey Neff's biomythology opens up the field of meaning found in natural forms. The very term she uses implies that there is what the Buddhists call "co-arising" in the development of the physical world and our impulse to make meaning of it. There is, in other words, no escape from narrative. Many theorists believe that the inability to escape from language and extrinsic meaning is a defining condition of post-modernism. What this point of view does, however, is not to determine what works of cultural production embrace the narrative, but rather to reshuffle the way in which we look at visual culture throughout time.

Amy Westphal's gigantic steel hoop skirt is explicitly about feminist narratives. Women were expected to wear these steel frames for fashion despite their inconvenience. Westphal, however, makes a massive steel sculpture of this form, parodying both the macho image of welded sculpture and the mid-century icon, Rosie the Riveter.

Three-dimensional art in New Mexico today crosses many boundaries and tendencies. Much art is still traditional sculpture—figurative or modernist—in well-known media. Some involves other sorts of materials like clay, glass or fiber that are often still classified as "craft" despite the sophistication of the product. Others function clearly in the mainstream of international post-modern trends: they engage in the same visual language that one sees in the art market the world over. A startling number use found or recycled objects to remind us to walk gently on the planet as well as to remember that histories are constantly generating and regenerating. Wilhelm Worringer claimed that the downfall of Empathy in art was hubris. Faith in the perfection of man, and in his ability to 'know' entirely through his intellect and sensory input, narrows his aesthetic world to variants of imitation. The opposite weakness, that of Abstraction, was to become dualistic and doctrinaire. Worringer believed that these two tendencies played themselves out throughout the history of art. The *techné* of artists in New Mexico resides not just in their skills, but in their ability to move fluidly between these fields of Empathy and Abstraction.

Aline Brandauer

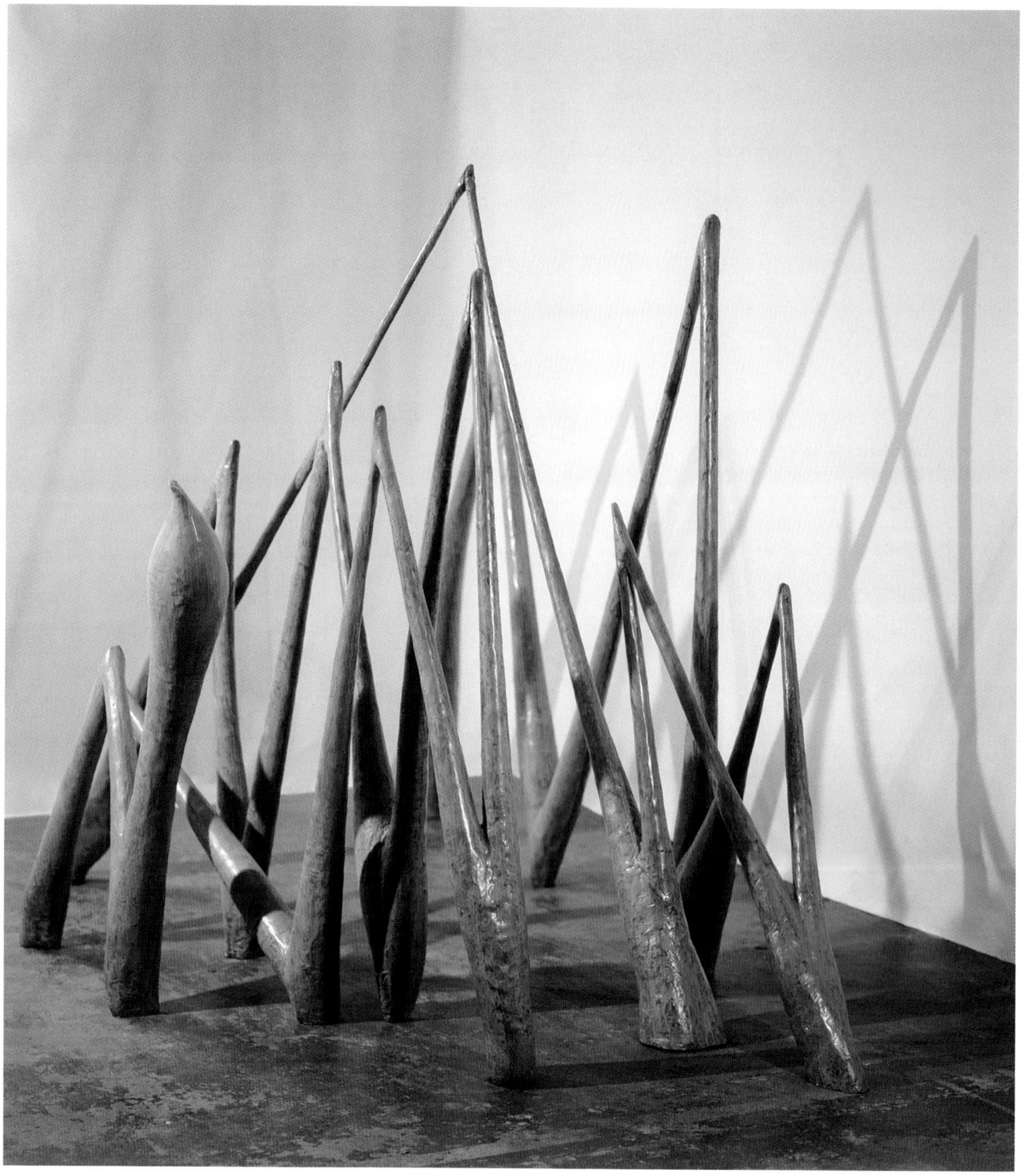

STACEY NEFF
Zig Zag, 2004
Blown glass, mixed media, fiberglass
6 x 11.5 x 7 Feet

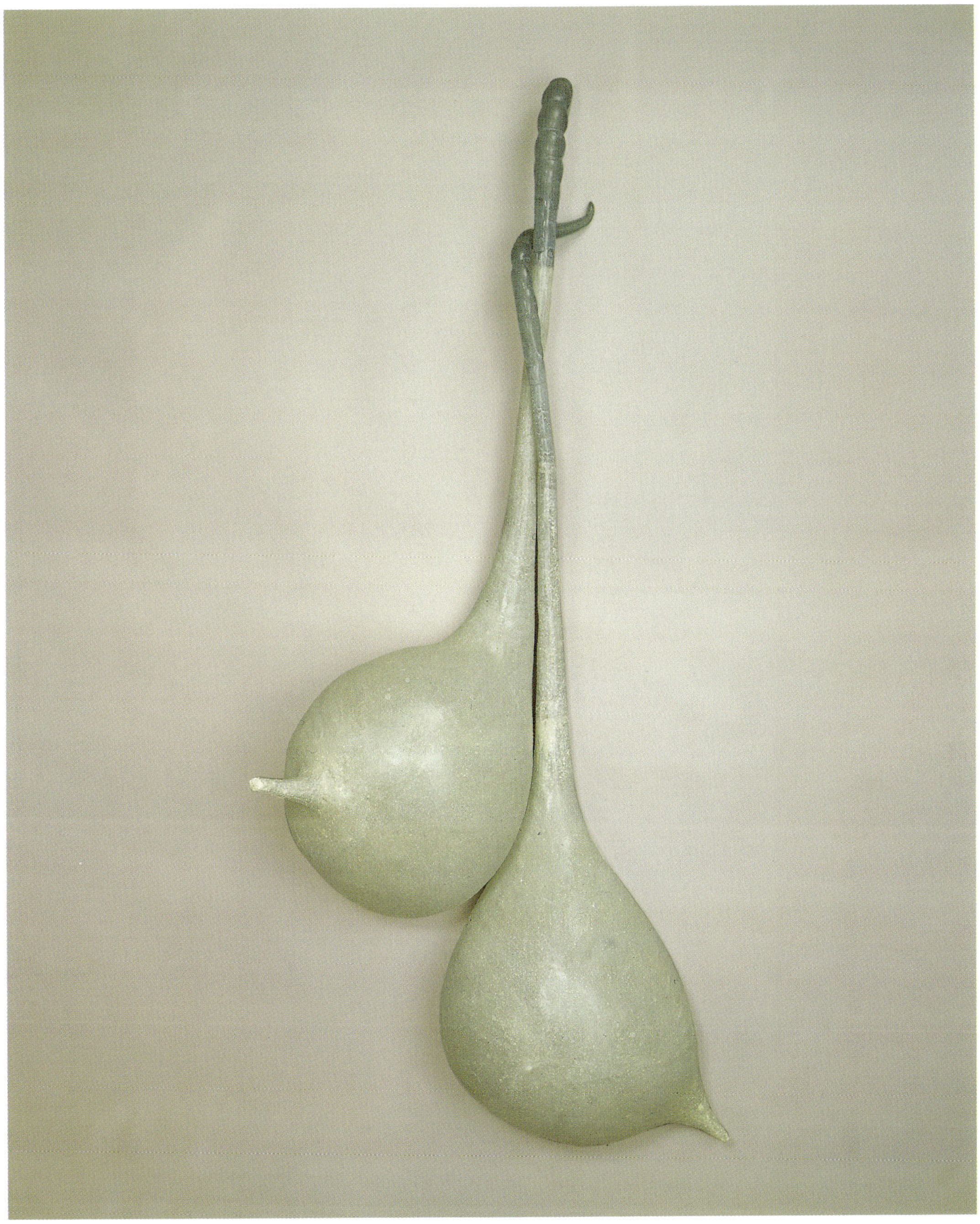

STACEY NEFF
Moon Pods, 2002
Blown glass, pigment, mixed media, steel
61 x 26 x 18 Inches

TOM JOYCE

At age fourteen he began working summers in a letterpress printing shop in El Rito, New Mexico. The printer also had a blacksmith shop set up in back to repair broken press parts and to forge other practical things for the village farmers. By 16, Joyce felt that forging iron, rather than printing, would be his life's work, so he left high school to begin applying himself full-time to learning more about blacksmithing.

Printing and forging—books and fire have always been in close proximity for Joyce. His work with books—titled after printer's terms—always involves systems of pressure and burning. Burning references vulnerability to loss and the fragility of many information storage systems. In ***Bridge***, charred volumes are suspended in place only by the weight of massive wood beams. Text is itself a compression, forcing everyday infinities into words on a page, blips of text on a screen, or zeros and ones on a disc. ***Quoin*** is a wedging system used to "lock up" the words once they're arranged on the press platen. Joyce is interested in the idea that right and wrong are not inherent in any technology, but rather hinge on how practices and beliefs are applied. Here he explores issues of re-pression and re-printing as they pertain to ideas of informational loss and preservation.

Through his bookworm love of learning, he has acquired a formidable knowledge of the world history of metalwork. From his easy disposition, his spellbinding forge and his imaginative intellect flows a seemingly endless array of transcendent forms.

His consummately conceived ***Skewed Vesicas***, made in response to the tragedy of September 11, 2001, are exemplary. These elegant objects are cast from an iron alloy Joyce composed himself, using ash from the World Trade Center site, healing earth from the Santuario de Chimayó, and sand from a Tibetan mandala made as a prayer for peace. Each, heavy to hold, memorial encases a beautiful concept of interiority. By removing each piece from the mold while the metal is still red hot, the sculpture chills on the surface and as a result, shrinks on the inside to open up a geode-like space in the center. Over time, water migrating through the alloy will condense within, filling each piece with tears of life sustaining liquid.

Joyce's commitment to the global and local community takes many directions. He conceived a lectern at the yet-to-be-realized United Nations World Center in San Francisco from pieces of dismantled nuclear weapons, gifted to the project from the United States and Russia. He constructed the gates for the Museum of Albuquerque's Sculpture Garden from steel and metal objects found along the banks of the Rio Grande. By implementing a mentoring program for "at-risk teens" for the duration of the project, Joyce has inspired more than a few young people to pursue the art of blacksmithing.

Interns aren't his only admirers; his recent MacArthur Foundation Fellowship is evidence of that, as well as his placement in collections worldwide. Dividing his time between private and public commissions, Tom Joyce is shaping history. The Archivists of American Art at the Smithsonian have recently asked him to be interviewed for inclusion in their Oral History Program. All artists are the sons and daughters of Hephaestus, the ancient Greek blacksmith to the gods; sometimes the apple just falls closer to the tree.

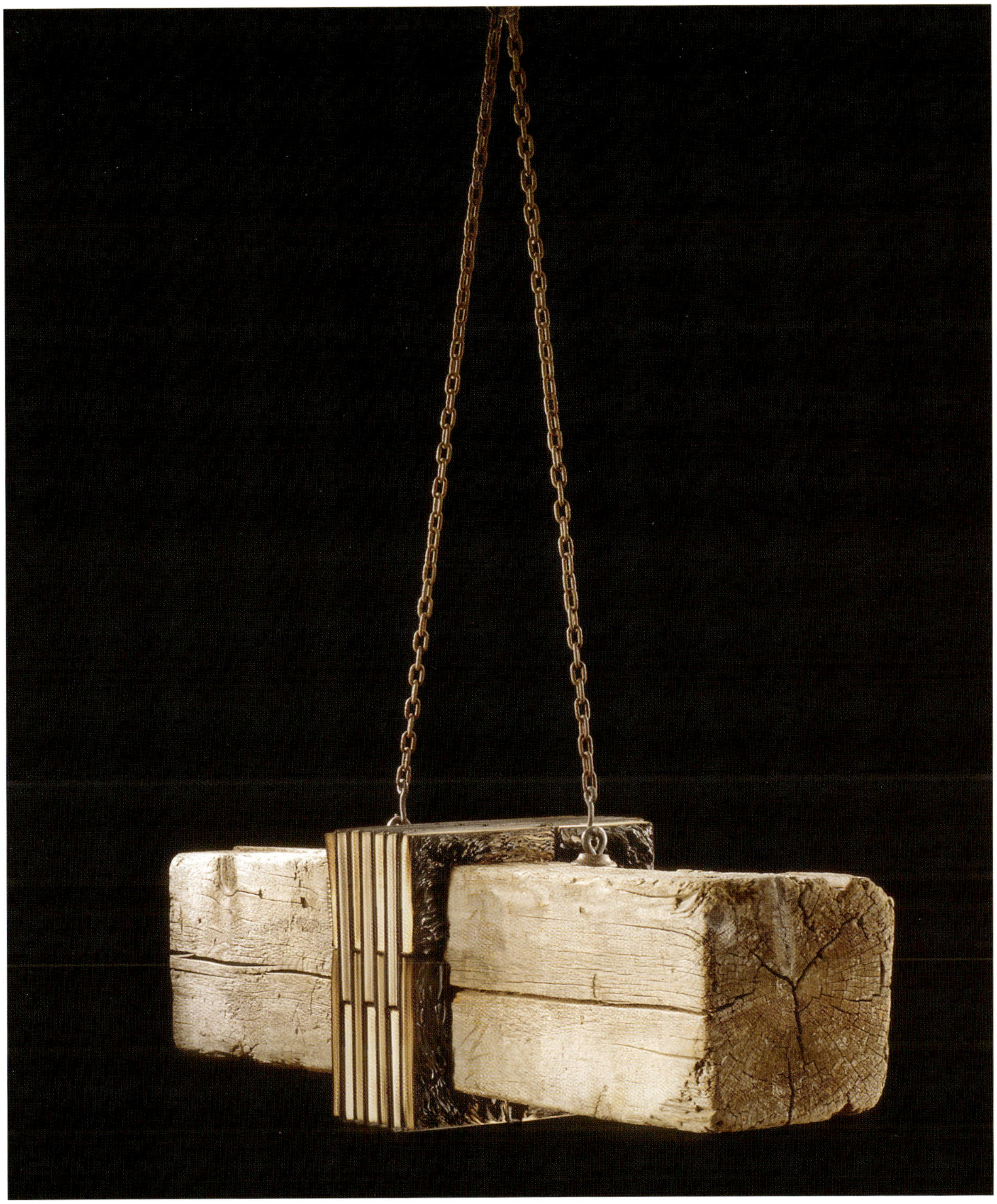

BRIDGE
WOOD, ENCYCLOPEDIAS & FORGED IRON
60 X 57 X 16 INCHES

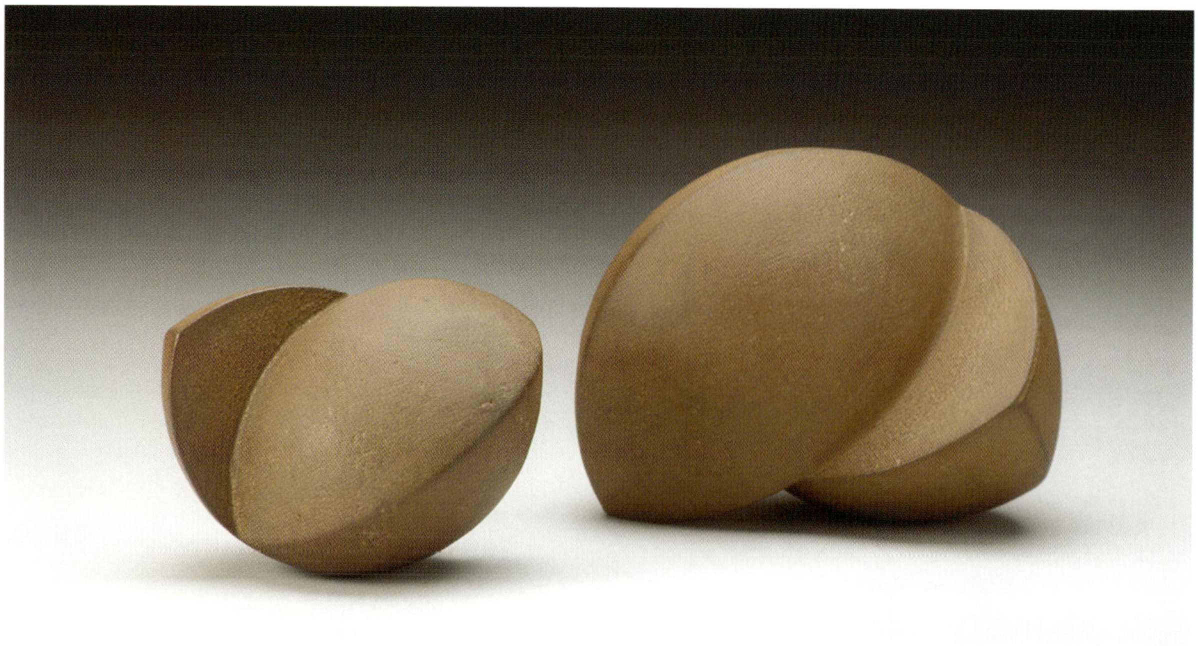

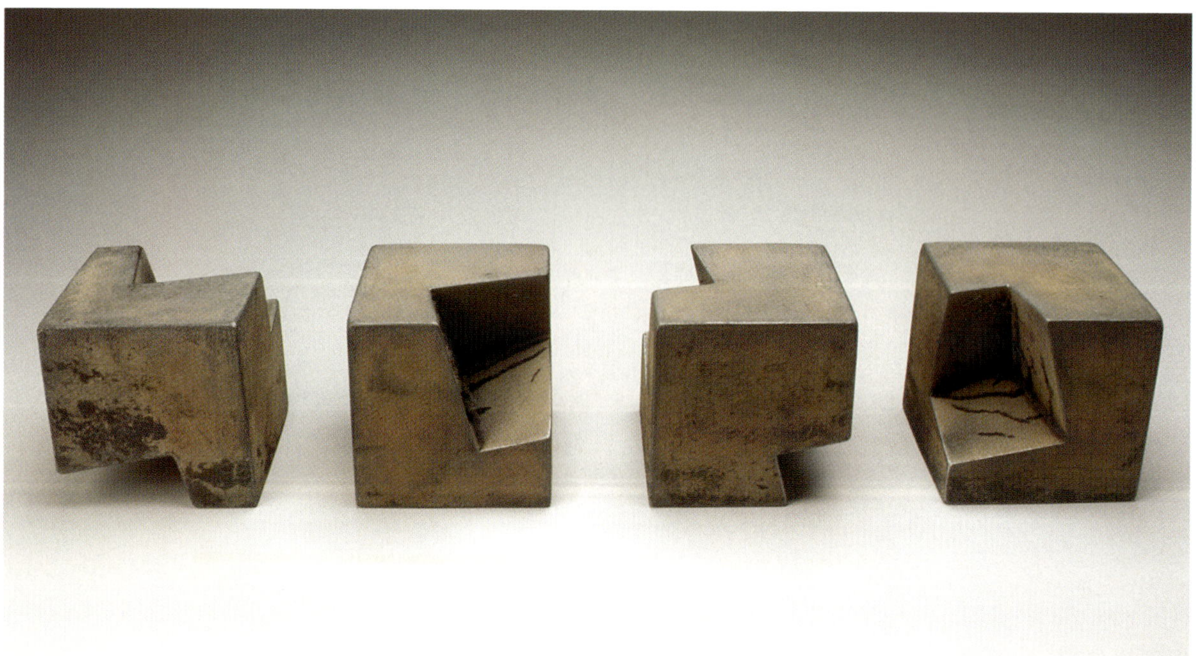

MEMORIAL SCULPTURE, SEPTEMBER 11, 2001
CAST IRON ALLOY MADE FROM WORLD TRADE CENTER ASH, SOIL FROM THE SANTUARIO DE CHIMAYÓ, AND SAND FROM A TIBETAN BUDDHIST MANDALA MADE AS A PRAYER FOR PEACE
8 X 8 X 8 INCHES

National Metal Museum, Memphis

NORTHEAST X SOUTHWEST
CAST IRON
6 X 33 X 6 INCHES

New Mexico Art in Public Places Acquisitions Program

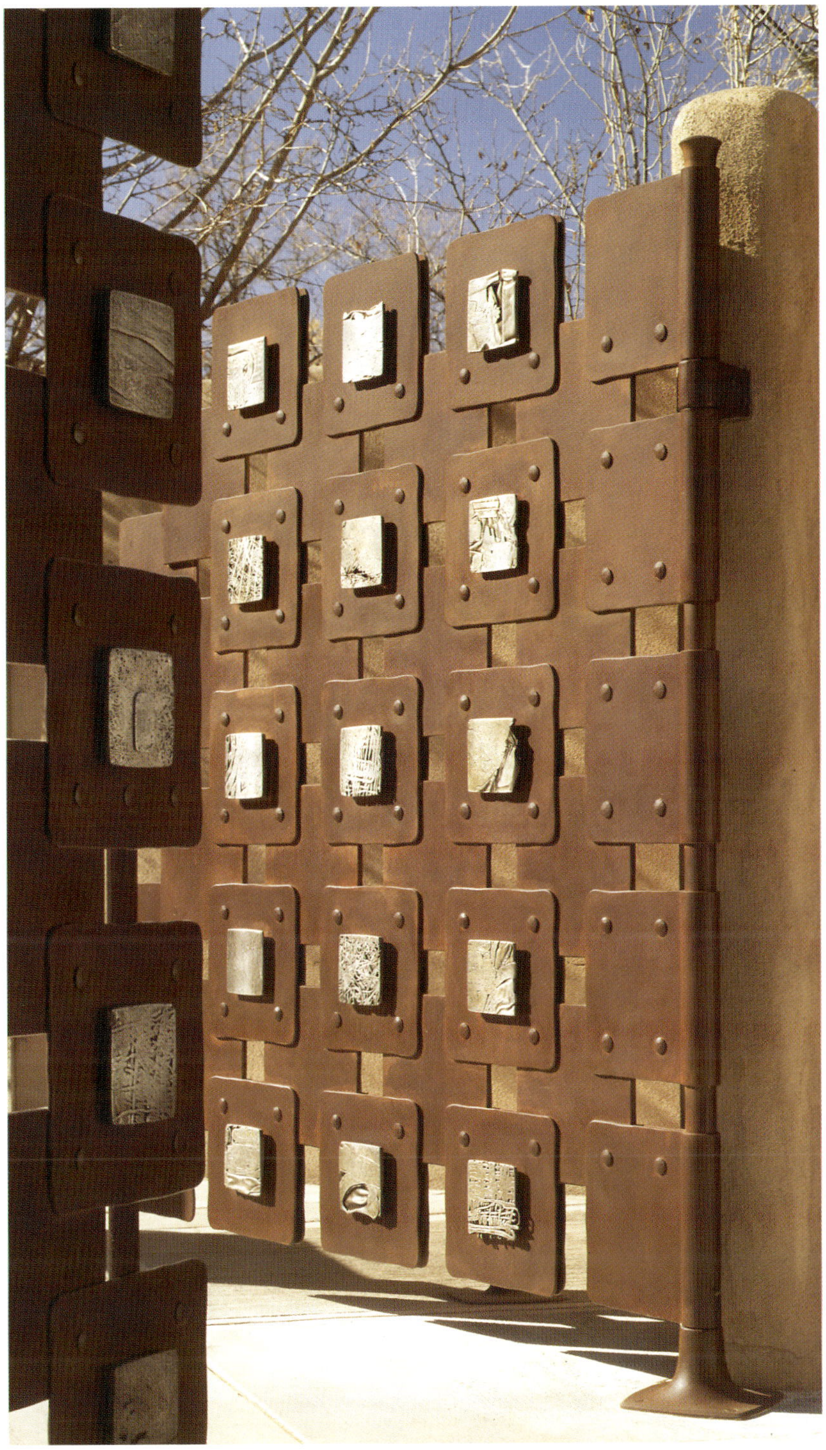

RIO GRANDE GATES
FORGED IRON & MATERIALS SALVAGED FROM THE RIO GRANDE
81 X 141 X 10 INCHES

Albuquerque Museum of Art

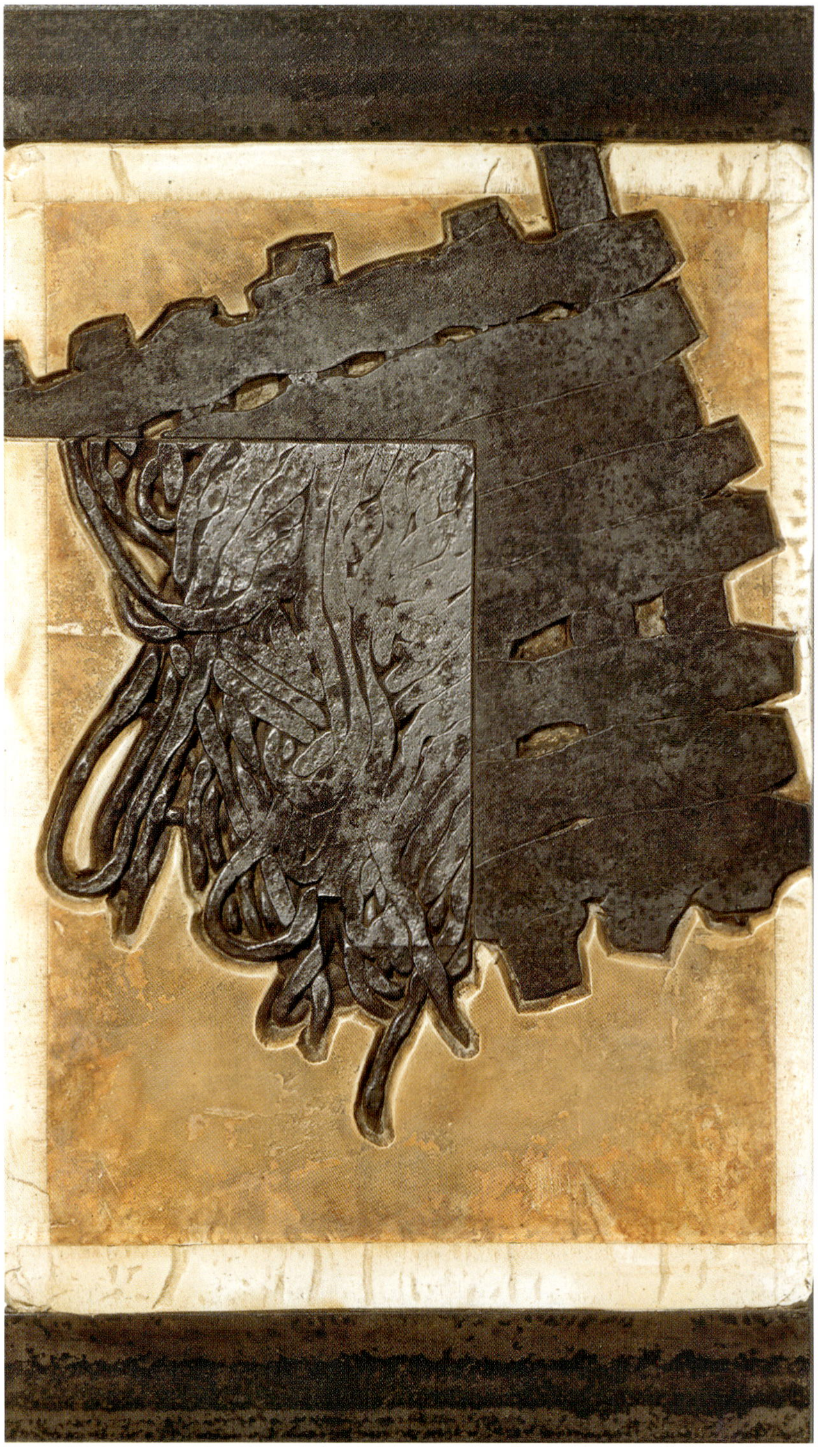

RIO GRANDE TABLET
PLASTER, FORGED IRON & MATERIALS
SALVAGED FROM THE RIO GRANDE
15 X 8.5 X 1.5 INCHES

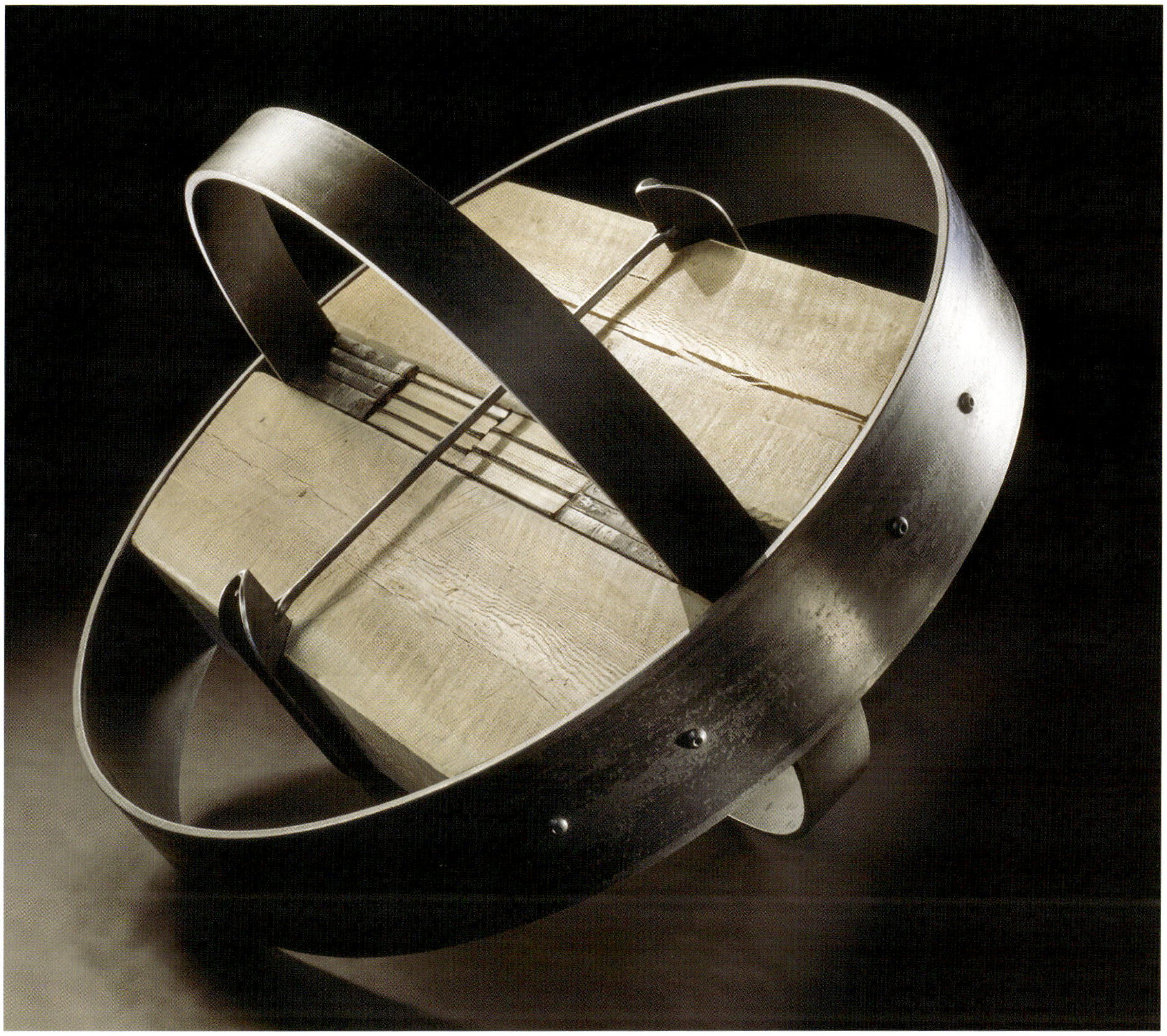

TOM JOYCE b. 1956 Tulsa OK. *Ed:* Life Experience. *Coll:* Minneapolis Institute of Arts; Albuquerque Museum of Art; Museum of Art and Design, New York; Detroit Institute of Arts; De Young Museum of Art, San Francisco; Mint Museum of Art, Charlotte NC; Museum of Fine Art, Boston; Museum of International Folk Art, Santa Fe; National Metal Museum, Memphis; Phoenix Museum of History; Smithsonian Institution DC; Southern Illinois Univ. Art Museum, Edwardsville IL; Standard Federal Bank Collection, Troy MI; Worshipful Company of Blacksmiths, London, England. *Awards:* MacArthur Foundation Fellowship, October 2003. *Representation:* EVO Gallery, Santa Fe.

QUOIN
WOOD, ENCYCLOPEDIAS & FORGED IRON
48 X 48 X 41 INCHES
Collection Amanda & Keith Innes

MICHAEL BERGT

Michael Bergt is best known for his painstakingly beautiful egg tempera on panel paintings of the human figure. He continues a modern tradition in this centuries-old medium that includes narrative masters like George Tooker and Paul Cadmus. While Bergt is essentially self taught, his immense talent and dedication caused Cadmus, his onetime mentor, to say of him, "The craftsmanship of Bergt's work is so assured that viewed alongside, say, a Crivelli or a Cossa it need feel no shame."

This accolade is no less true of his marvelous, sensitively sculpted bronzes. Actually, his work in this medium holds its own when placed next to the whole of art history. This is an extremely rare thing to say of any contemporary artist, but in the case of Michael Bergt it is entirely apt. His subject matter is humanity, plain and simple, and he has a spectacular ability to make a viewer think and feel, through pared down narratives that reveal the mythic and magical within the everyday.

His work makes a very convincing case that there is far more aesthetic substance to be discovered by reassessing art history, rather than by blindly rejecting it for the sake of endgame strategies. Standing before a Bergt painting or sculpture one has the sense that the game is over—there's nothing left to reject or react against—and that we might do well to return to the wondrous and disturbing human verities of body and soul. He is completely open to the pluralistic possibilities of post-modernism and admires art and artists of all sorts, but he has the self-assurance and humility to know what he's here to do. Perhaps this is why he does it so well.

His figures fit into forms he has slyly described as "fit or fat," though in either case his bronzes achieve a visceral sense of volume and weight. Gaston Lachaise, Fernando Botero, and the anonymous artists of Greek antiquity come to mind. In fact, he quotes the latter in *Transformation*, but as usual gives things his own inventive twist. Here we see a standing figure in the stylized pose of an archaic male *Kouros*—hands closed, arms at the side and one foot forward. This figure, however, steps into the future on the left foot rather than the right, and in an even more radical reversal, this figure is female, when this pose was always reserved for male nudes. Finally he adds a pair of wings in the form of giant hands. As is so often the case in Bergt's approach, she is both archetypal and angelically new.

Harmoniously resolving oppositions is one of Bergt's potencies. Witness his "everyman" turning atop the two-headed steed of *Paradox*. Like Bergt, he goes in two directions at once—back into the deep dark past and forward into a future that only this protean artist can imagine.

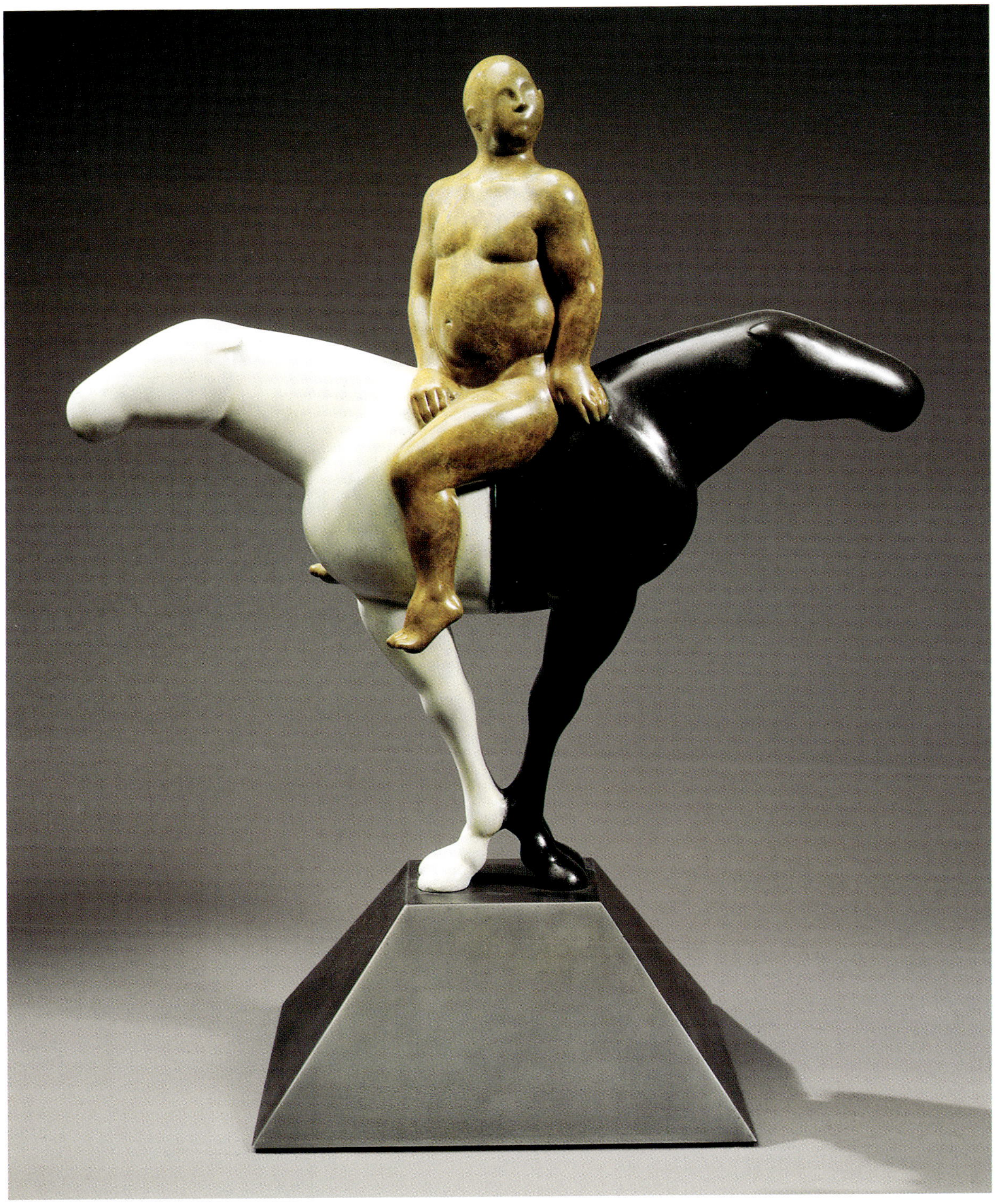

PARADOX
CAST BRONZE ON STEEL BASE
25 X 21 X 12 INCHES ON BASE

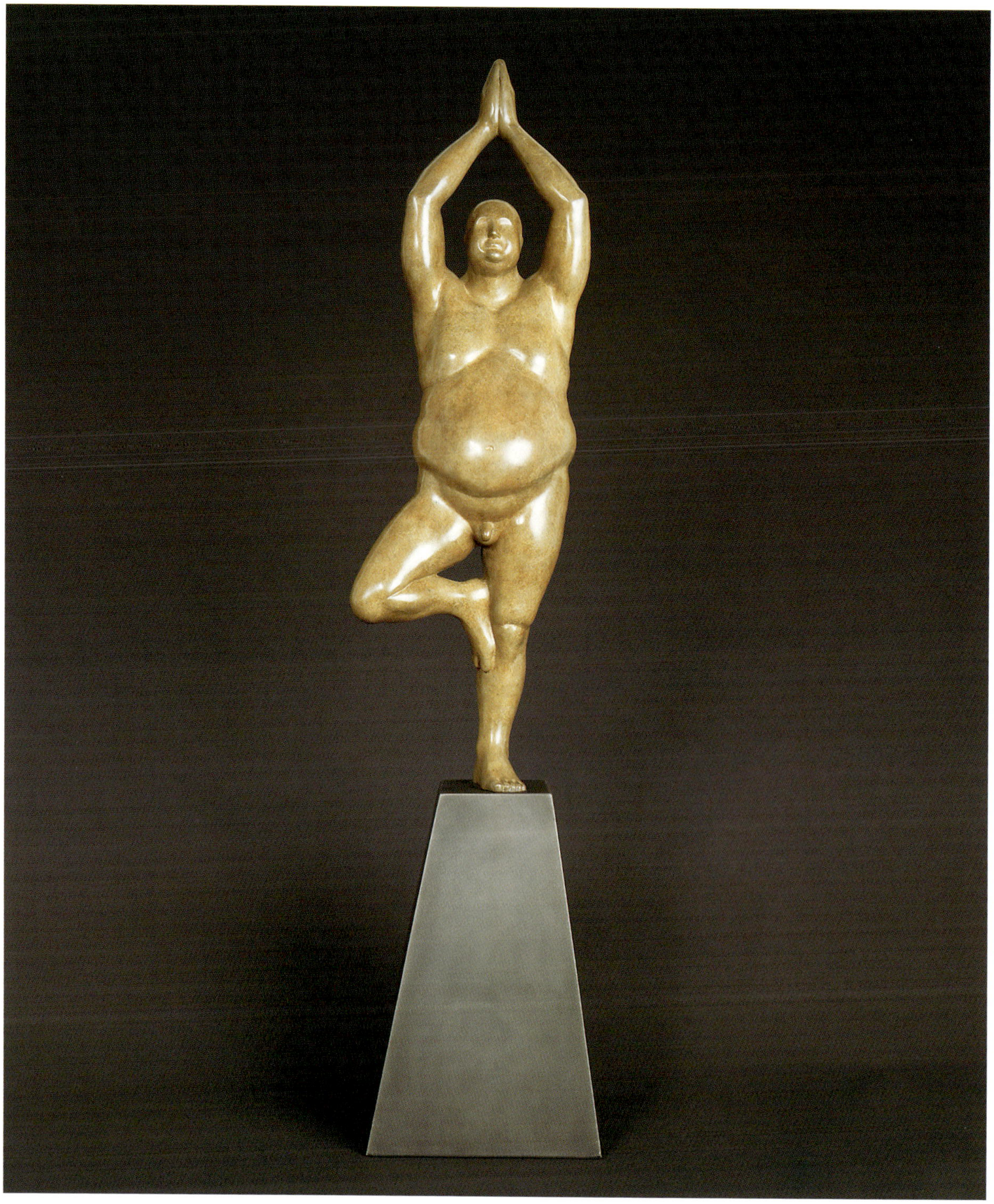

YOGA MASTER
CAST BRONZE ON STEEL BASE
38.5 X 8 X 8 INCHES ON BASE

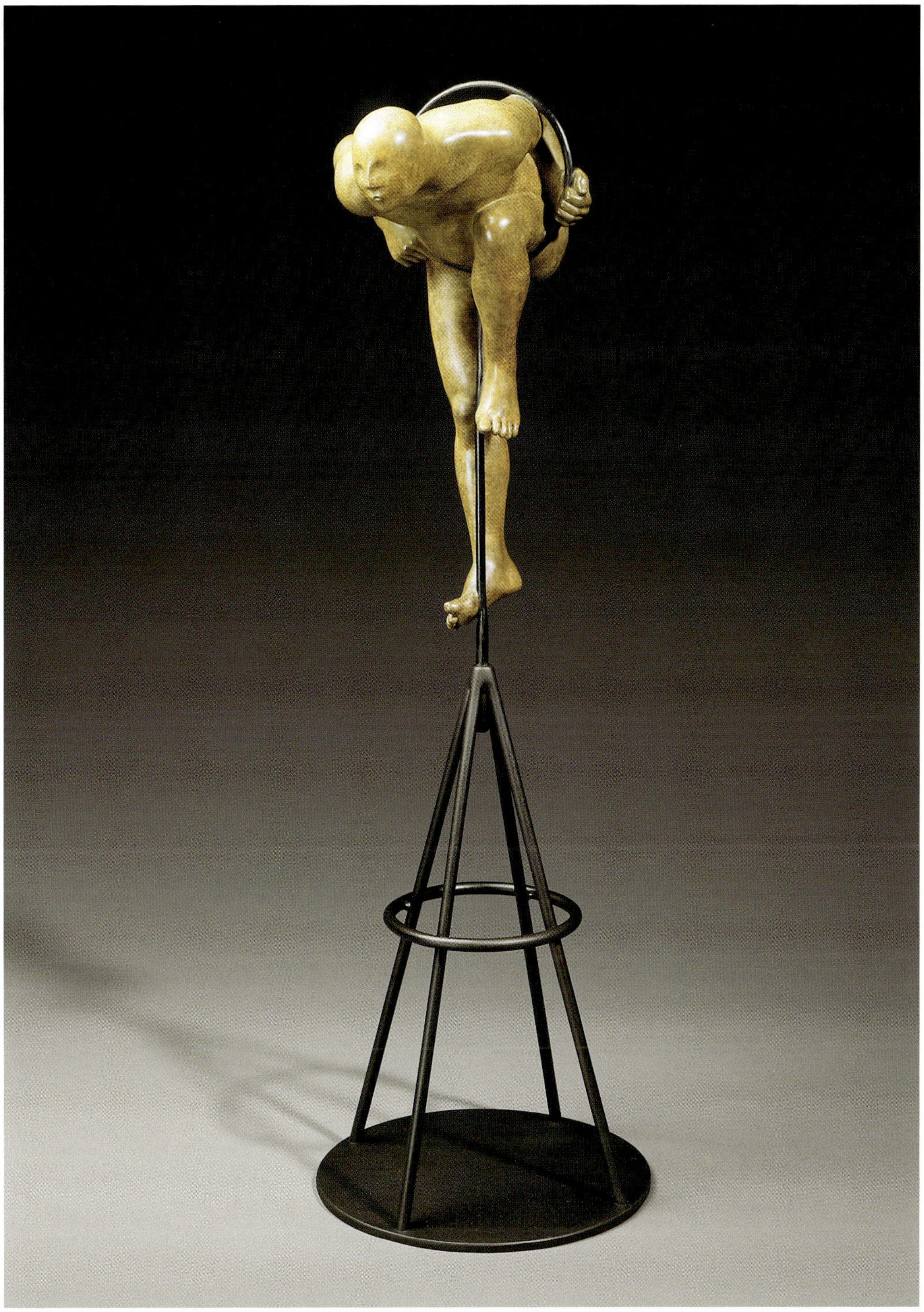

IN THE LOOP
CAST BRONZE ON STEEL BASE
35 X 16.5 X 16.5 INCHES ON BASE

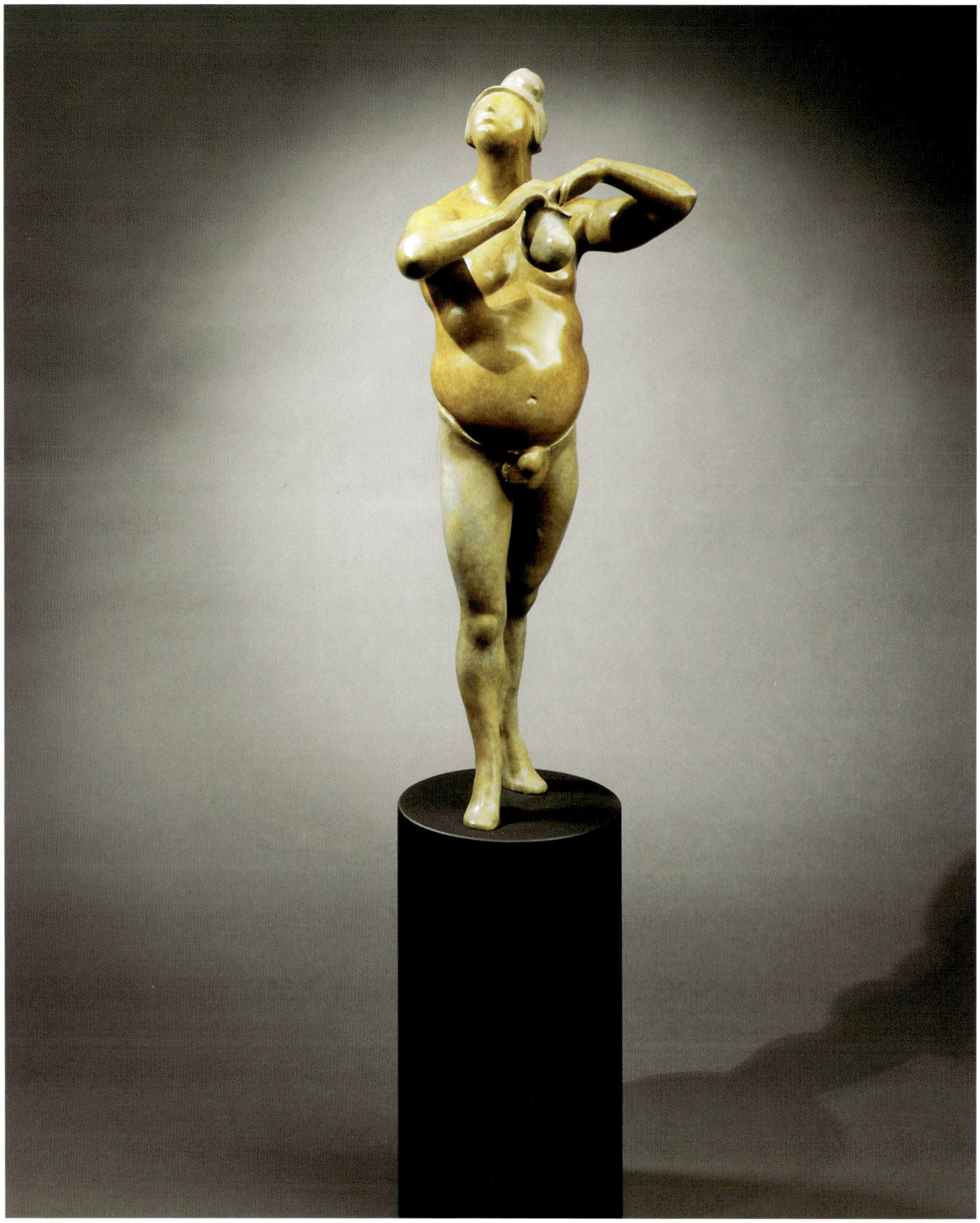

IN THE BAG
CAST BRONZE ON STEEL BASE
33 X 9.5 X 6.5 INCHES ON BASE

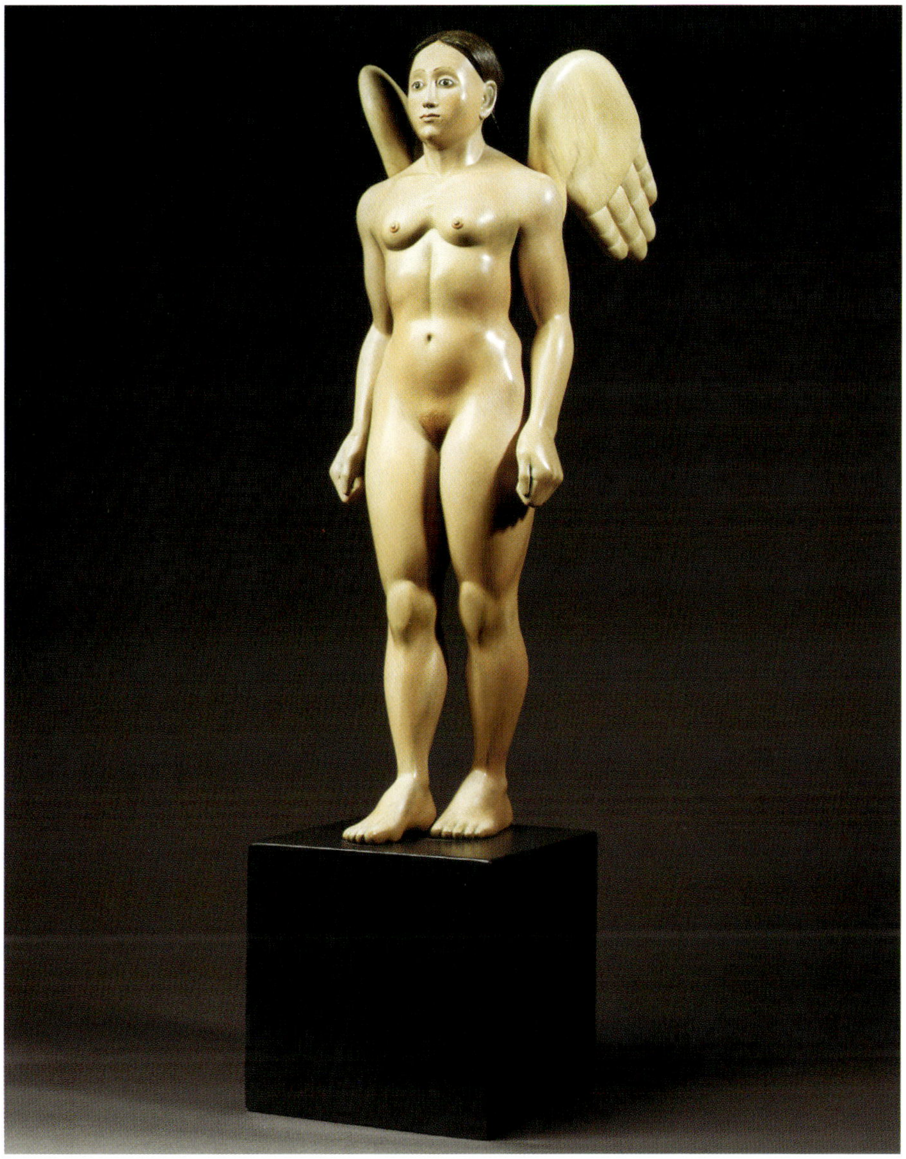

MICHAEL BERGT b. 1956 Deshler NE. *Ed:* Self Taught. *Coll:* California Palace of the Legion of Honor, The Achenbach Collection, San Francisco; Colorado Springs Fine Art Center; De Young Museum, San Francisco; Evansville Museum IN; Fons d'Art del Diari Avui, Barcelona, Spain; Kalamazoo Institute of Art MI; Michigan State Univ. Art Museum, East Lansing MI; New Mexico Museum of Fine Art, Santa Fe; Palmer Museum, State College PA; West Publishing (Art and Law Purchase Award) Eagan MN; Frye Museum of Art, Seattle; Arnot Museum of Art, Elmira NY. *Representation:* Turner Carroll Gallery, Santa Fe.

TRANSFORMATION
CAST BRONZE ON STEEL BASE
32 X 8 X 11 INCHES ON BASE

LINDA FLEMING

Diagram a thought in space and steel. Take the most electric, ethereal energy of the human paraphernalia and assemble a giant metal model of it. Let it get rained on and rust, the better to weather all your ideas. Live with the concept, out in the backyard or down in the basement or up on the balustrade, and best of all, illuminate your thoughts to see what kind of shadows they cast.

Linda Fleming, tireless sculptor and thought diagramist, in her most recent solo show activated the gallery space with a compelling cast of cast shadows alongside and abstracted from her signature steel sculptures. These flat silhouettes, liberated from the forms light used to create them, on the first glance fool the eye, positing fictional illuminations in the way the Nike of Samothrace hangs in a fantastic gust of imagined wind, or how the gaze of Michelangelo's *David* creates Goliath. On second look they read as abstract symbols afloat on the wall or flowing on the floor in a flattened graphic space—beautiful single characters in the quicksilver calligraphy which good sculpture, like Fleming's, so often makes of light.

Her sculptures are pieces of a magical technology, energized by transcending dichotomies, starting with form and space, interior and exterior, rounded and geometric, technological and natural, heavy and weightless, monumental and microscopic. They are built for the purpose of attuning the human apparatus to awe. They are time machines to ancient futures and alternative ages. Fleming's work takes flight in the mind as well as in the gallery or sculpture garden. She generously charges imaginary as well as physical space (the classic definition of sculpture).

It works something like this. Since these sculptures resemble sixteenth century drawings of theoretical universes, or an explanation of pre-natal cell division or the structural shape of a bizarre solar system, you might be given the idea of a spirograph space mandala expanding in all dimensions, causing you to consider the paths of a satellite wobbling in orbit or an entry to a U.F.O. design competition or of some grand discarded piece of rusting core technology from the defunct civilization the aliens later find on Earth. Maybe your meditation comes to center on an oversize iron lotus bud aglow to the sky with a geometric light made of love which spreads softly over the planet and on into the galaxy.

While all the above are possible points of departure for a flight in a Fleming dream encapsulator, her work eternally returns to its own inner resource. Its power to expand is as unlimited as thought itself because it issues from a strong generative center. Fleming charges the soundlessness of steel to achieve a palpable, activated quietude. In the end, it is this silence that speaks most eloquently for her art.

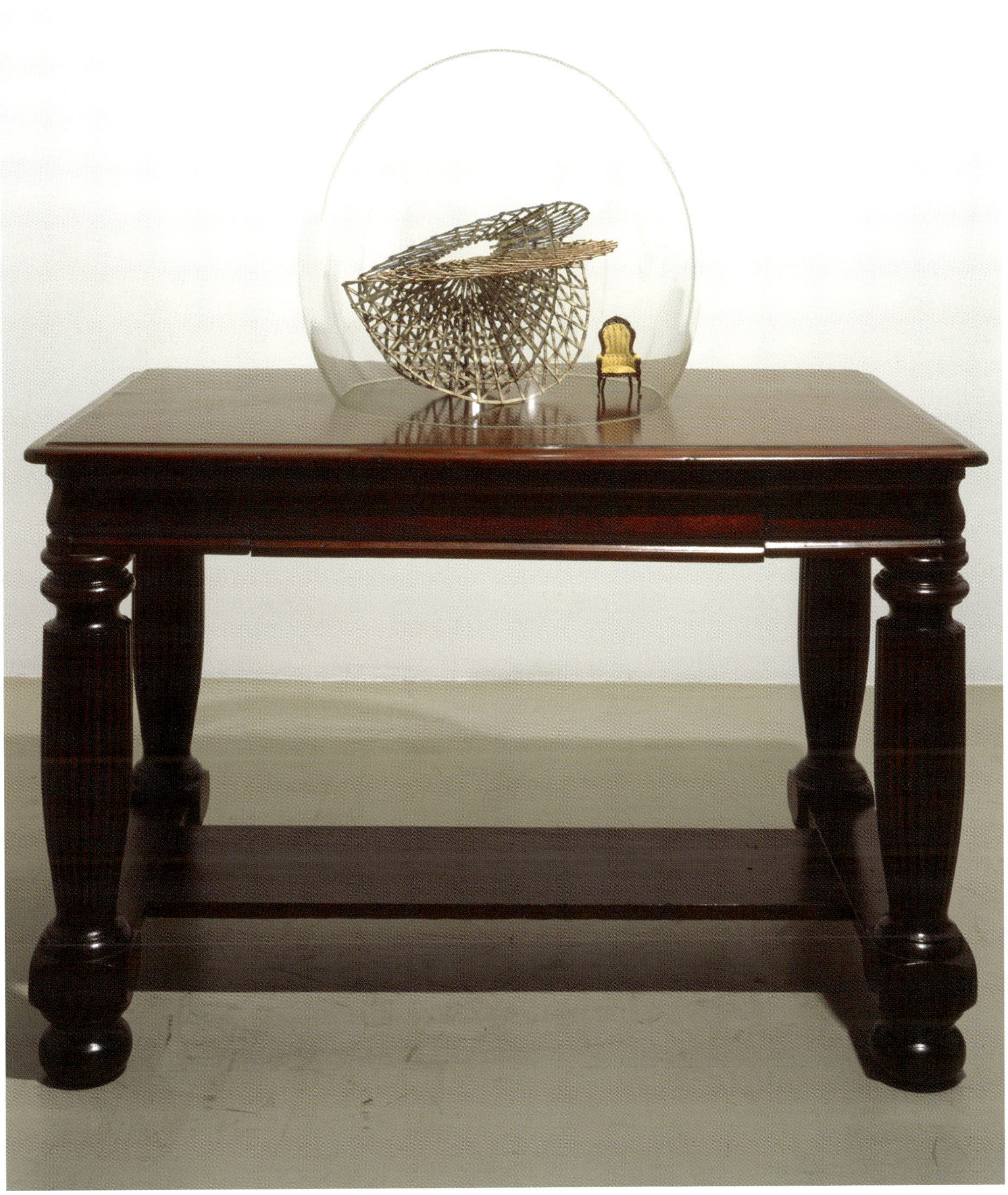

PARALLEL UNIVERSE: INTRICACY, 2003
BALSA WOOD, GLASS & MINIATURE FURNITURE
22 INCHES (DIAMETER OF GLOBE)

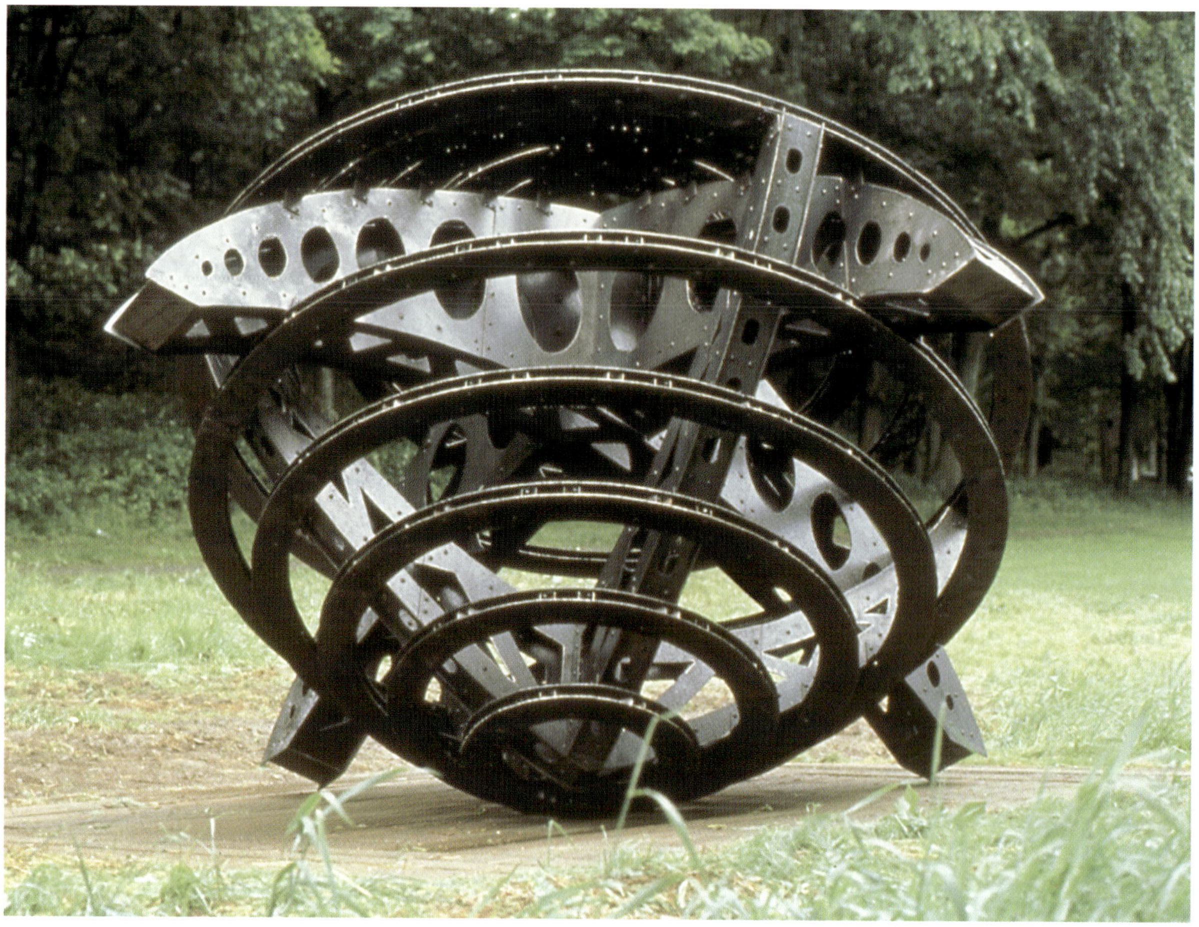

CLOAK OF MOTION, 1993
STEEL
92 X 132 X 132 INCHES

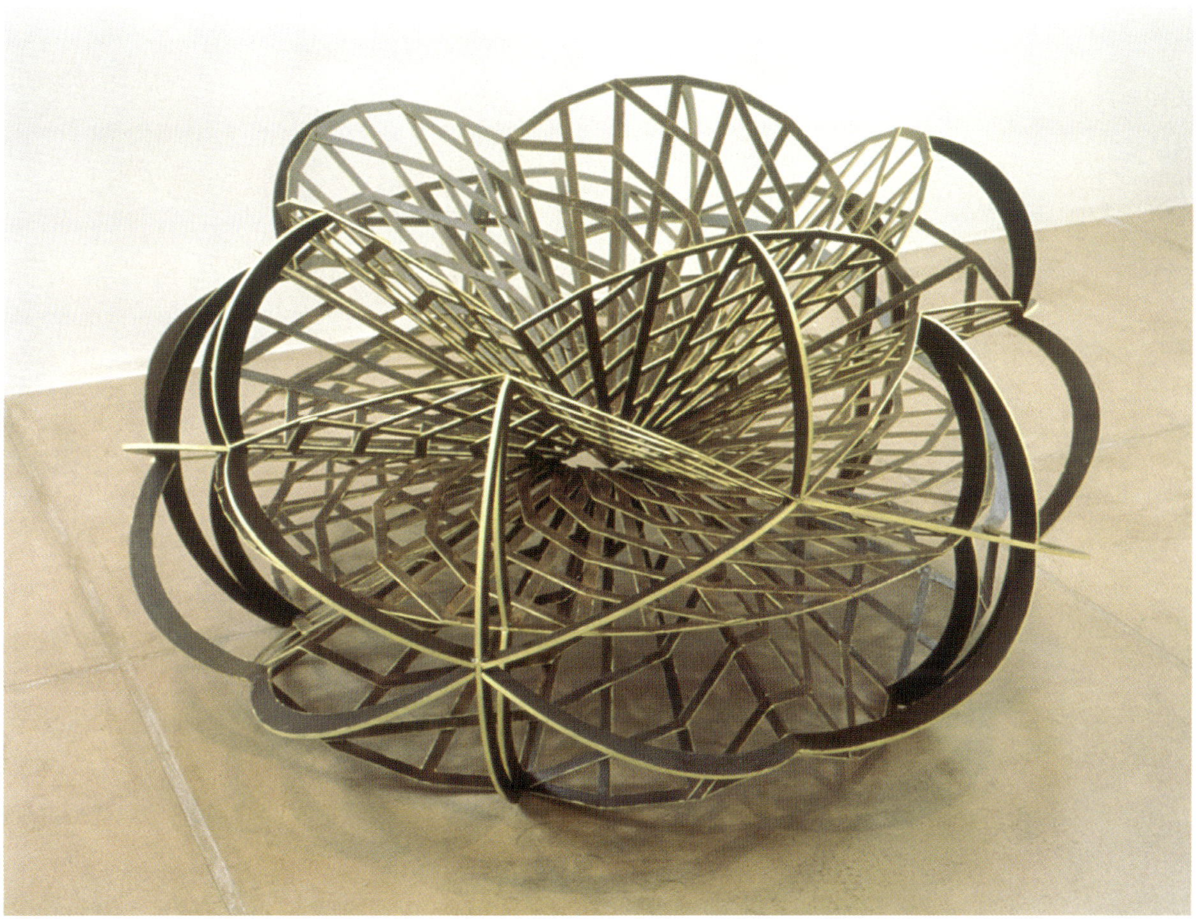

GREEN LACE, 2004
STEEL & ENAMEL PAINT
31 X 60 X 60 INCHES

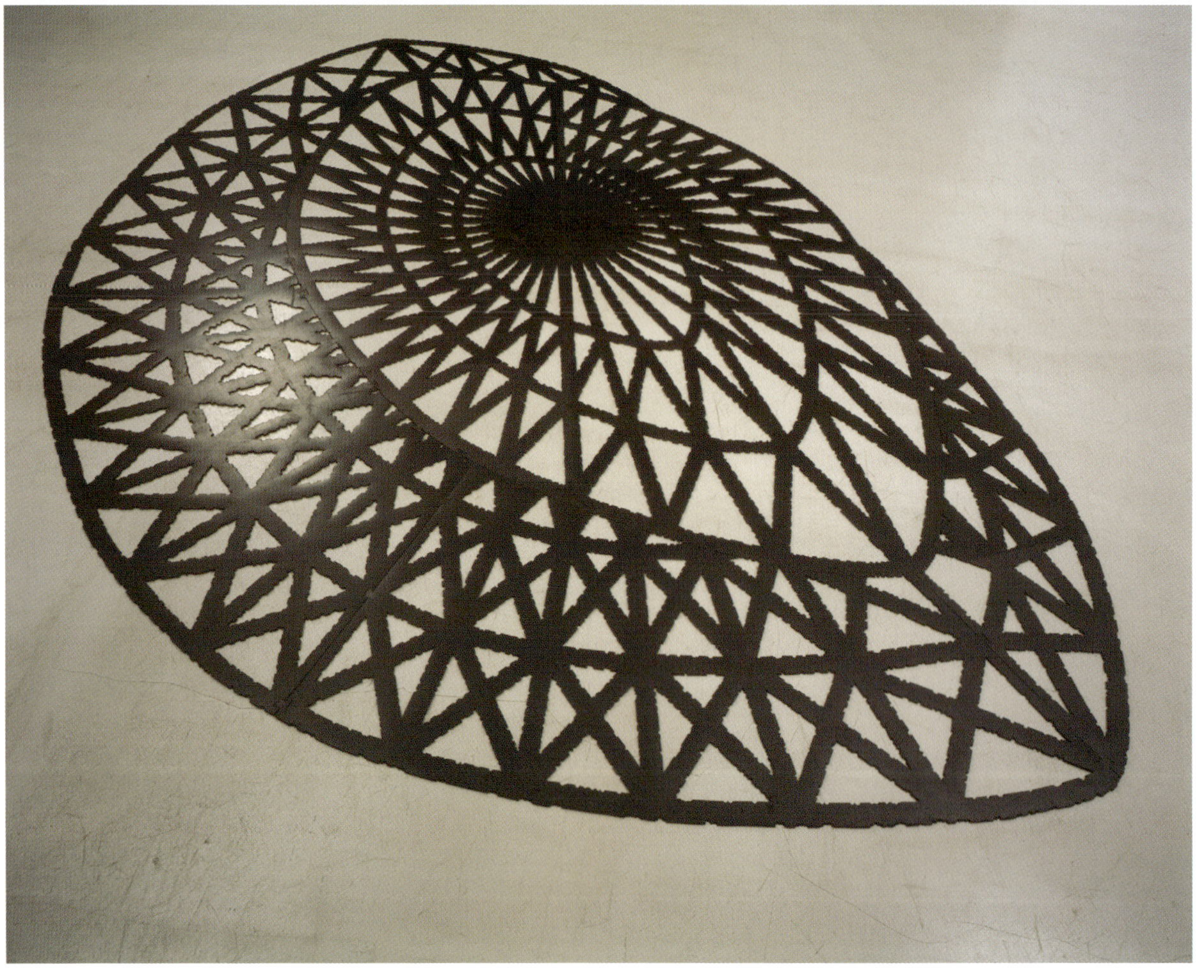

DARK MATTER, 2003
NEOPRENE RUBBER
116 X 172 INCHES

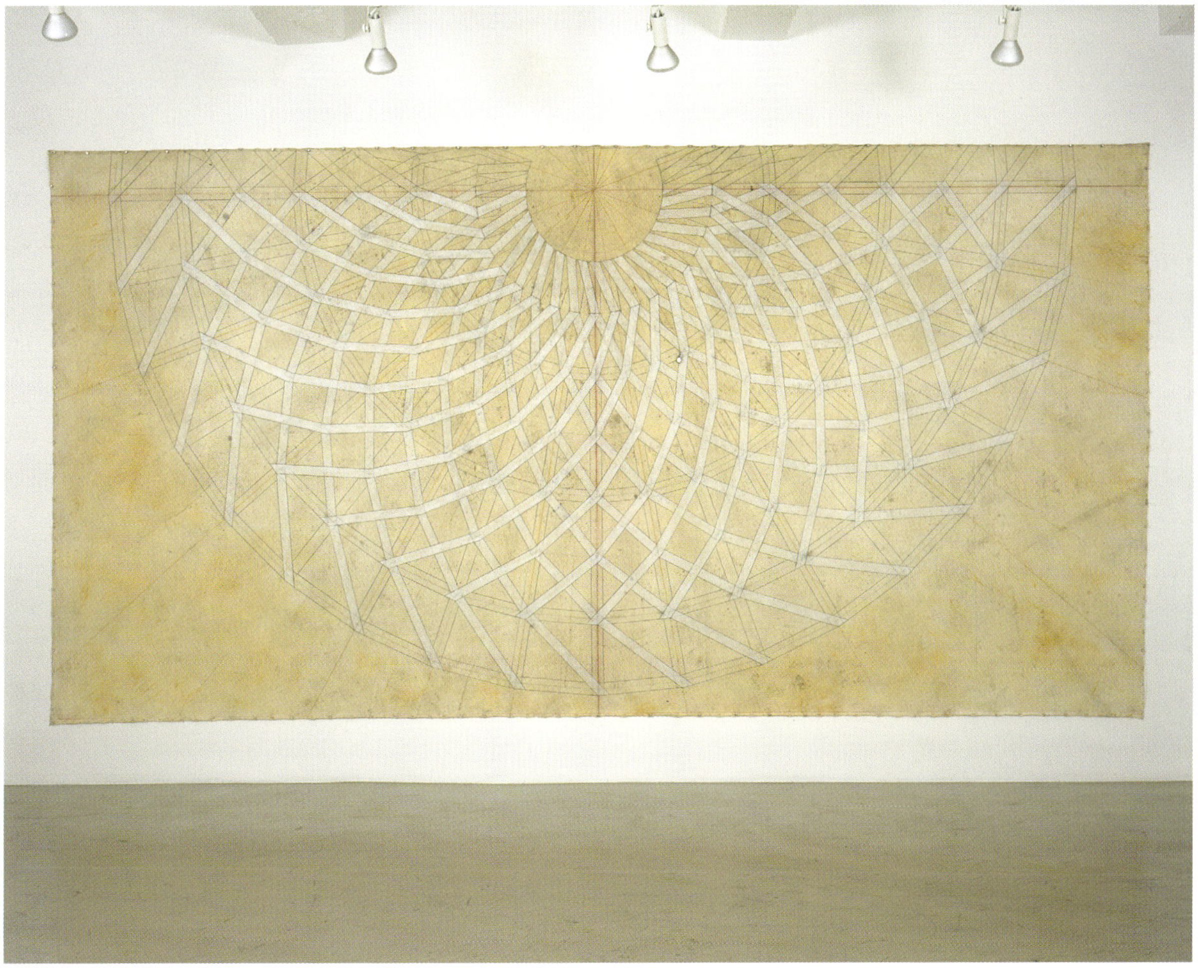

LINDA FLEMING b. 1945 Pittsburgh PA. *Ed:* Carnegie Mellon Univ. *Coll:* Albuquerque Museum; Berkeley Art Museum CA; First Bank, Miami FL; Stanford University Museum of Art CA; Neiman-Marcus, San Francisco. *Representation:* Linda Durham Contemporary Art, Santa Fe.

TEMPLATE, 2003
CANVAS, GRAPHITE, PIGMENT & VARNISH
76 X 189.5 INCHES

MALCOLM ALEXANDER

Malcolm Alexander's art could be referred to as an erotica of volumetric sensuality or simply the crafting of caresses. The sculptor's abstracted torsos suggest a worshipful response to the eternal feminine. Balancing rounded surfaces with hard edges, positive volumes with charged negative space allows him to arrange aesthetic counterpoints of movement and stasis, softness and strength, luxury and limit. Had Gaston Lachaise applied a cubist's multidimensional sense of touch, he might have ended up where this formidable artist has arrived.

Born in Michigan, Alexander brings decades of success to his current work. His formal education happened at Art Center College of Design in Pasadena, but he truly became an artist through the mentoring relationships he developed with Taos legends Doel Reed, Howard Cook, Bettina Steinke, Emil Bistram, and Leon Gaspard. For nearly thirty years, Malcolm Alexander's speciality was in representational work, including monumental portraits and figure groupings. He became well known for sculpting sports giants like Joe Dimaggio and Johnny Bench, actors like Jimmy Stewart and art collectors such as Harrison Eiteljorg, whose namesake museum is in Indianapolis. His list of corporate commissions impresses, including an 18-foot Alaskan Pipeline Monument, *Valdez*, and another equally massive monument commemorating the 25th Anniversary of Alaskan Statehood in Fairbanks. Starting in the mid-80s Malcolm Alexander opted to forego his genius at capturing likenesses in favor of abstracting the human form by filtering it through his emotional landscape. Piercing and polishing a sensuous harmonic of anti-form and earthly ore, the artist achieves a dynamic interpenetration of space and substance. He understands, like Michelangelo, the use of convexity—pushing swollen surfaces to the fore—and the corollary of concavity—how it can be made to activate a spatial solidity, making the invisibility of air appear denser than the lithe suppleness of shaped metal.

Malcolm Alexander's incredible understanding of the invisible originating is everywhere apparent in his sensual sculpting of negative space. His is an essential love song of presence and absence created by scale defying blocks of holy smoothness. The eye feels the same sweet topological glide, the slip into invisibility that is so pleasurably attained before certain monumental geographies.

Malcolm Alexander's purest abstractions suggest a virtuosic minimalism, a master of bronze at the top of his form. His work possesses a timeless naturalness while providing intense interaction with the here and now. His creations are simultaneously organic and beautifully architectonic. Whether placed in a landscape setting or in an interior, the shadows and highlights, edges and voids take on ever-changing dimensions as the sun crosses the sky. Malcolm Alexander's abstractions manifest the passion of human nature at its ennobled finest.

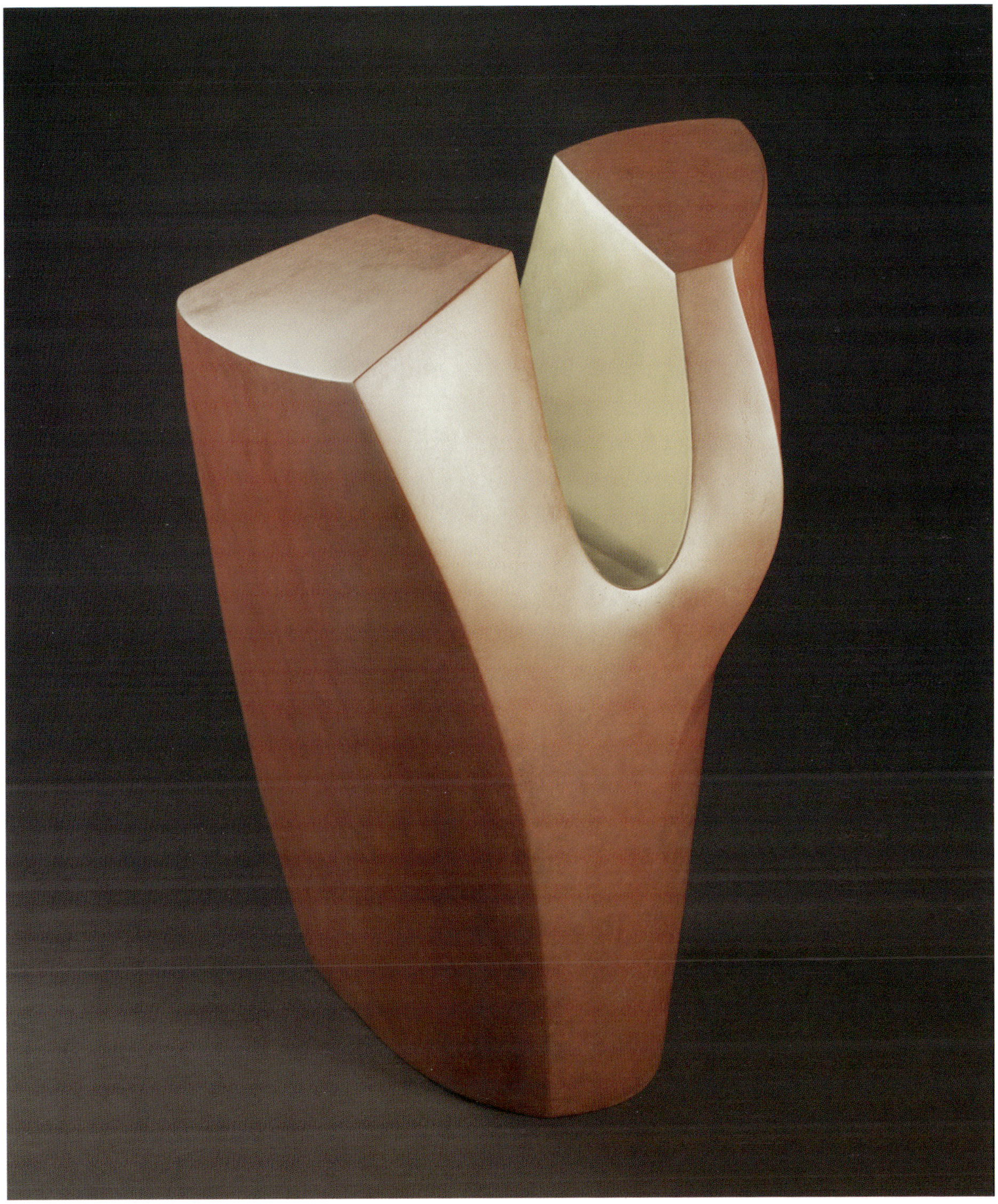

COMPLETION
BRONZE
20 X 13 X 13 INCHES

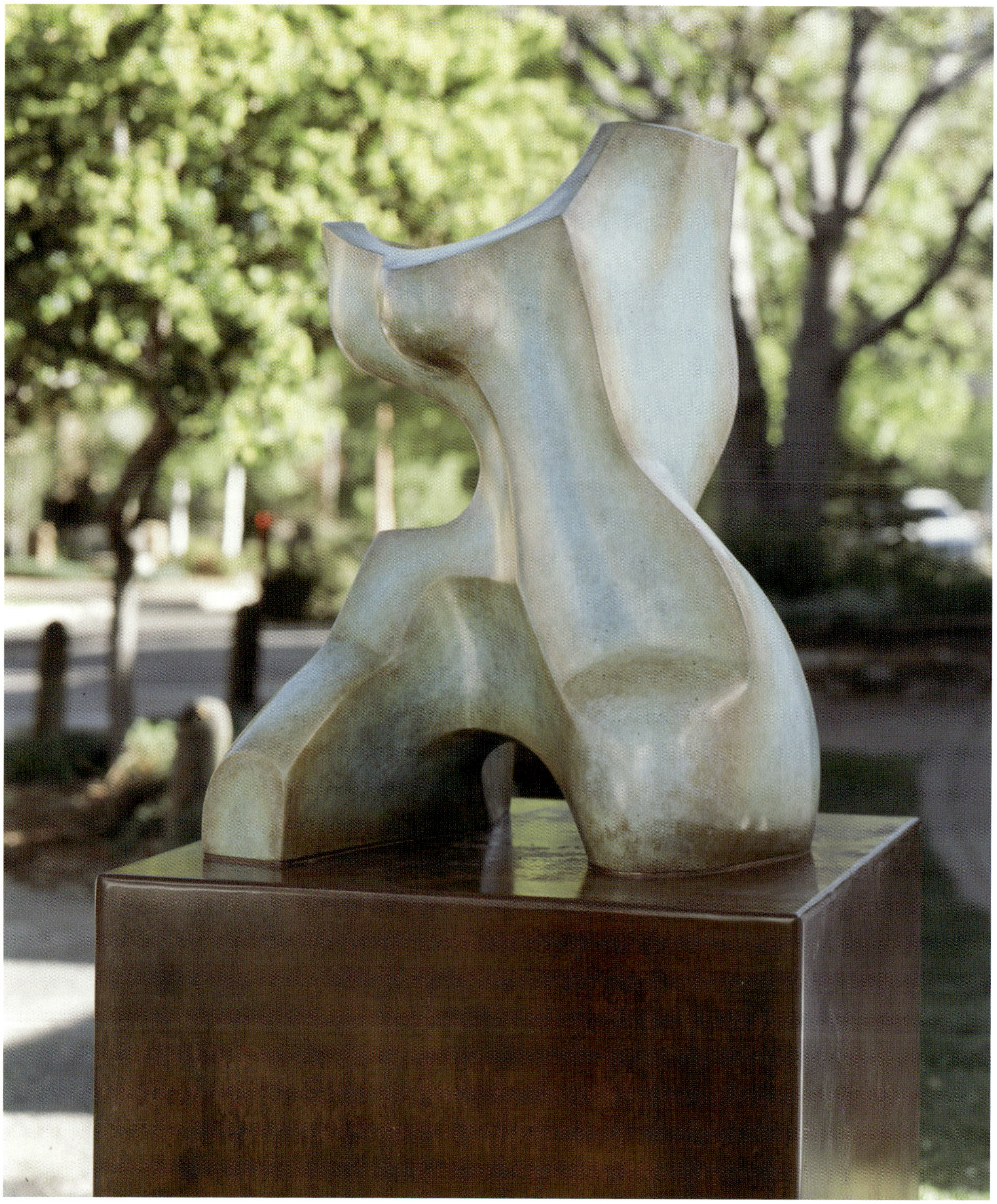

INNERMOST
BRONZE
34 X 28 X 24 INCHES

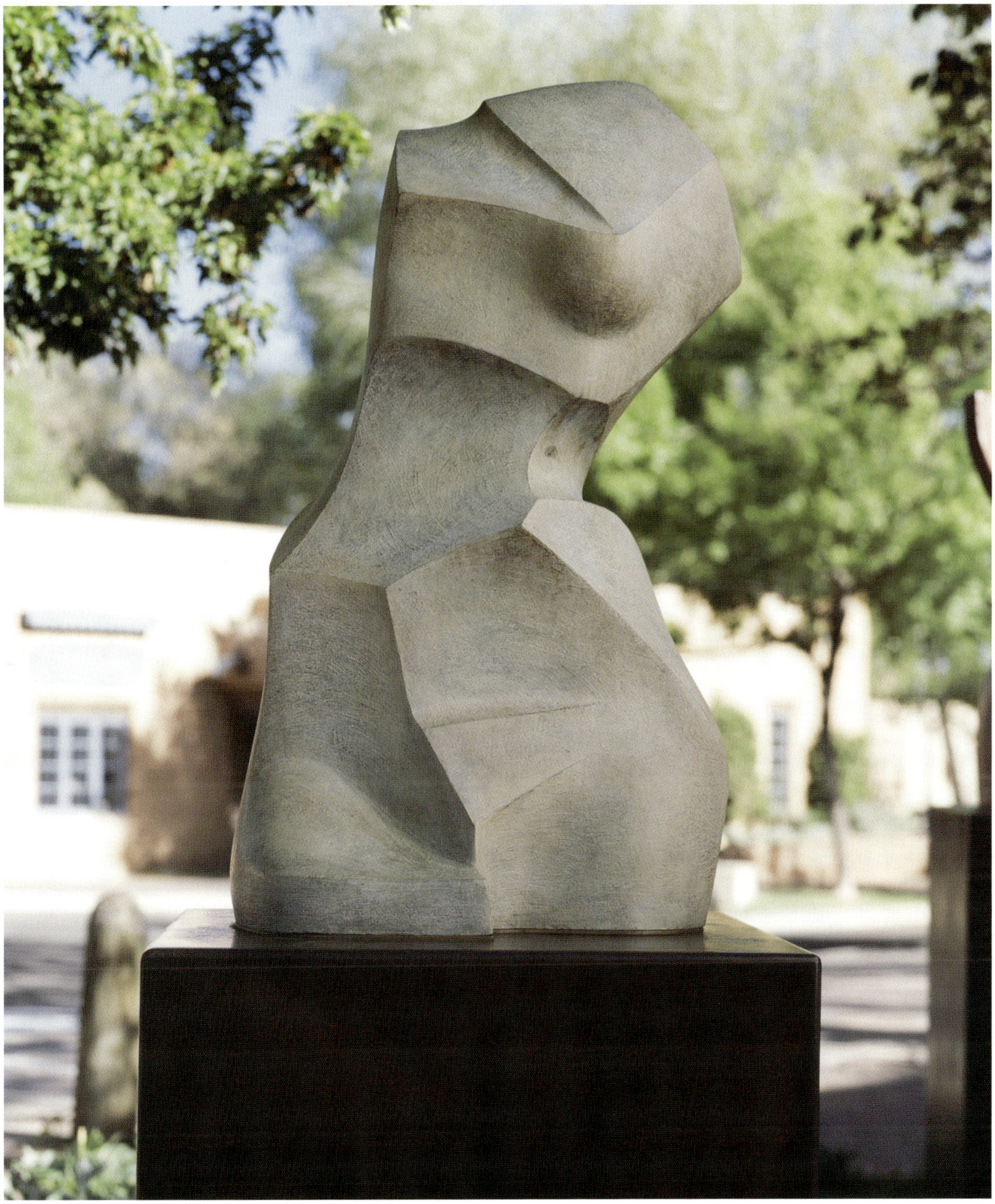

ISHTAR
BRONZE
30 X 20 X 19 INCHES

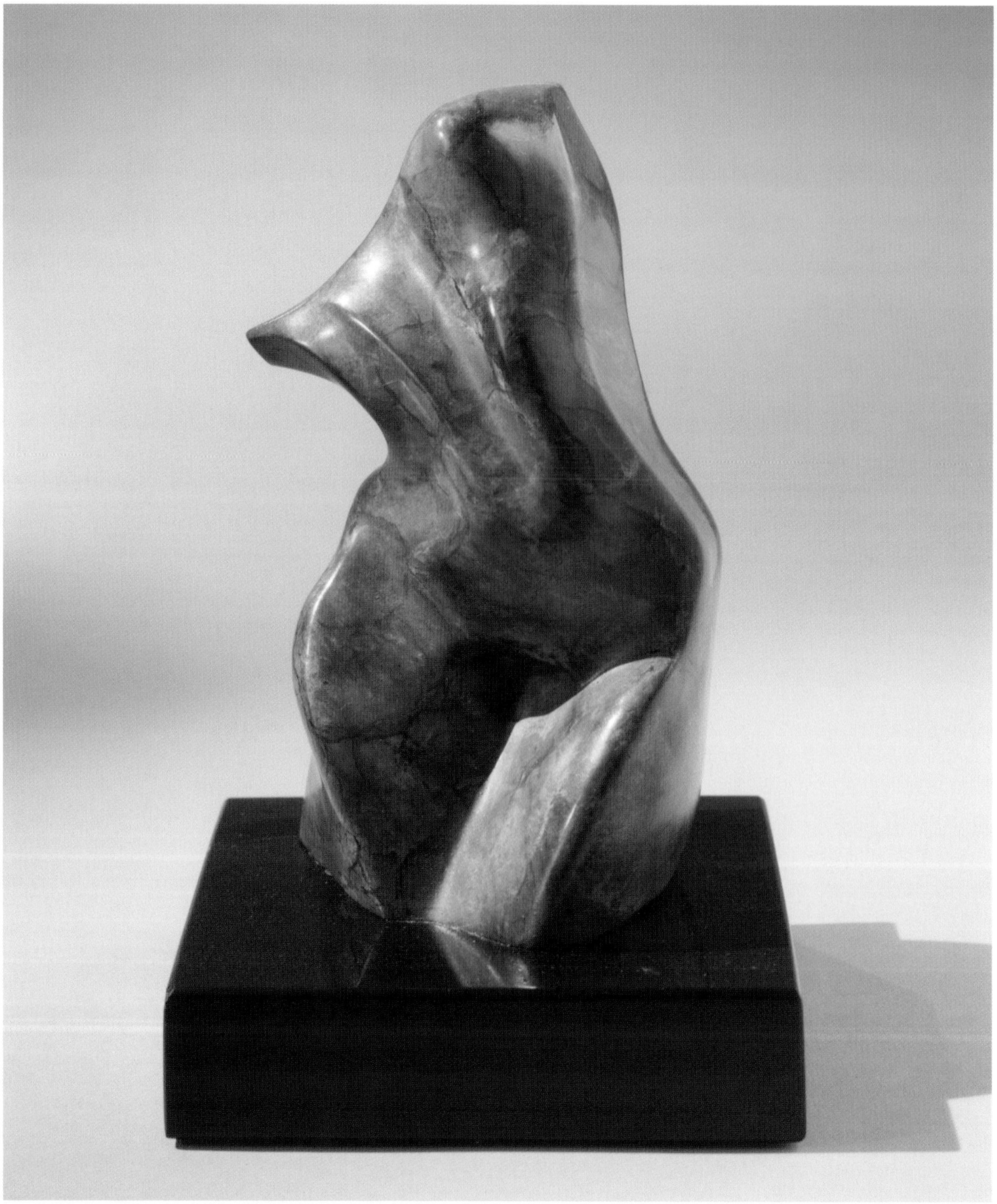

LOTUS
BRONZE
26 X 15 X 16 INCHES

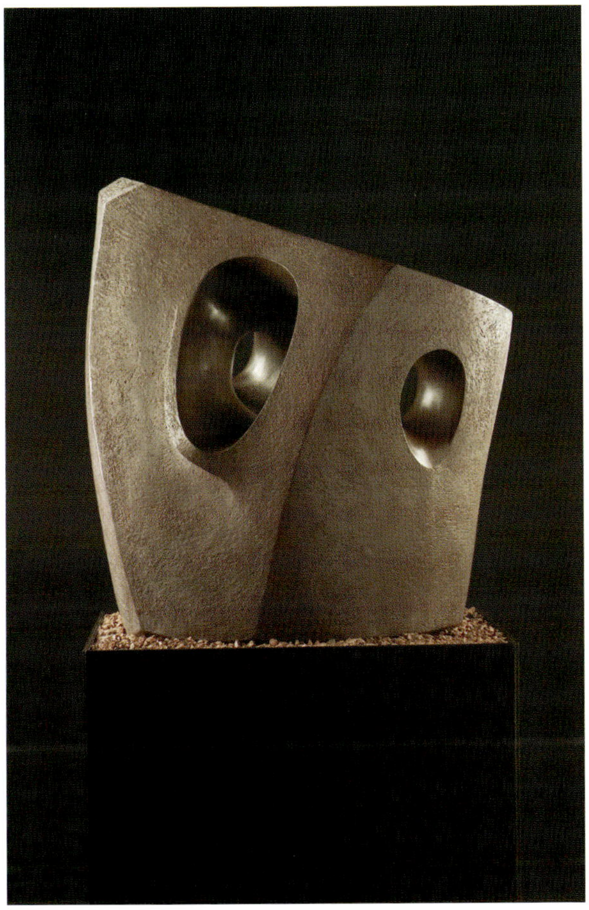

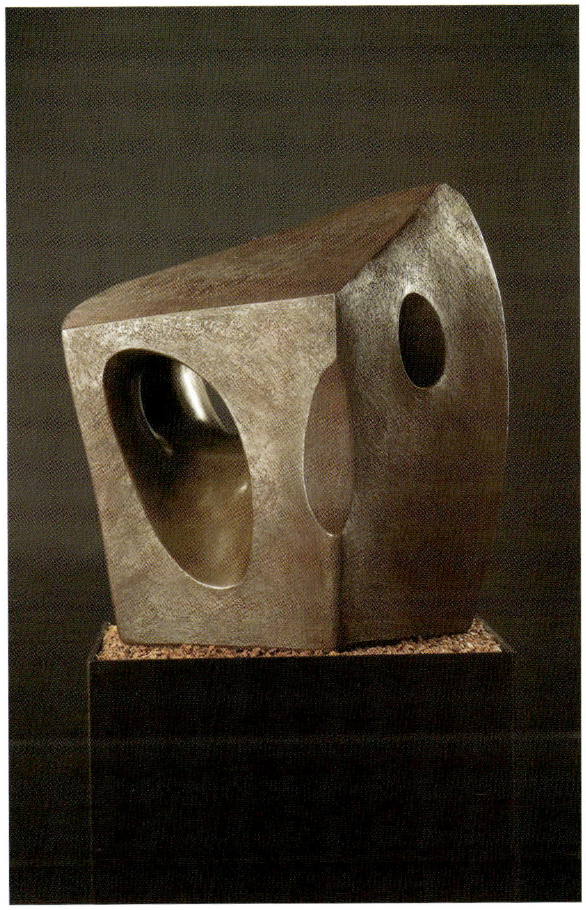

MALCOLM ALEXANDER b. Detroit MI. *Coll:* Houston Museum TX; Los Angeles County Museum CA; Olympic Museum, Greece; Smithsonian Institution DC; Atlantic Richfield Oil Company; Exxon Oil Company, Houston; Supreme Court Judge William O. Douglas; Phillips Exeter Academy; Weyerhauser Industries, Seattle; Bowie Kuhn, Commissioner of Baseball; James Stewart, Actor. *Representation:* Ventana Fine Art, Santa Fe.

TERRESTRIAL
BRONZE
25 X 22 X 21 INCHES

JAMES WESTWATER

James Westwater is the post-Pop, post-military-industrial purveyor of *Pinklings*, little pink ticklings at our wasteful underbellies and corporate complicity. The artist posits these love lozenges across a wide variety of found forms, or spreads his message by splooging objects with pink latex paint. Westwater refers to these harmonized stoppages as "non-logo brandings of failed idealisms." Practicing a schematized system of blotting out wholes and portions, he intervenes between viewer and image in an *arte-povera* lambasting of "signature style" and brand name consumerism.

Peace is pink. Blood is red. Blood is the inside color of the incarnadine animal. White is the energy of innocence and spirit. Red is the dusk and twilight place on the color wheel, where flesh and spirit meet as one. Pink is the balance of red and white. The longing for peace with our selves and our overwhelming material world is what Westwater will not let us forget.

In his earlier *Pills* series, Westwater's "non-logo" tended to function as a sort of ironic cancellation. *Pills* and *Bubbles* continue to appear in the current body of work, but under the *Pinklings* umbrella, the emptying-out has become a filling-in. There is still an elemental cynicism at play, but absence is now replaced by fullness. For example, with *Globe*, the addition of finger-daubed pink atmospheric phenomena not only cancels out, but also makes us see beyond the conventional mapping of geo-political boundaries, that ruling diagram imposed by history's winners. In this simple, paint-driven exercise, Westwater speaks for the archetypal artist-underdog, the seemingly powerless everyman, wishfully changing the world. Somehow he succeeds, like a breath of fresh air, overriding the dead, spherical grid of cartographic separatism, and resuscitating something spontaneous and hopeful.

By adding and altering identifiers, the artist collapses signification upon itself. To participate as a viewer in Westwater's pink project is to establish a resonant field of overlap, where de-signification and re-signification rapidly alter and expand our appropriated rhythms of seeing and deriving meaning. That's the cerebral part, the picto-mental feedback loop, the infinite invert of the advert, and the weird sounds it makes. In other words, these switched up visual-linguistic interventions can really make your mind tango.

Take three seemingly disconnected objects—a cell phone; two pairs of glasses, mounted Janus-like; a statuette of a meditating woman—and subsume each in pink paint. Westwater does not render them un-seeable, he causes them to be seen again. Their new formal unity allows similarities to emerge. All three might be described as mechanisms for assisting sight and communication: A phone makes manifest people, places and events in places where one isn't; glasses extend vision, mitigate the blinding light, and allow observation without being seen; and the Buddha-like statuette is a graven image used to jumpstart metaphysical sightings. What *Cell, Glasses*, and *Meditating* all address are issues of blindness and sight. What we want to see and what we don't, what we're willing to look at and what we're not. These concerns are at the very core of James Westwater's work.

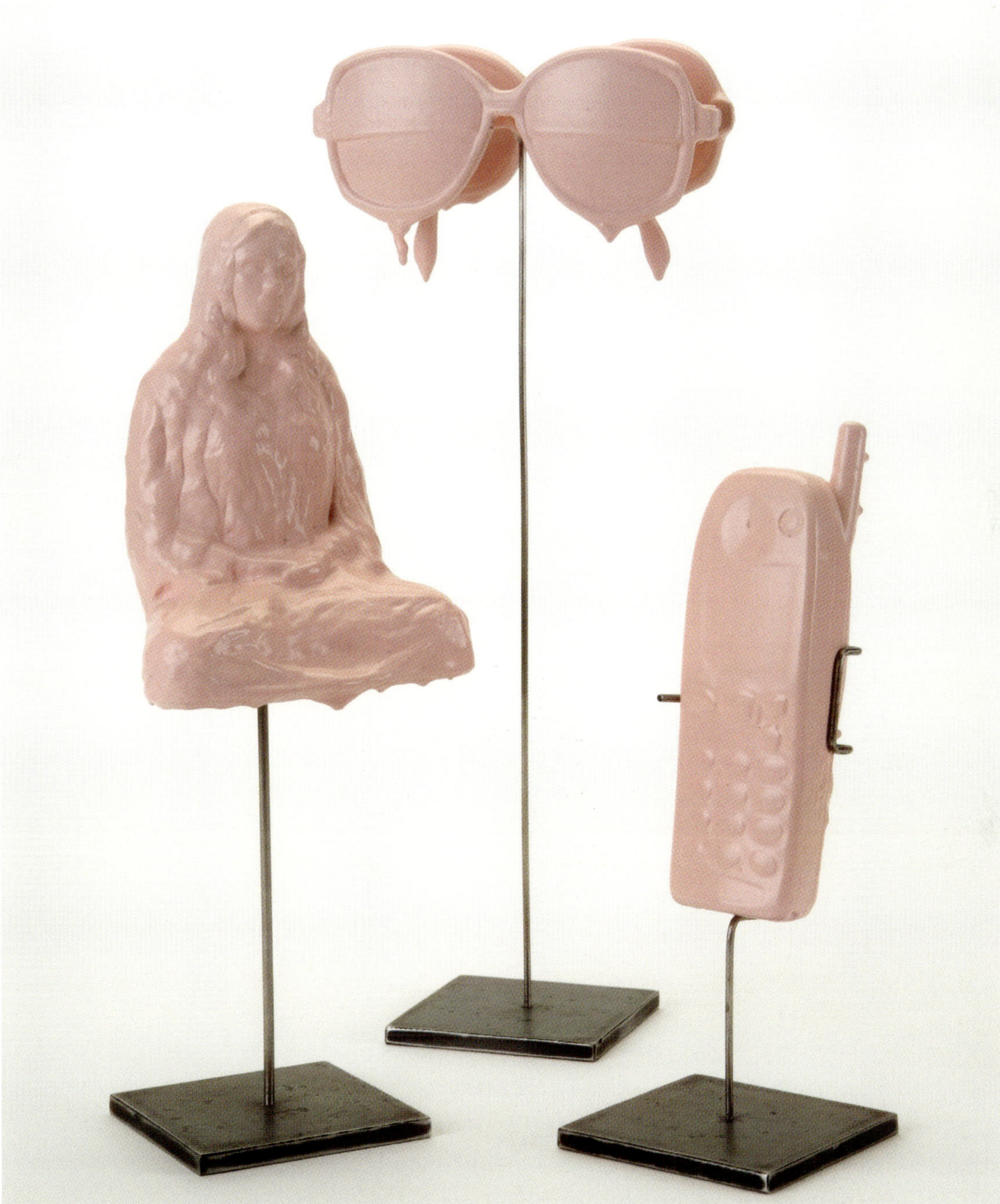

MEDITATING, 2004
ACRYLIC LATEX ON POURED STONE, WITH STEEL STAND
11 X 4 X 3 INCHES

GLASSES, 2004
ACRYLIC LATEX ON PLASTIC & GLASS, WITH STEEL STAND
13 X 6 X 3 INCHES

CELL, 2004
ACRYLIC LATEX ON PLASTIC & METAL, WITH STEEL STAND
8 X 3 X 3 INCHES

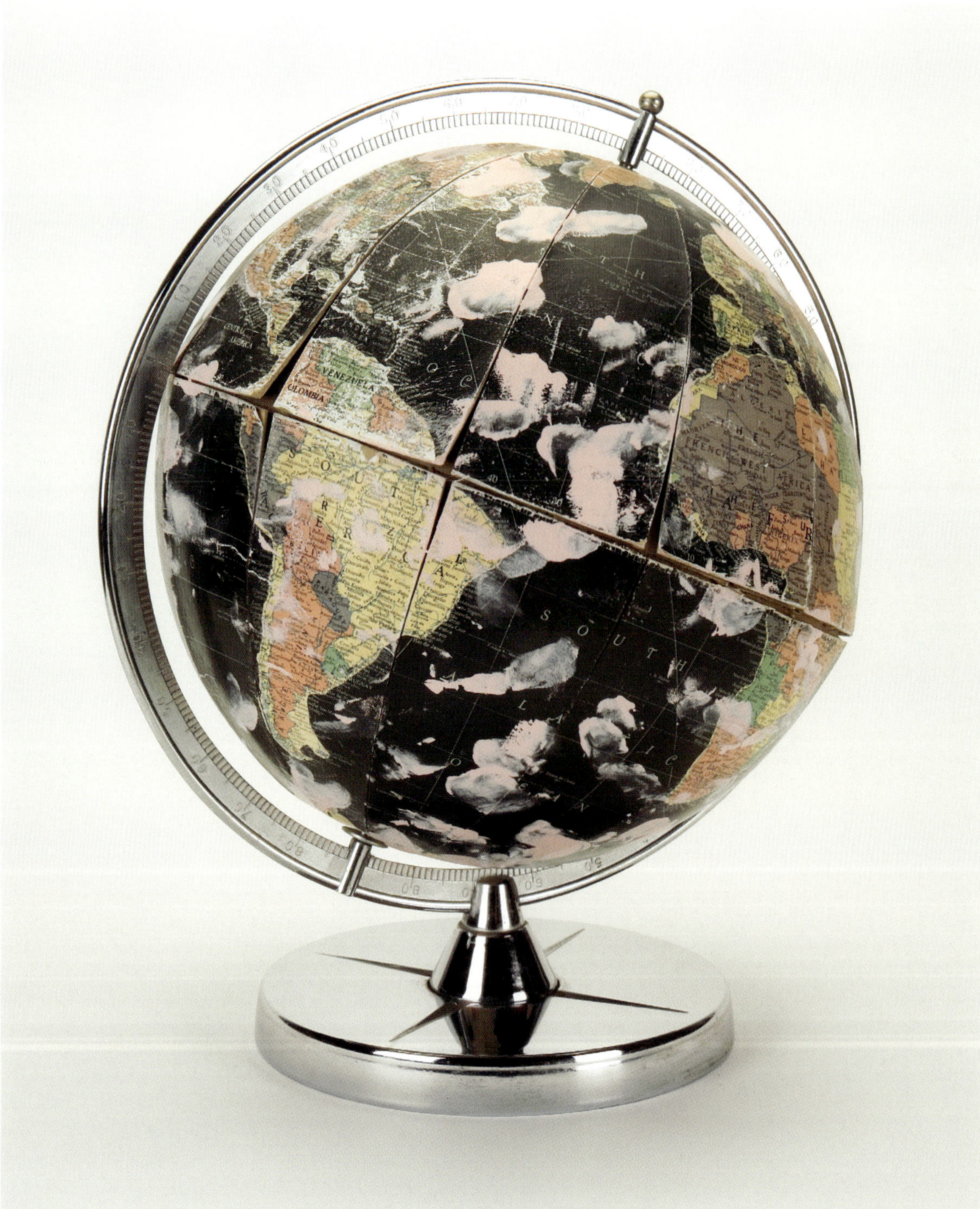

GLOBE, 2004
ACRYLIC LATEX ON PRINTED CARDBOARD
WITH CHROMED STEEL STAND
16 X 14 X 12 INCHES

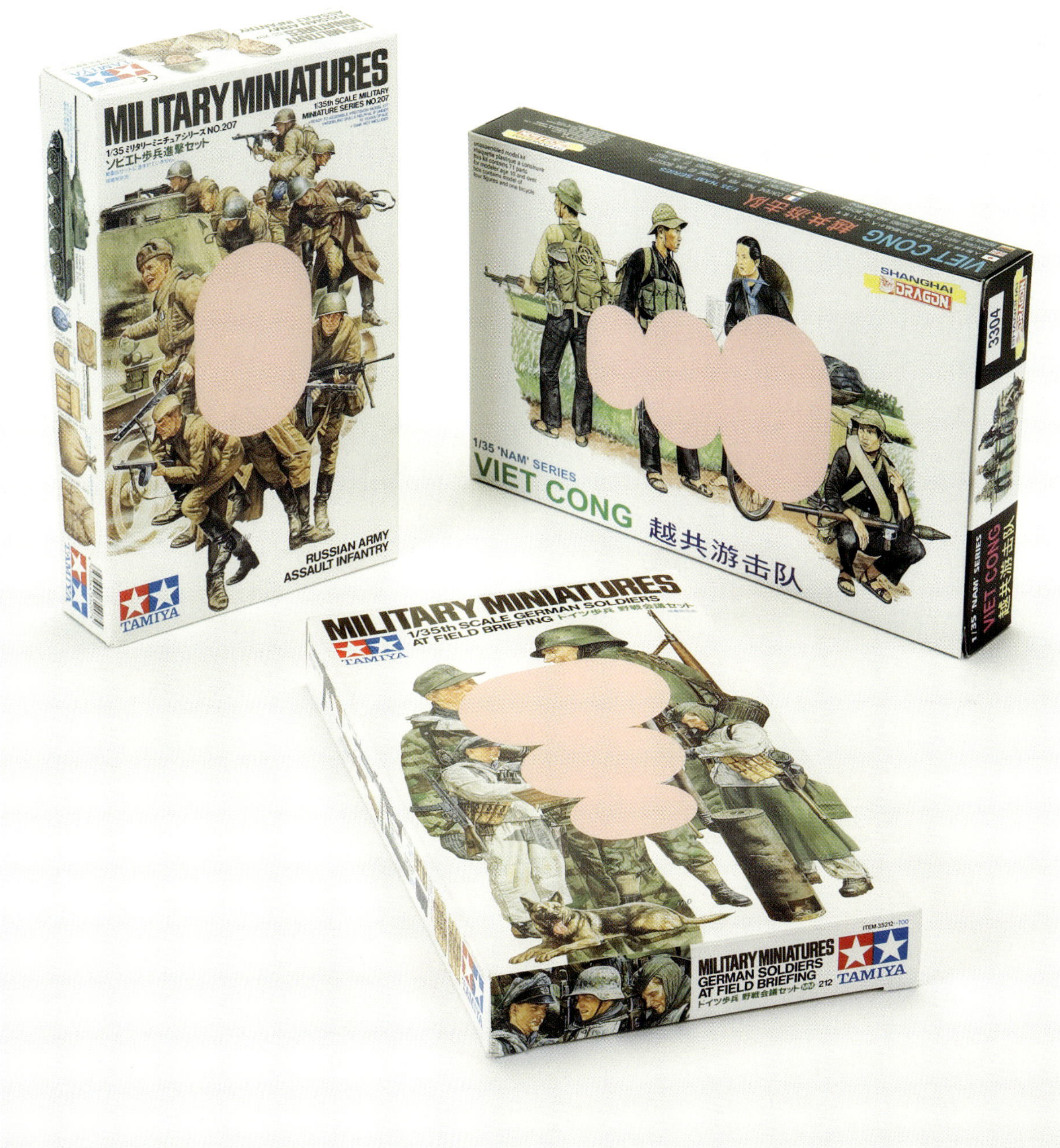

RUSSIANS, 2004
ACRYLIC ON PRINTED CARDBOARD
9 X 6 X 2 INCHES

VIET CONG, 2004
ACRYLIC ON PRINTED CARDBOARD
6 X 10 X 2 INCHES

GERMANS, 2004
ACRYLIC ON PRINTED CARDBOARD
10 X 6 X 1 INCHES

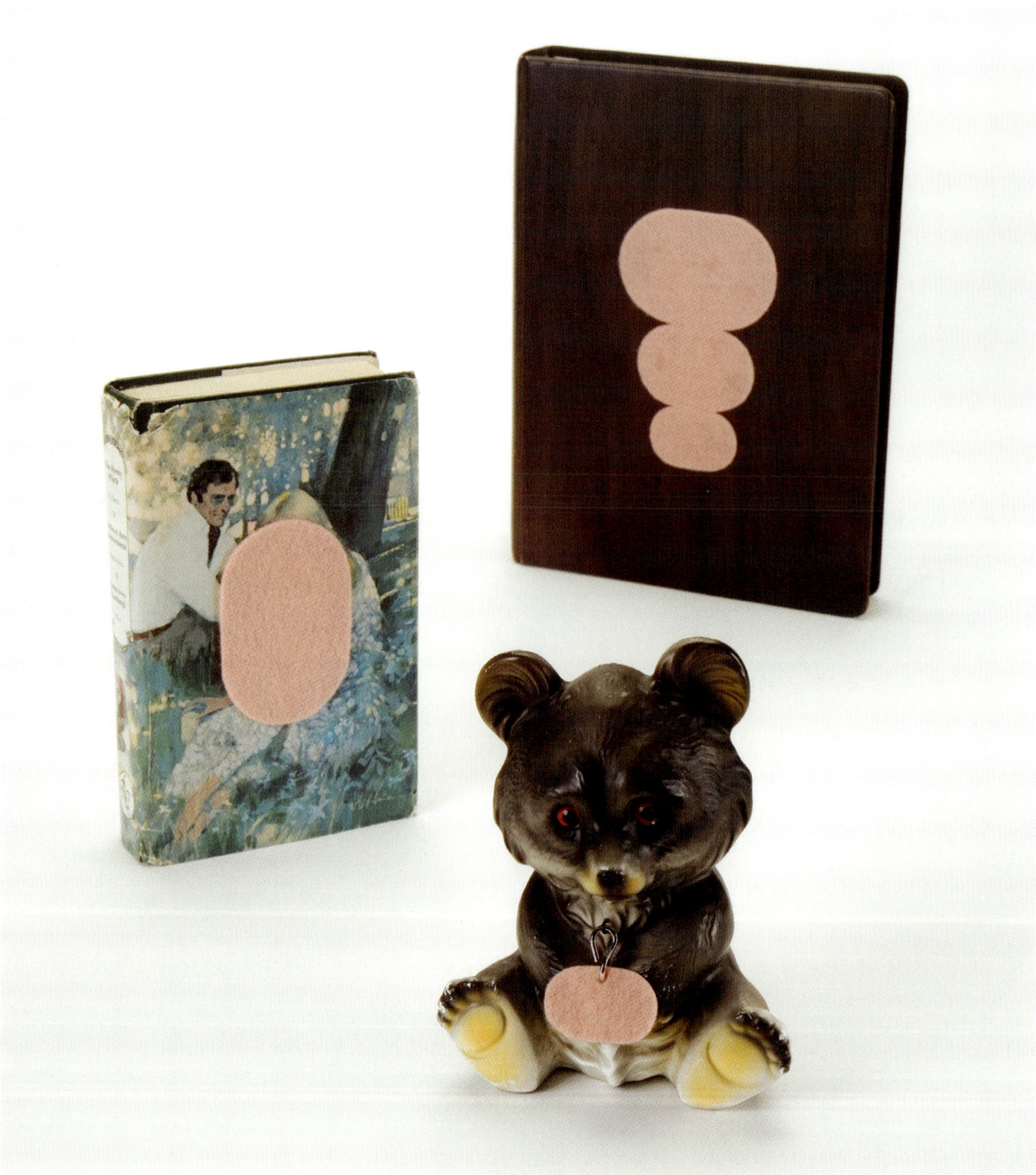

BOOK, 2004
FELT ON PRINTED PAPER & CARDBOARD
7 X 5 X 2 INCHES

BINDER, 2004
FELT ON PRINTED PLASTIC WITH PAPER & STEEL
10 X 8 X 2 INCHES

BEAR, 2004
FELT, CARDBOARD & STEEL ON CERAMIC
6 X 5 X 3 INCHES

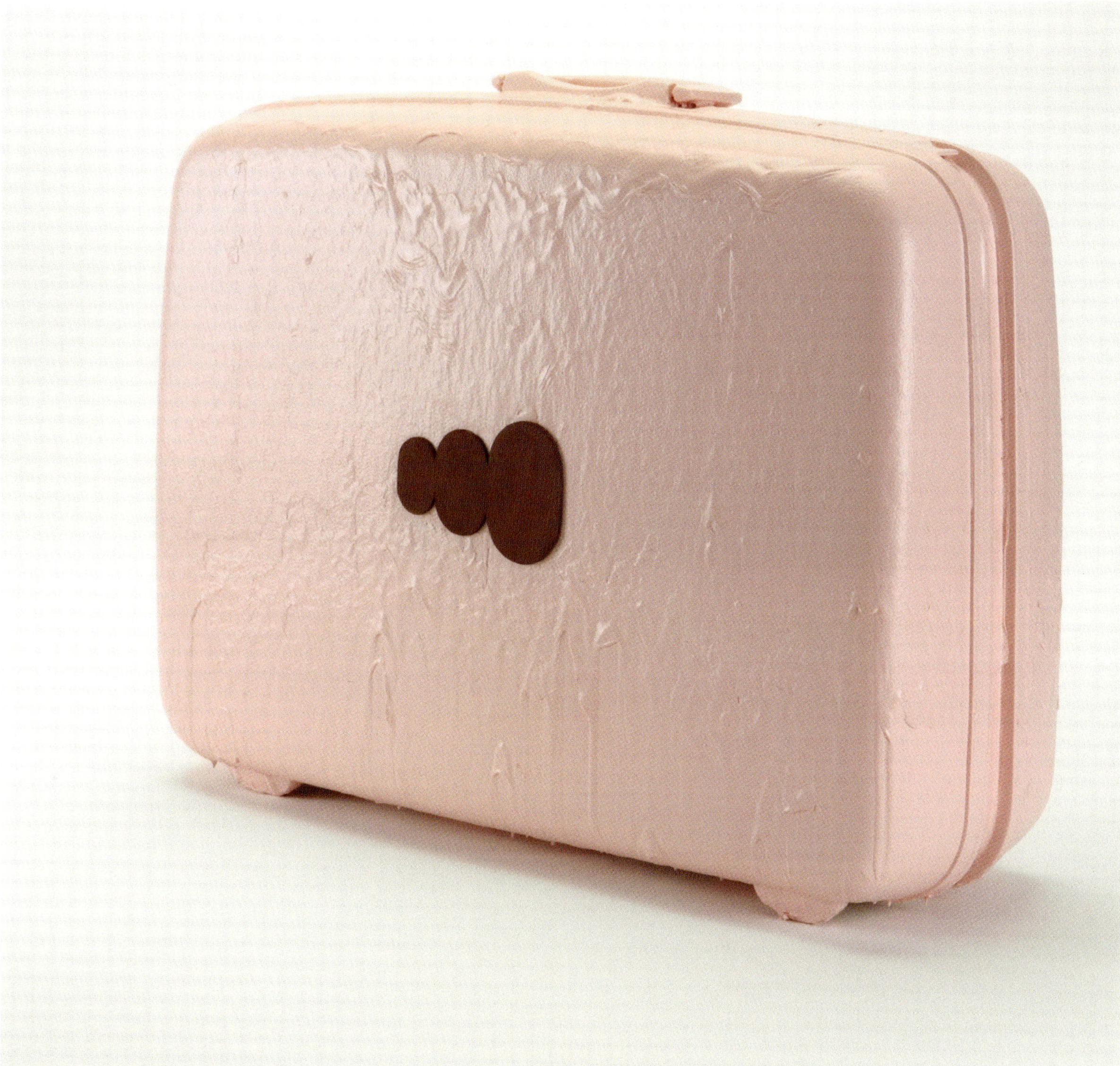

JAMES WESTWATER b. 1962 Salvador, Brazil. *Ed:* Suffolk College and Manchester Metropolitan Univ., England. *Exhib:* Lothringer Dreizehn, Munich; Sun and Doves, London; Kiron, Paris; Ahra Lee, New York; Robert Berman, Los Angeles; MoCA, Fort Collins; SITE Santa Fe; Linda Durham, Galisteo. *Coll:* Museum of Fine Arts, Santa Fe; Komar and Melamid, New York; Drew Barrymore, Los Angeles; Geoff Waring, London; Denys Arcand, Montreal; Pélé, Rio de Janeiro. *Representation:* James Kelly Contemporary, Santa Fe; Klaudia Marr Gallery, Santa Fe; Rule Gallery, Denver.

SUITCASE, 2004
ACRYLIC LATEX & RUBBER
ON PLASTIC, ALUMINUM & STEEL
18 X 23 X 7 INCHES

ANDREA VOLKOFF-SENUTOVITCH

What matters in the art of living, and concretely in the art of sculpture, is how you work the transformations. Which cup of change, chance and intention is poured into which, to reach the golden admixture at the heart of all art?

Andrea Volkoff- Senutovitch has figured that alchemy out by exploring, archiving, collecting, reworking, manipulating and assembling cast-off and discarded objects and antiques into *meta-objets d'art*. Charging the air around them with a formless presence has become her obsession. This secret intimate life of objects, their memories, the imprint left over time by the owner's soul, the resonant energies that become their psychic patina, and how these vibrate together, holds her committed attention. Andrea Volkoff-Senutovitch is a serious, spiritual, sculptural mixmistress. In the same way a good DJ assembles found materials to make a room take flight, the vibe off her best work has a papable intensity that has sent New Orleans voodoo healers into rapturous song. That's some serious juju.

Her father was Russian, though she was born in Santa Fe, and at one point she studied Orthodox Icon painting. One day she had finished painting her peacock feathers, just as instructed, a little more quickly than the other students, and decided to embellish them a little. The teacher became very upset, demanding to know what she thought she was doing. He then asked her to leave the class and not return. This early encounter with authority (in the form of the exacting rules of a seventeen hundred year old religio-artistic tradition) ended her only brush with formal art education but fueled her fire to make whatever she wanted to make.

The Dreamer, her first assemblage, was created that evening. From an open book in an ornate frame emerges the hand of an antique saint holding an ivory ball, an emblem of the innocence required to reconfigure one's religion.

Andrea Volkoff-Senutovitch's sculptures come from the mind's delight in fantastic hybrids. It runs through fairy tales, Bosch and Archimboldo. Artistically her ancestry includes Man Ray, Rauschenberg, Broodthaers, Boltanski, and of course, Duchamp, while her project is closest in feel to Joseph Cornell's in it's ability to present syrup-free sentiment and give a heartfelt nostalgic longing for a past you never had.

Her sculptures exist on a human scale (she's outside the box now and in the room with you), impressing upon the viewer their everyday reality while at the same time inducing an hallucinogenic fever of symbolic imagining, magic code deciphering and intuitive interpretation. Her meanings are ultimately archetypal so they reside at the boundary of the conscious and unconscious mind, and to be truly grasped must be sought in the self. Speaking of the sacredness of intuition in the work of creating her alchemical constructs she says, "I believe the individual elements have a soul of their own. When assembling them I know instinctively if something doesn't belong. When a piece is placed correctly I can feel it, there is a smile, a sigh, a fit."

ANDREA VOLKOFF-SENUTOVITCH

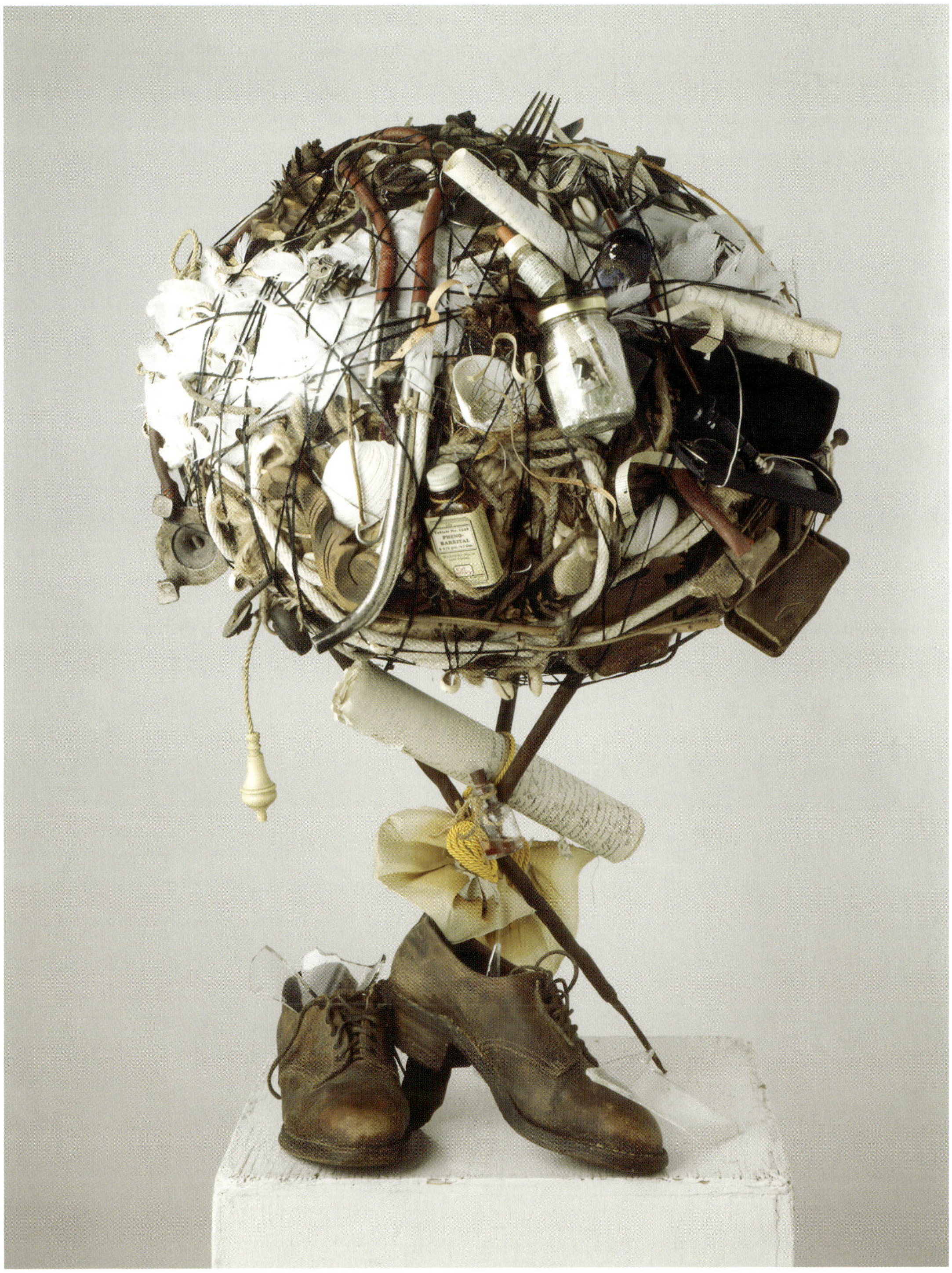

UNCLE JOE'S EGG
GREAT UNCLE JOE'S FETISH FILLED WITH OBJECTS
HE MIGHT HAVE COLLECTED AS A CHILD AND
DURING ADULTHOOD, 2000
WRITING, EYEGLASSES, MEDICINE BOTTLES,
SHOES & BROKEN GLASS
28 X 20 INCHES

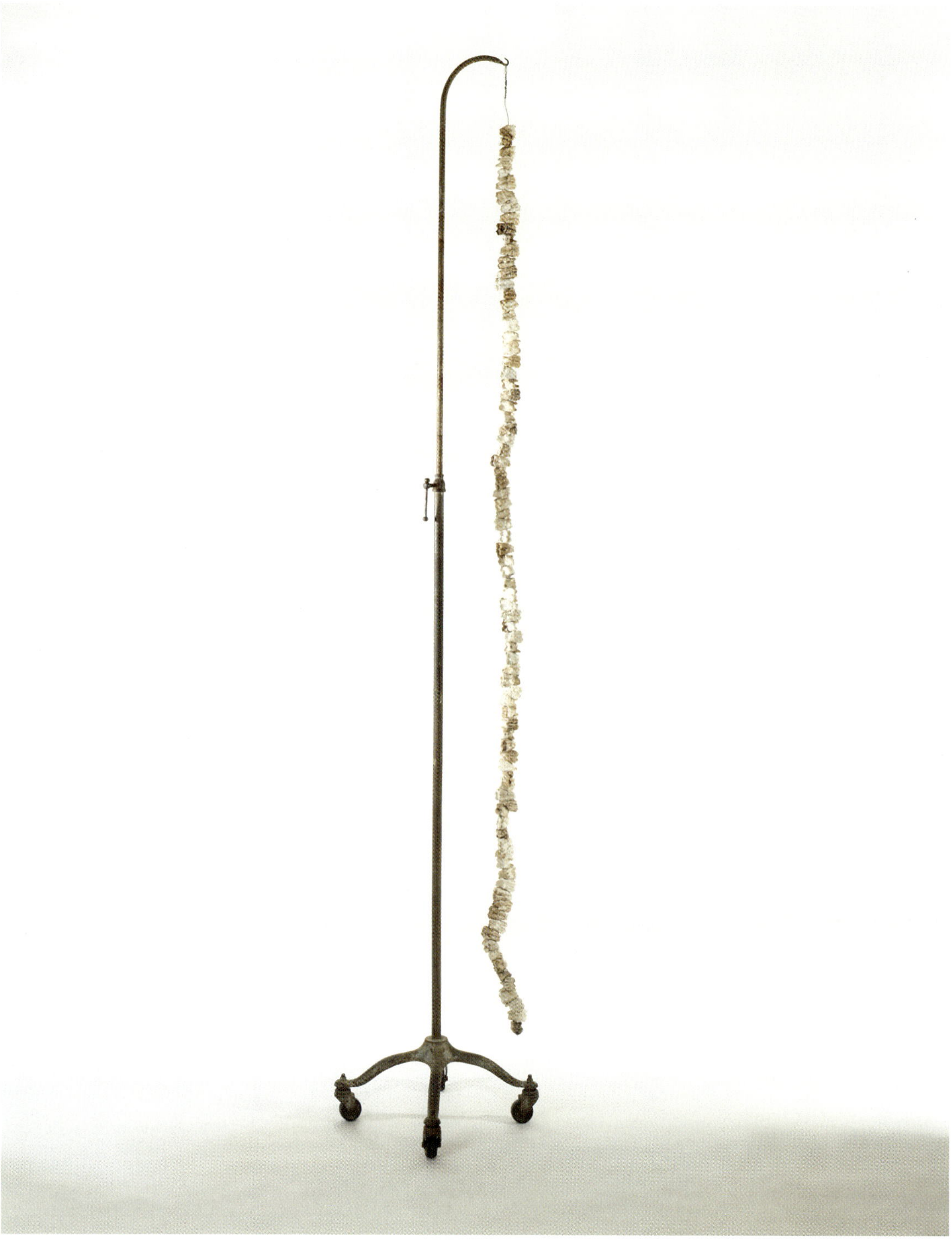

TROJAN HORSE, 2004
CAST HORSE TEETH ON WIRE HUNG FROM
AN ANTIQUE MEDICAL IV STAND
72 INCHES

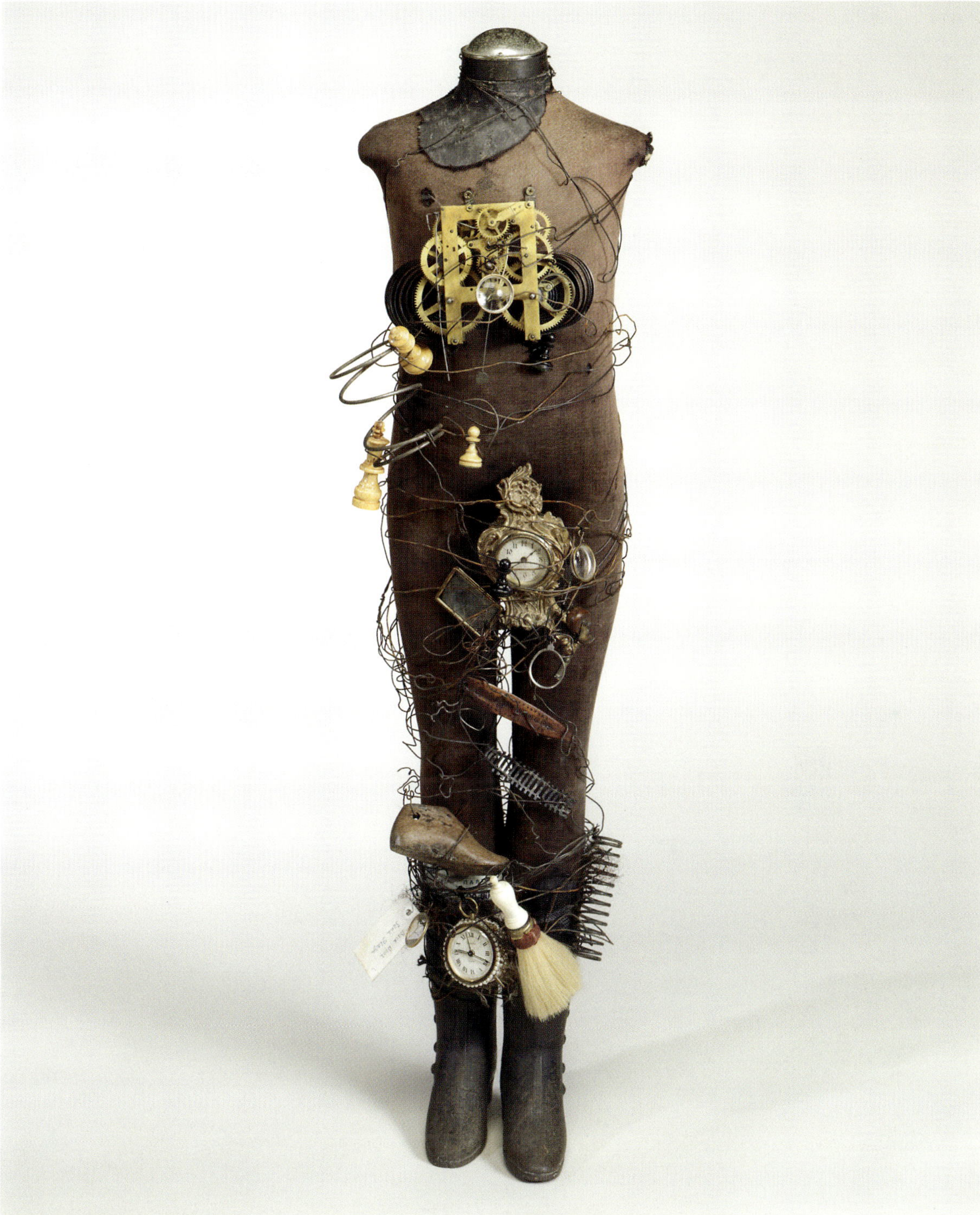

VICTORIAN CHILD'S MANNEQUIN FROM
SALEM, MASSACHUSETTS, 2003
TIME PIECES & FOUND OBJECTS
48 INCHES

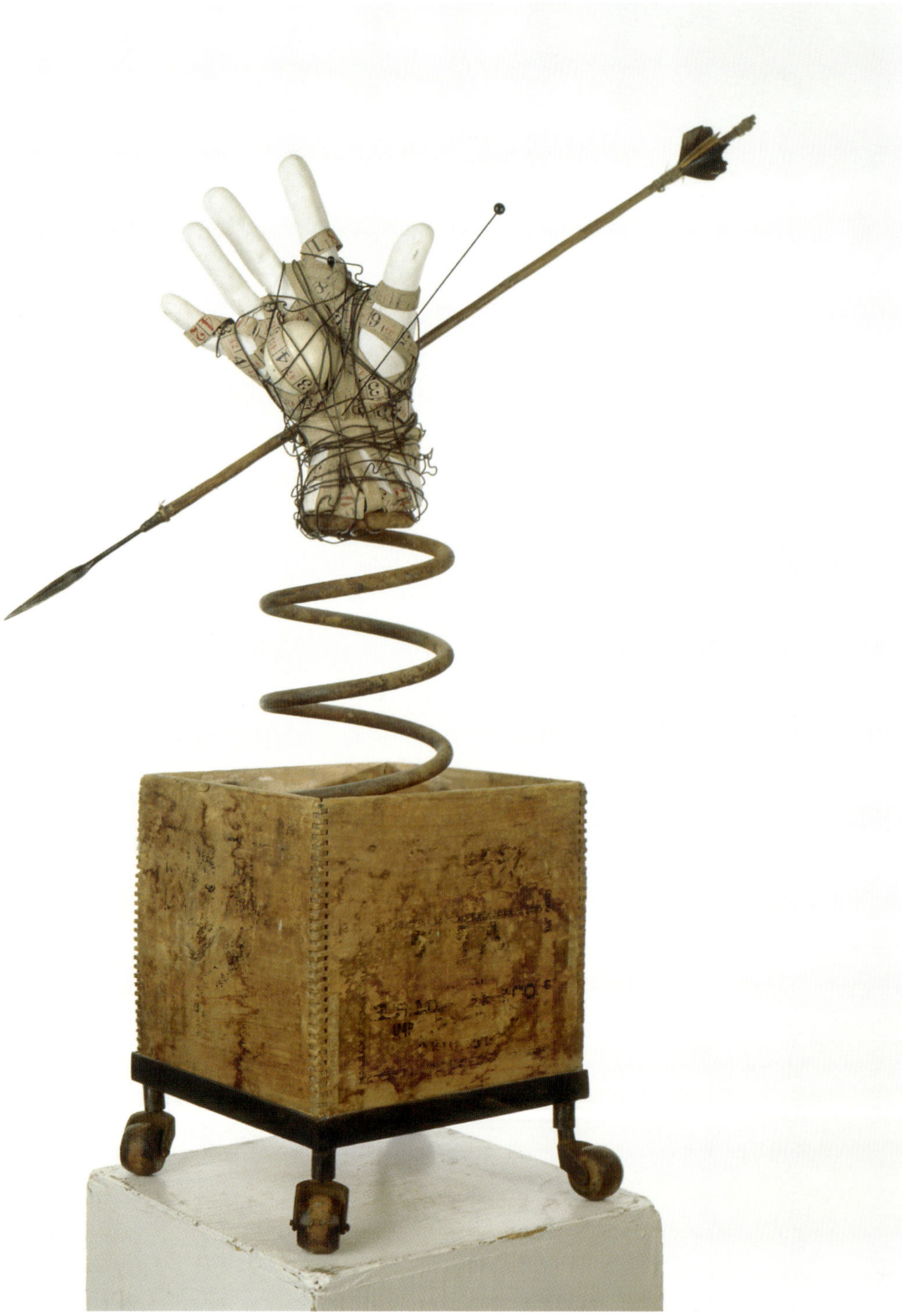

REACHING OUT, HAND IN BOX, 2000
ANTIQUE JAPANESE TEA BOX ON WHEELS,
PLASTER HAND, OLD MEASURING TAPE, AFRICAN
HUNTING ARROW, VINTAGE HAT PIN & WIRE
36 X 26 X 19 INCHES

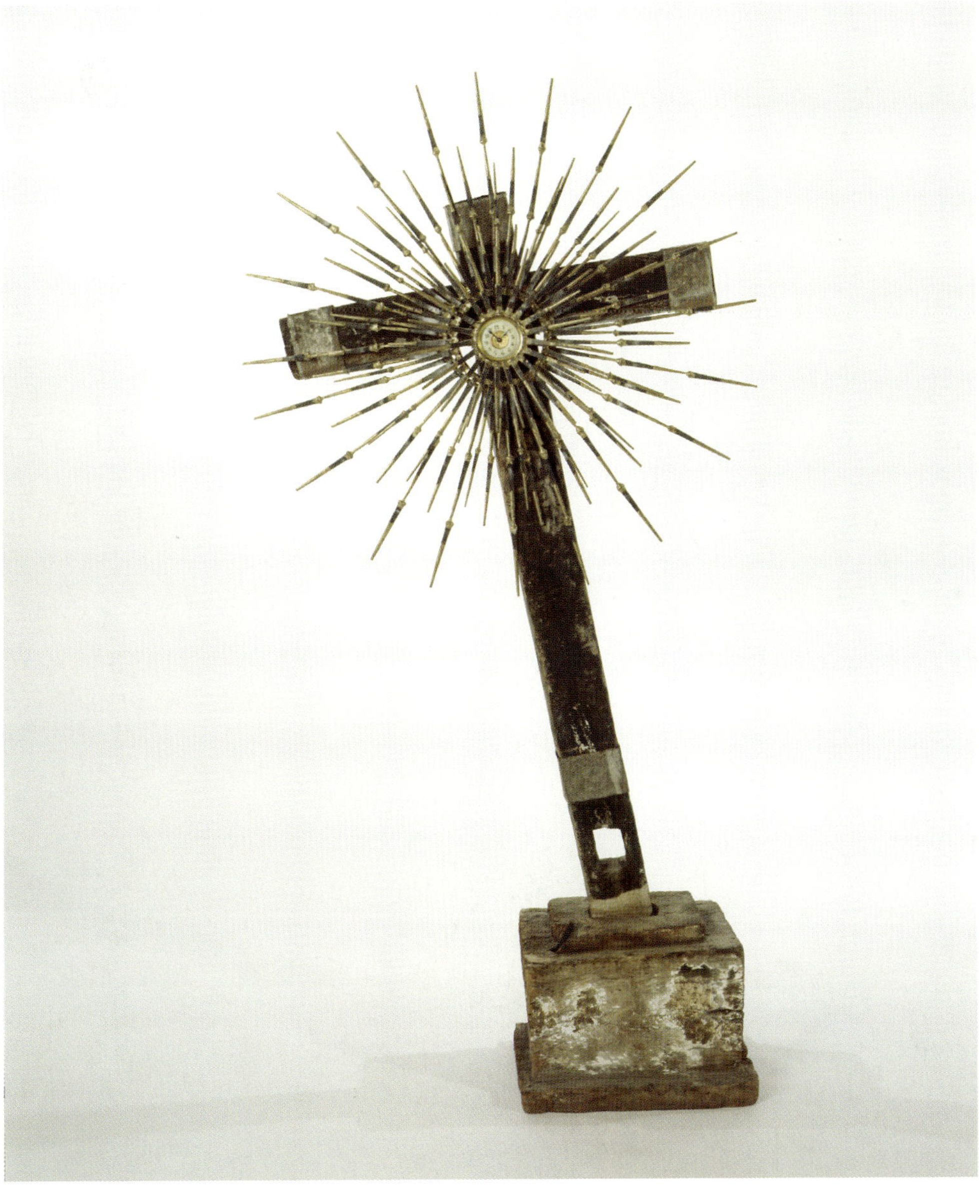

ANDREA VOLKOFF-SENUTOVITCH b. 1961 Santa Fe NM. *Ed.* Univ. New Mexico. *Coll:* Robert Stivers: Marion Wasserman; Michael Diaz; Pat Hall. *Exhib:* Winterowd Fine Art, Santa Fe; Russian Egg Auction, Museum of Fine Arts, Santa Fe; Cross Show, Museum of International Folk Art Shop, Santa Fe; Group Exhibition, Barristers Gallery, New Orleans; FOCA Artist Exhibition, LewAllen Contemporary, Santa Fe; Recycled Art Juried Show, First Place, Santa Fe. *Representation:* Barristers Gallery, New Orleans; Winterowd Fine Arts, Santa Fe.

CROSS WITH IDEA, 2001
ANTIQUE MEXICAN CROSS ON PLINTH, BRONZE
STARBURST & FRENCH CLOCK IN CENTER
48 INCHES

TRACY KRUMM

Wall Curtain; Saw Blade

The elements are listed in the artist's marvelously literal title. Hanging on the wall from the blade of an old logging saw is the folded ghost of a curtain crocheted from copper wire. The great thing about this particular piece of Tracy Krumm's is not that it questions assumptions about an arbitrary line dividing the handicrafts of women from the traditionally patriarchal Arts with a capital A. This it does with *bravura*, as does all of Krumm's work, but the great thing in this piece is that Tracy Krumm relishes that line as she obliterates it, playing both sides splendidly close to the chest, knowing she holds the winning hand.

Her first card is the scent of prairie grass and more than a strand of pioneer romance. *Wall Curtain; Saw Blade* is an homage to every blanket ever crocheted by nimble fingers on autumn evenings, as if the same astral thread ran through them all and straight into Tracy Krumm's art. A thread through conversations and the ease of mind in the silences as night falls and one by one they go to sleep. A thread through your fingertips, a soothing chant of touch, running like a prayer of gratitude to all aunts, *abuelas*, and ancestors practicing these crafts.

And at the same time, the piece is an airy work of sophisticated minimalism, an *arte povera* object drawing, and it ups the ante with a bit of a rectangular jab at painting's near death experiences. "Hang it up, painter boys," the work asserts with complete confidence, "Crocheting's still going strong," and has finally found its wildest maverick in Tracy Krumm.

Besides delightfully deflating gender biases, and puncturing the puffed paradigms that meaninglessly divide arts and crafts practices, Krumm constructs a fascinating mechanics of abstracted emotion and sculptural play. Her works can be read as enlarged cooking implements, they can literally be baskets, or they can look like mechanisms from a lost world of machinery. Some are sweet, delicate, and diaphanous while others have a sinister edge of bondage and gothic torture. Almost all would function nicely as lobster traps.

There is a rare humor here too, and a Dr. Suessian sense of whimsy. Another pole of her work expresses itself in pieces like *Long Tapered Bag or Semi-shroud Coil*. A figurative sense animates these symmetrical pieces, scaled to the body, dropping from the ceiling like marionettes. The formal and literal tensions compound in a way that brings a suspended feeling of expectant life to their taut verticality. This all-encompassing vitality is at the heart of Tracy Krumm's project.

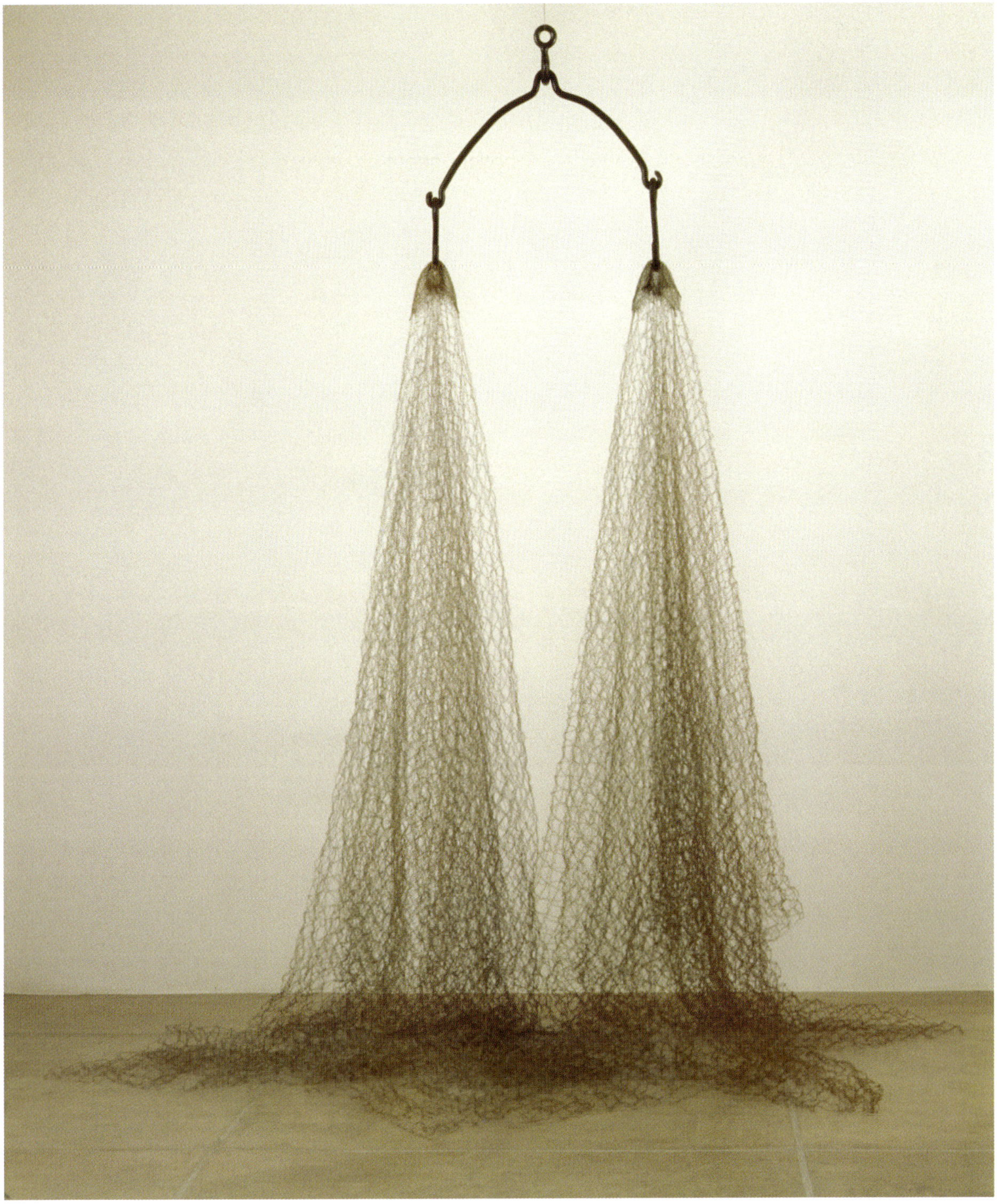

BALANCED, 2003
CROCHETED & FABRICATED METAL & FOUND OBJECT
121 X 114 X 82 INCHES

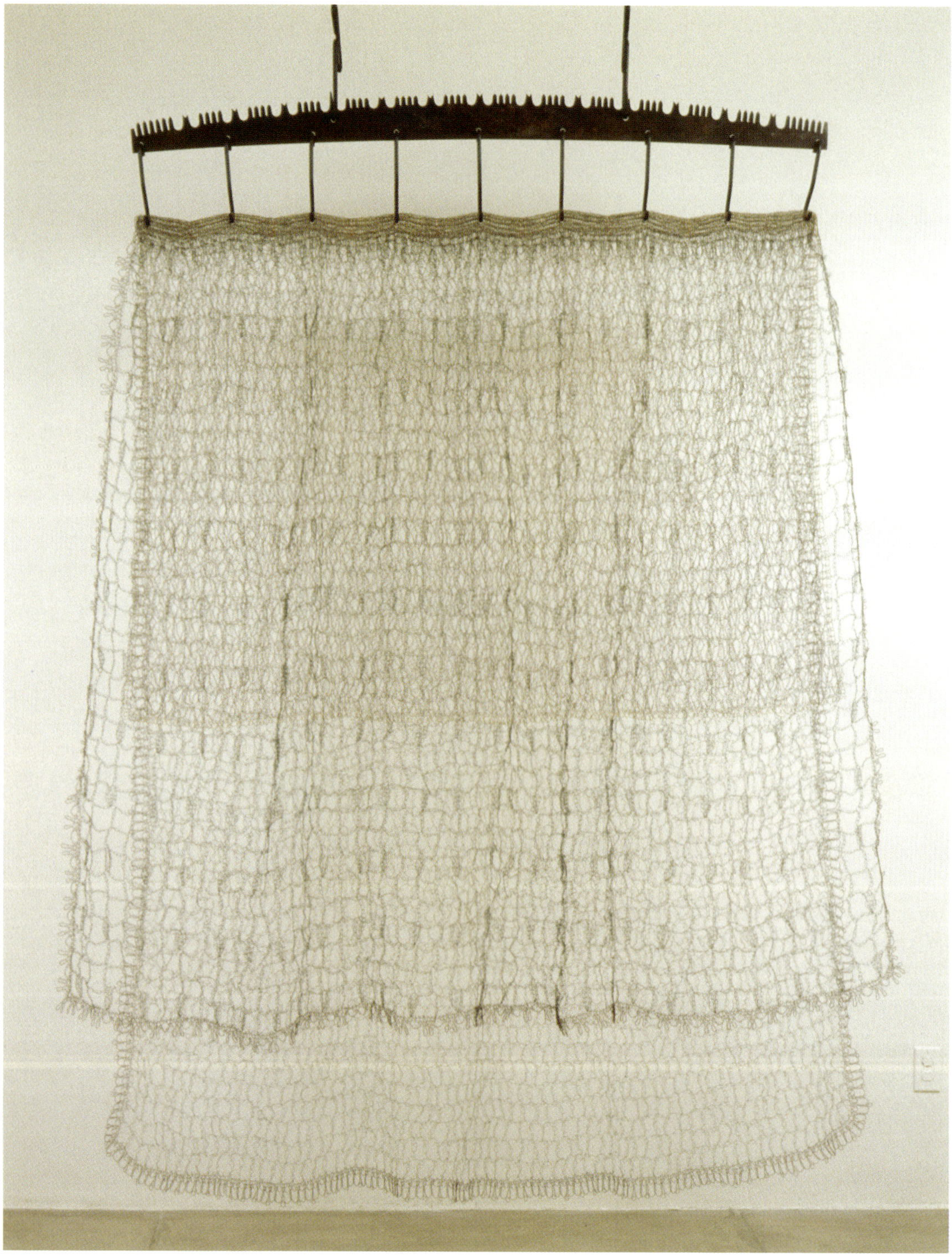

WALL CURTAIN: SAW BLADE, 2002
CROCHETED & FABRICATED METAL & FOUND OBJECTS
104 X 78 X 10 INCHES

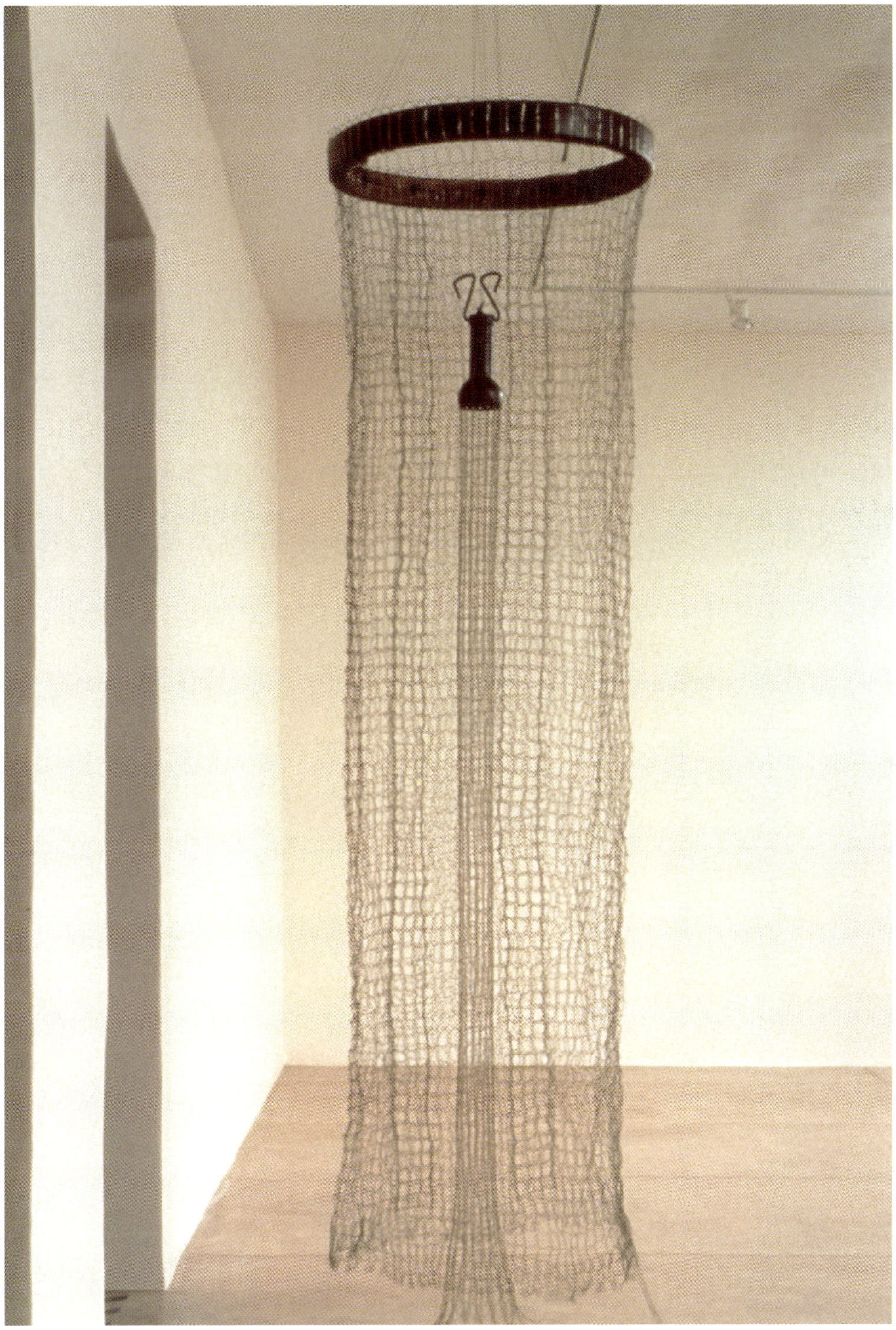

SHROUD: WAGON WHEEL/BLOOMING BELL
CROCHETED & FABRICATED METAL & FOUND OBJECT
110 X 31 X 31 INCHES

TRACY KRUMM

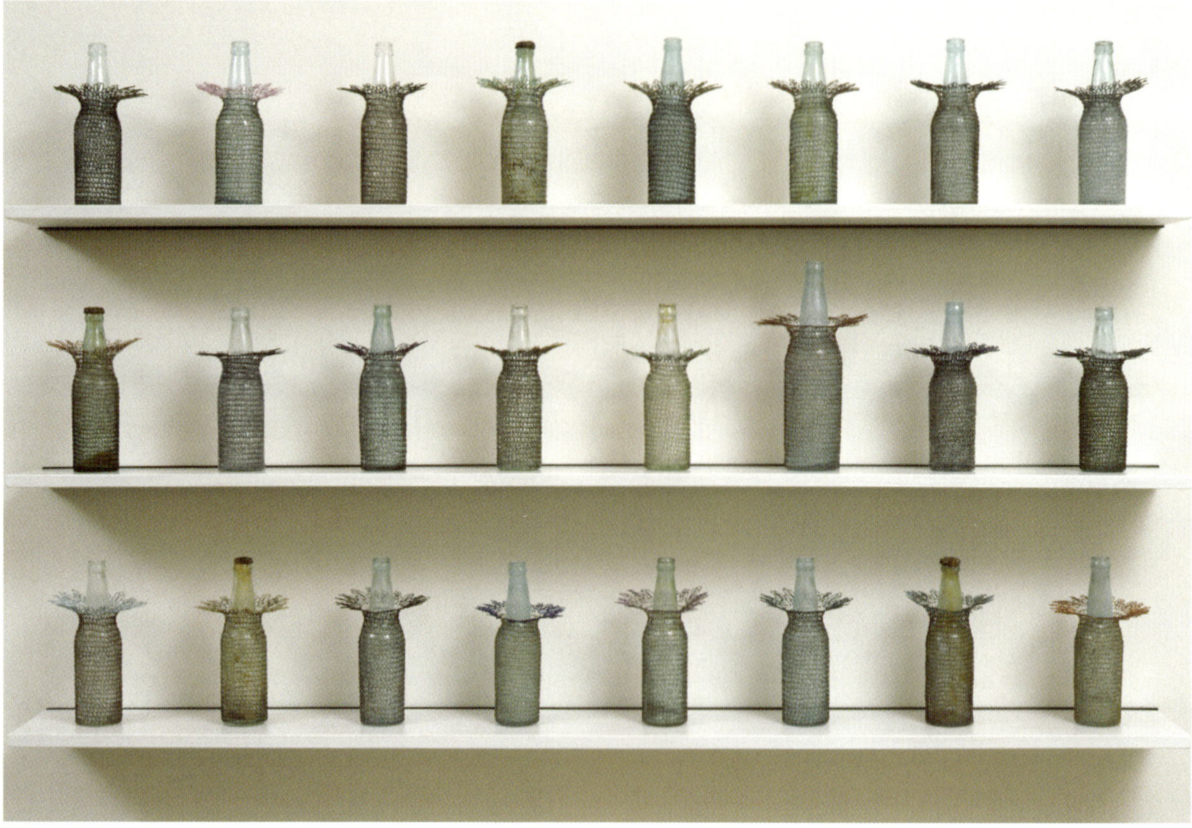

TWO DOZEN, 2003
CROCHETED & FABRICATED METAL & FOUND OBJECT
42 X 68 X 8 INCHES

TRACY KRUMM

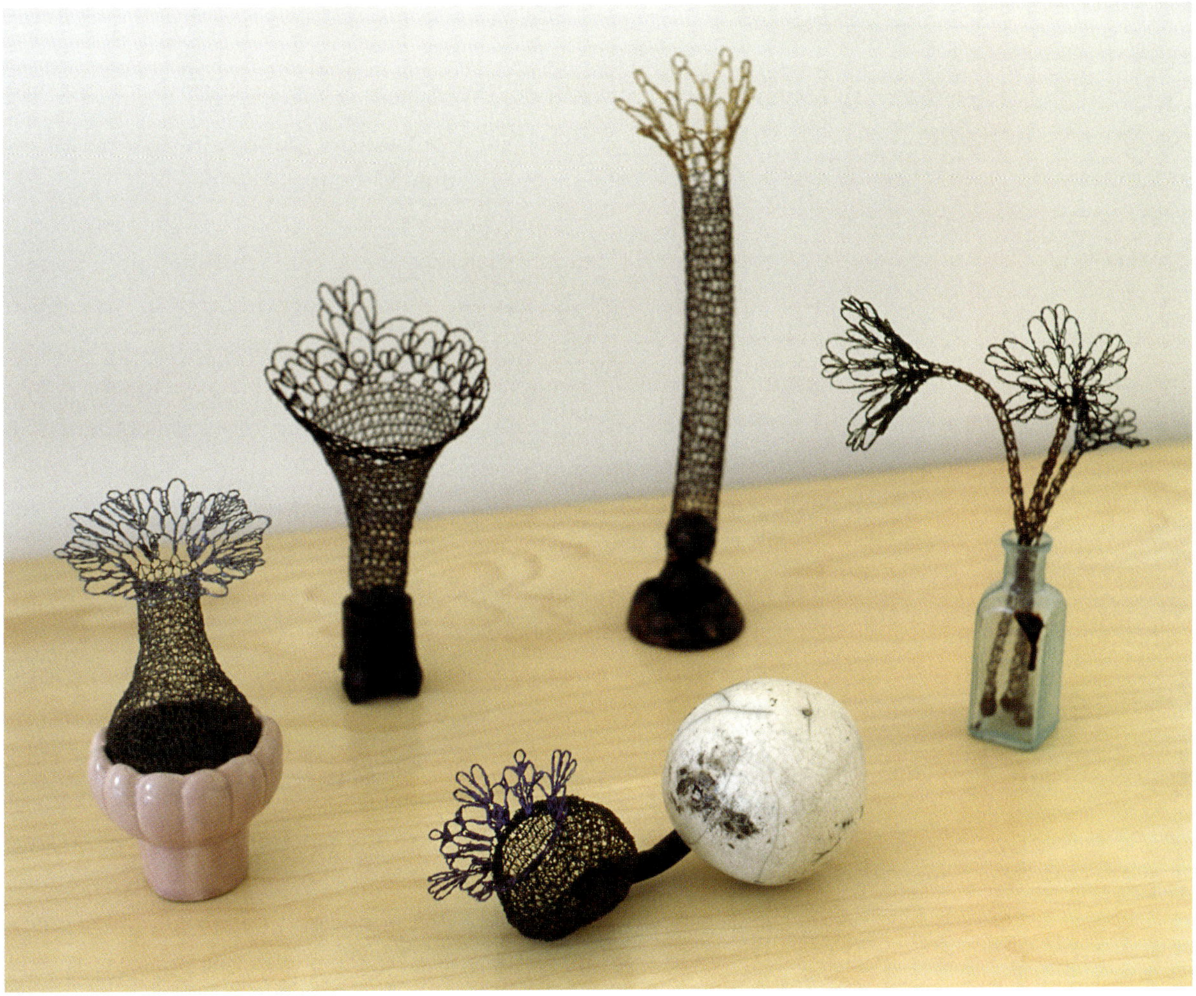

TRACY KRUMM b. 1963 Kenosha WI. *Ed:* MFA Vermont College; BFA California College of Art and Crafts, Oakland; Evergreen State College, Olympia WA. *Coll:* Atlanta Airport Hilton; American Craft Museum, New York; Ed Broida Trust, Santa Fe; Clorox Corporation, Palo Alto CA; Concepts, Santa Fe; Denver Art Museum; Elements, Chicago; Ford Motor Company, Serramonte; Kaiser Permanente Hospitals CA; Lark Books/ Fiberarts, Asheville; Marin General Hospital, San Rafael; Minnesota State Arts Board, St. Paul; Museum of Fine Arts, Santa Fe; Shadow Agency, Minneapolis. *Representation:* Linda Durham Contemporary Art, Santa Fe.

LUCKY BLOOM AND OTHERS, 2002
FABRICATED METAL & FOUND OBJECTS

BARBARA ZUSMAN

Barbara Zusman's power to see through appearances to the essence of things raises the question of what constitutes essence. Is essence a perfect Platonic form existing in an invisible dimension towards a shadow of which human perception strives? Or is essence a perfume, an auric phosphorescence, an invisible but perceptible encoding of uniqueness? Is essence something deep inside that has to do with character, virtuosity, and soul?

Existence precedes essence is what Sartre said, reversing Plato's poetry. Maybe essence is a particularly resonant linguistic echo, vibrating inside and out, expanding beyond time and sounding through an ungraspable sea of ever changing constructs. Is essence a buoy of truth in the fog of other words, or is it the shape of the enveloping fog itself?

This questioning of essence is what makes the work of Barbara Zusman essential. Her sculptures grasp certain aspects of the truth of a thing which otherwise might go unknown. They demarcate zones of associative slippage through multiple categorical levels including those that would seek to demonstrate the difference between nothing and something. Perhaps essence is the medium that allows this skipping along from A is to B is to C which is the core of simile, metaphor, analogy, allegory, and a million other mental mapping systems. Is essence eternal or can it be rewired, remixed, and rewound.

Or is it what you wind up with, a distillation after an arduous process of removing the inessential. Perhaps this is why Barbara Zusman's closest artistic forbearer is minimalist Eva Hesse. Zusman operates with the tactility and contained emotion that guided Hesse's mature work. The iconic wall pieces, *Square to Round*, for example, could almost be 3D realizations of obsessive Hesse drawings.

Zusman's unwrapping of the invisible spaces that her wood supports create is mind bogglingly intense. Each edge of coffee stained muslin meticulously overlaps the next by as little as a millimeter resulting in soft organic forms that look like they arrive through some kind of natural process, the way a snail or clam secretes a shell over time, or a caterpillar becomes a chrysalis. In Zusman's case a cyclical accretion, or nesting instinct takes over. This is where the essential slippage starts, at the point of zen hypnosis derived from Zusman's infinite spiraling linearity and its resulting forms.

You are reminded of a ritual wrapping of a body, a tactile incantation endlessly repeated, an Egyptian mummification, a symbolic stele in the language of a lost nomadic tribe, a compulsive fetishism of sculptural space, an haptic topography, a vulvic topology, a sensuous, winding geography, an anthropological anthropomorphic essence, a birth process, a sustained soul swaddling, and a cocoon for an unknowable, unbirthed, interior life which blooms in the mind's ear. And the beautiful epitaph the great poet Rilke wrote for his own gravestone and the flower that killed him—

Rose, o pure contradiction,
desire to be no one's sleep
beneath so many lids

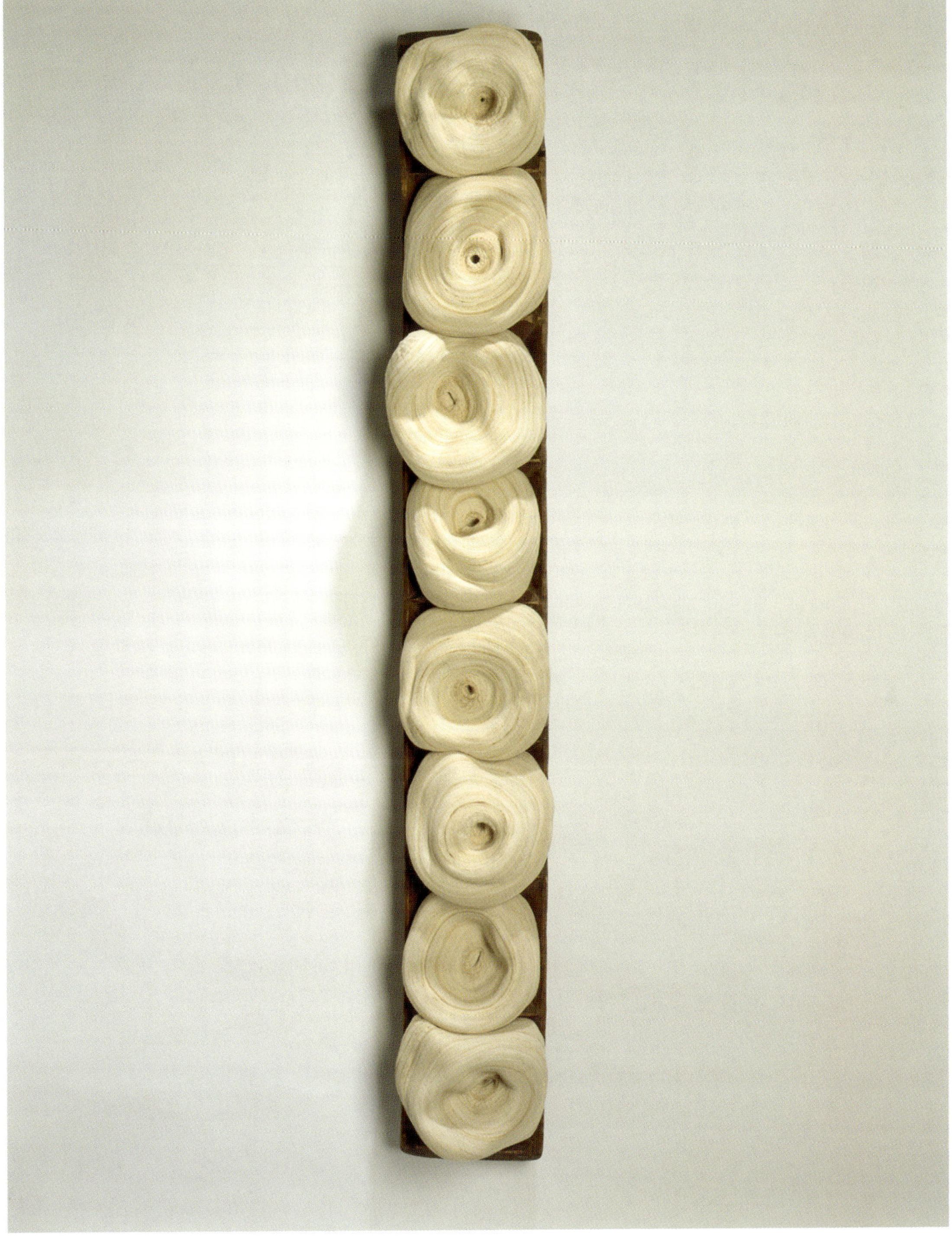

MULTIPLE NESTS
COFFEE ON MUSLIN ON FOAM, FOUND WOOD
80.5 X 8 X 10 INCHES

BARBARA ZUSMAN

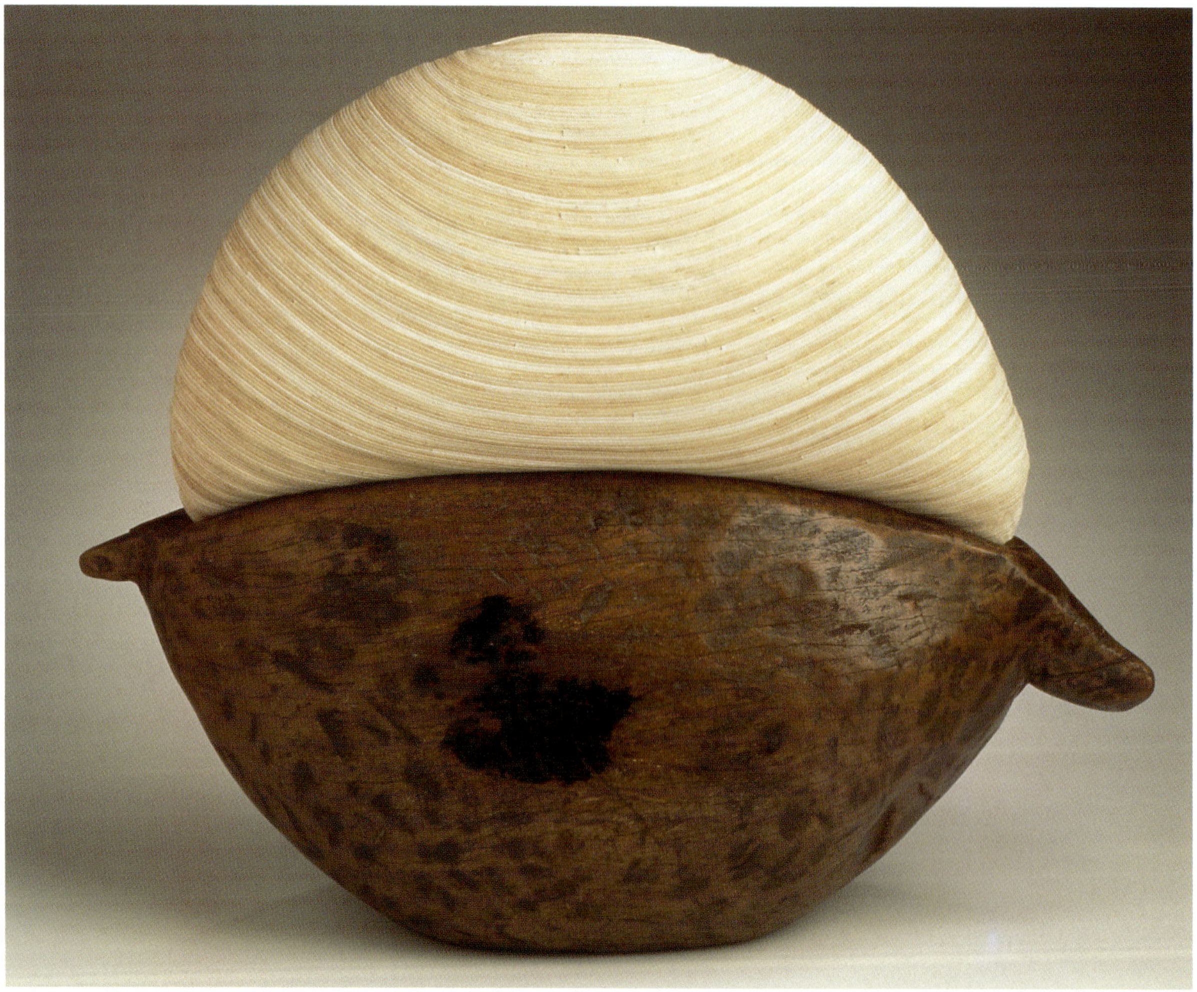

BIRD, 2003
MUSLIN ON WOOD
21 X 25.5 X 10 INCHES

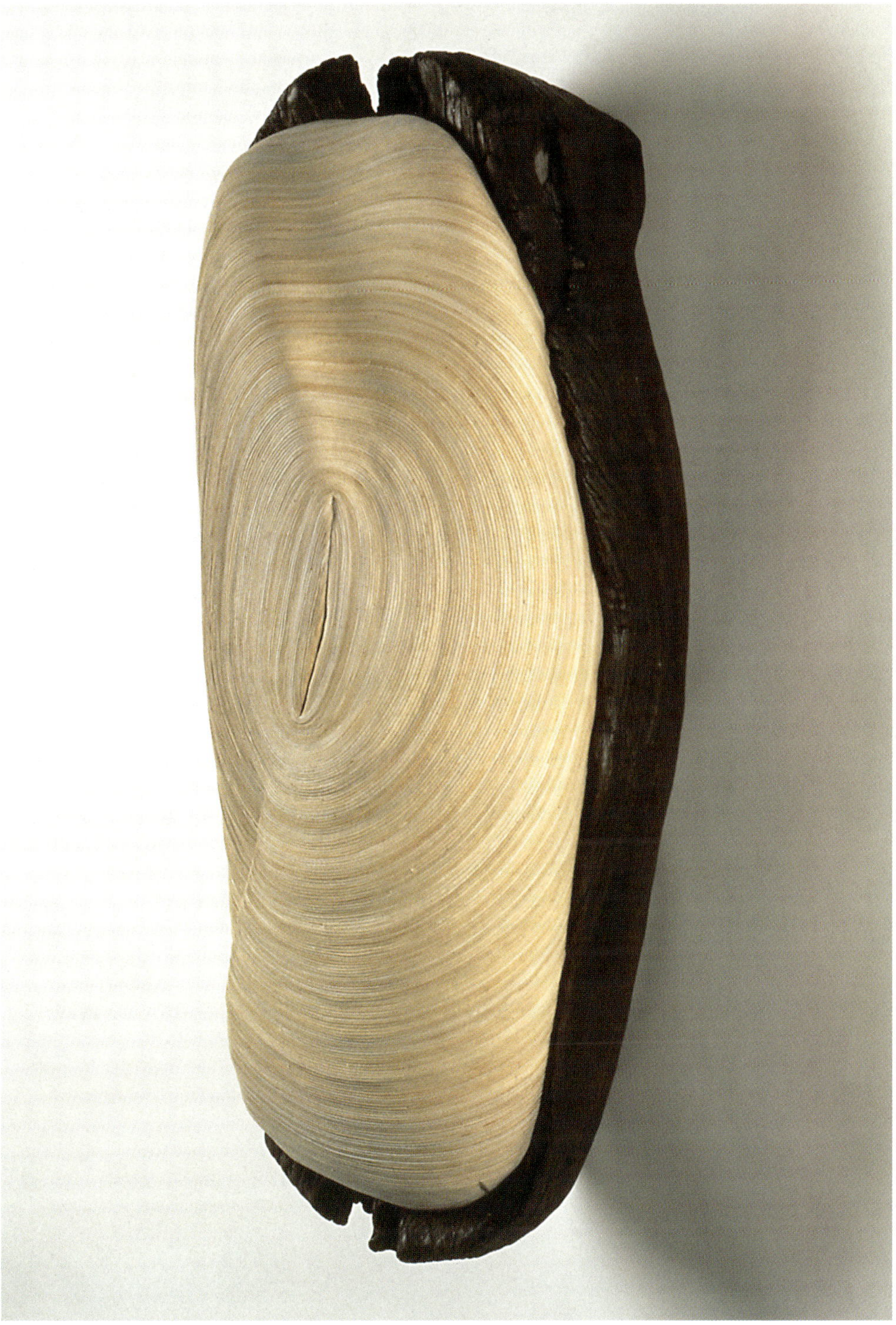

OVAL, 2003 (SIDE VIEW)
MUSLIN ON WOOD
30.5 X 14.5 X 11.5 INCHES

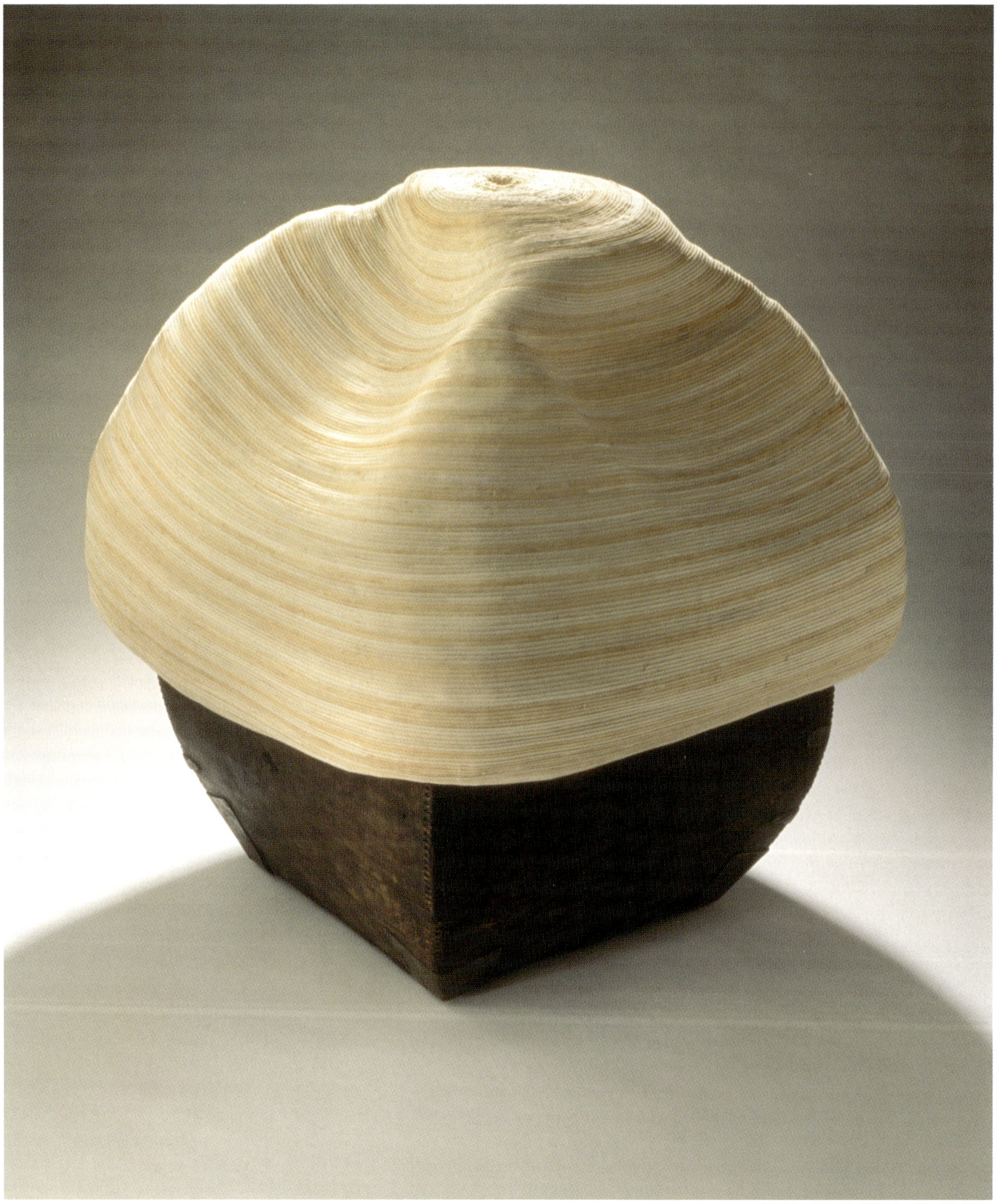

OVERFLOW #2, 2003
COFFEE, MUSLIN, FOAM & FOUND WOOD
20 X 20 X 19 INCHES

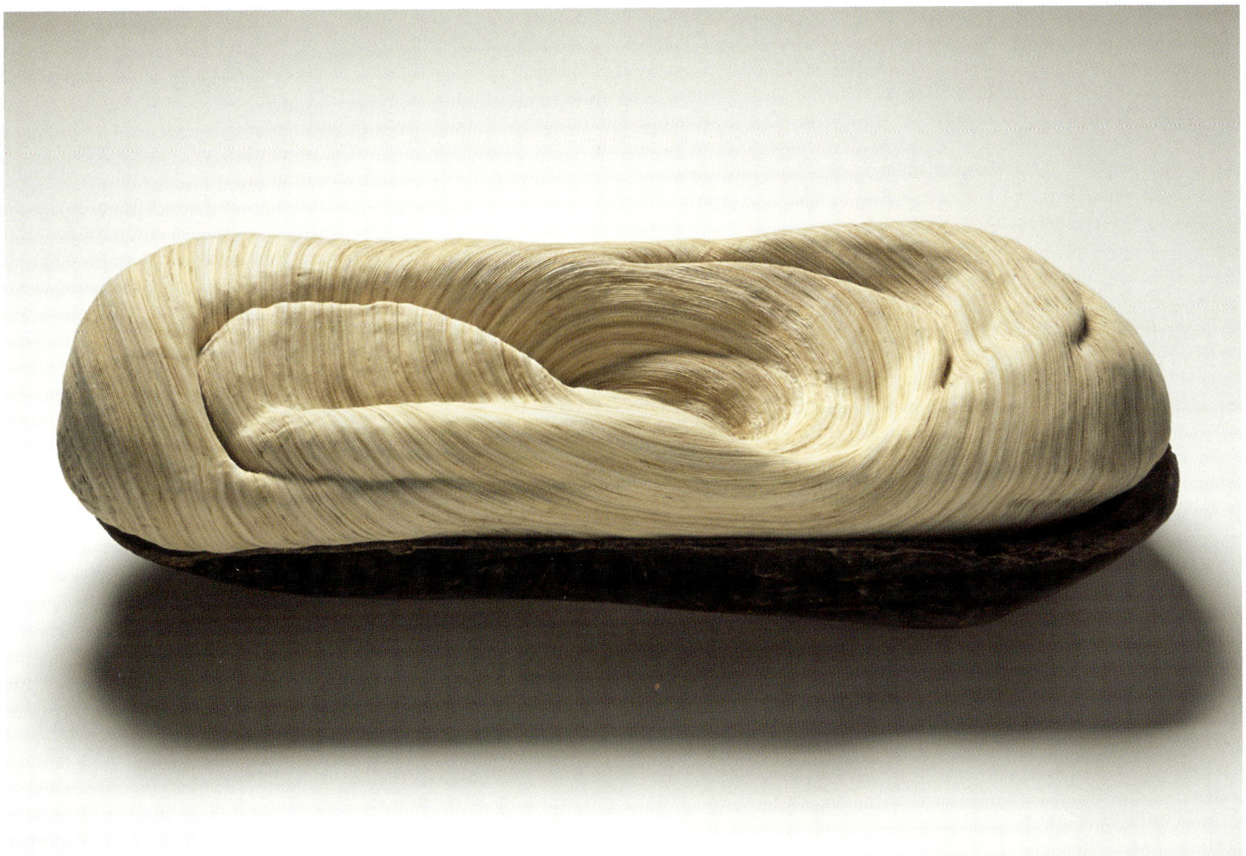

BARBARA ZUSMAN b. 1944 Chester PA. *Ed:* BA and MFA Program, Portland State Univ. OR. *Coll:* Museum of Fine Arts, Santa Fe; Scottsdale Center for the Visual Arts; Cannon U.S.A., Lake Success NY; Pacific Northwest Bell Telephone Company, Seattle; Eberhard Faber Company, New York; City of Portland; Seattle Light Company; Rainier Bank, Seattle; Ed Broida Trust, Santa Fe. *Representation:* Linda Durham Contemporary Art, Santa Fe.

CRADLE, 2001
MIXED MEDIA ON FOUND WOOD
11 X 41.5 X 16 INCHES

DOUG GRAY

The four elements—fire, water, air and earth—the sun, the rain, the wind, and rock—may be associated with different aspects of the person. Fire is spirit, enthusiasm—the creative will that you feel in your gut. Water is the ocean of emotion—assuming every shifting shape in an endless florescence, centered in the wellspring kindness of the heart. Air is for breathing ideas, words—your intellect magnificently housing and inhabiting vast imaginary worlds inside and outside your communicative cranium. And Earth is the involuntary, organic, interlock with life—the skeletal structure of desire and fecundity grounded around the base of your spine.

Sculptor Doug Gray makes work fired by inspiration, rising from earth into air, tapping into deep aquifers of feeling. His stone and wood constructs are at once emotive, intelligent, earthy, and alight.

Nido de Corazón puzzles together, from equal parts of stone and space, a nest for the heart, that rhythmic section of sea which evolution put outside-in in each of us. In the beginning we only felt what water feels. Gray's series of interlocking marble plinths connecting stilt-like legs of ash appears extremely vulnerable, and simultaneously protective. Here is an airy pragmatics of compassion, a lesson in staying light and open to the burning joy of this world, while also staying cool and solid with your feet firmly on the clay. It's clearly a matter of delicate balance.

All of Doug Gray's work is about the process of making. You almost see the work construct itself before your eyes. Nothing is hidden here. Though there is magic, there are no tricks, no sleight of hand. The balance is found by being truly in your body in each moment. Each finished piece is a happy accident—what resembles luck and ease is hard work and openness to opportunity. The work is about a solid connectivity between stone and spirit, between the earth and all your *chakras*.

If the steadiness needed to overcome *gravitas* and hold the heart aloft is the true subject of *Nido de Corazón*, the figure suggested by *Awakening: From the Cradle to the Grave* is the wave master who maintains that self-same equilibrium. Still as marble and onyx ought be, yet he moves and ripples within the most abstract of fabrics, robed arms raised in a prayer on the air. Whether priest or priestess is of no matter, whoever the spirit of the stone may be. He has subjugated the mind to serve the truth of the heart, has satisfied the belly, has strengthened the spine, and seems apt at any moment to issue auric flames of transformational soul-magic from the crown of the head.

Suffice to say, contemporary stone-carver, Doug Gray easily interlocks all the elements in perfect play.

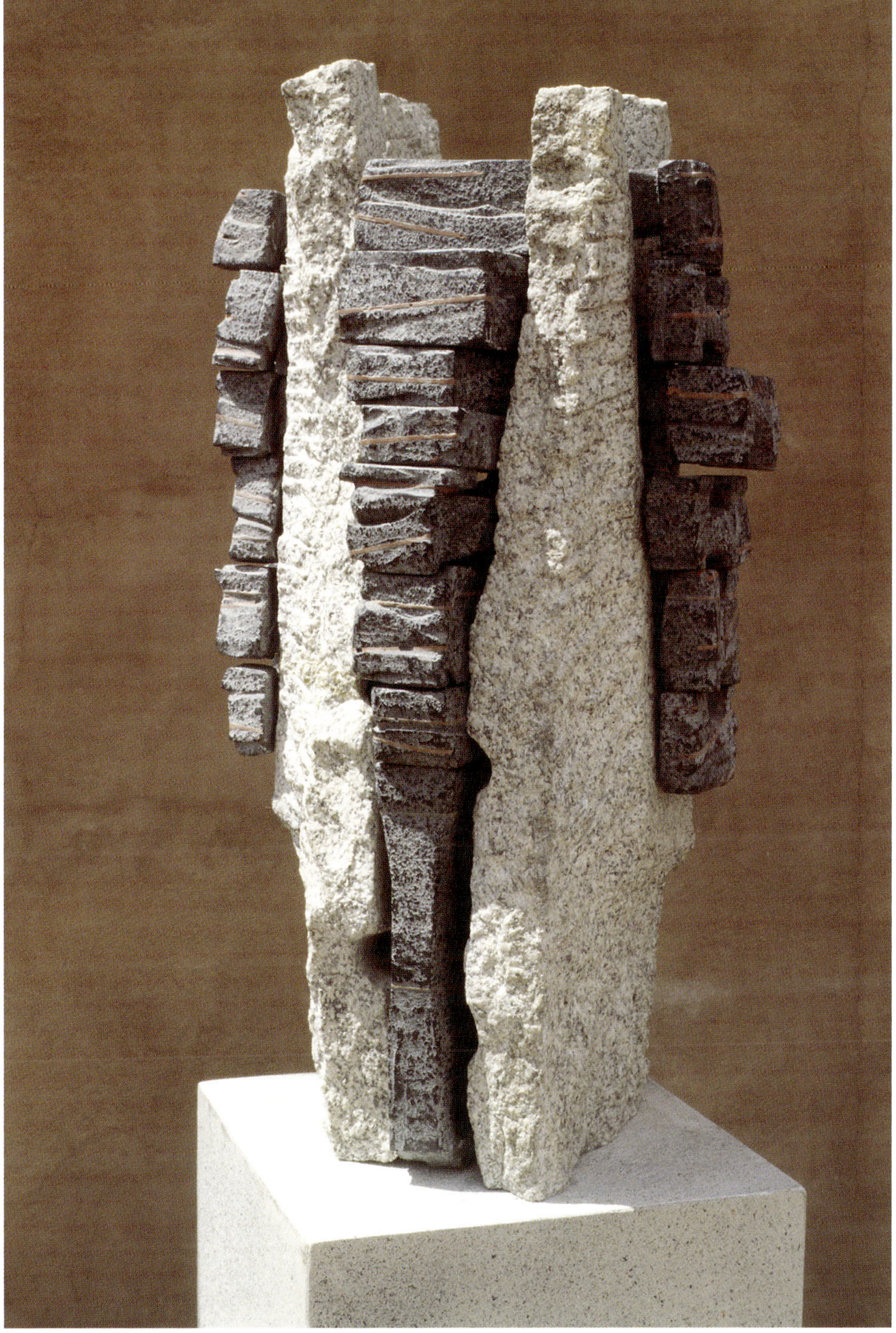

CORALITH, 2000
MARBLE & GRANITE
27 X 15 X 13 INCHES

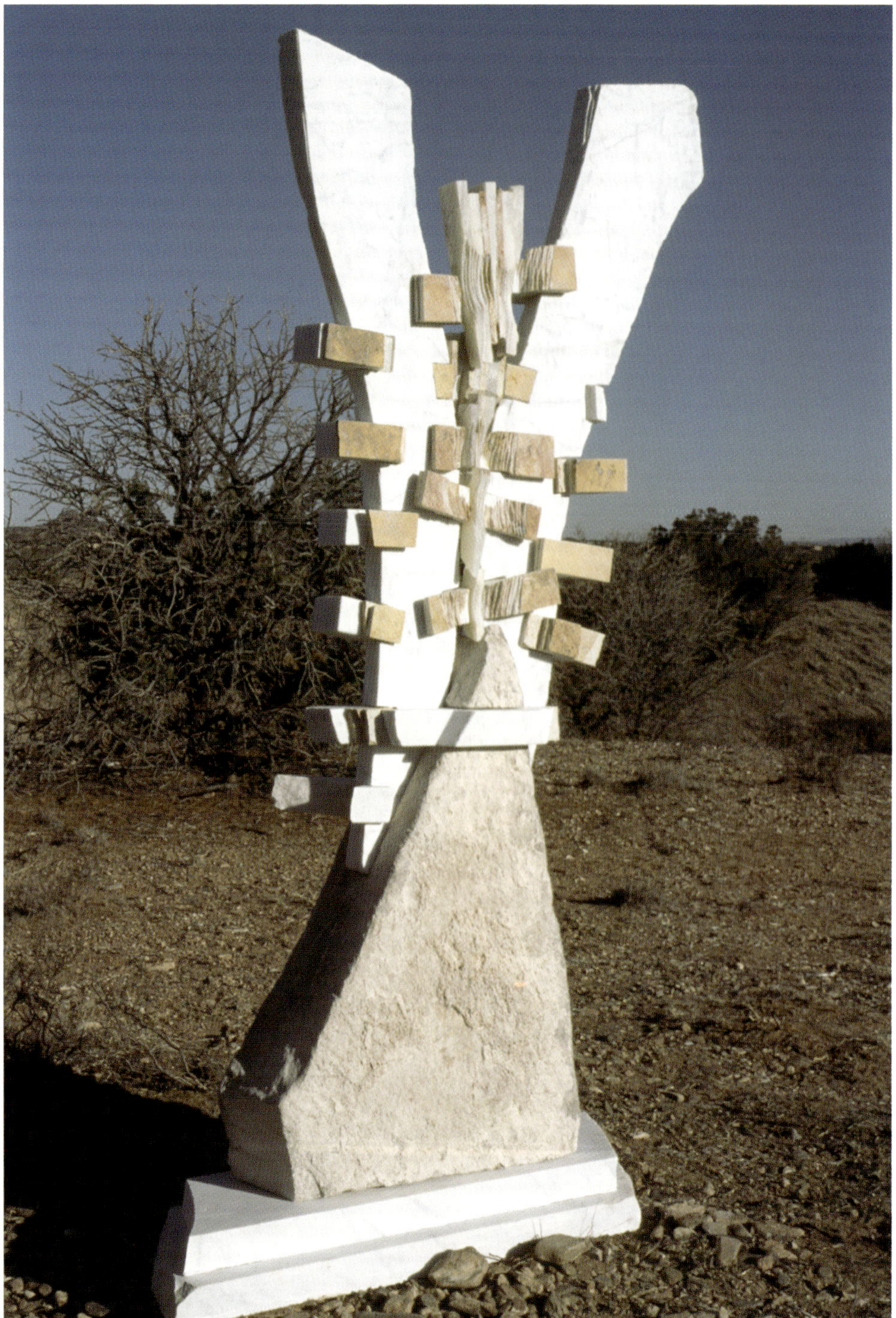

AWAKENING: FROM THE CRADLE TO THE GRAVE, 2003
MARBLE & ONYX
64 X 29 X 12 INCHES

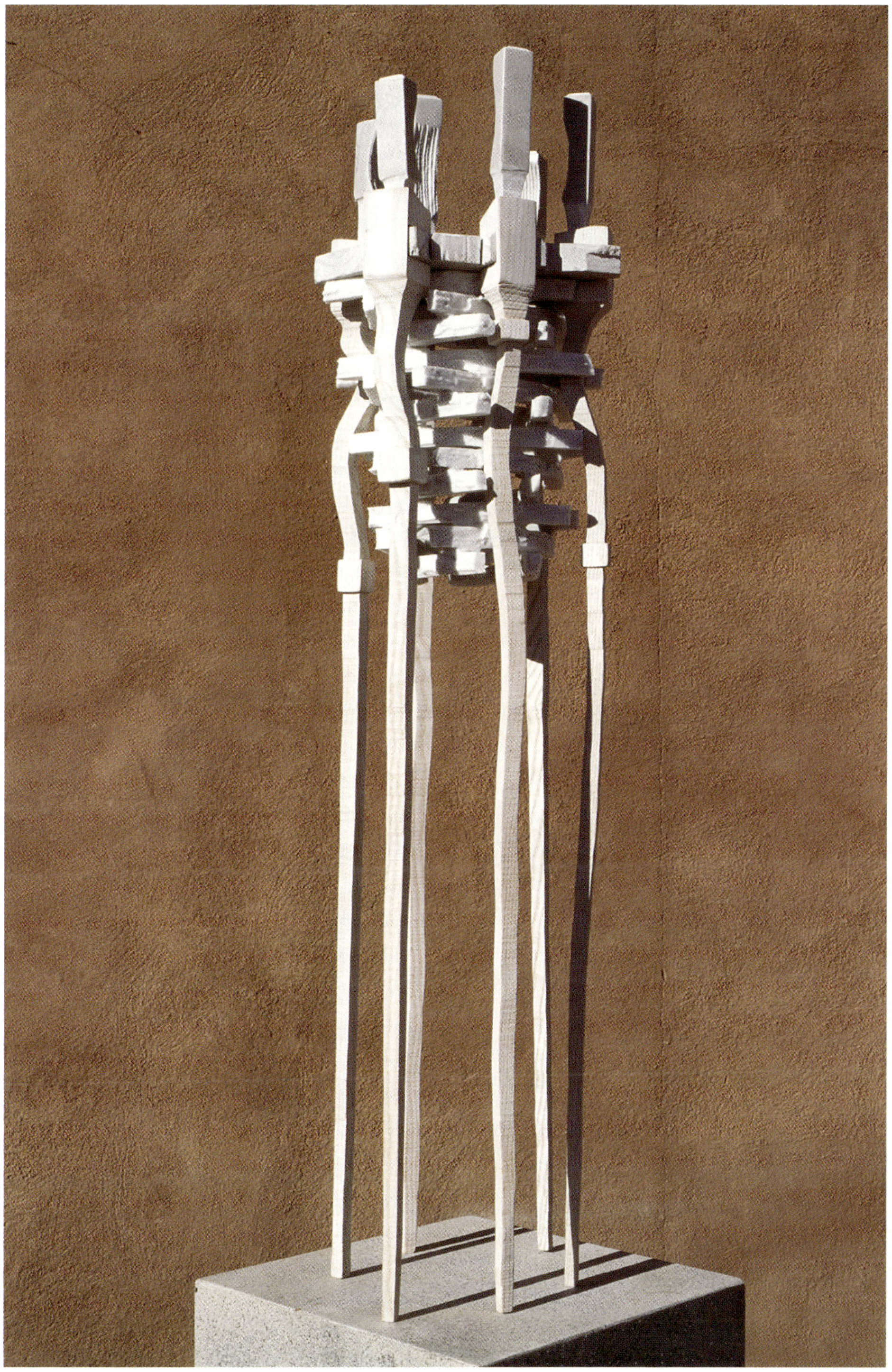

NIDO DE CORAZÓN, 2003
ASH & MARBLE
37 X 9 X 10 INCHES

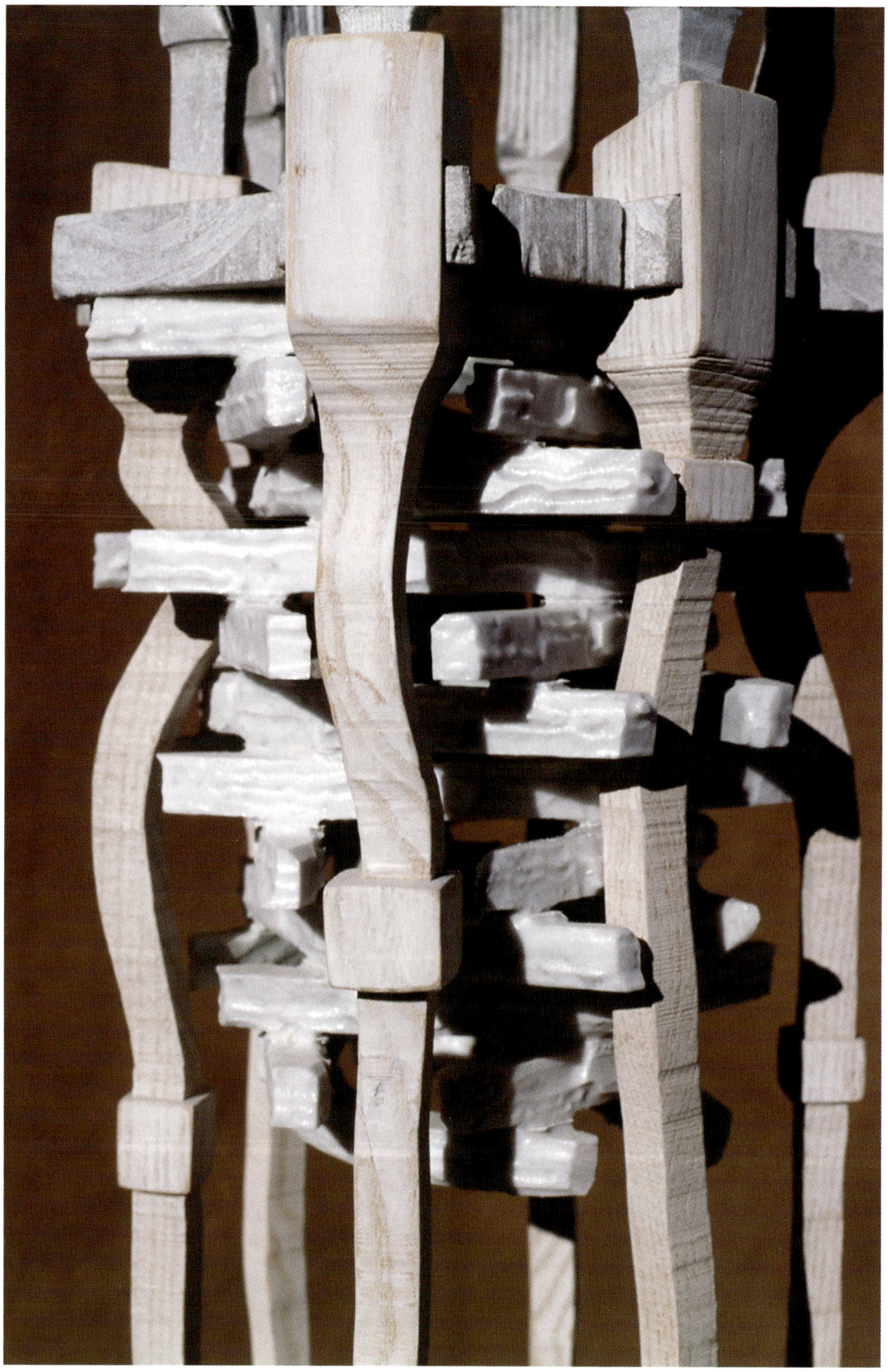

NIDO DE CORAZÓN, 2003 (DETAIL)
ASH & MARBLE
37 X 9 X 10 INCHES

DOUG GRAY

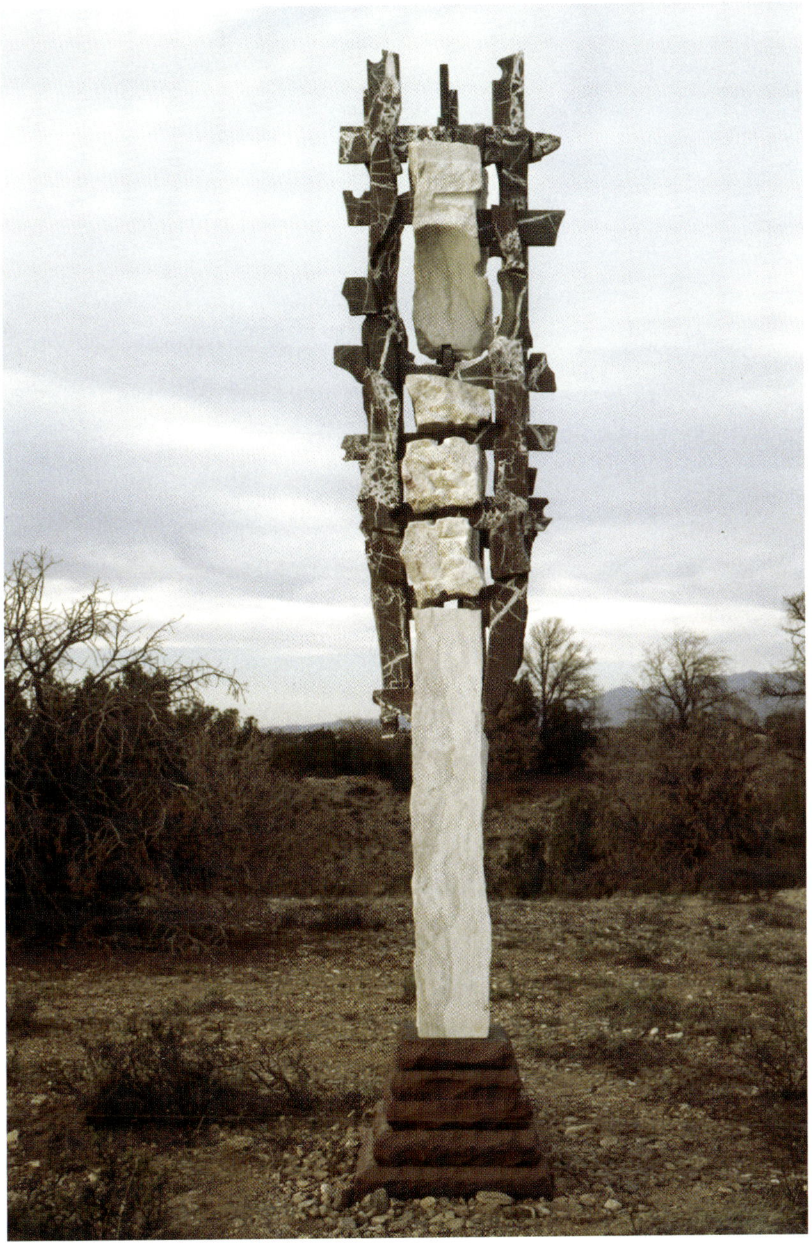

DOUG GRAY b.1961 Pittsburgh PA. *Ed.* MFA Pennsylvania State Univ., University Park PA; BA Trinity College, Hartford CT. *Coll:* J.E. Lee, Las Cruces NM; The Las Cruces Museum of Fine Art. *Awards:* City Arts Grant, Baltimore. *Selected Exhibitions:* Fourteenth Annual College of Santa Fe Juried Outdoor Sculpture Exhibition; *The Terrain*, Las Cruces Museum of Fine Art. *Representation:* Gallery 234, York PA.

MOTHER'S BLOOD
MARBLE
96 X 18 X 16 INCHES

ERIKA WANENMACHER

She can walk through walls and embody the four elements. Her magic casts serious spells and her medicine can cure the common cold. Her reverence for the natural, the supernatural and the *conjunctio* is profound. She's gone head to head with Kali, the annihilator. She takes the form of a whirling energy vortex sweeping up everything in sight and turning it towards the purposes of her craft. She's Erika Wanenmacher, grand infinite initiate, culture witch, and high priestess of the imagination.

Her Santa Fe studio is legendary for its pure complexity and the wild assortment of creatures and objects that find their ways there, or have been birthed into being in its alchemical fires. Or both. She escaped the twentieth century unscathed by the hungry sparseness of white wall Modernism and hasn't looked back. She's a maximalist, like her Fluxus forebears, the wizards of Dada, and Joseph Cornell. She's got everything she needs to weave trance-inducing narratives and pull off astounding feats of spellbinding art.

Viewing an Erika Wanenmacher show is like being led to an archetypal folkloric precipice inhabited by plant and animal allies charged with nothing less than the prayerful task of total planetary healing through imaginative anarchy. It is from this vantage, deep in the uncharted mountain region of the unconscious, that through a sudden clearing you are able to see the meadow that human beings have come from, and what we've been, and then out on the horizon, how much more we can be when we harness our creativity to the will of our hearts. As in Jungian psychology, in the curing of addiction, or in car repair, things can't change for the better until the problem is visibly addressed. Hurling fiery pinwheels of illumination into black holes of denial is a big part of any good culture witch's job.

Like a skilled spider, Erika Wanenmacher spins political content into her mystic web in a way that more resembles practices of artists and magicians outside the U.S. Think Czech art or Maurizio Cattelan, where there is no denial of the political, nor conceiving of politics as the only subject. Erika Wanenmacher's entire *oeuvre*, from punk 'zine origins to her one woman show at Site Santa Fe is politically active on a continuum that runs from "only by inference" to being pointedly, poignantly clear. Her carvings, boxes, objects, rituals, installations, masks, magic lantern slideshows, enormous wings, and *Fool's* x-ray are fabulous and practically constitute the artifacts of a culture all their own; and then, after the manner of Wonderland, a beautifully distorted mirror culture of the one we usually inhabit. Using castaway materials from Los Alamos National Labs, Goodwill, and wherever her real and imaginary wanderings lead, her work reflects a wake-up call in a language assembled from the occult edges of ancient wisdom.

Whatever direction Erika Wanenmacher's endless experimental, multi-media art making steps off into next, it is the skillful, seamless merging of the hardcore here and now with a complex, chaotic meta-physic (her changeling ability to exist in so many multiple dimensions simultaneously) which beguiles and bewitches the most.

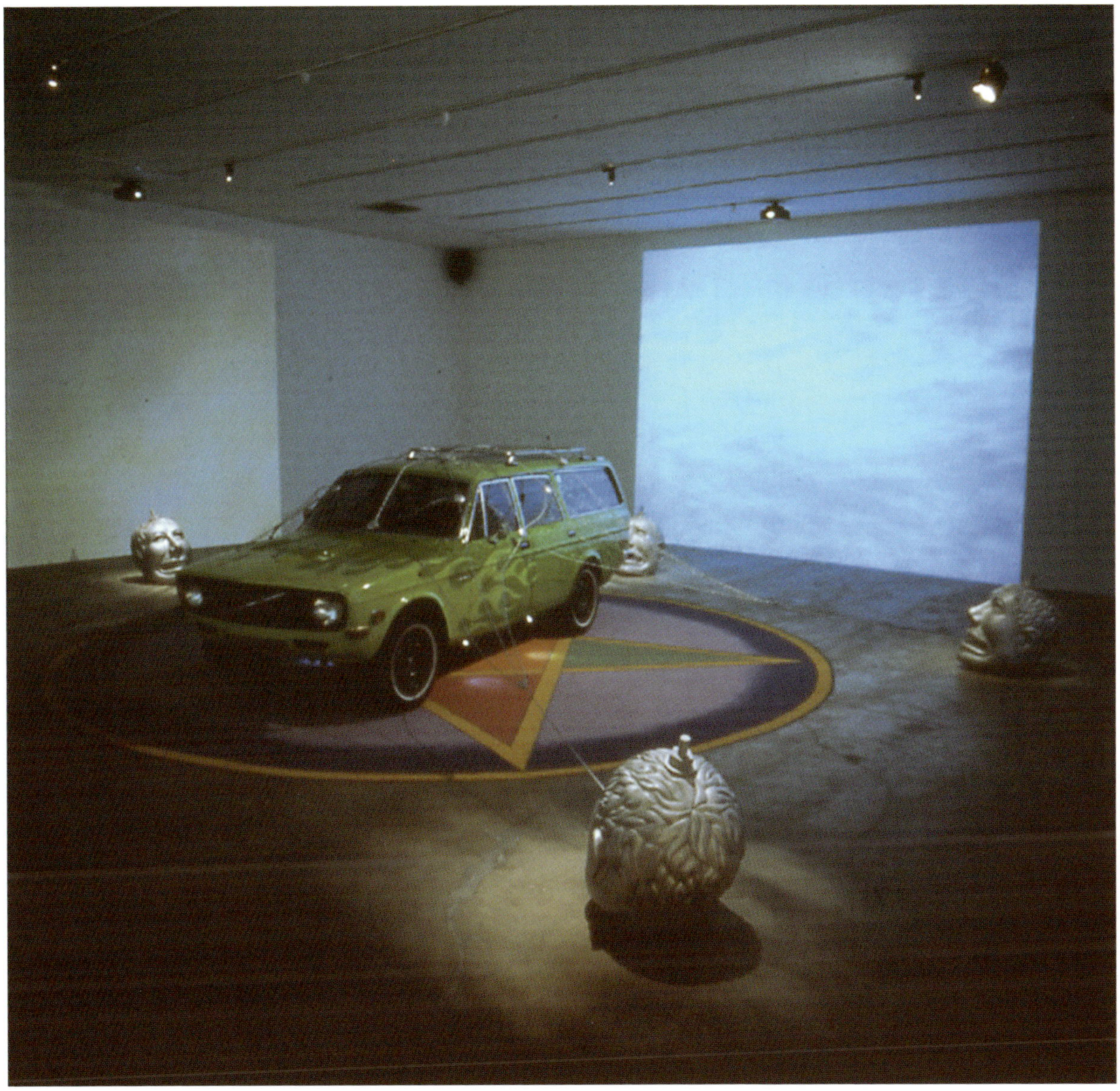

GRIMOIRE INSTALLATION, 2001
MIXED MEDIA WITH VOLVO HOTROD,
SAND PAINTING, ALUMINUM CASTINGS,
AUDIO & VIDEO

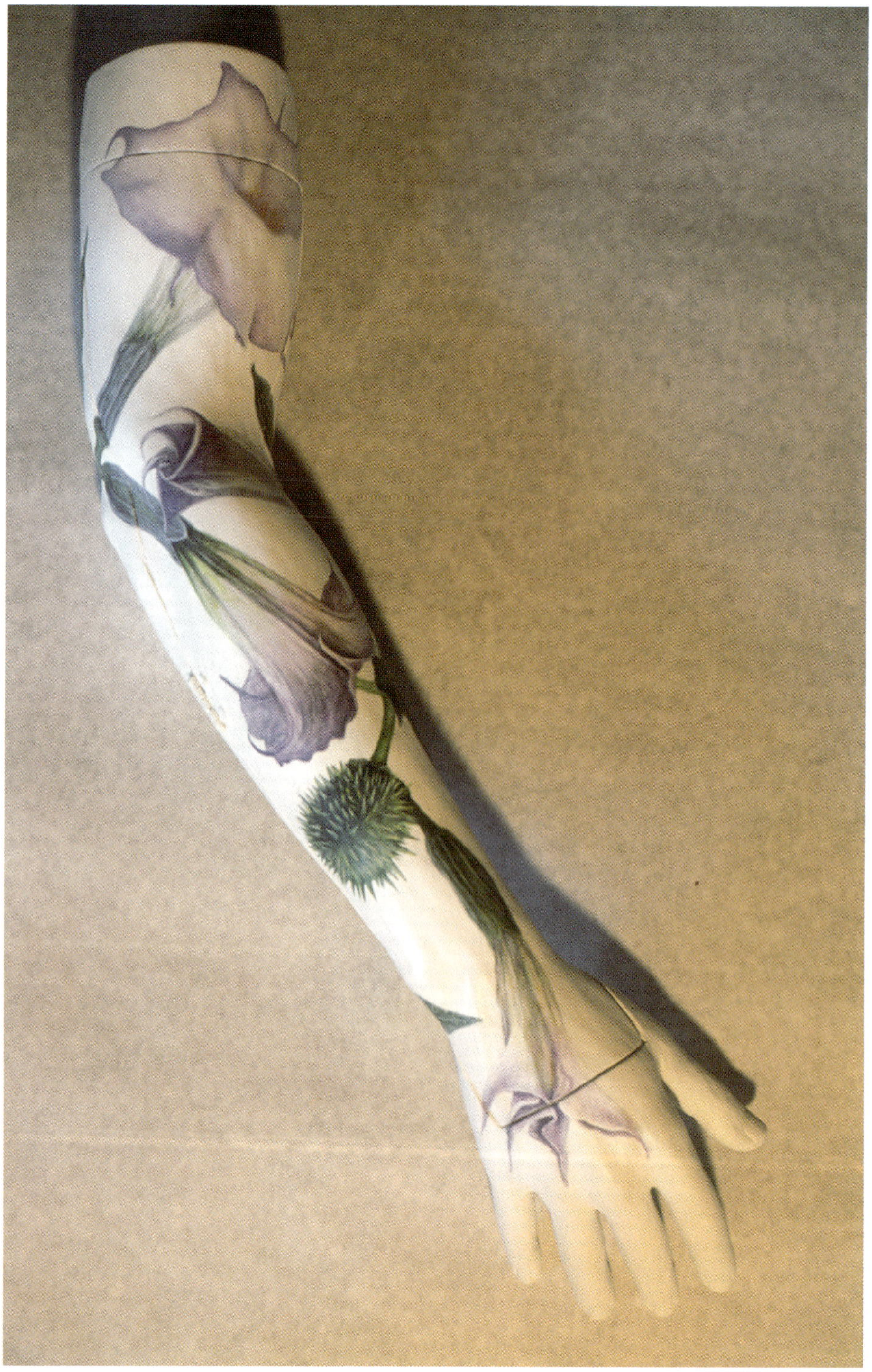

DATURA ARM, 2002
MIXED MEDIA ON WOOD
24 X 8 X 5 INCHES

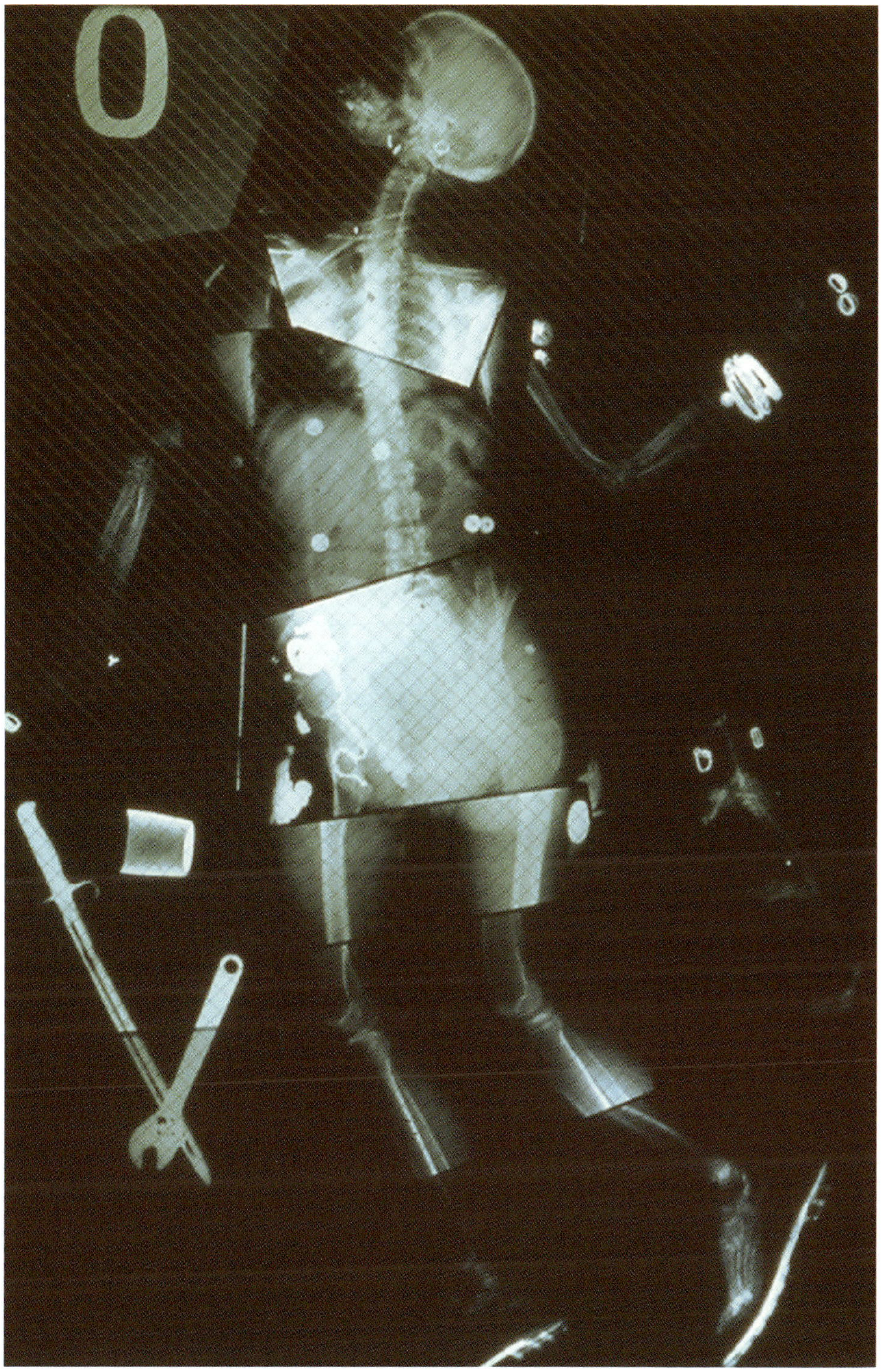

THE FOOL, 2001
X-RAYS, SAFETY GLASS, COPPER & LIGHTS
60 X 48 X 6 INCHES

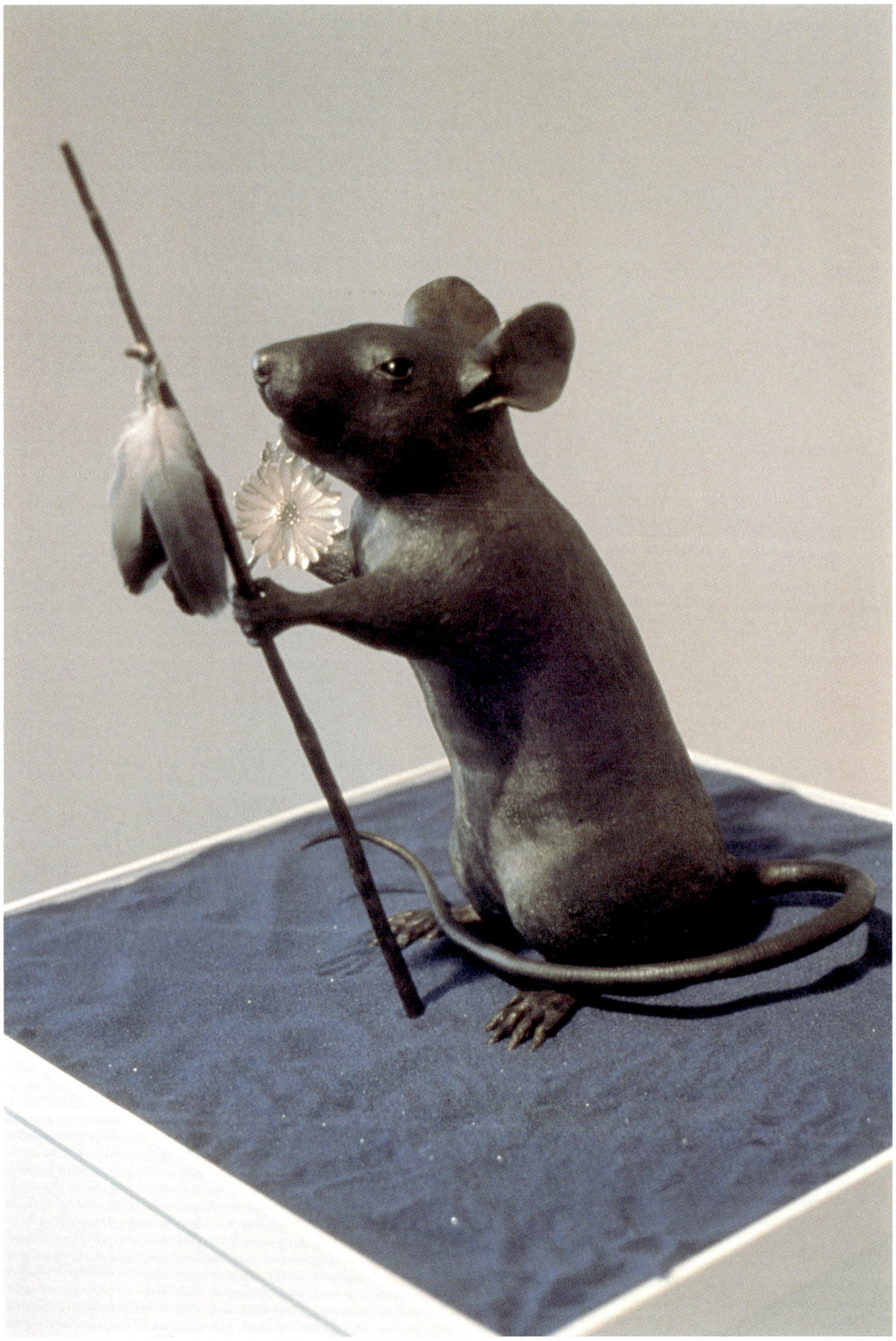

RAT WARRIOR, 2003
CAST BRONZE, STEEL & PIGEON FEATHERS
17 X 10 X 12 INCHES

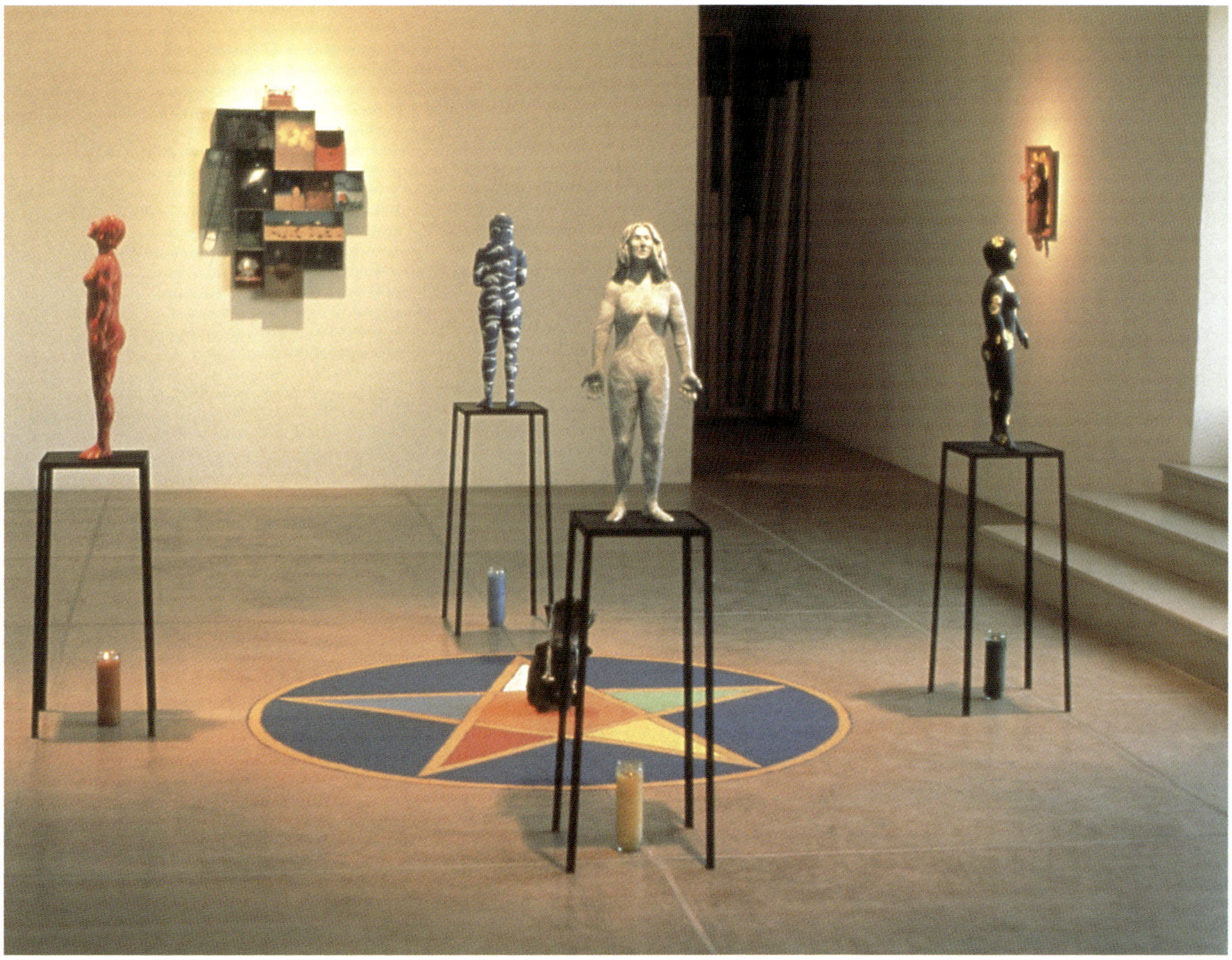

ERIKA WANENMACHER b. 1955 Berea OH. *Ed:* Kansas City Art Institute MO; Feminist Studio Workshop, Los Angeles. *Coll:* Fisher Landau Center, Long Island; Pacific Enterprises Collection; Wagner and Webb Architects; Suby Bowden & Associates, Santa Fe; Museum of Albuquerque; Museum of Fine Arts, Museum of New Mexico, Santa Fe; Stephane Janssen Collection; Ann Janss Collection. *Representation:* Linda Durham Contemporary Art, Santa Fe.

GOOD WILL INSTALLATION, 2003
MIXED MEDIA

JENNIFER JOSEPH

The eye is the faculty that allows Jennifer Joseph to recognize unnerving beauty in the strangest of places. Using everyday objects like steel rings, tiny shells, plastic tubes, glow in the dark vintage icicle ornaments, cotton cosmetic pads, acupuncture needles and ceremonial incense charcoal, she builds objects, arrangements and installations that seem to exist in gravity-defying spaces and glisten with a strange form-dissolving light. There is a strong suggestion of an everyday, experiential spirituality which worships these visual rhythms, the spiral and geometric patterns inherent in this complex natural world, even when Jennifer Joseph's jumping off point is the use of materials that are utterly manufactured and familiar. Her work is a manifestation of that fractal mindset where science, rather than debunking the metaphysical, exposes more readily than ever that the magnitudinous intermixture of fire, water, air, and earth, stirred by time, which we call the universe, is simply a trick of the light, bouncing electrons which vanish as quickly as they are perceived and formed from an infinite invisible spirit.

The void is the new humanism. Awe and reverence for the pure and utter mystery, the unknowably vast beyond that puts forth the dizzying wonder of the universe and the intense beauty of our blue green star, are the only reasons to be kind to nature's most and least refined of creatures—your fellow human—simply because he, she, they, we, you too, are of the multiplicities, the ten zillion emanations—all worthy of high respect—born of that oneness.

The openness to wonder is a high human virtue and the core of the multi-media work of artist Jennifer Joseph. The power of wonder can be dangerous sometimes, but fearlessly practiced on a regular basis with appropriate discretion, especially in the realm of art, leads to the development of a remarkably open eye.

In the archetypal language of early mythologies, the world of perception, our material experience, is described as a vision, a hypnagogic image, behind the lid of the closed eye of a sleeping deity. This material world then vanishes like a dream you can't remember, when the goddess wakes up—when she opens her eyes to the intricate beauty of the truth of the beyond. In Jennifer Joseph's art this is the here and now.

JENNIFER JOSEPH

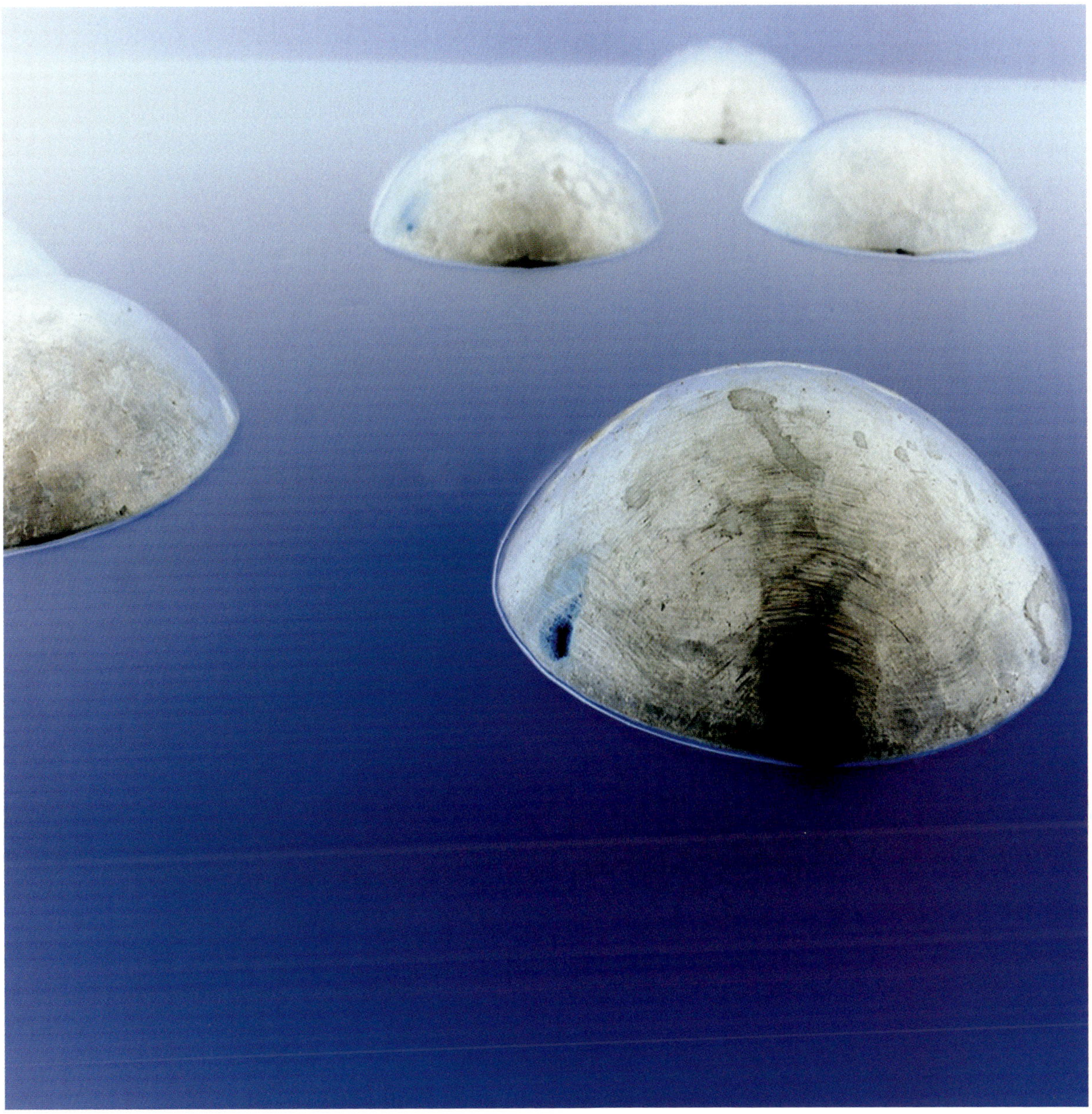

UNTITLED, 2001
STERLING SILVER
2 INCHES

JENNIFER JOSEPH

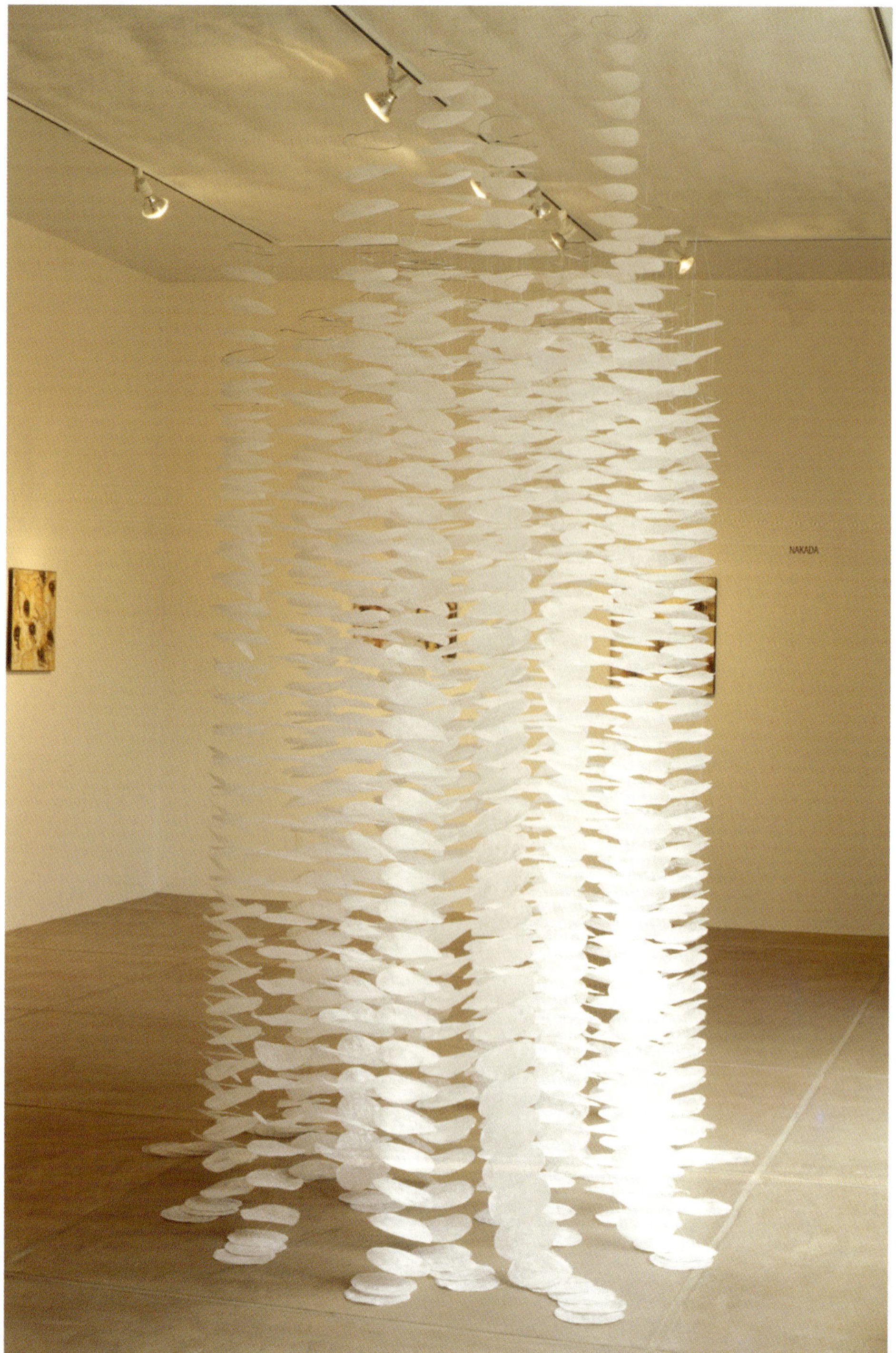

FOREST
HANDMADE PAPER
100 X 84 INCHES

JENNIFER JOSEPH

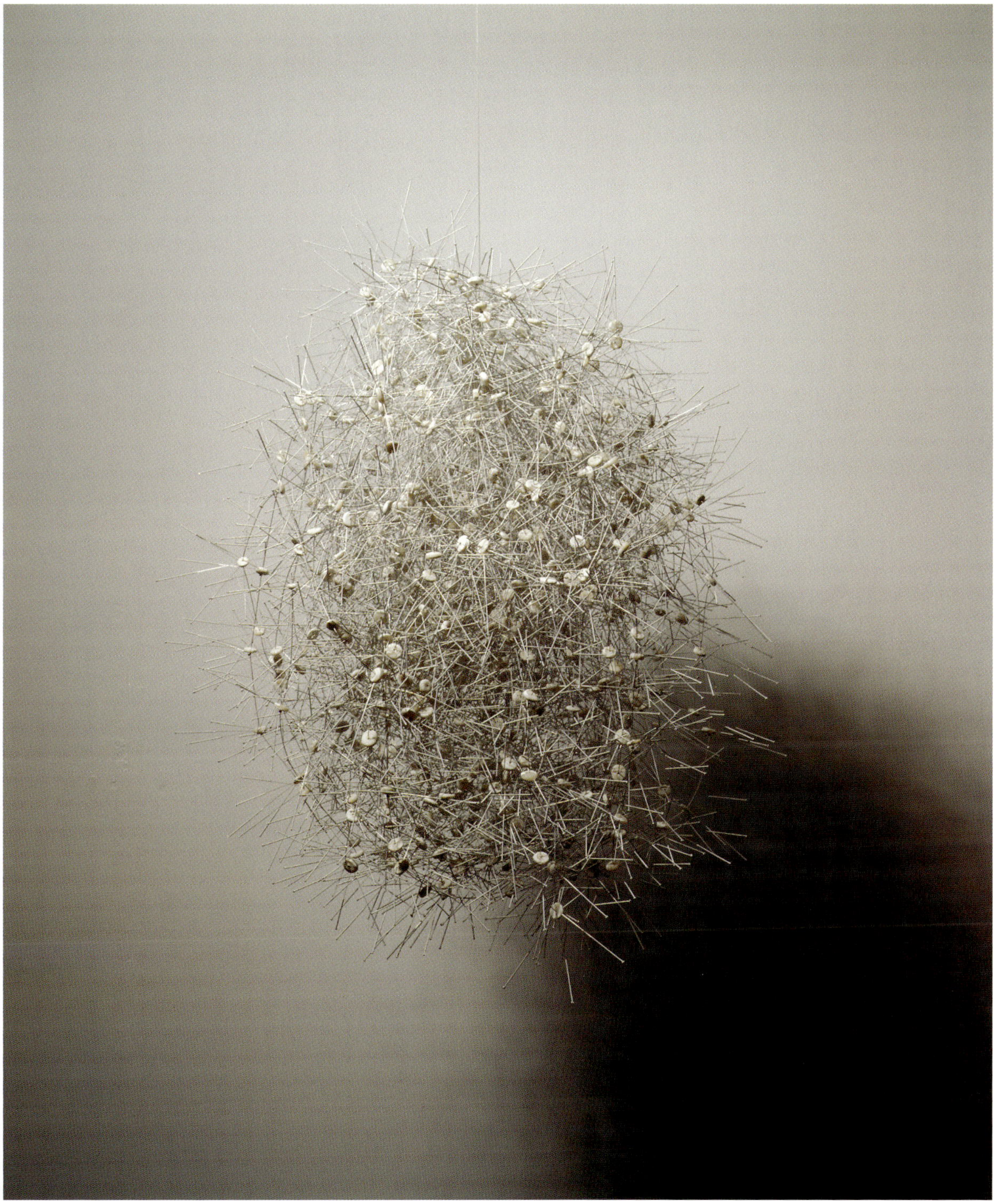

#9, 2003
ACUPUNCTURE NEEDLES, SYNTHETIC CLAY
& MIXED MEDIA
26 X 16 X 16 INCHES
Collection of Cindy and Doug Ring

JENNIFER JOSEPH

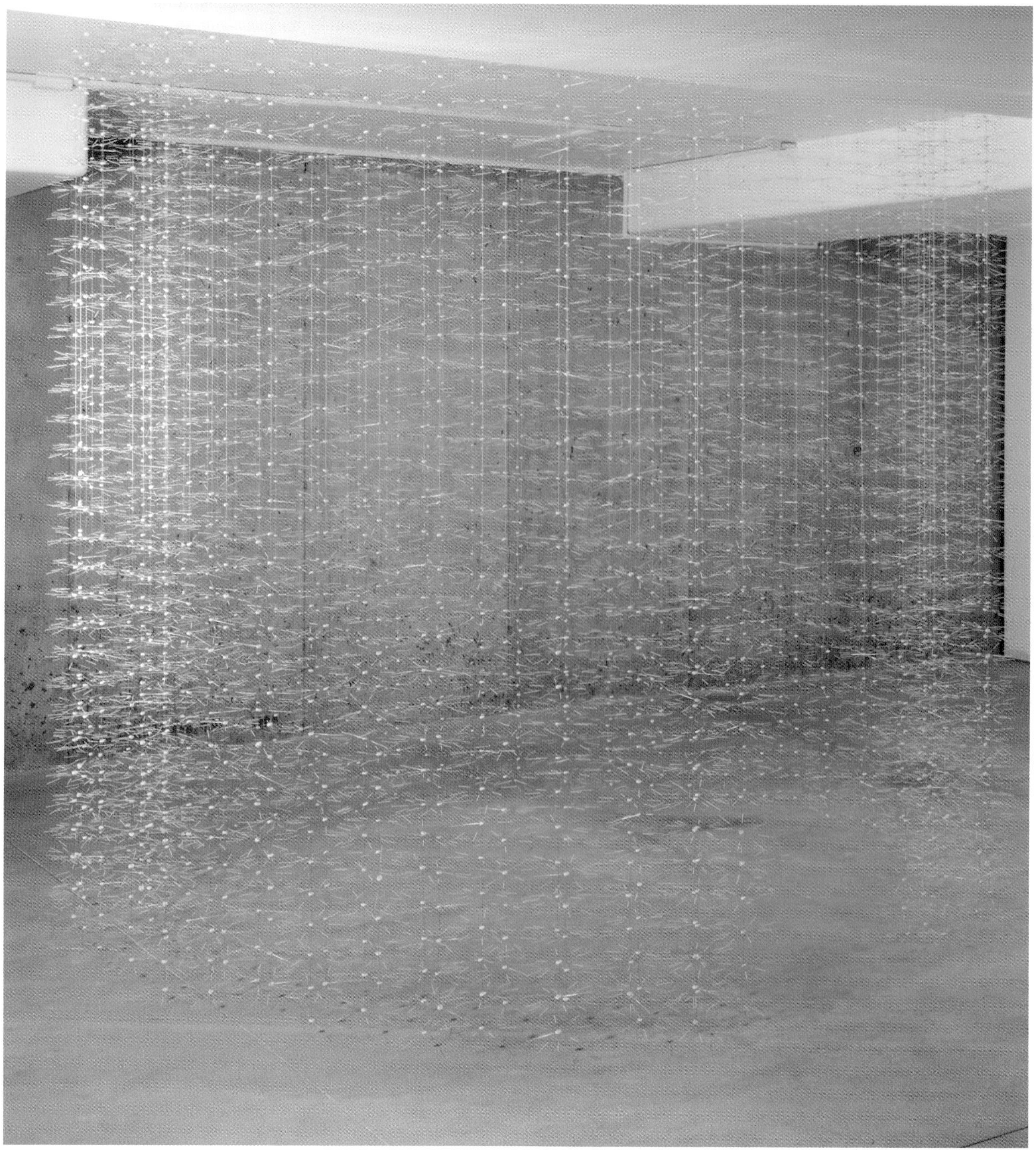

#11, 2003
ACUPUNCTURE NEEDLES & MIXED MEDIA
96 X 96 INCHES

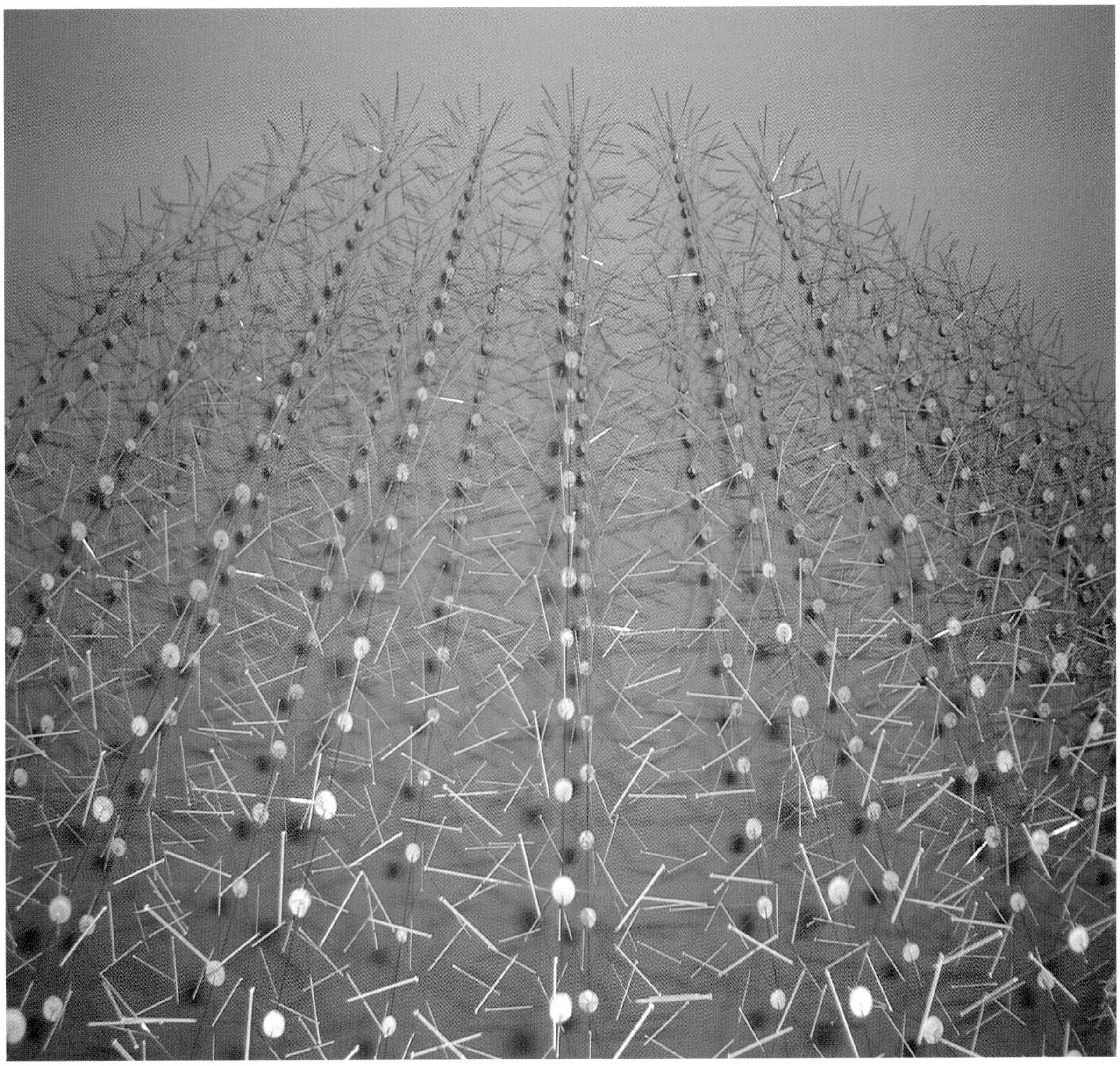

JENNIFER JOSEPH b.1966 USA. *Ed:* BFA Moore College of Art and Design, Philadelphia PA. *Coll:* Acsys Corporation, Atlanta; Allan Bedwick, Tokyo; Sandy Besser, Santa Fe; Bobrow and Assoc., Los Angeles; Dr. Luther Brady, New York; Leslie and Richard Dilworth, Santa Fe; Diversified Information Technologies, Scranton PA; Elizabeth Glassman, Chicago; Hallmark Corporation, Kansas City MO; Megan Fox Kelly, New York; Orthovita, Inc., Malvern PA; Doug Ring, Los Angeles; Naomi Sachs, Santa Fe; Olivia Beckwith-Smith, New York; Swiss RE, New York. *Representation:* EVO Gallery, Santa Fe.

#11, 2003 (DETAIL)
ACUPUNCTURE NEEDLES & MIXED MEDIA
96 X 96 INCHES

MARY BENNETT

Written words obscure as much as illuminate. You write something down to remember it, and then you put it aside and forget about it. In libraries and booksellers' shops around the world, for every book that is read, tenfold linger dusty and unopened like so many shuttered windows. Some most likely look out onto scenes of shining clarity and preternatural wisdom, others open only upon a dense gray fog of inscrutable verbiage. It is this ambiguous nature of writing that allows the object of the book to stand both as symbol of authority (the Bible and the textbook come to mind) and a divine means of escape, a line of flight across the desert away from all oppressive systems. Words, Languages, Books can entrap or enrapture.

Mary Bennett's books definitely do the latter. Much of her work consists of finding and elegantly altering reading materials through origami type folding, careful shredding, or other rearrangement. What does it mean to give books a sculptural presence? For one thing it often means a denial of legibility or a severe dismembering and reassemblage of the body of the text. It expresses a radical skepticism about words and language, and the information they contain, and/or, however paradoxically, a reverence, an homage, to textual and intellectual possibility.

Bennett commits herself time and again to the act of readerly deconstruction. Her extraordinary ability to physicalize her chosen texts, to turn them into art objects, is on the one hand the ultimate expression of the idea that you ought not believe everything you read, and simultaneously establishes an extra-textual realm of creativity, alive with concrete, poetic possibilities that says believe anything you read as long as you don't stop with the text. If the book can be reinterpreted, reread as an object, then, Bennett suggests, with Borgesian logic, every object can be read as a book. Once you open the pages of your life to this possibility you may find you have more truthful correspondences with your shower curtain than you find in an epistolary record of Marco Polo's Adventures.

The desire to destroy what you love most, or to love to the point of destruction is behind all rituals of sacrifice. Bennett loves books. She loves them so much she has to shape them, bend them, tear them, fold them, and generally exploit their inherent sculptural options. She kills them to bring them back to a three-dimensional life. Because she cares so much for the world of ideas she is compelled to reseat the author in authority and give thinking, real thinking, visceral forms that throw us, as readers, back on ourselves. The message is: read books voraciously, certainly, but more importantly, for true knowledge, read the text of your own body in the world.

MARY BENNETT

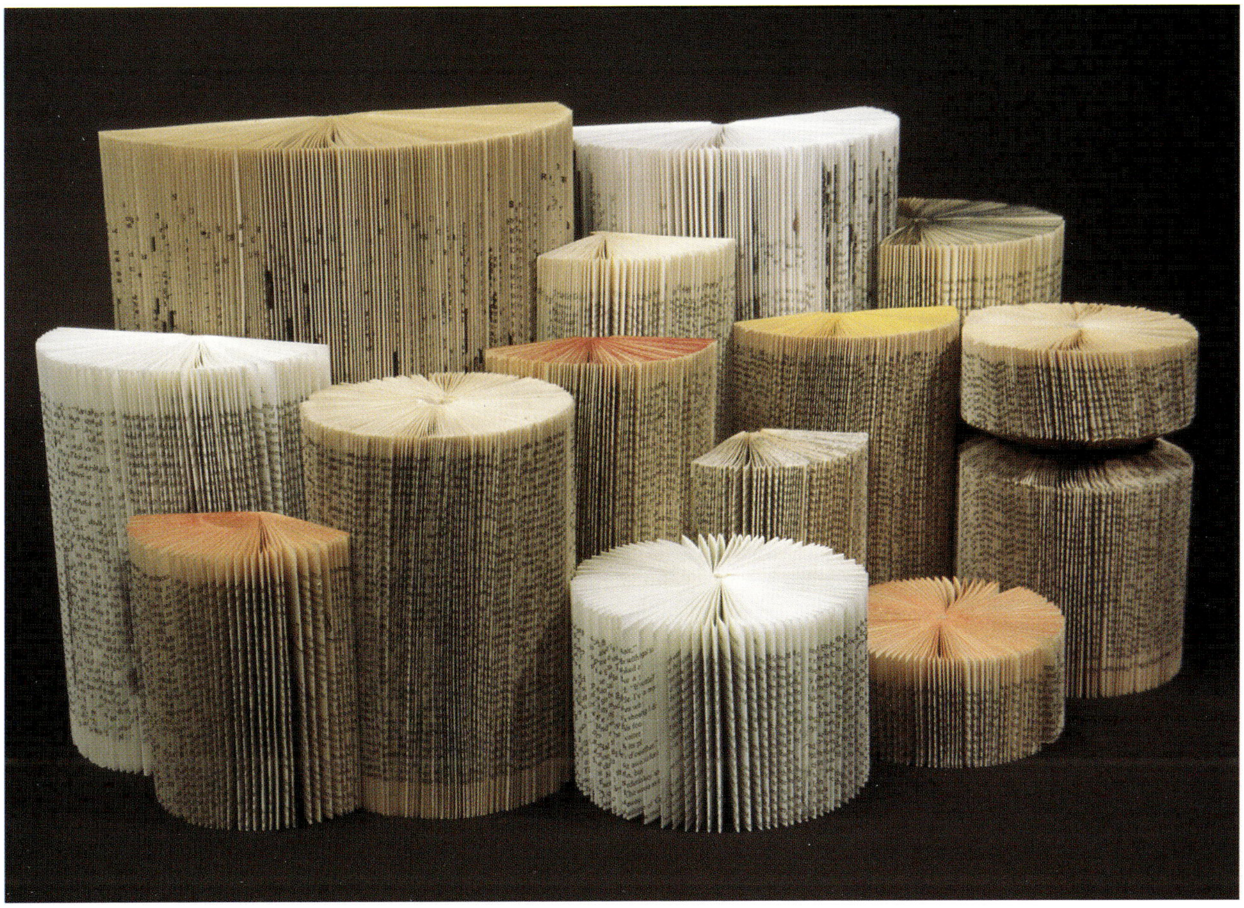

UNTITLED, 2003 (INSTALLATION)
ALTERED BOOKS & MIXED MEDIA
DIMENSIONS VARIABLE
Collection of Amanda and Keith Innes

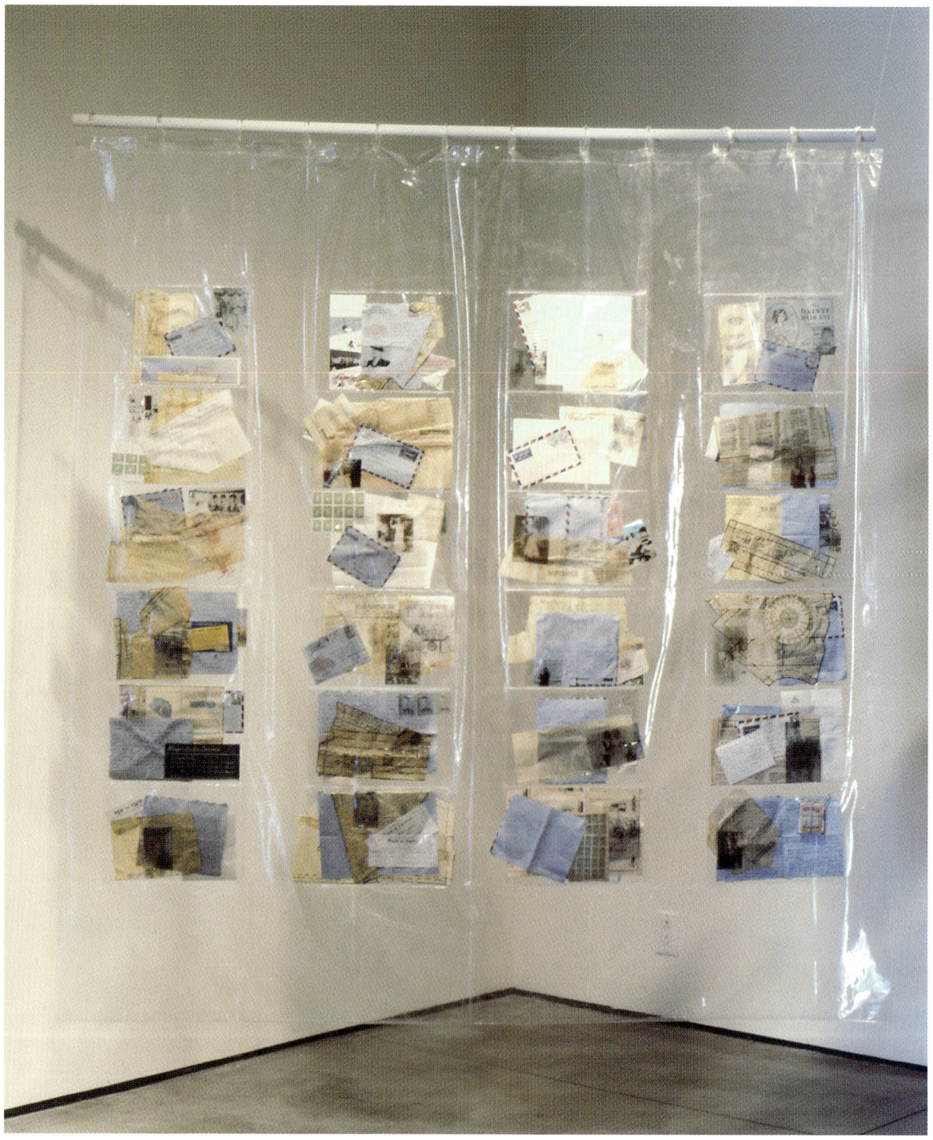

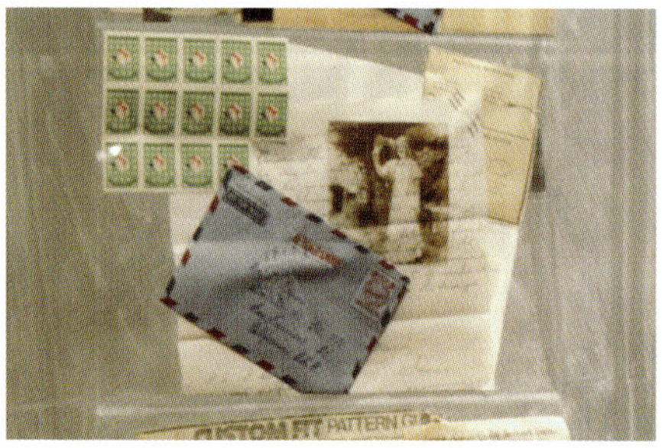

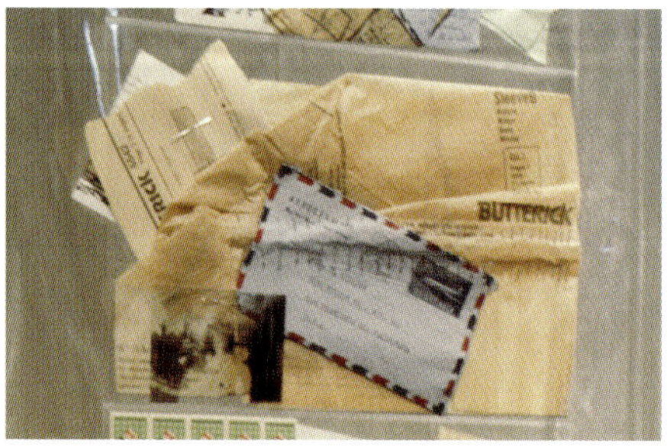

DOWN UNDER, 2003
SHOWER CURTAIN & MIXED MEDIA
6 X 3.5 FEET
Collection of Sandy Besser

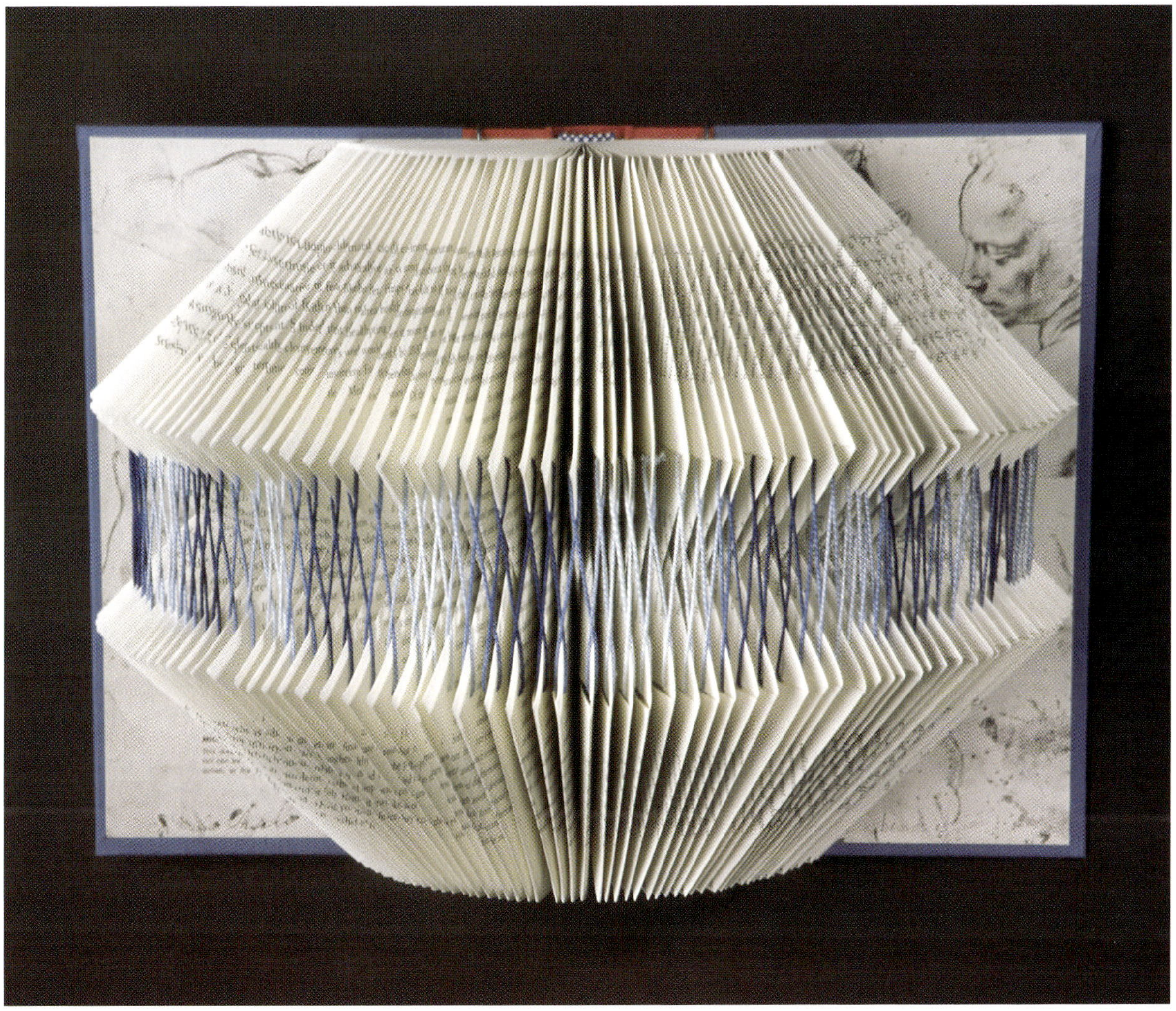

MICHELANGELO, 2003
ALTERED BOOK & MIXED MEDIA
7.5 X 10.5 X 9 INCHES
Collection of, Sandy Besser

MARY BENNETT

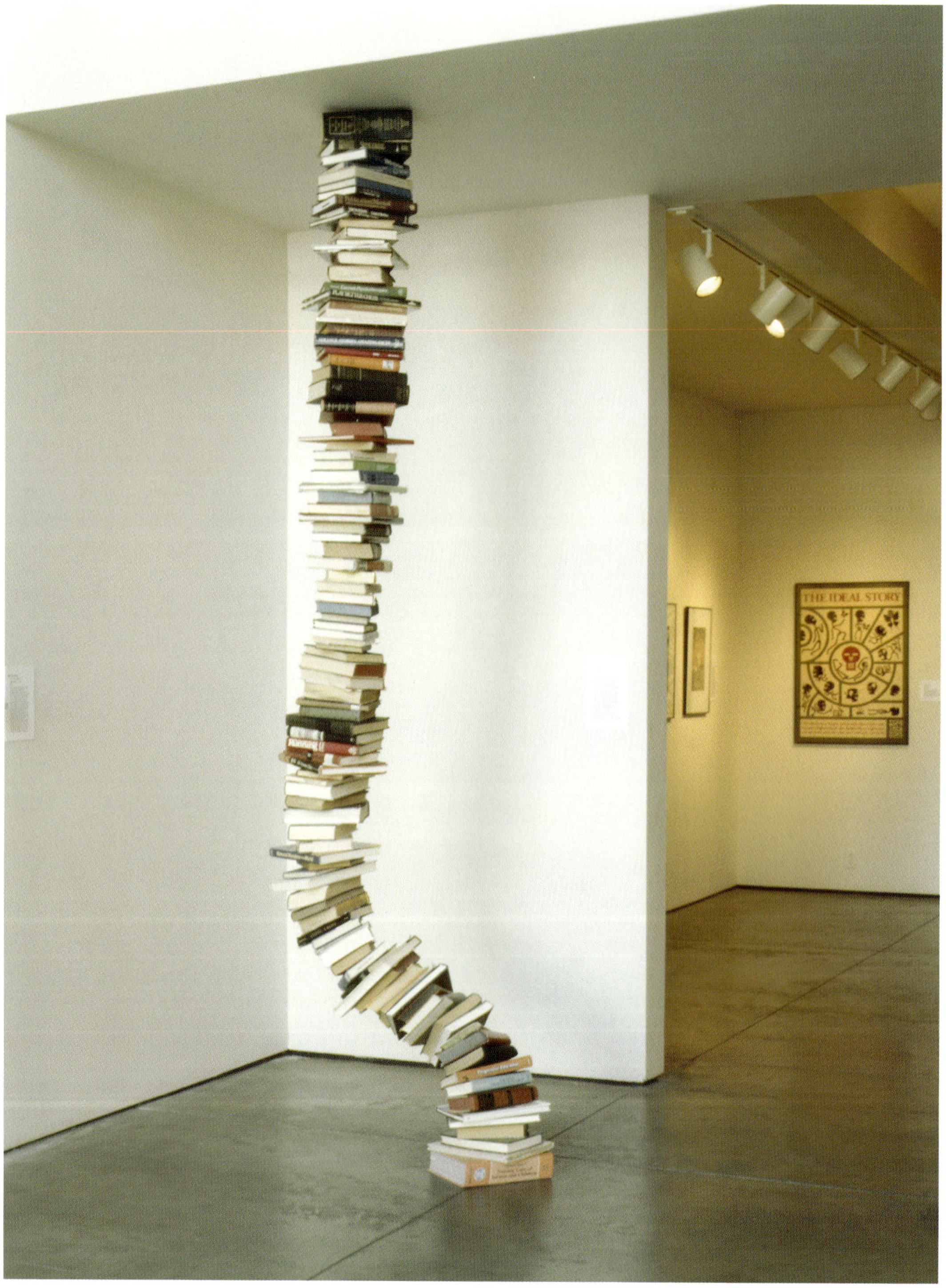

BOOK TOWER, 2004
MIXED MEDIA W/BOOKS
DIMENSIONS VARIABLE

Private Collection

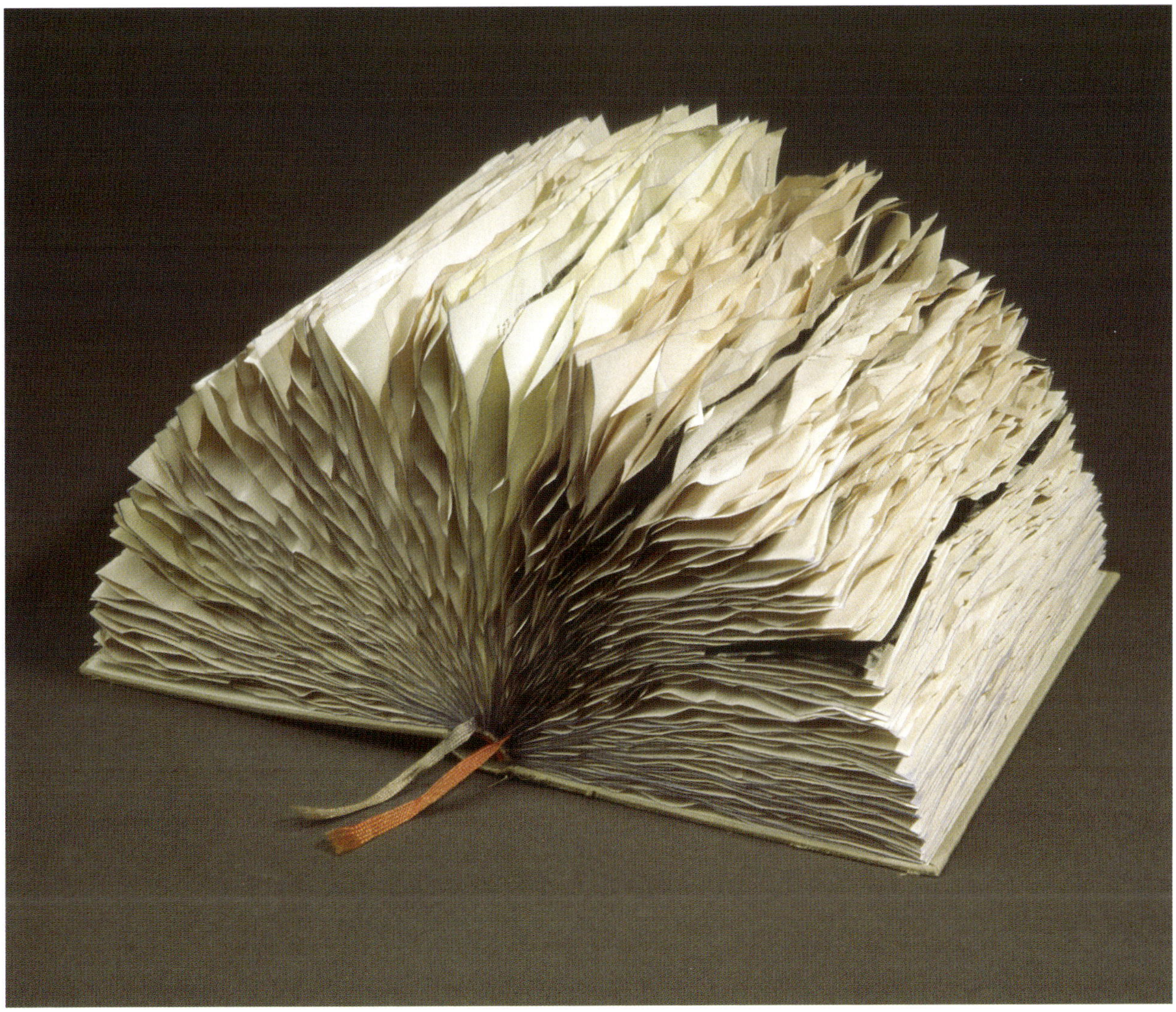

MARY BENNETT b. Everett WA. *Ed:* BA Creative Arts, San Francisco State Univ.; MA Inter-Arts, San Francisco State Univ.; BA History, Univ. Washington, Seattle; MBA Univ. Washington, Seattle. *Coll:* National Museum of Women in the Arts, DC; Museum of Fine Arts, Santa Fe; Mimbres Valley Learning Center, Luna County, Deming NM; John Wiley & Sons, Hoboken NJ; Boston Symphony Orchestra, Boston; Seattle University WA; Advanced Micro Devices, Mountain View CA; City of Boston MA; San Francisco Public Library CA; Mission Economic Development Association, San Francisco; City of Oakland CA; Boone and Associates, San Francisco; Marc Lumer & Co., San Francisco. *Awards:* State of New Mexico, Emerging and Practicing Artists Purchase Initiative. *Representation:* EVO Gallery, Santa Fe.

THE MANUAL OF MODERN PHOTOGRAPHY, 2003
ALTERED BOOKS/MIXED MEDIA
6 X 6 X 12 INCHES
Collection of Ann Tenenbaum

GAIL RIEKE

Travel. Unpack your bags. Live like a dawning global nomad. Open the windows of far away cities. Open your e-mail. Open your sketchbook on an old rock wall. Open the shutter on your camera. Open your trumpet case by the steps, or just clap your hands. Open your eyes and fingertips to all the ways people practice the art and accident of being alive.

Gail Rieke's project has the recurring motif of the artist as sojourner.

Each piece of rice-paper parasol, delicate fabric, found ephemera, or elegant envelope is possessed of its own temporal territory. As if time were no less seamless, but instead of being understood as the triad: past, present and future, were seen as a profusion of contiguous facets, a cubism of time zones. Think of how bits of next week might shine through the present. Picture the past sliding and sparkling across the surfaces of multiple futures. Your great grandfather's watch, so long unwound, has perchance stopped time itself.

Gail Rieke's objects have this sense of enwrapping time and nurturing it. In her elegant assemblages, time is captured in a bird nest or the spiral concavity of a shell, stored in the holes of a button, folded in silk, bundled like dry grass, or lies await in a dry seed pod.

Color, that sweetest wonder of visible mystery is her primary organizing principle. For the viewer attuned to the subtleties of these frequencies, Rieke's work holds unlimited, indescribable delight. Color exhibits the sheer wonder of the wide world more accurately, is more effectively true in open-endedness and emotive qualities, than perhaps any other ideational system. Only a musical modality might represent color's equal as a sensory portal to the awe of being alive.

Gail Rieke is well known for her exquisite work and for collaborating with her husband Zachariah. Objects and surfaces cross-pollinate. Each artist's work is distinct, yet intimately connected. Both are collected worldwide, having shown in excellent galleries for years. The two artists also take turns exhibiting by invitation on alternating Augusts, and show year round by appointment in the gracious spaces of their Santa Fe home.

Here, in the back room of Gail Rieke's studio, is the apotheosis of her travels, an installation titled, *Suitcase Wall.* She packs an entire orchestration of hues, vibrant tones, melodic lines, arias, and cantos, with the stunning, lucid intimacy of a caress. A tactile model too approaches the dulcet tones of color and music. Gail Rieke's is a sonorous Proustian poetics you can see and touch.

If the world ended tomorrow, *Suitcase Wall*, better than any other hominid repository, with its open-ended inclusivity and Gail Rieke's highly evolved sensibility, might just well exhibit the best idea of what this trip has really been all about.

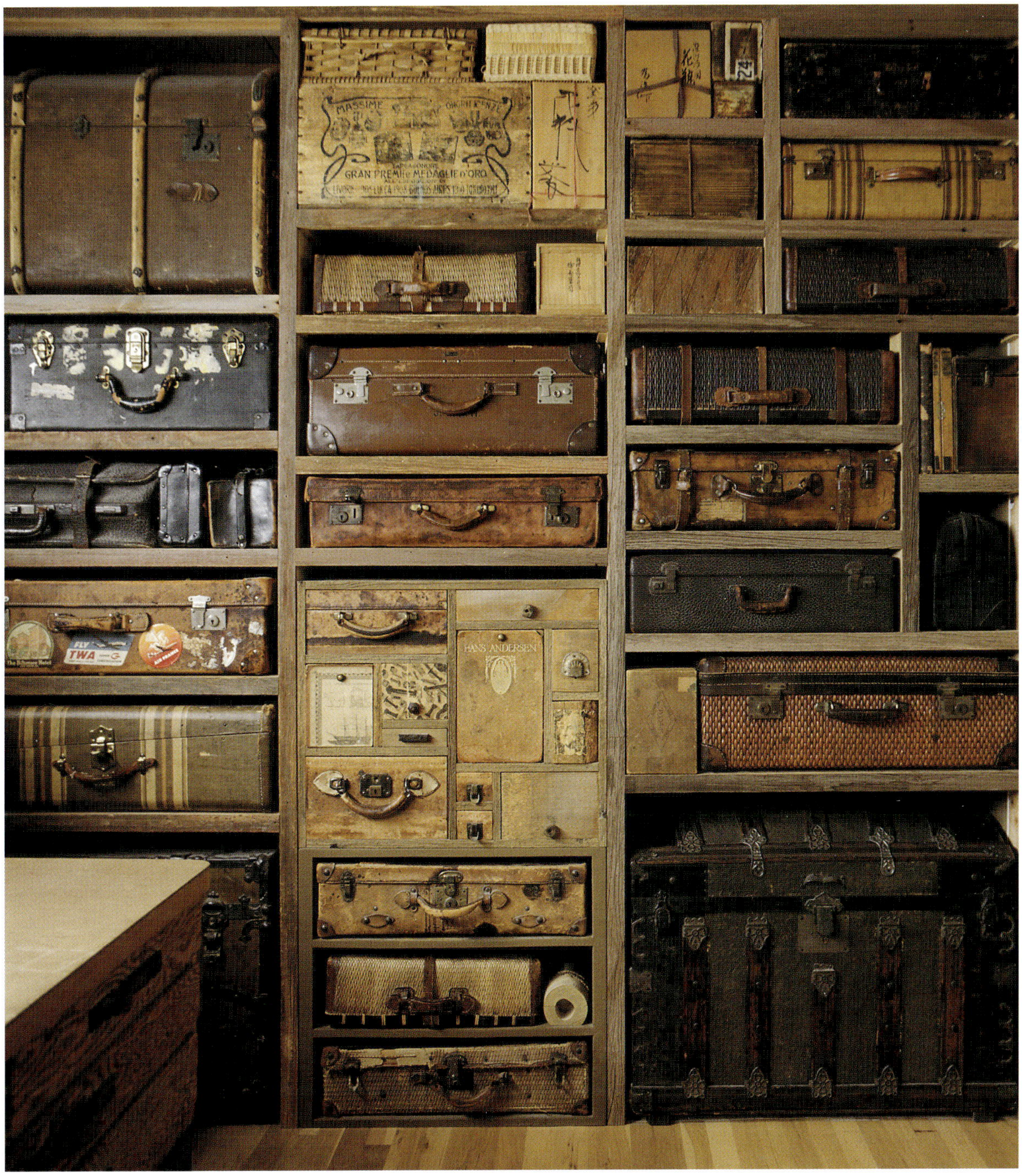

SUITCASE WALL
COLLABORATIVE INSTALLATION
GAIL AND ZACHARIAH RIEKE

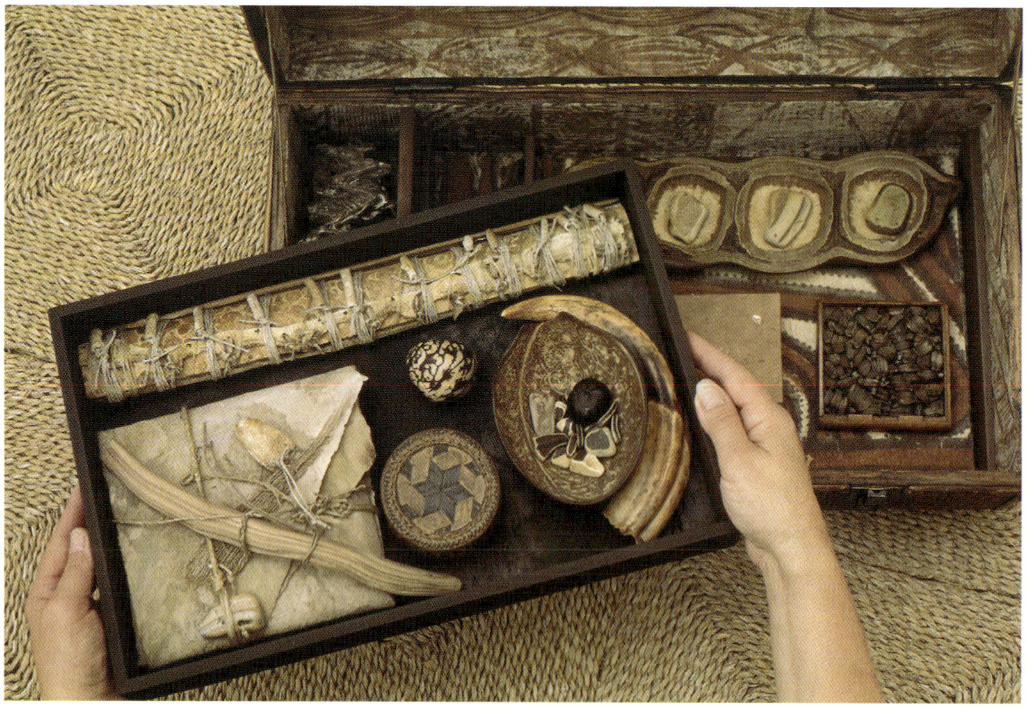

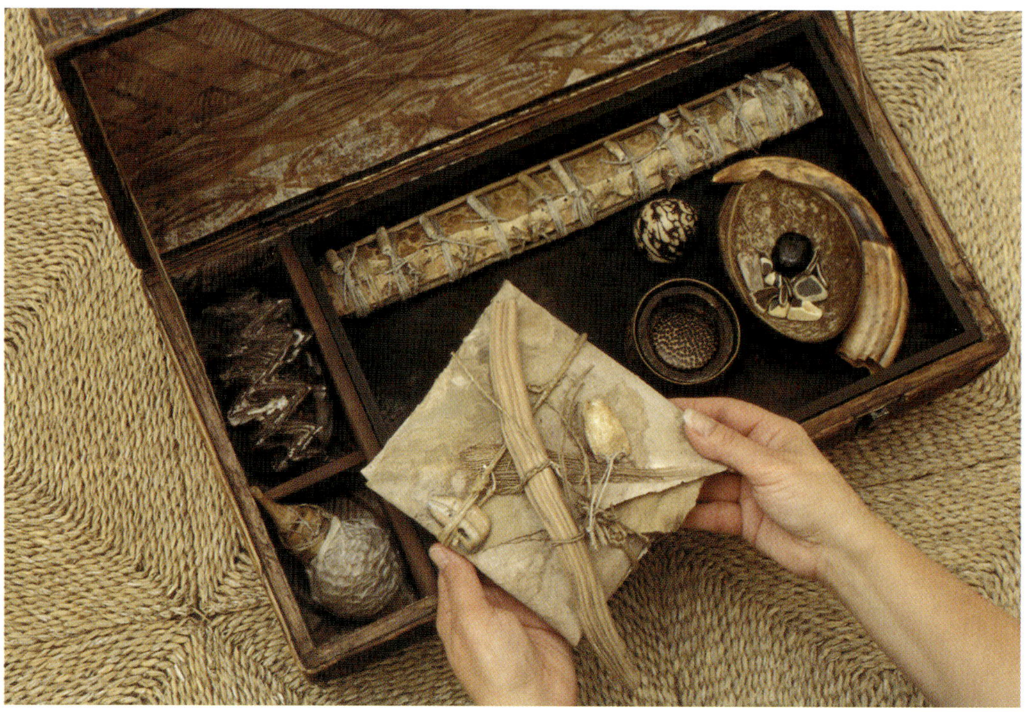

TROPIC JOURNEY
MIXED MEDIA ASSEMBLAGE
VIEWS 1 & 2

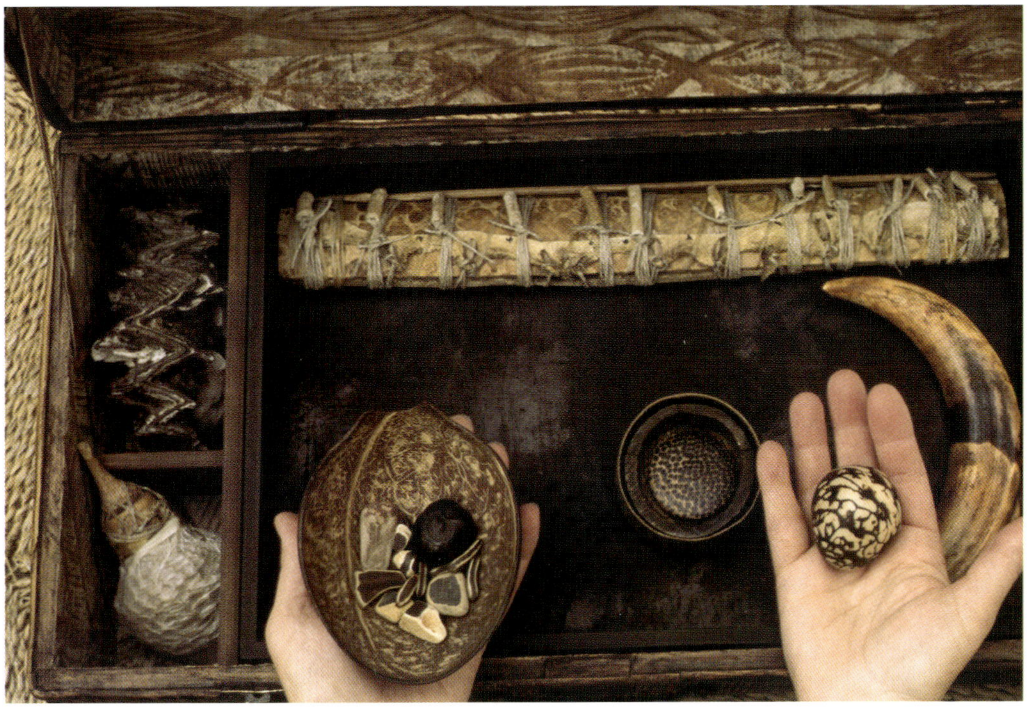

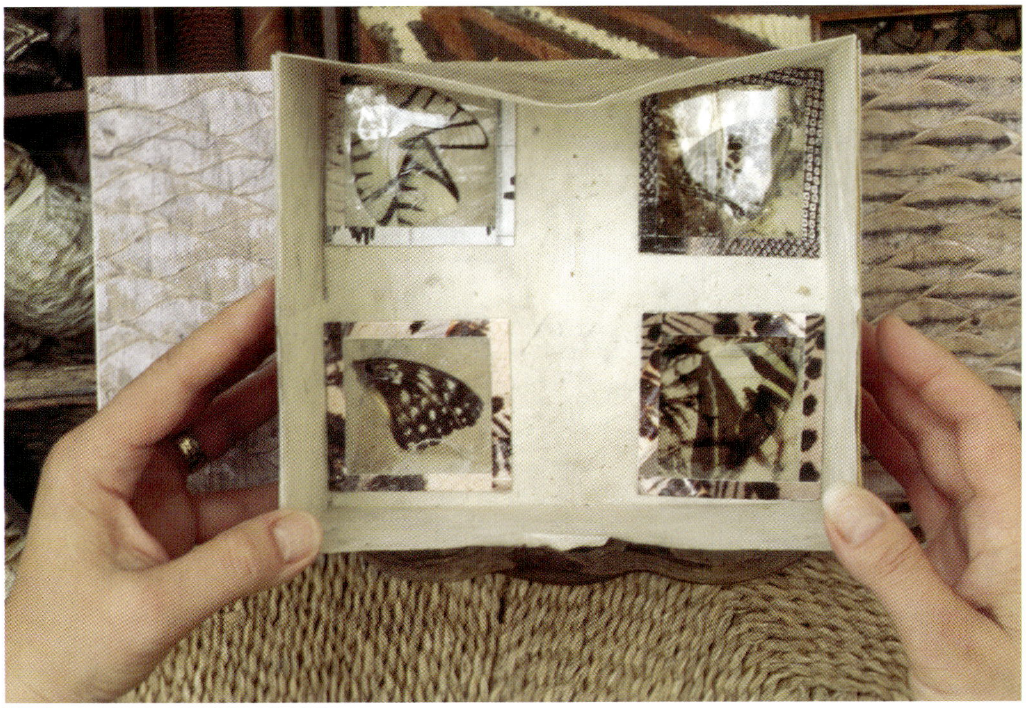

TROPIC JOURNEY
MIXED MEDIA ASSEMBLAGE
VIEWS 3 & 4

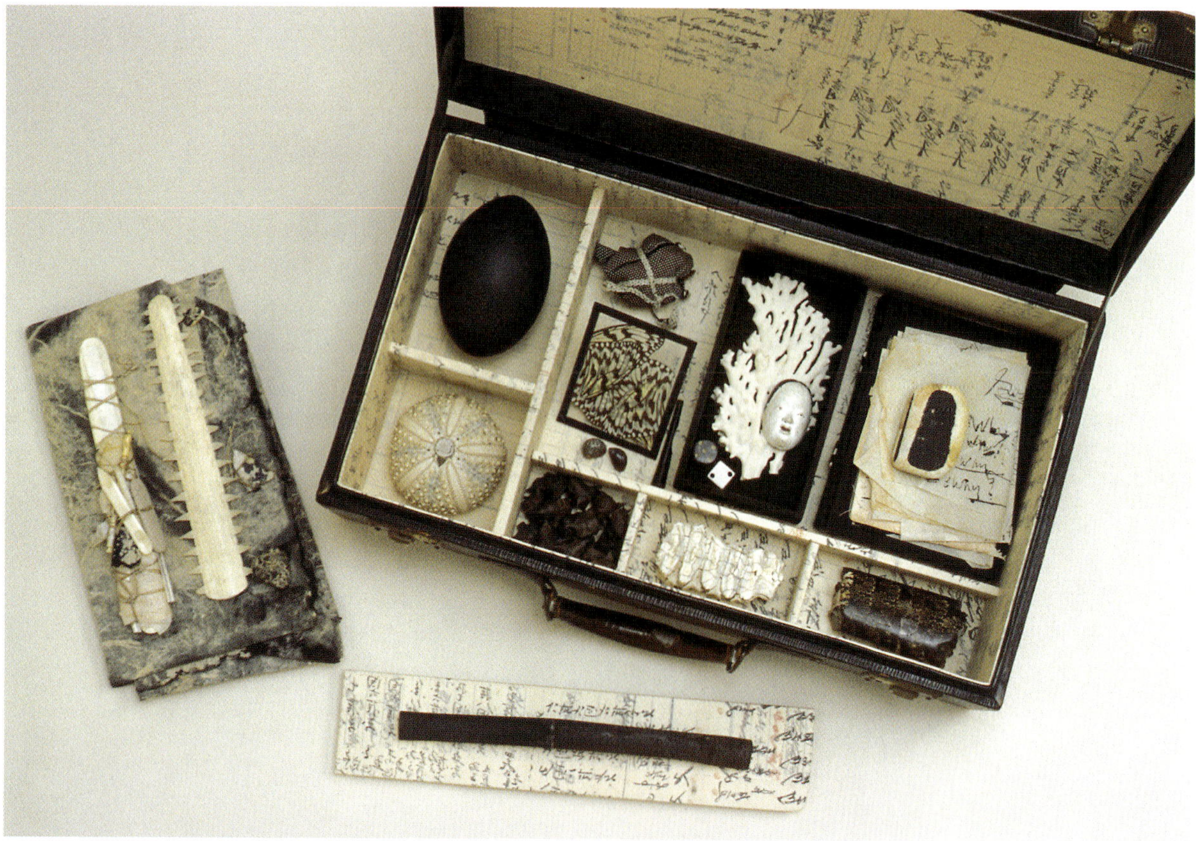

VALISE
MIXED MEDIA ASSEMBLAGE
17 X 20 X 17 INCHES

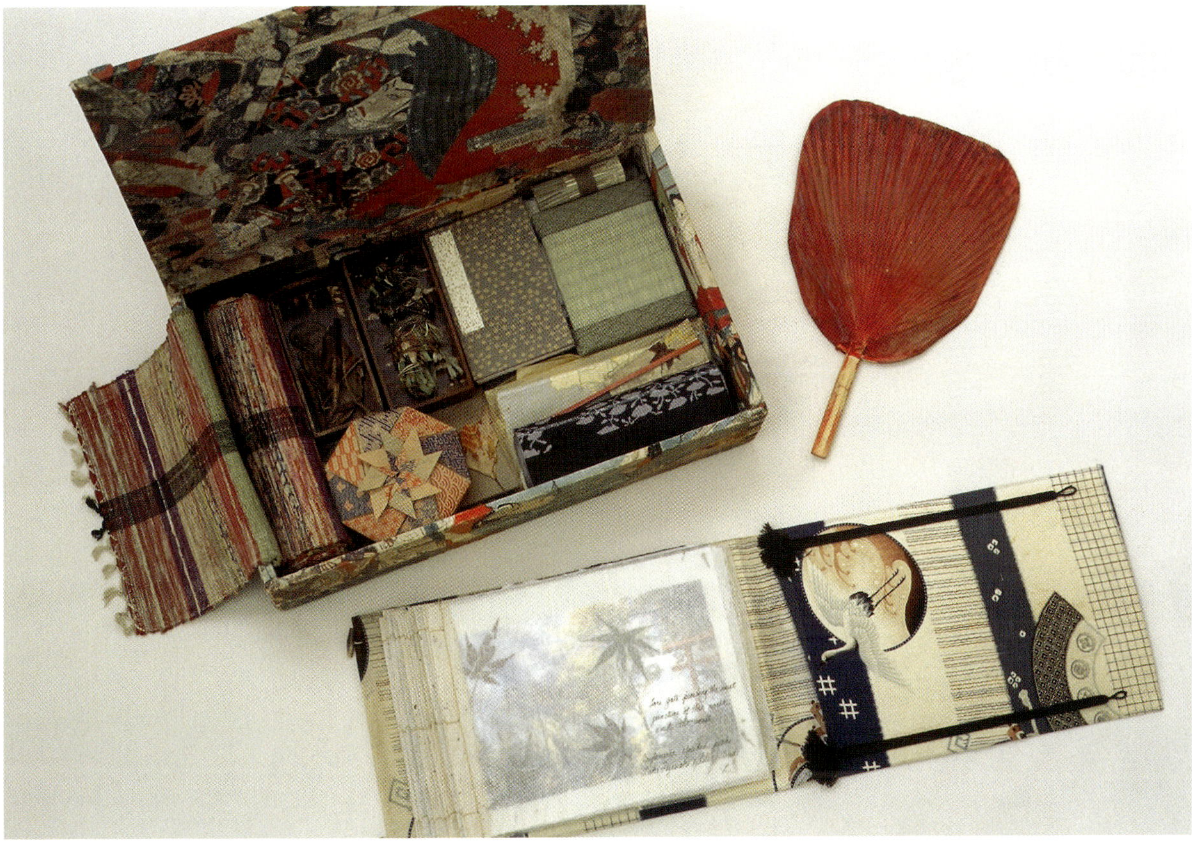

GAIL RIEKE b. 1944 Mount Vernon NY. *Ed:* BFA and MFA Univ. Florida at Gainesville. *Coll:* Museum of New Mexico; The Albuquerque Museum; Sheldon Memorial Art Gallery of the Univ. Nebraska; Roswell Museum NM; Fiberarts Magazine; Santa Fe Institute; Univ. Florida.

TOHOKU TRAVEL JOURNAL
MIXED MEDIA ASSEMBLAGE
13 X 20.5 X 5 INCHES

TOM WALDRON

It is hard to have spent much time art watching in Santa Fe without at least once being entranced by a Tom Waldron sculpture. His work is quiet, unassuming, understated, and massive. The experience is one of watching the work slowly and subtly change in space-time as you move around it, or as you shift your body, your head, your two eyes.

In a public place, or someone's living room, a Waldron sculpture sneaks up on you because the perceptual glide across its rounded surface is so pleasurably intriguing that you find yourself in the midst of it—wondering what's happening—before you even recognize it as an art experience.

Waldron's changing volumes have been described as perceptually ironic, but this misses the point. While the disjunctions of irony often attend humor, there are ways to laugh that are not quite so arch. Interacting with a Waldron you might find it funny to find no corner where you expected one, or to watch a three-sided form turn into a four sided one. And it can make you laugh to shift quickly back and forth in front of one of Waldron's large steel forms and watch it jump like jello in its quarter inch steel skin. But this would be a little like taking a turn in the road and thinking it ironic because you'd suddenly come across the delightful vision of a lake where you hadn't expected one.

Waldron's engaging work is more about a serious kind of artistic pleasure-play with perception than it is about irony. He grew up in the northern plains State of Minnesota—"Land of 10,000 Lakes"—where irony would constitute having a hard time finding one. Waldron's curvilinear geometry could easily represent mathematical models of how liquid fills space.

His work is like water in that it can seemingly accommodate any impossible shape, coming to rest in large pockmarks left by boulders dragged across the earth's surface by the ice of glacial recess and pooling in concavities atop the selfsame stones when it rains. His work is like water in that it cannot be compressed; the quarter inch shell between a Waldron's interior and the world is precise in delineating exactly how much space the piece takes to exist. His work is like water in that it's presence can be placid and soothing, or deeply ominous, and that either way it can have purity. And his work is like water in the smooth play of light across soft planar geometries. It can be still and moving at the same time. Maybe the irony is that Waldron has chosen to live and work in the desert.

Still this elemental quality aligns Waldron with the great abstract sculptors of Modernism. From Brancusi, to Henry Moore, to Richard Serra, Tom Waldron may well be the last best minimalist in the West. His art is a sort of pared down cubist abstraction turned inside out and his concerns are as calmly expressive and as rigorously formal as any of them. His project is a deepening of Modern form, an act of scaling it to the body, revitalizing Modernist Universality from the inside out. What is it to be a Modernist in a post-modern world?

What kind of post-modernism wouldn't allow you to be?

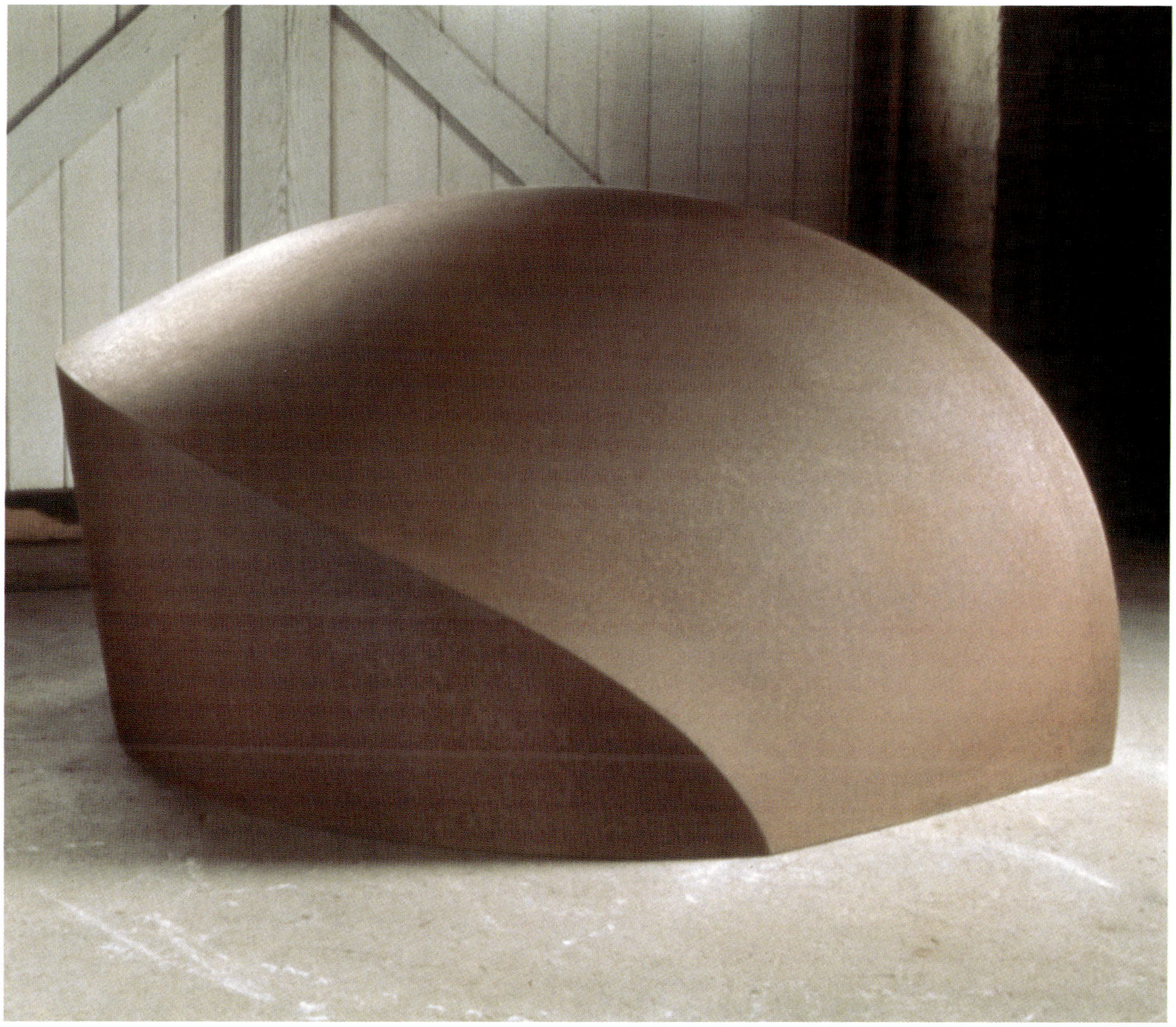

FLOOD, 2001
STEEL
35 X 71 X 57 INCHES

TOM WALDRON

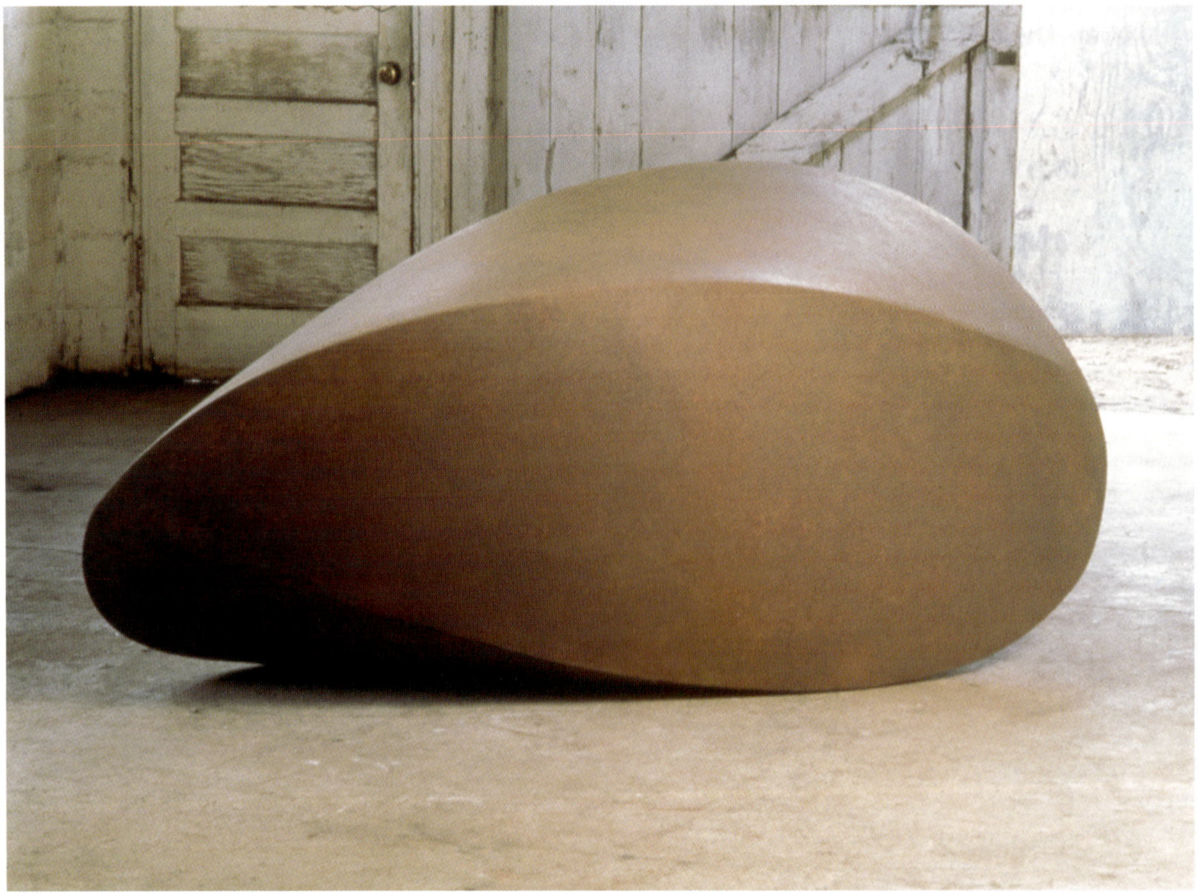

MATCH, 1993
STEEL
38 X 64 X 24 INCHES

TOM WALDRON

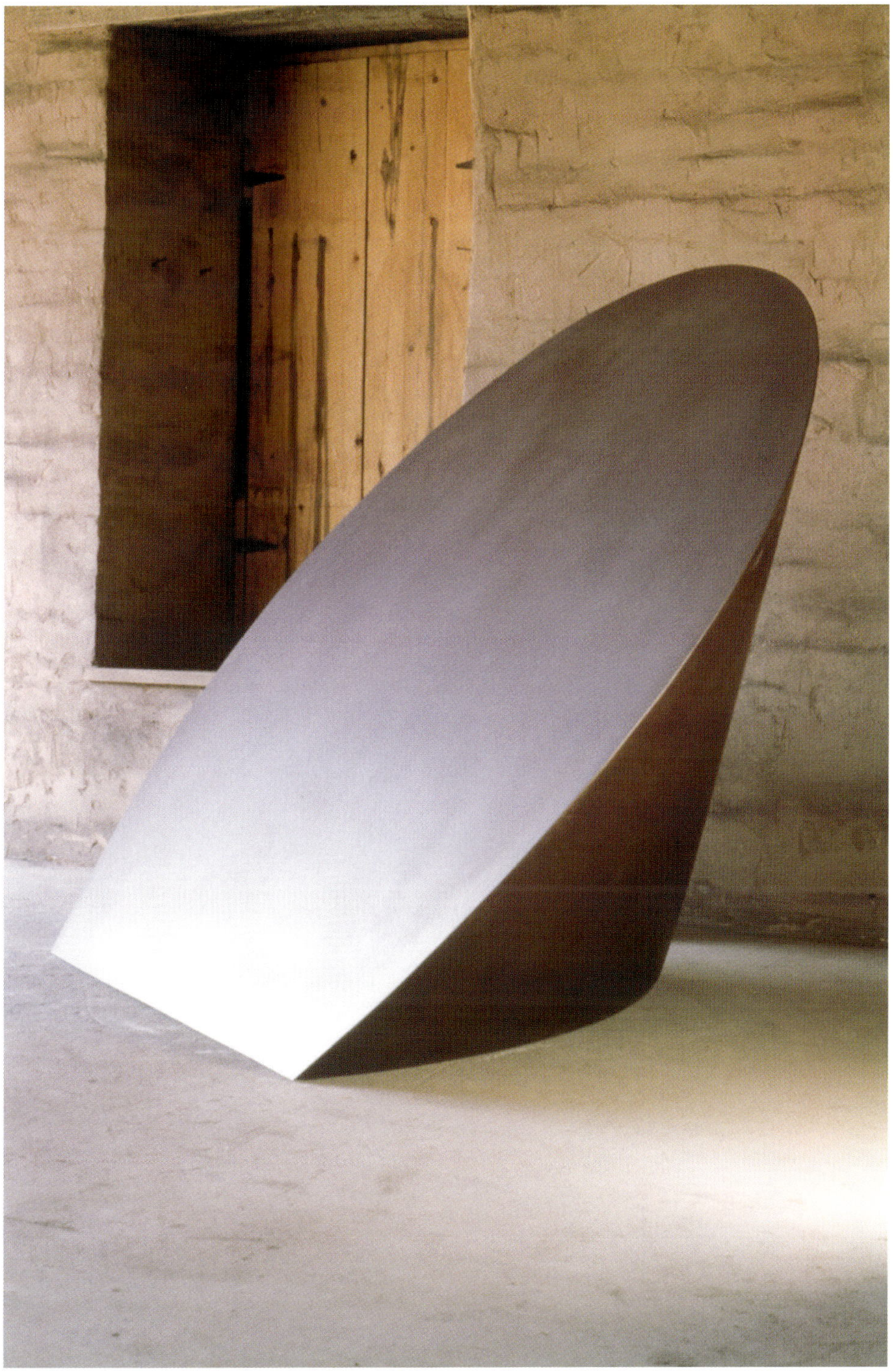

LOOM, 2001

STEEL

63 X 90 X 49 INCHES

TOM WALDRON

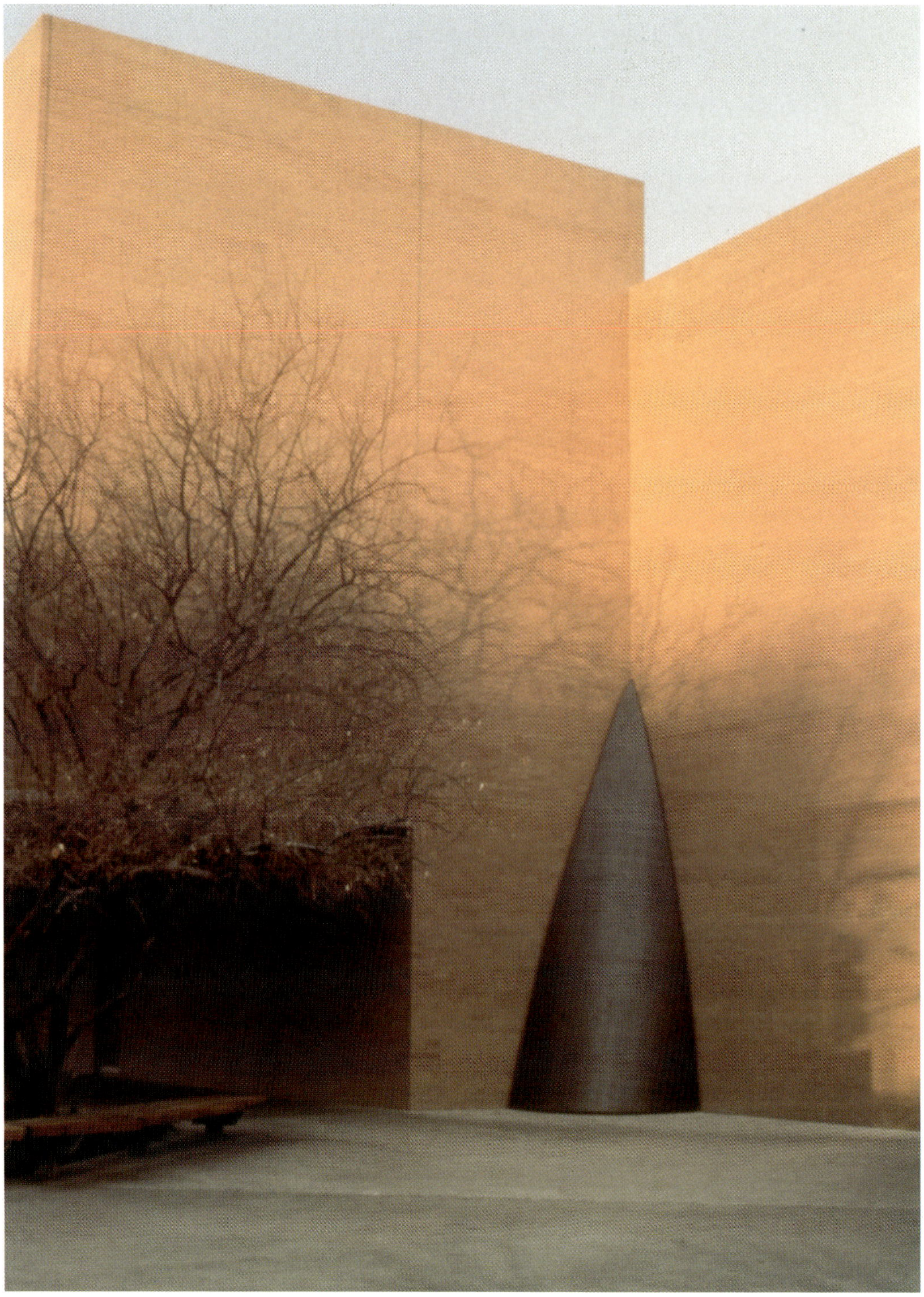

CONE TEN, 1994
STEEL
16 X 6 X 4.5 INCHES

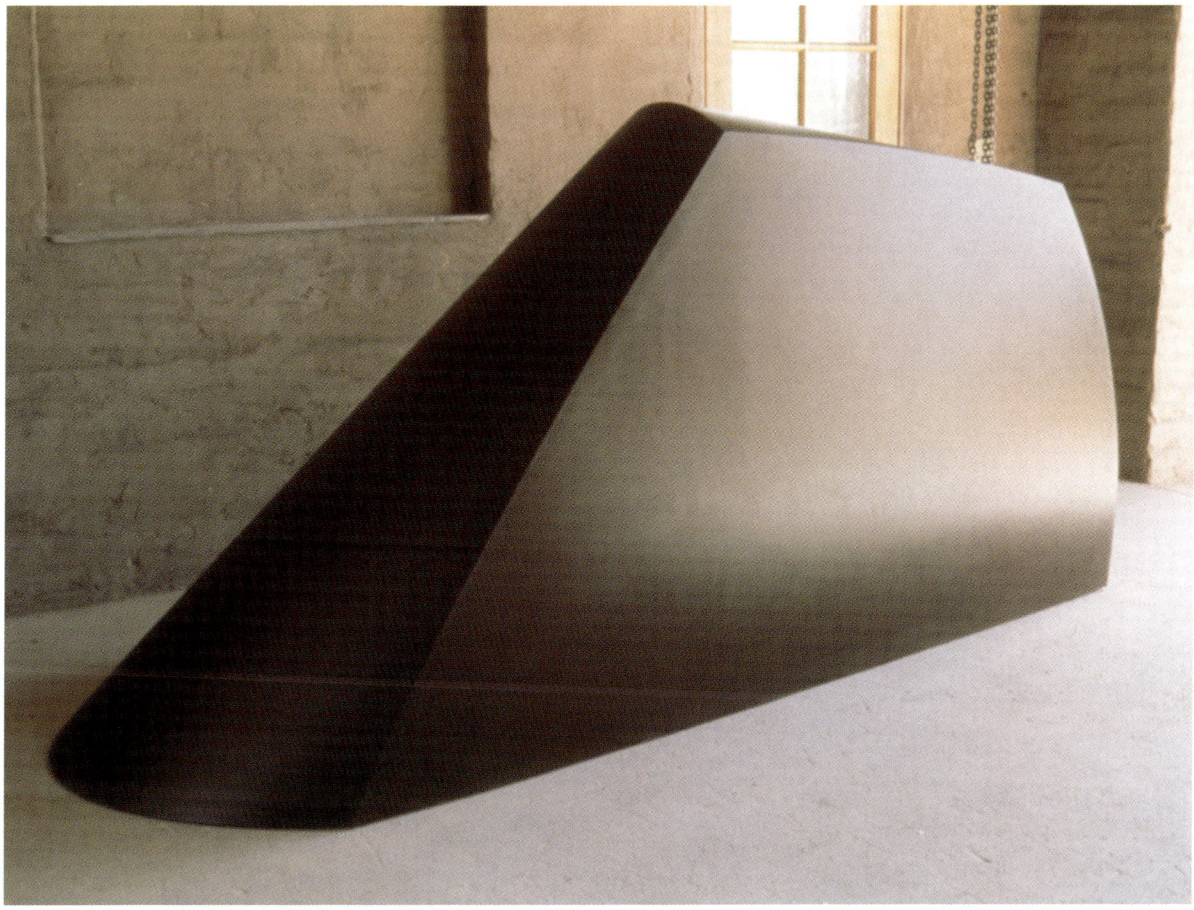

TOM WALDRON b. 1953 Minneapolis MN. *Ed:* BA Univ. Minnesota; Notre Dame; Univ. New Mexico, Albuquerque. *Coll:* Univ. New Mexico, Gallup NM; New Mexico Museum of Fine Arts, Santa Fe; Albuquerque Museum of Art. *Representation:* Linda Durham Contemporary Art, Santa Fe.

DART, 2001
STEEL
50 X 100 X 42 INCHES

PRISCILLA ROBINSON

All the world is an energy in constant spiral flux. All that matters is how you transform the world. Perusing the list of materials Priscilla Robinson puts into her handmade paper/mixed media work, one comes across this lovely English word: aspidistra—the houseplant immortalized by prescient writer, George Orwell. By the act of putting this plant matter—nandina, oak, and tree leaves as well—into a piece like *Transformation,* she literally joins her domestic surroundings to the gallery wall, making of the ordinary, something extraordinary.

In the alchemical something-from-nothing art of papermaking, the process of pulping organic matter is associated with the late autumn of the year, the endless and ever-beginning most secretive point of nature's cycle when the crops are tilled back under the earth to magically compost under winter snows to provide the nourishing material for the upcoming summer of forms. The hand of the papermaker and plant nurturer alike creates from a soup of natural substance, through cooking, watering and drying processes, fundamental change in the world around them.

The seeds of Priscilla Robinson's abstracted forms lie already in the matter sea of her paper pulp, and take only the artist's patient skills to blossom into full-blown life. Priscilla Robinson was trained as a painter, and her cast paper reliefs are paintings in a sculptural dimension. In a mixed media, paper and wrought iron piece like *27 Resting Butterflies,* she gathers her strength to engage the physical space of the viewer in a mode of transform and transport. Is this a section of the wing-drying moment at the long end of dawn, before migratory flight? Or the first physical actualization of life beyond caterpillar consciousness? Or is it an origami invitation to afternoons spent in the topsy-turvy gravity of butterfly time?

As materials from her Taos garden find their way into her Hollander beater, so nature and her cycle of birth, growth, death, decay, and rebirth inhabit the center of Priscilla Robinson's centrifugal output. Have a dream of flying upward on the great white wings of *Transformation* in an open expanding spiral. Aspidistra and all, these scale-defying wings are the skin shed by a changeling angel, or a moth you might ride to the moon.

Priscilla Robinson's communion with the natural world governs her artistic intentions. Whether rhythmically undulating, or rectangularly situated, her muses live in the spectacular soaring heights and sunlit sights of the Southwest. Donning and shedding their resplendent robes, the seasons observe in succession the processes of *Procession.* The artist evokes rites of planting and passage, spectacular celebrations of abundance, and generous days of atonement and gratitude whereby the great gardener might return us to respect for our planet and ourselves.

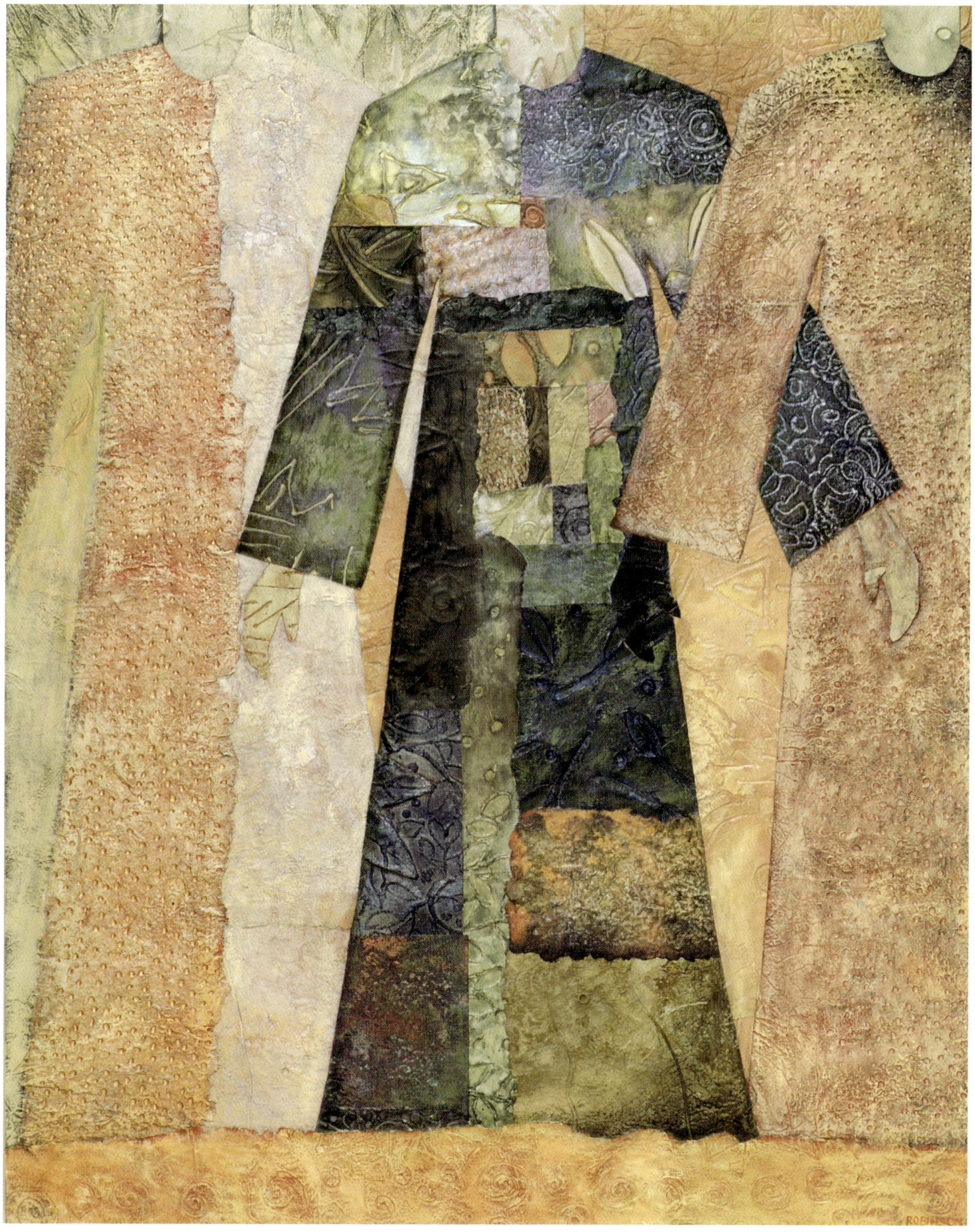

THE PROCESSION
ACRYLIC ON HANDMADE PAPER
OF COTTON & ABACA
60 X 48 INCHES

PRISCILLA ROBINSON

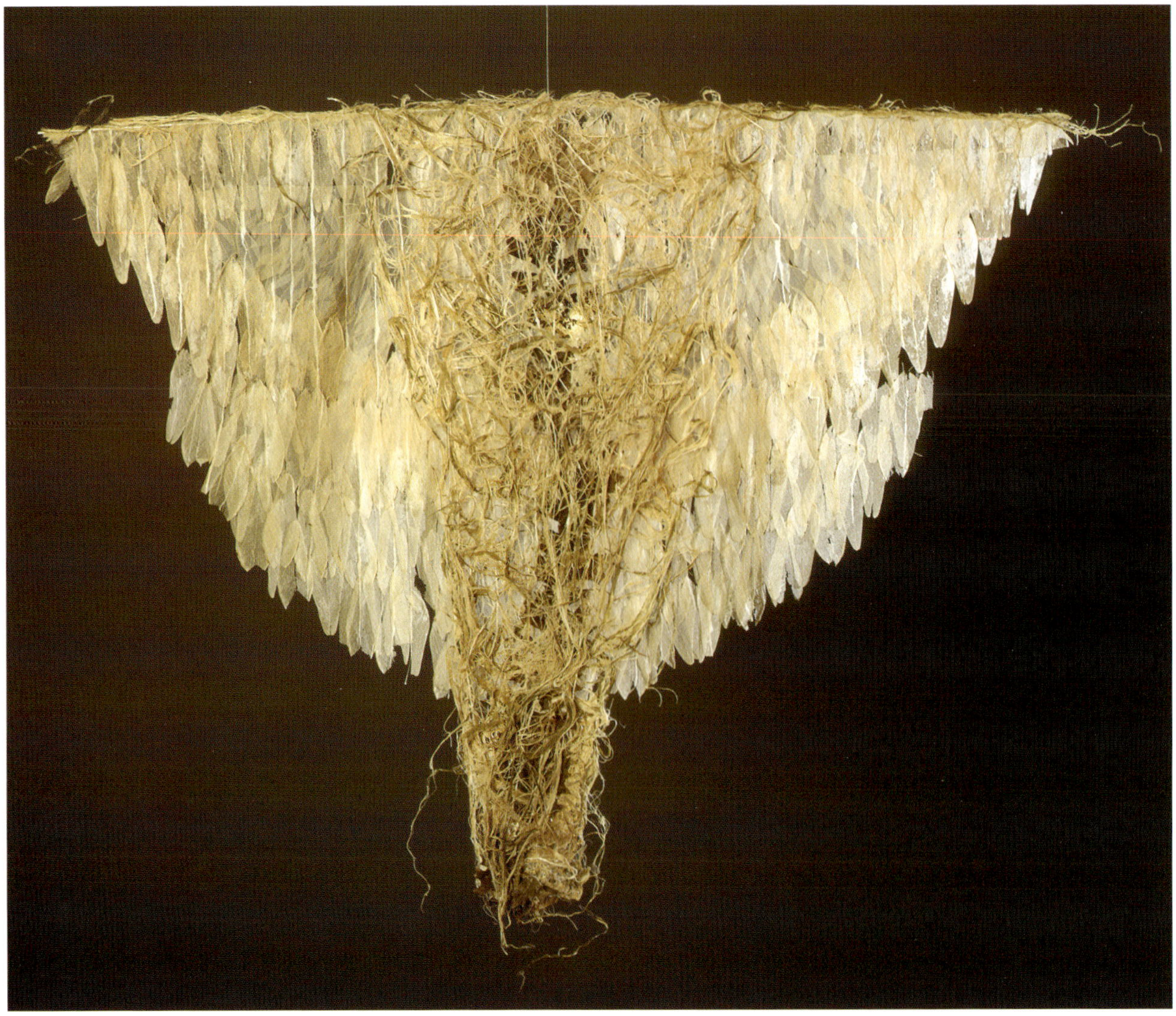

TRANSFORMATION
HANDMADE PAPER OF NANDINA, OAK,
ASPIDISTRA & VARNISH TREE LEAVES
36 X 48 INCHES

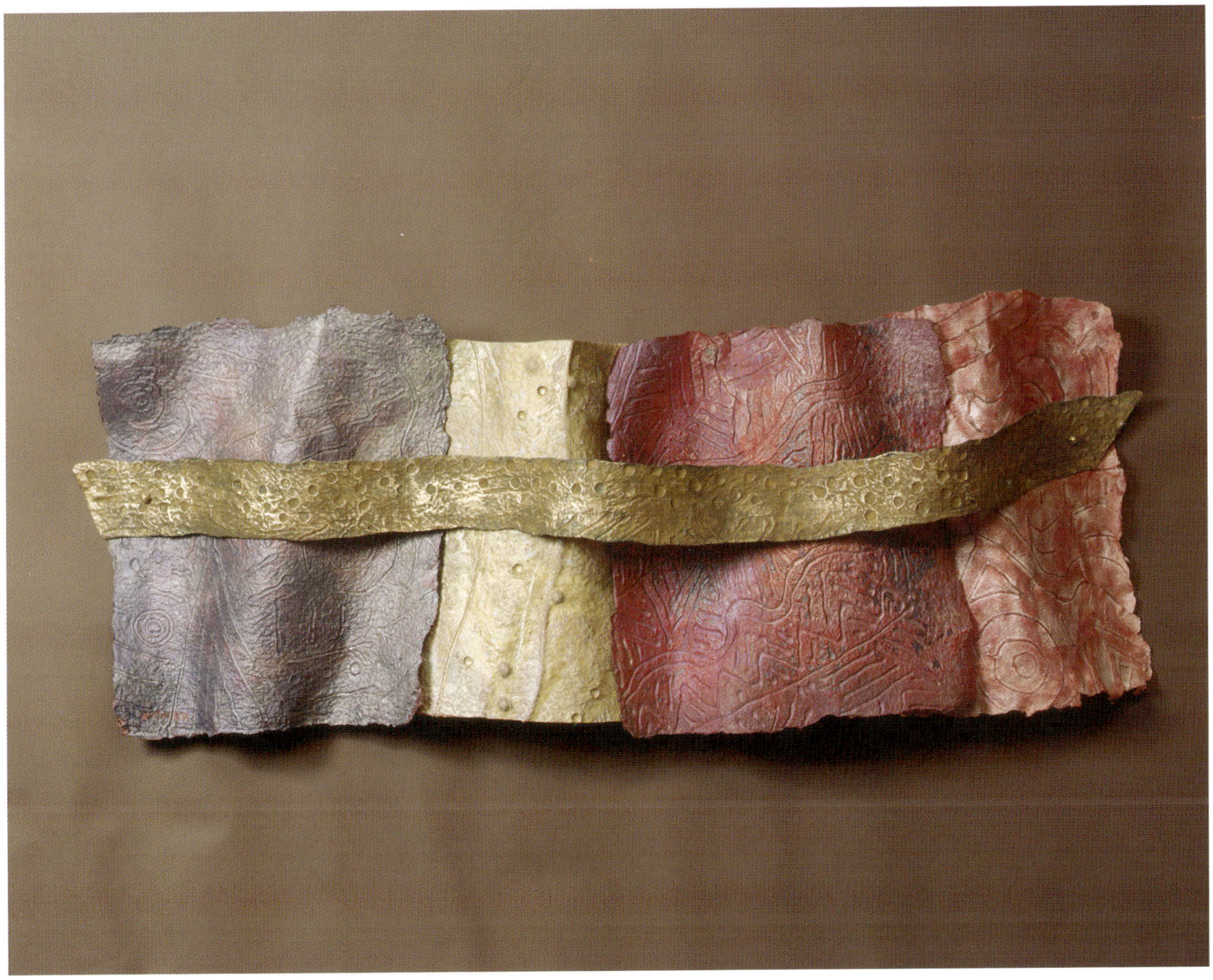

FREE SPIRIT
ACRYLIC AND BRONZE LEAF ON HANDMADE PAPER
OF COTTON & ABACA ON FIBERGLASS
15 X 41 X 4 INCHES

PRISCILLA ROBINSON

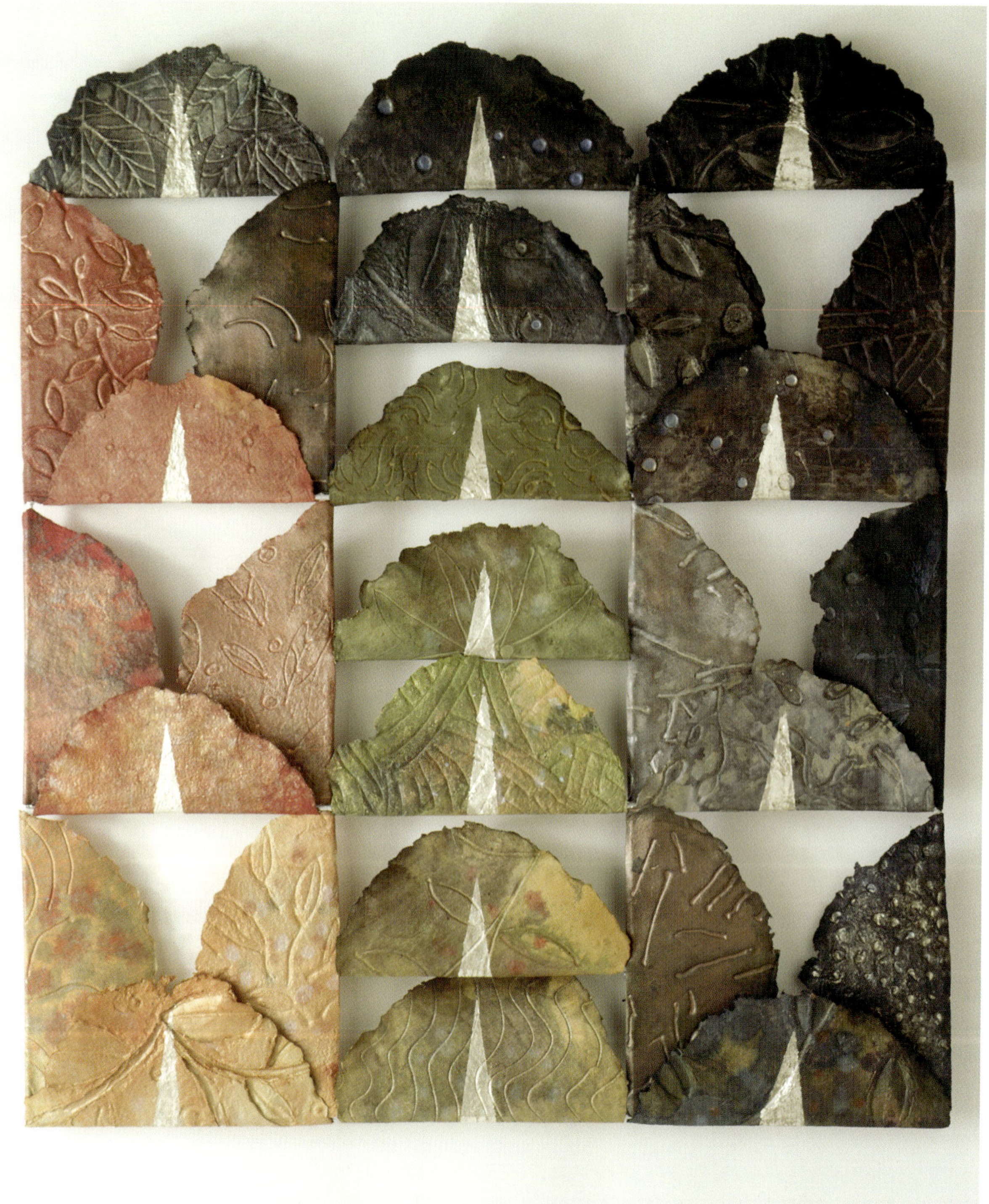

27 RESTING BUTTERFLIES
ACRYLIC & WHITE GOLD LEAF ON HANDMADE PAPER
OF COTTON & ABACA ON A WROUGHT IRON GRID
42 X 36 X 2 INCHES

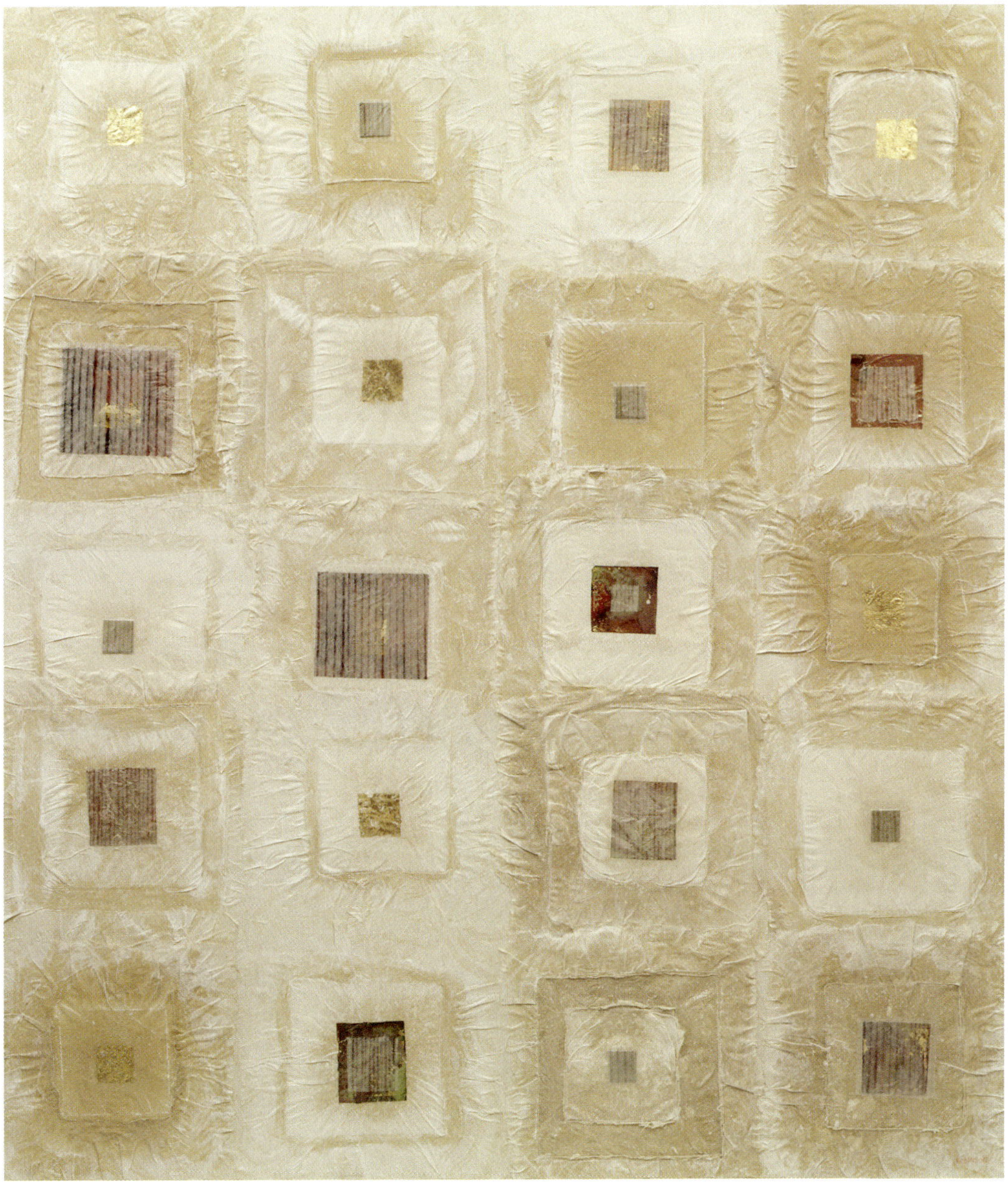

PRISCILLA ROBINSON b. 1948 Washington DC. *Ed:* BFA Univ. Arizona. *Coll:* Abbey of Spineto, Tuscany, Italy; Royal Library, The Hague, The Netherlands; Museum of the Valley, Charmey, Switzerland; Chevron Pipeline, Houston. *Coll:* Shell Oil Company, Houston; Tokyo Electron America, Austin; Frost Bank Plaza, Austin. *Representation:* New Directions Gallery, Taos; Wally Workman Gallery, Austin; National Art, Houston.

FIELDS
ACRYLIC & GOLD LEAF ON HANDMADE PAPER
OF OVERBEATEN FLAX
62 X 54 INCHES

SYDNEY K. HAMBURGER

Polyvalent postmodernist Sydney Hamburger creates a psychic architecture of ritual and renewal. Her corten steel, aluminum, cedar, bronze and/or bamboo structures define open-ended spaces of refuge from an increasingly troubled world. Her willingness to confront and contend with the complexities of contemporary conflicts—social, cultural, and spiritual- makes her that rarest of artistic personalities—an articulate visionary.

Speaking of her constructivist environments she states her intentions clearly, "I feel at various times, vulnerable, isolated and exposed to grave dangers. My art is an effort to mitigate and to dissipate these anxieties for myself and my viewers." If postmodernism has a patron saint, he is surely that great writer of being, Samuel Beckett. Evidence of his influence is felt variously in the work of recent masters, Philip Guston, Bruce Nauman, Susan Rothenberg and Ed Ruscha. Sydney Hamburger, with her concerns for our failing cosmologies, and her discovery within sculptural space of a place for being, ought to be included in this legacy.

Her "safe spaces" are frameworks, forays and multi-dimensional architectural drawings in the air that suggest housing, hogans, temples, tree houses, teepees, caves and cathedrals—all places wherein people have successfully sought respite from troublesome times. Many would function excellently as stage sets for Beckett's theatrical works, and are often peopled by amusing fetishistic characters fashioned from feathers, twigs, and plastic ties like the kind that link new flip-flops together, or sales tags to t-shirts. Suggesting a new urban primitivism, or consumerist voodoo, Sydney Hamburger sees, like Beckett, a real connection between humor and spiritual sustenance. Still, as the French classicist Montaigne said, "Oneself and one's companion are sufficient theatre." Bemusedly exploring her constructions alone, *sans* drama, is indeed superbly soul satisfying.

Giacometti comes unavoidably to mind. His sublime use of the spindly was well ahead of its time and Hamburger practices a similar linearity in her establishment of spatial boundaries and volumetric indicators. *Sila's Baldacchino* with its reference to Bernini and the Baroque, explodes from the center like a stripped down, self supporting shrine to the sun, while *Fragus* spins on its center like a compass, tracing a circle in the sand and simultaneously scoring the sky.

These amazing pieces project outward, suggesting motions of expansion, although this is simply the residual effect of their true movement inward toward still centers housing intense interior spirits. Their greatest growth happens as a journey into inner landscapes, positing places of reflective contemplation within infinite abodes. It is Sydney Hamburger's sincere and laudable contention that "...we most desperately need to confront the magic and uncertainty of our lives... so that we can learn and grow." This, she rightly believes, in Beuysian terms, is, "the best hope for human salvation." She is does a beautiful, subtle and spectacular job of creating habitations for hope.

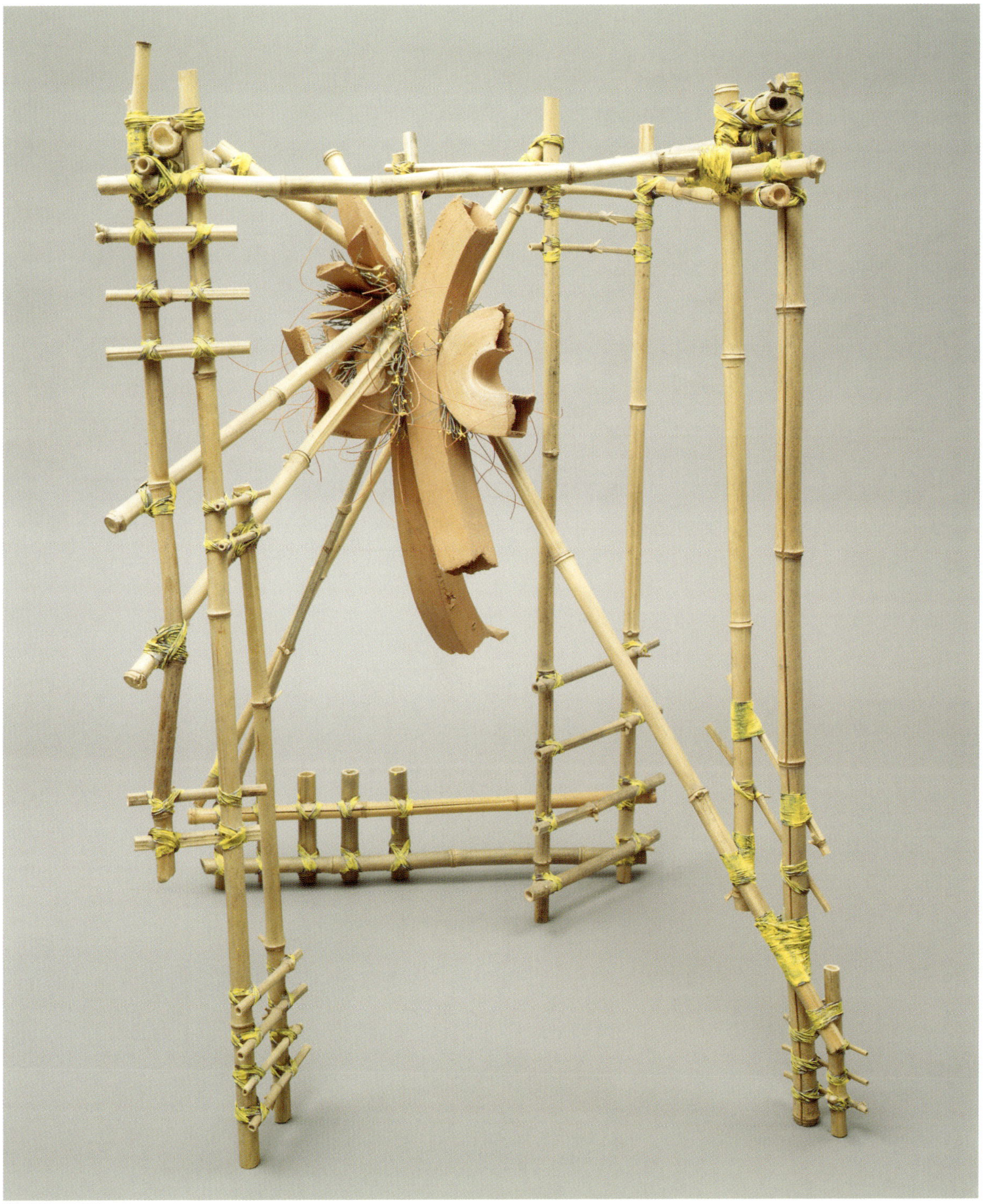

SILA'S BALDACCINO
BAMBOO & TERRACOTTA
42 X 28 X 28 INCHES

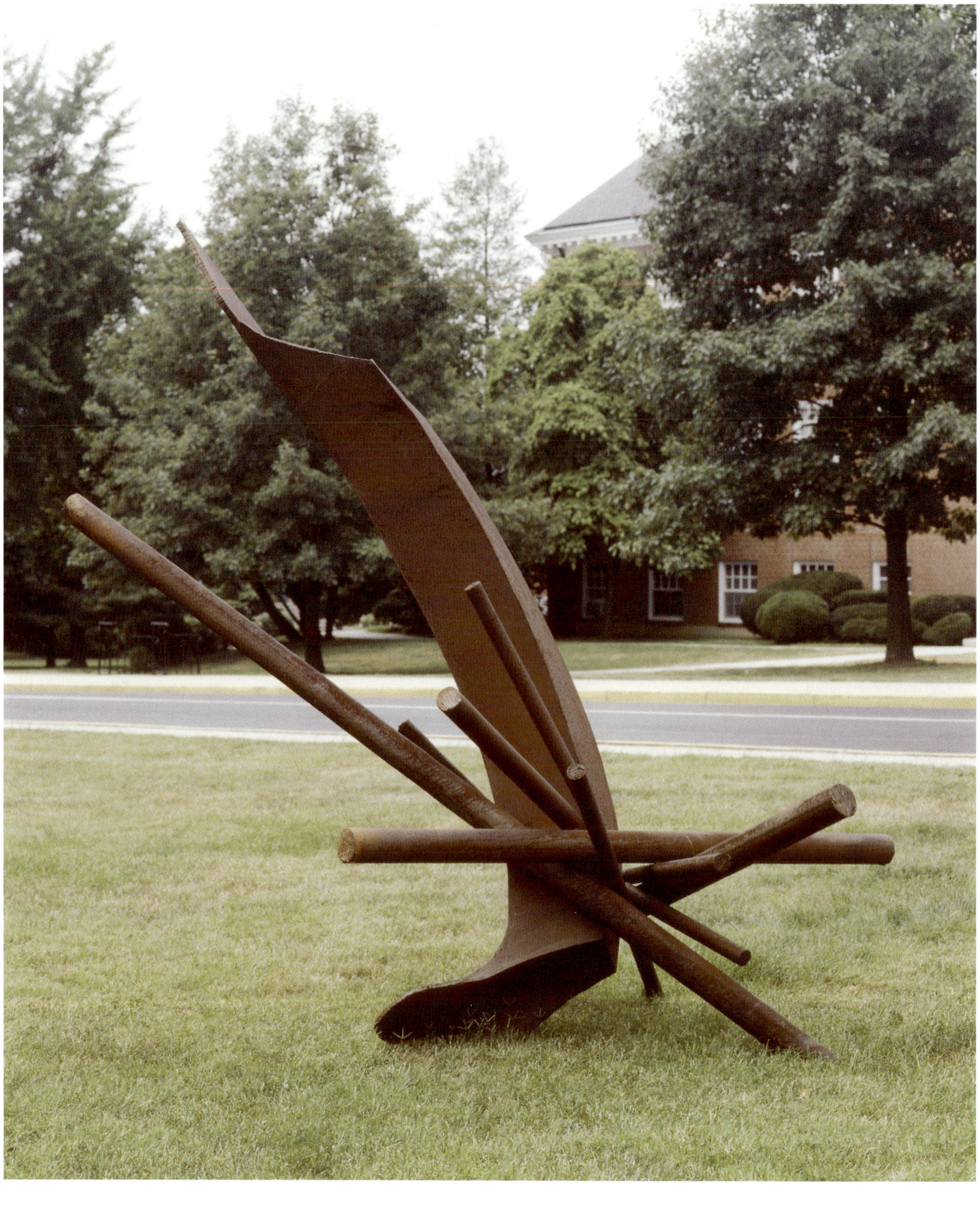

FRAGUS
CORTEN STEEL
194 X 96 X 72 INCHES

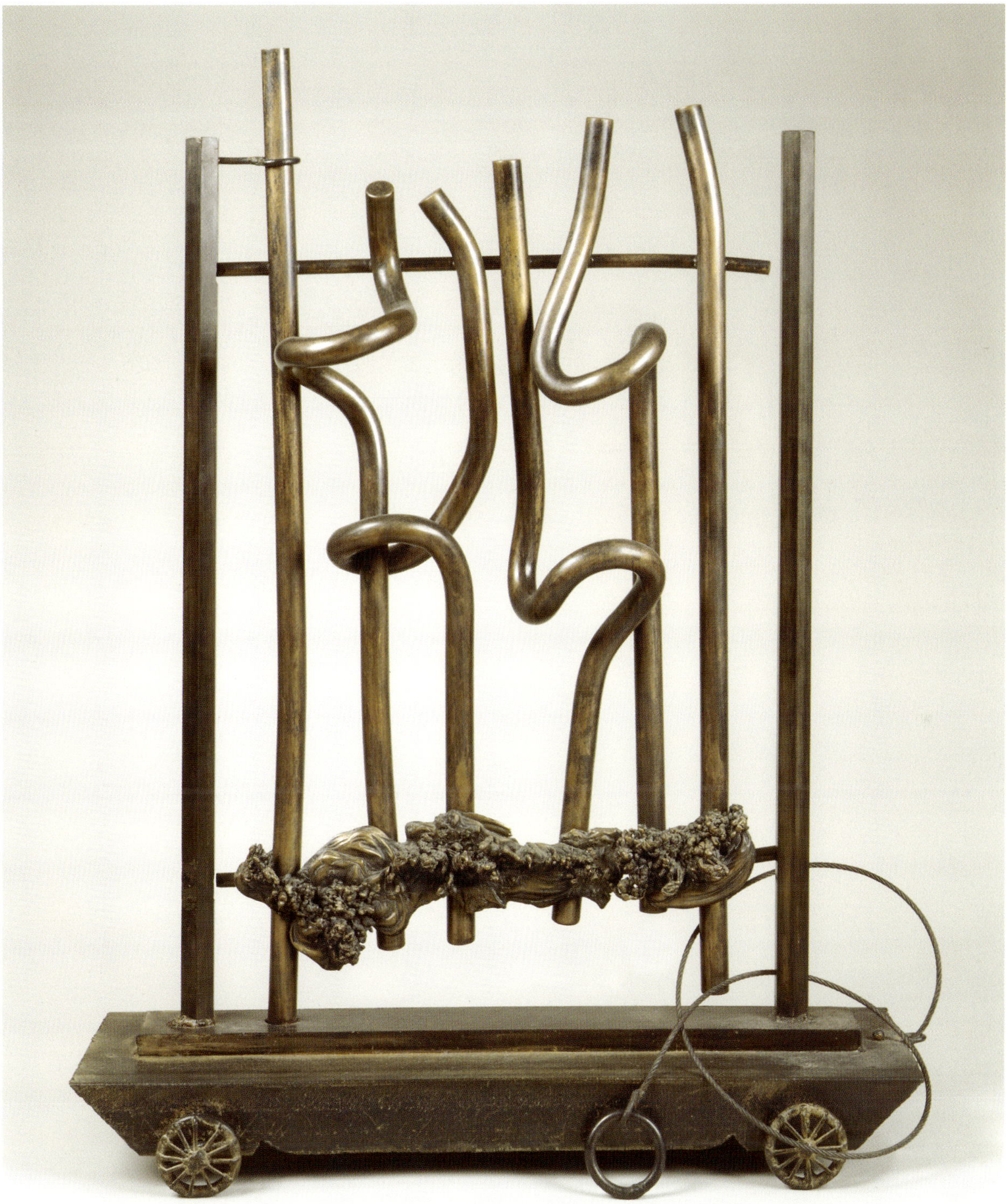

HOLOCAUST GATE TOY
BRONZE
36 X 21 X 7 INCHES

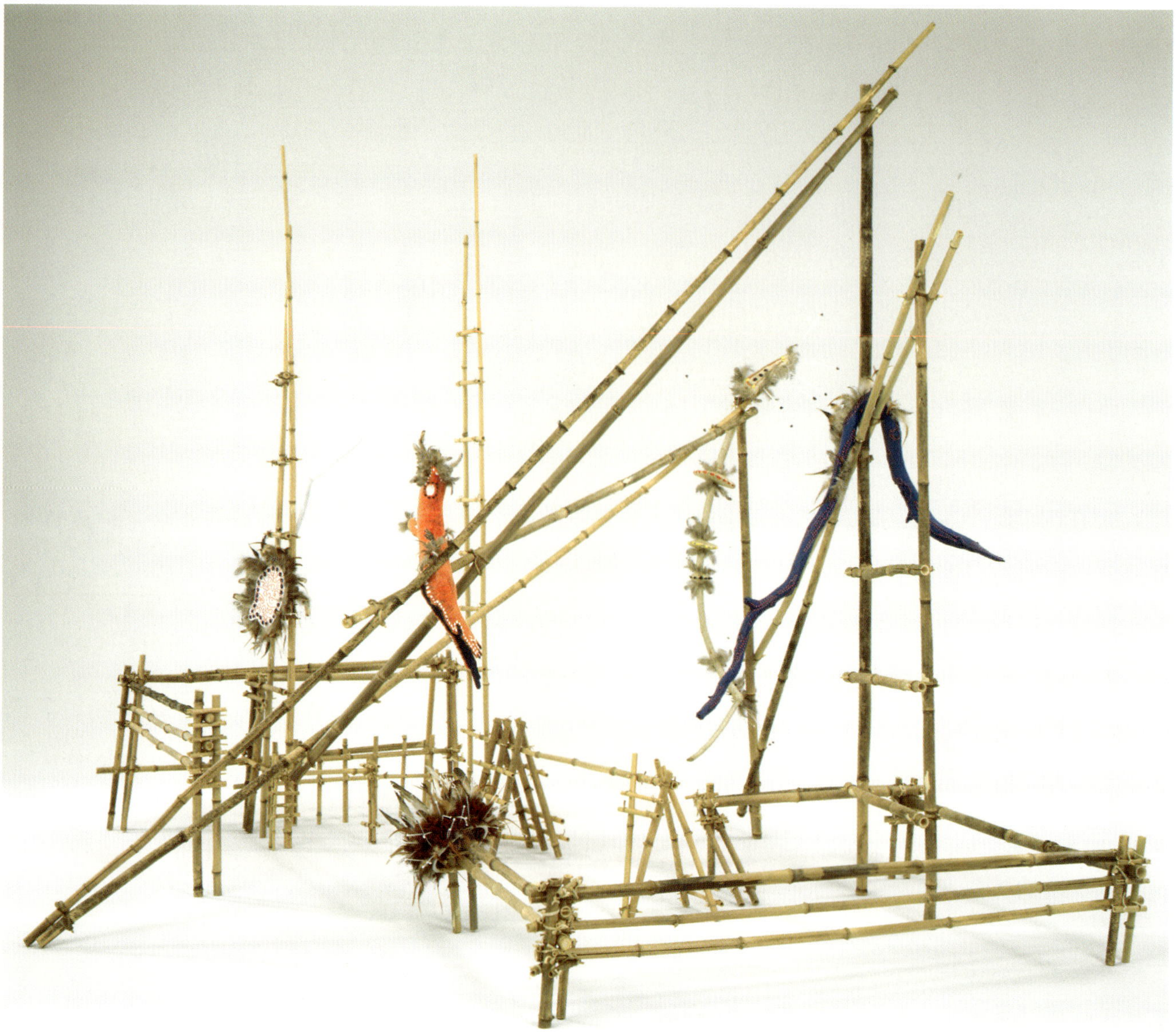

TAPOP'S CLOSET
BAMBOO & MIXED MEDIA
89 X 102 X 102 INCHES

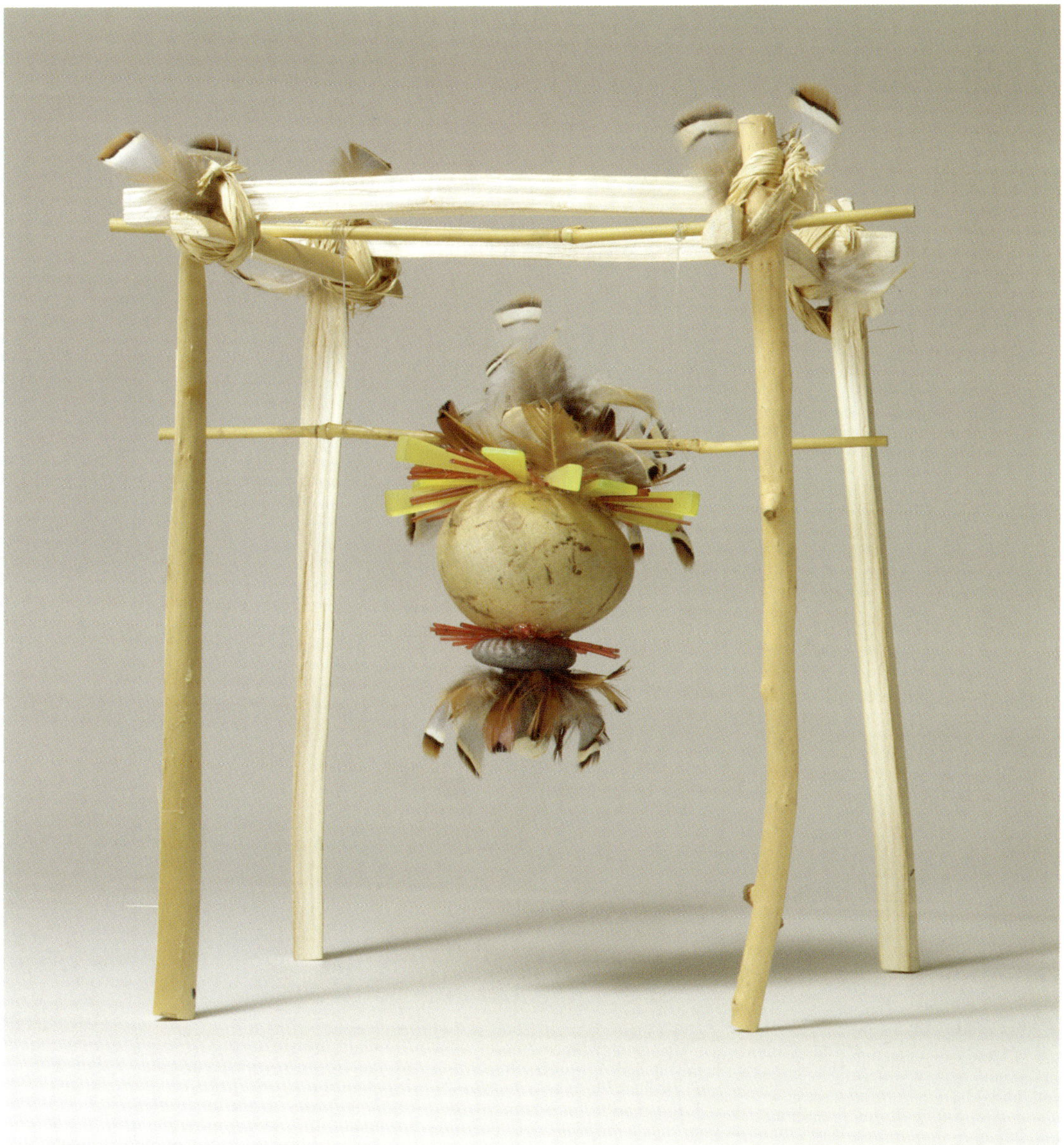

SYDNEY K. HAMBURGER b. 1935 New York. *Ed:* MFA, BA Towson State Univ., Baltimore; Honorary Doctor of Fine Art, Hood College, Frederick MD; Maryland Institute College of Art, Baltimore; Johns Hopkins Univ., Baltimore; Oxford Univ., England. *Coll:* Washington County Museum of Fine Art, Hagerstown MD; The Macdowell Colony, Peterborough NH; The Talbot Bank, Easton MD; Grace Hartigan; Pepita Seth; Amalie R. Rothschild. *Representation:* Von Schlegell Fine Arts.

THE EGG AND I
BAMBOO & MIXED MEDIA
54 X 31 X 29 INCHES

JOHN GELDERSMA

John Geldersma's art is intensely and immediately human. He merges the sophistication of minimalism with an organic concern for color, natural forms and the human spirit.

Geldersma was born in New Orleans, Louisiana, and grew up in the "West Bank," a working class town on the other side of the Mississippi River. The connection between artmaking and ritual was impressed upon him early in the form of homemade Mardi Gras floats and costumes, the rich Roman Catholicism of the region and the world of Voodoo.

He left Louisiana to get his MFA degree from Rutgers, in New Brunswick, New Jersey, where he studied with Robert Morris and had easy access to the New York game. It was 1965 and heavy hitters like Dan Flavin, Donald Judd, and Sol Lewitt were in full swing with the new idea of minimalism. Ever anti-hierarchical, Geldersma included in his thesis show a bi-planar geometric piece constructed of chicken wire and colored paper rosettes (like a Mardi Gras float), to which he gave the hilarious title, *Fuzzy Morris.* This seamless merger of realities, Geldersma's bayou past and the rigors of minimalism, are the hallmark of his mature work.

Once you come unstuck in time and space as Geldersma has, you see that the entire past, and any geographies or cultural influences, are fair playing fields. This revelation fueled the early modernist revolutions and remains true to the post-modern day. In his art, Geldersma, like the French artist Rousseau, is a self-made primeval man, a nomad of the spirit, an accomplished and sophisticated culture-traveler.

Today, a connection to natural forces distinguishes Geldersma as an artist of the Southwest where natural beauty has been a source of art for ages. African Art and ritual objects pared down to pure presence inspire his primitive minimalist aesthetic, like the high desert sunshine that burns away all non-essentials. His *Spirit Poles* rise in wavy organic lines to taper into the vast unknown; like the spires of Chartres Cathedral, they bring the eye to the point at which the material world vanishes and the spirit world begins. If anti-expression is part of your definition of minimalism, then the *Spirit Poles* won't do, but otherwise they fit the bill. They are vessels for the soul, upright indicators of a world beyond the senses from which every perceivable thing grows and returns. With carved wood and paint, Geldersma creates images that resonate in the psyche across time and space, Jungian archetypes that speak an ancient and universal language.

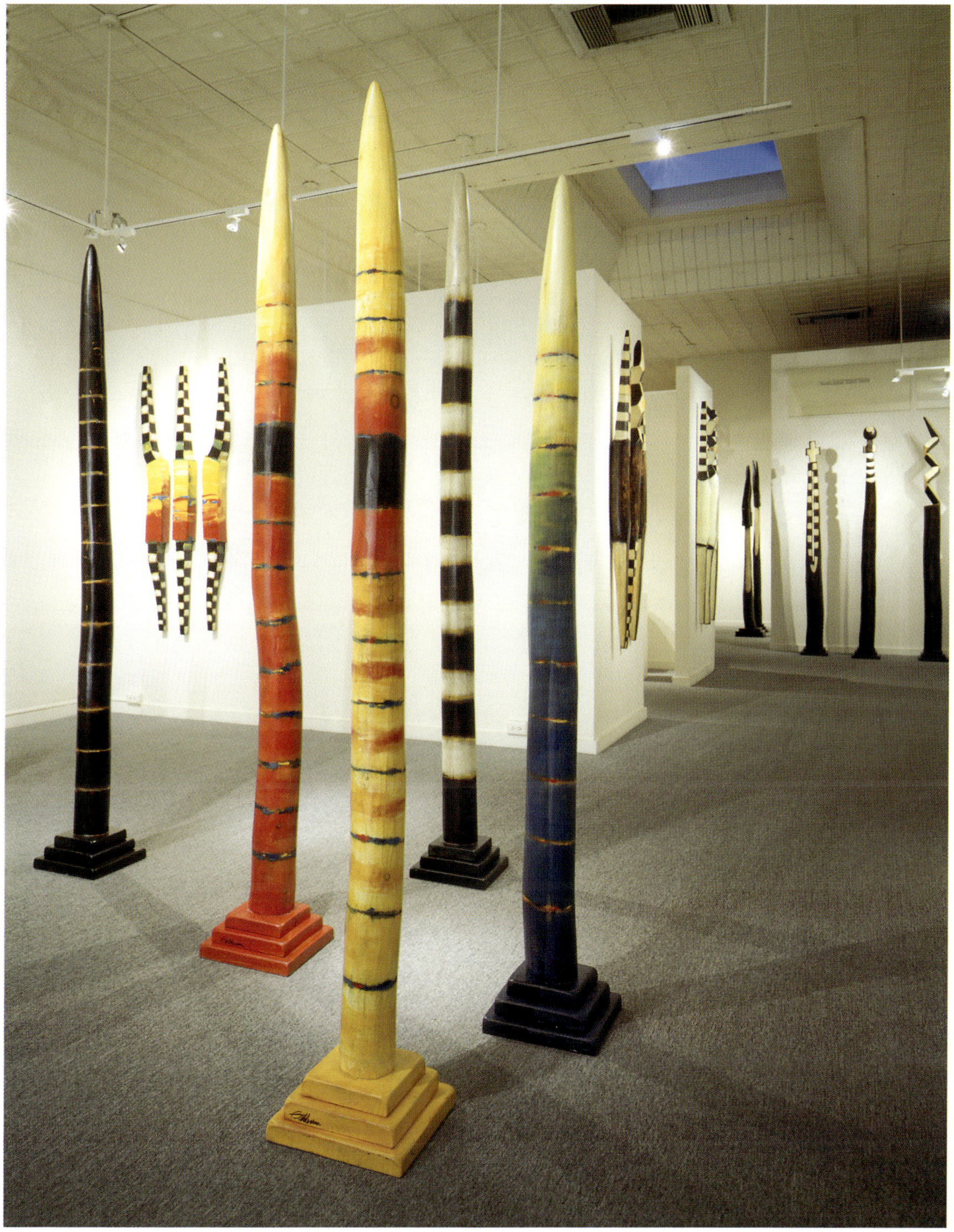

INSTALLATION, 2000

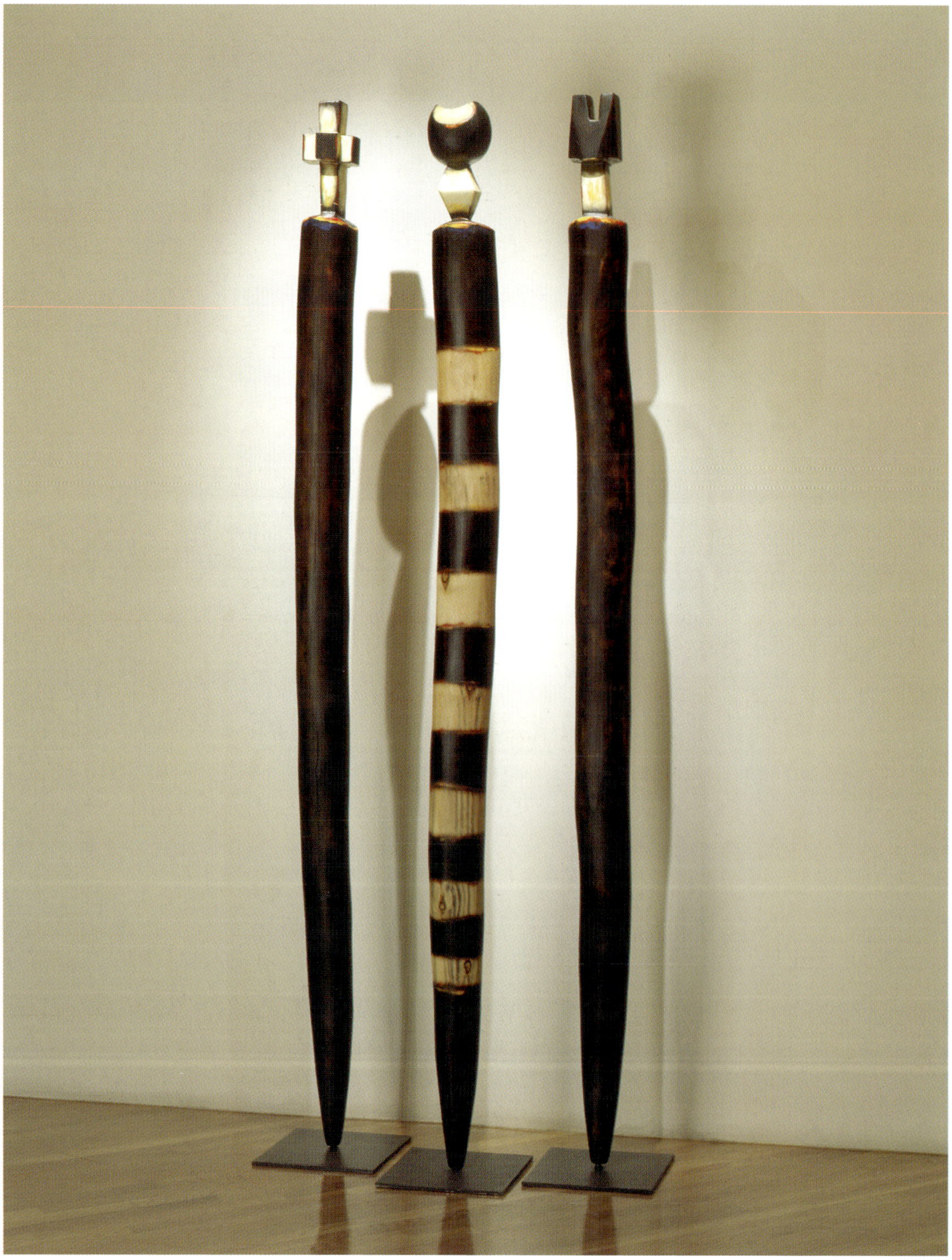

INVERTED SPIRIT POLES, 2004
BURNED & PAINTED ASPEN
97 INCHES
BASE: STEEL 12 X 12 INCHES

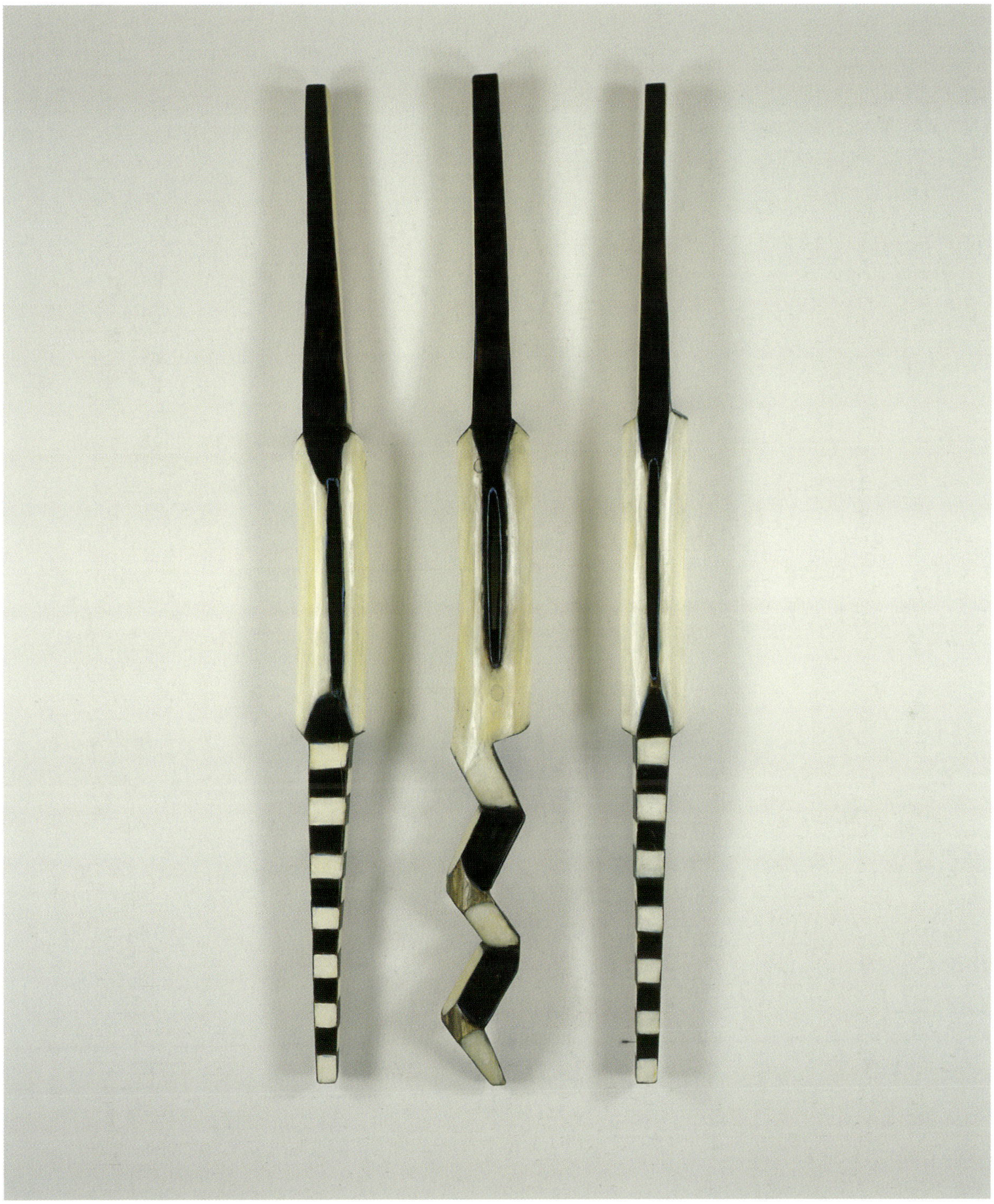

TREE SHIELDS, 2000
BURNED & PAINTED ASPEN
72 X 30 INCHES

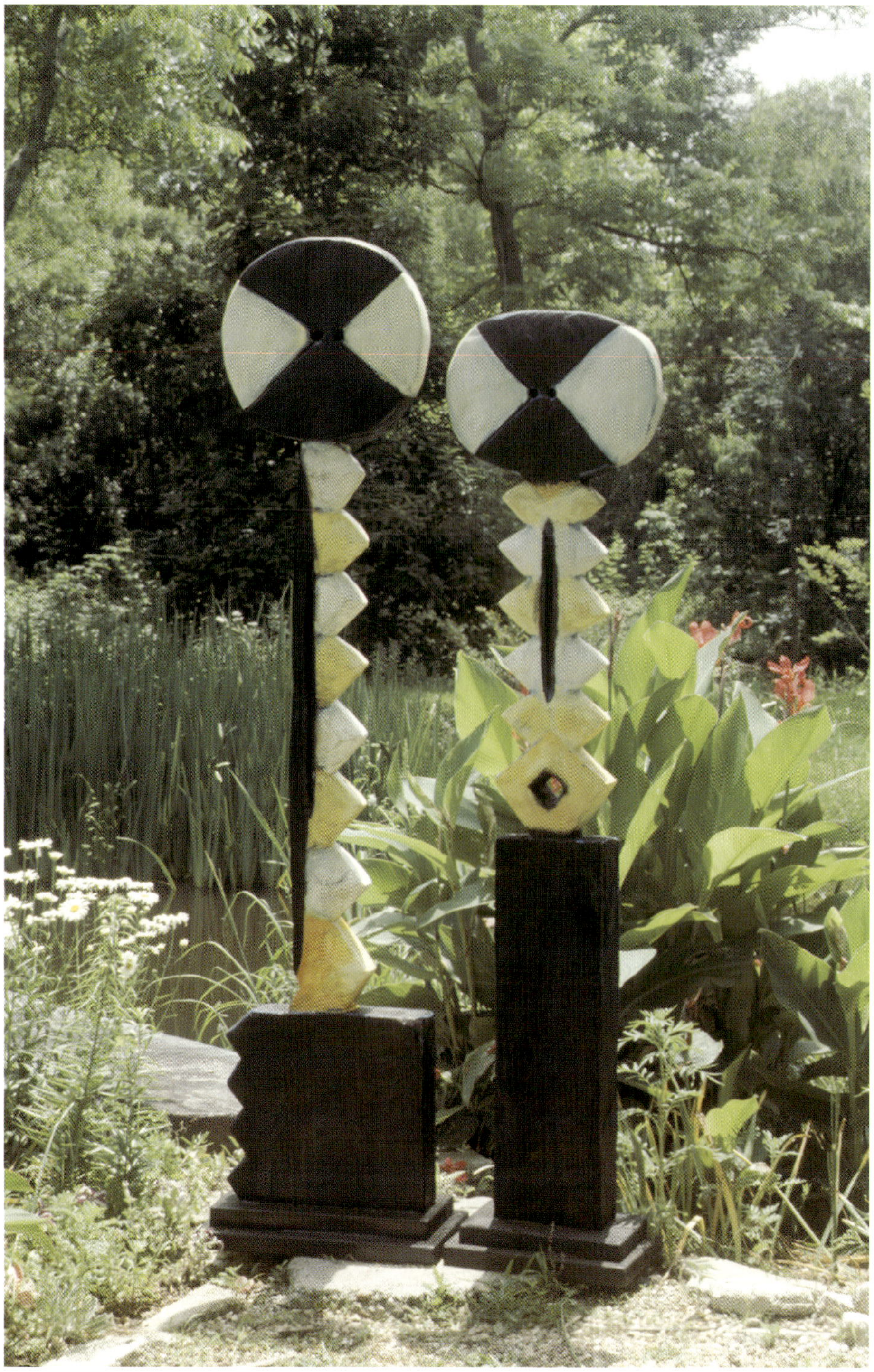

GUARDIAN FIGURES, 2004
PAINTED & BURNED PINE
MALE: 89 INCHES
FEMALE: 80 INCHES

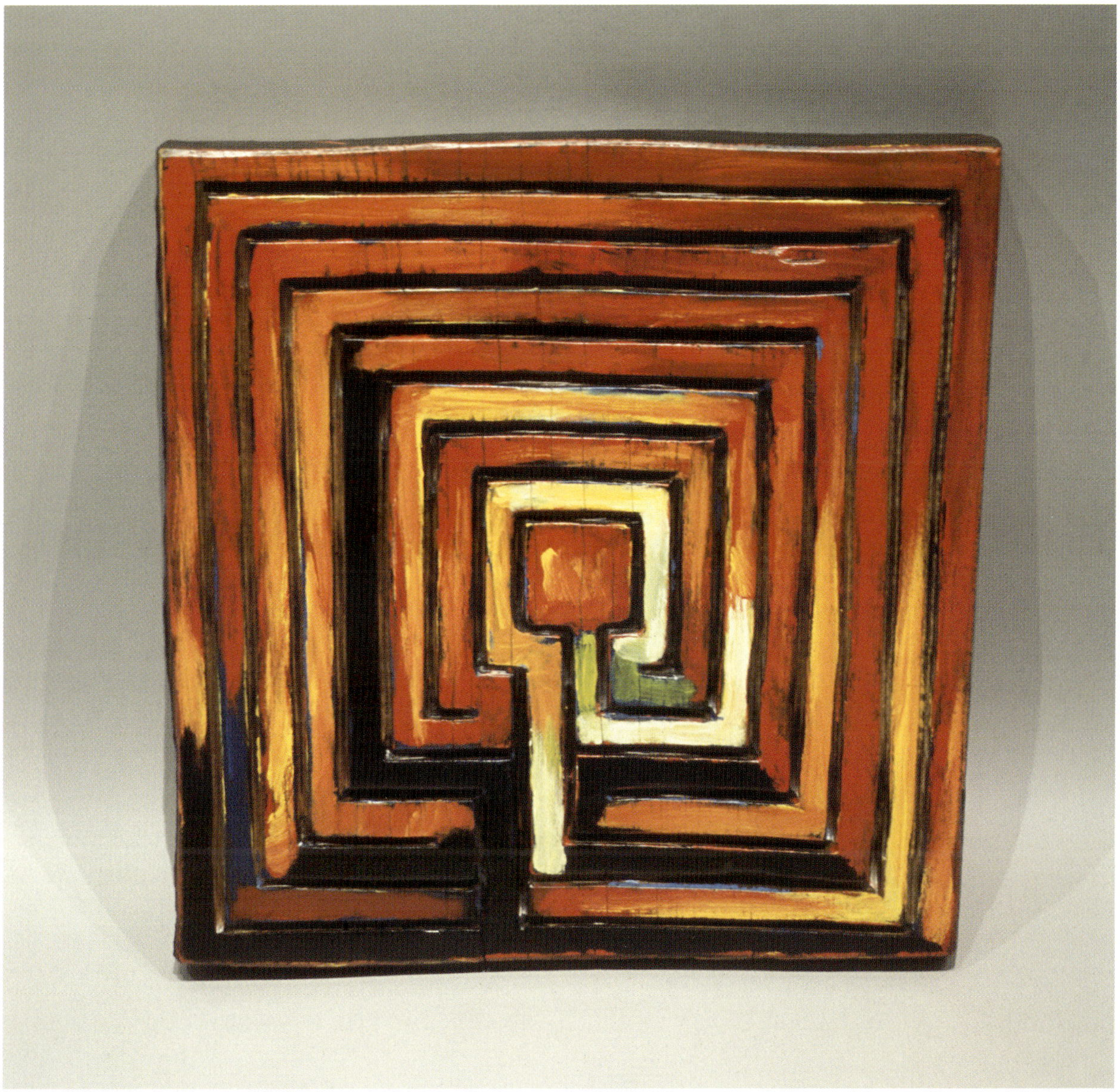

JOHN GELDERSMA b. 1942 New Orleans. *Ed:* MFA Rutgers State Univ. NJ; BFA Univ. Southwestern Louisiana, Lafayette. *Coll:* The Ogden Museum of Southern Art, New Orleans; Paul & LuLu Hilliard University Art Museum, Lafayette. *Public Coll:* Lafayette Surgical Specialty Hospital, Lafayette. *Representation:* LewAllen Contemporary, Santa Fe; Jean Albano Gallery, Chicago; Marguerite Oestreicher Fine Art, New Orleans; Galerie R. Treger, Paris.

LABYRINTH, 2004
BURNED & PAINTED PECAN
20 X 20 INCHES

MUNSON HUNT

Artemis, the ancient Greek goddess of the hunt, would retire with her dogs to her lunar abode when she desired solitude from the drama of Olympus. She guards over birthing as an attribute she retains from her earliest Asian incarnations as a multi-breasted mamma deity, and because she has the strongest mind and body of the female Olympians. For the same reason she was favored by the Amazons.

Reverence for moonlight brought Druidic rites, Dionysian ritual and Aztec sacrifices, but was associated (by bizarre logic) in Medieval Christianity with Satan's madness. Eve's descendents won't be oppressed, leaving the moon of the Western mind still tonight to the culture's lunatics. A short list includes: witches, warlocks, feminists, fabulists, ravers, revelers, authors, *amorati*, and most importantly, the artist.

Munson Hunt is as deeply attuned to the play of moonlight on cloud-life as any follower of Artemis, plucked from her mythic, mystos past and plugged into 21st century New Mexico, would be. *Natural Displacement*, her installation of chain saw sculptures against a tripartite video projection titled *Inner Entrapment*, presented a woman in a white flowing dress walking away from the viewer, across a desert meadow. Beneath a harvest moon and a bright night sky of fast-forwarding clouds, she strides expectantly into the distance only to endlessly reappear up close again, from another angle to repeat this action. Finally, sometime after anticipation gives way to meditative acceptance, rain comes, and the thrice split screen dissolves into one.

One is left with the sound of rain and the mute presence of the rounded forms Hunt hews from massive wood ashlars with her electric chainsaw. She derives their sculpted shapes from drawings and lovely clay studies that sing similar songs of live silence. If only we all had such character and could stand so bravely exposed, cracks, crevices, and all. One piece still sprouts mushrooms from the original tree. They suggest vessels, bellies, boats, and planetary bodies, yet exist in an abstract universal space all their own.

Munson Hunt courts the strong and subtle lights of night and day as they play across the dark burnt, and graphite-rubbed sheens of her surfaces. Like many of the best sculptors, *primitif* to post-modern, she's a force of nature.

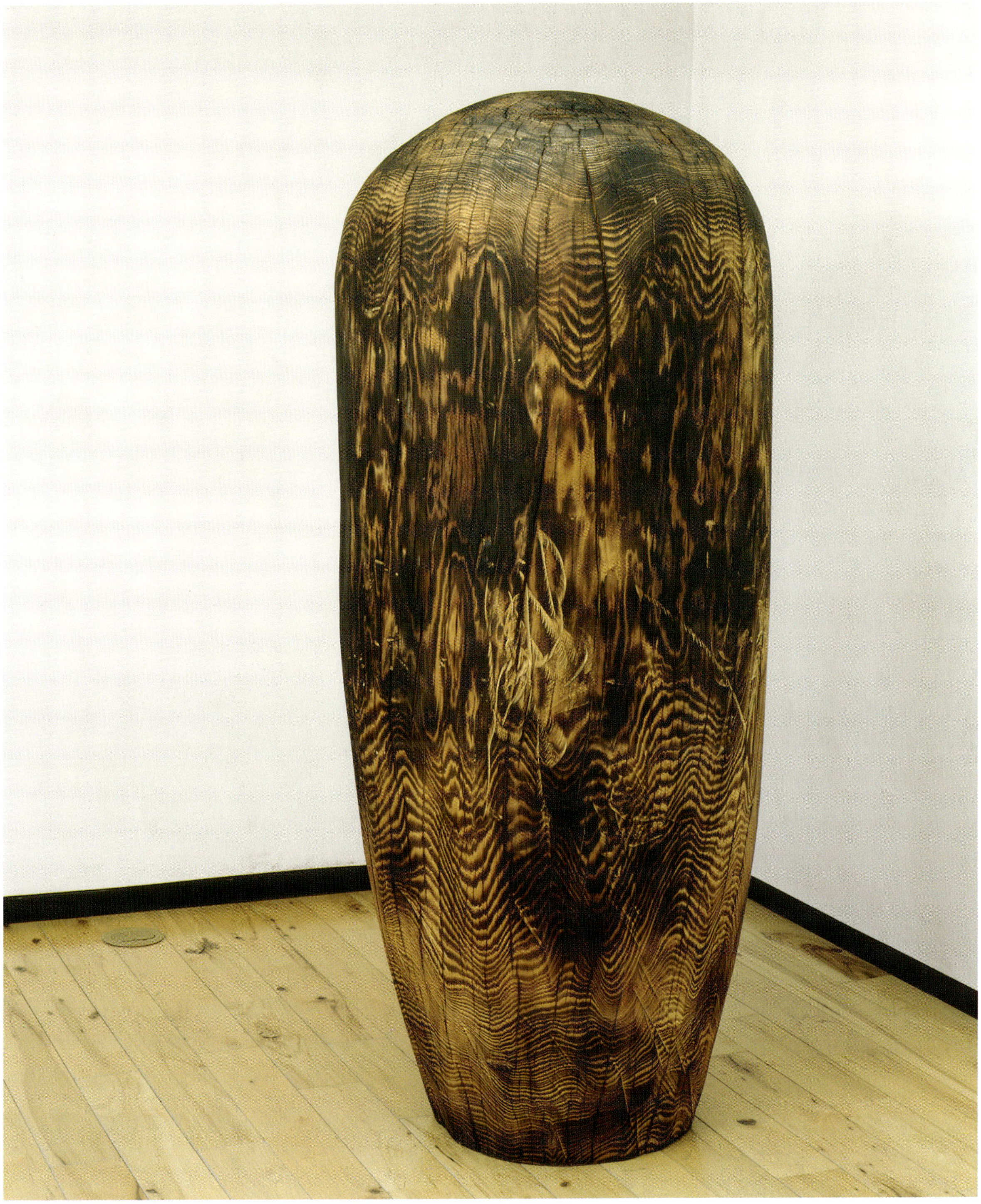

UNTITLED
PONDEROSA PINE WITH A BURNED FINISH
72 X 32 INCHES

MUNSON HUNT

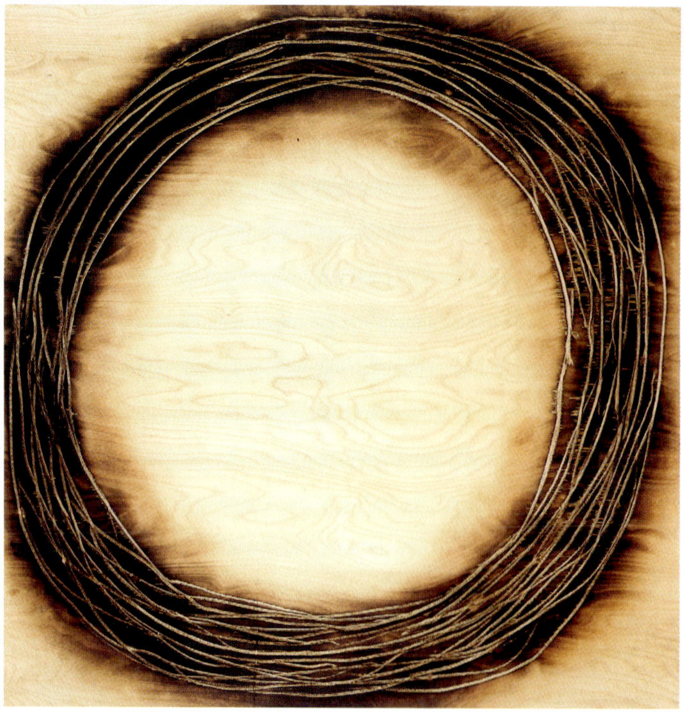

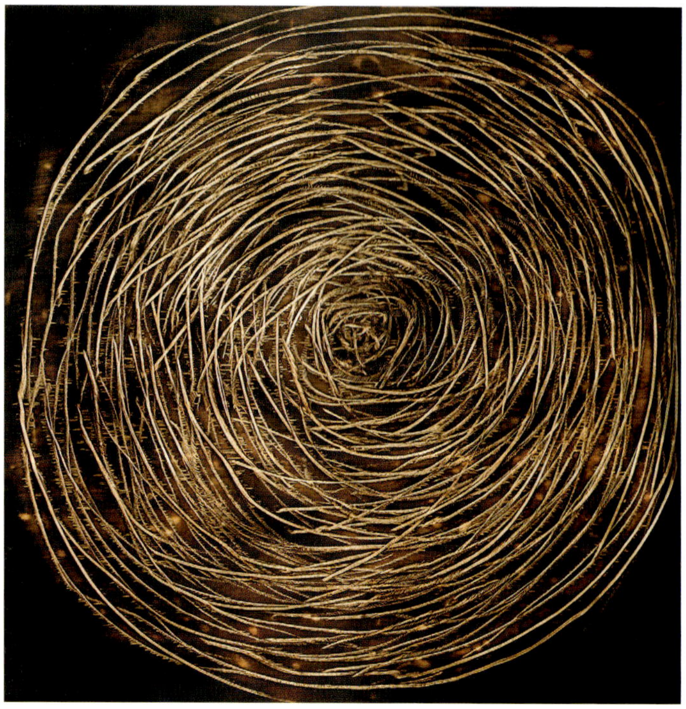

PLYWOOD
CHAINSAW DRAWINGS
WITH A BURNED FINISH
60 X 60 X 1 INCHES

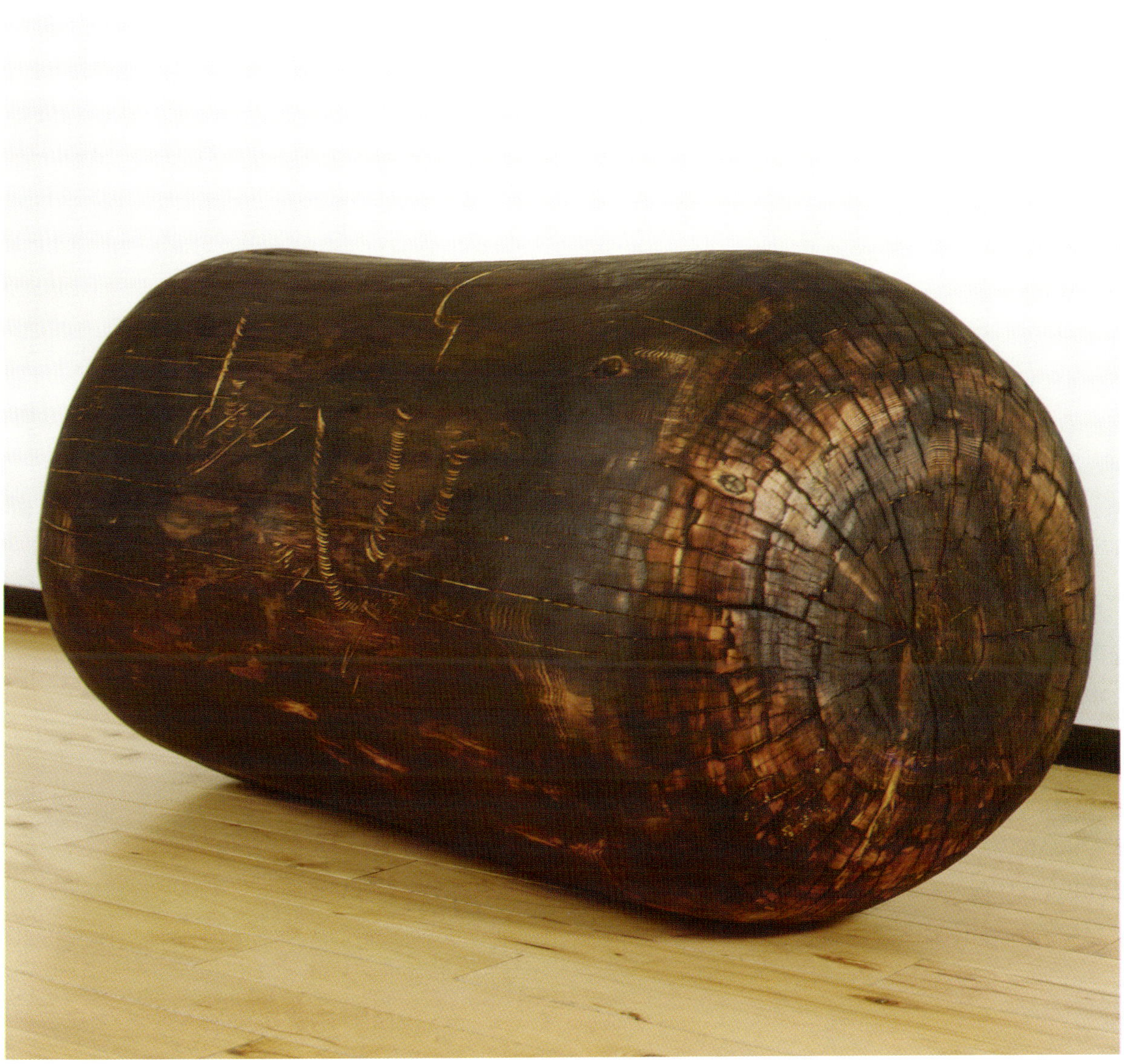

PERDITION
PONDEROSA PINE WITH A BURNED FINISH
53 X 27 INCHES

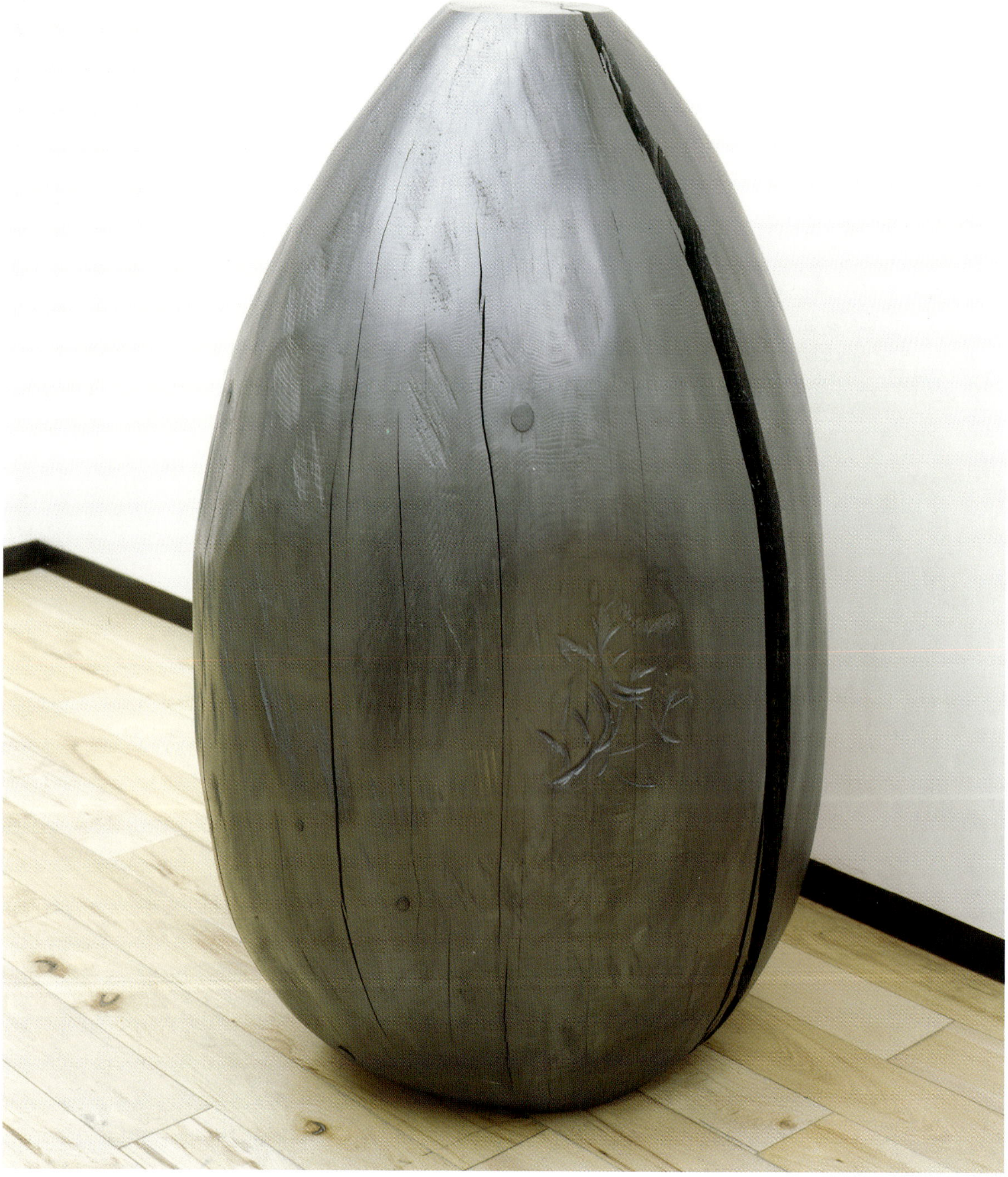

INHALE
WHITE FIR, GRAPHITE & OIL
49 X 25 X 25 INCHES

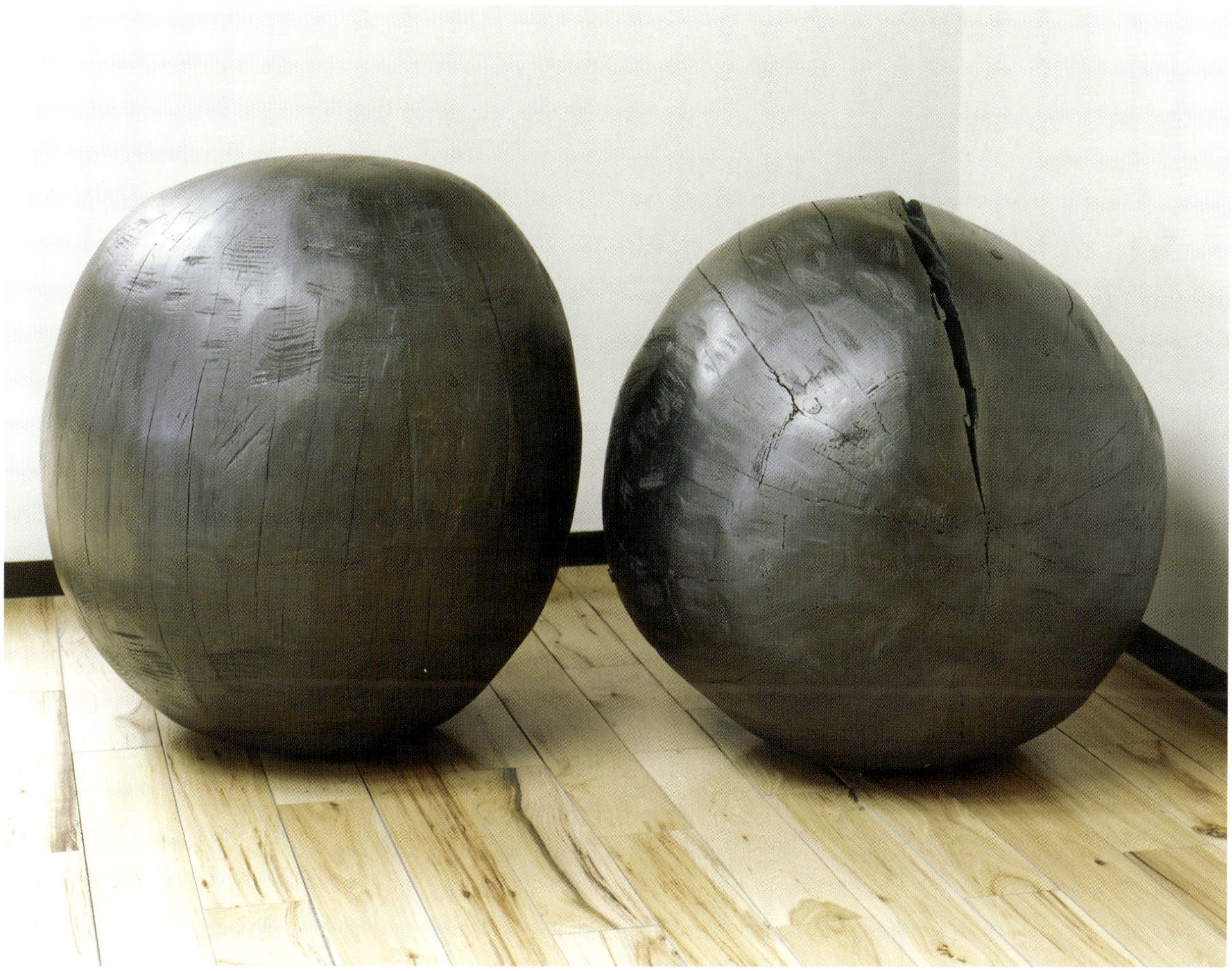

MUNSON HUNT b. 1962 Stamford CT. *Ed:* BFA Parsons School of Design. *Coll:* New Mexico Arts Permanent Collection; Jaqueline Bolli, Italy; Jerry & Alice Kruse TX; Kathy Barancik MO. *Representation:* Chiaroscuro Gallery, Santa Fe and Scottsdale.

A PAIR OF BALLS
WHITE FIR, GRAPHITE & OIL
34 INCHES (D)

HEIDI LOEWEN AND BRALDT BRALDS

Following food, shelter and friendship, art is the most enduring human essential. Its necessity is often underrated but no civilization, from the Stone Age to the urban grid, exists without art. As Manet advocated, art is for art's sake, but it is no contradiction to say that art's primary purpose is soul satisfaction. Heidi Loewen achieves this in her beautiful and exceptionally skillful porcelain art.

Heidi has thrown plenty of vessels that have seen fabulous catastrophe. Luckily, her son Hans says, "No Mom, this is great. Just create more wild forms." Hence a new transition in her art occurs. As Dali says, "Almost every accident is sacred."

Heidi's home in the country has two grills, one for filet mignon, and the other for her masterful *pot fumé* technique. The smokable organics or "cooking ingredients" as she calls them include chili peppers, papers, wood shavings from her sculptor friends, bananas, ponderosa pine and a few secret ingredients. How does she get that amazing teal overtone? Straw and pine needles create surprise calligraphic notations and her sumptuous surfaces are often intricately carved or "chattered." These carvings are as unique as snowflakes and the smoked pine scent often lingers for months. She accents her pieces with gold or white gold leaf.

Heidi Loewen's atelier and modest showroom on the corner of Guadalupe and Johnson streets is where she met Braldt Bralds, the Dutch painter and world-renowned illustrator when he signed up to study the wheel. The two *maestri* formed an instant friendship. She calls him "Rembraldt." He asked to paint in her studio loft and the two secured a civilized collaboration creating soul-satisfying art at heart. Another happy connection occurred when Braldt met his future wife when she took clay classes from Heidi.

You've seen Braldt Bralds' oils on the cover of *Time*, *Newsweek*, *Rolling Stone* and *Der Spiegel* to name but a few publications. His magnificently detailed images are probably in your kitchen on boxes of Celestial Seasons tea. He has executed several postage stamp designs for the United Nations and the U.S. Postal service. In 1989 he received the coveted Clio award and it's safe to say contemporary life wouldn't quite look the same without him. As is his birthright, he works in a Dutch Realist mode, and Jan van Eyck's got nothing on him when it comes to presenting the minutiae of texture and light in oil paint.

In Soho and Santa Fe's best galleries he has exhibited paintings documenting the secret life of stones, some more than a billion years old, suspended before deep, luscious landscapes using raffia, copper wire, rope or fabric. His collaborations with Heidi Loewen are surreally spectacular. She makes an exquisitely trimmed and chattered platter often thirty inches wide. With painstaking detail, wearing a jeweler's magnifying helmet, Braldt applies his *trompe l'œil* composition. Their collaborations must be seen to be believed. Children want to feel the sticks, stones and intricately placed wires to see if they are real.

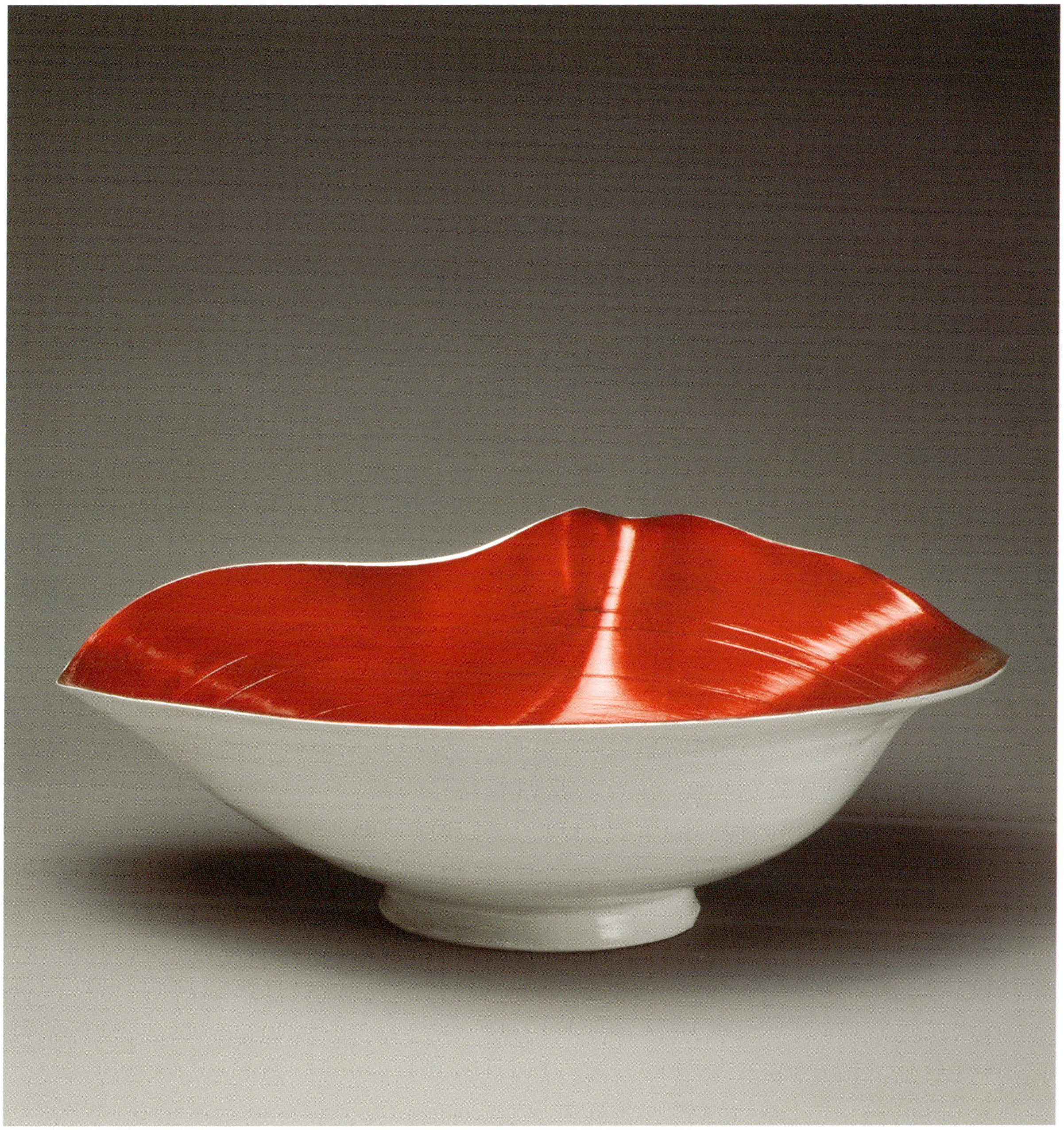

KISS ME NOW
PORCELAIN, 23 KARAT GOLD LEAF & OIL
22D INCHES

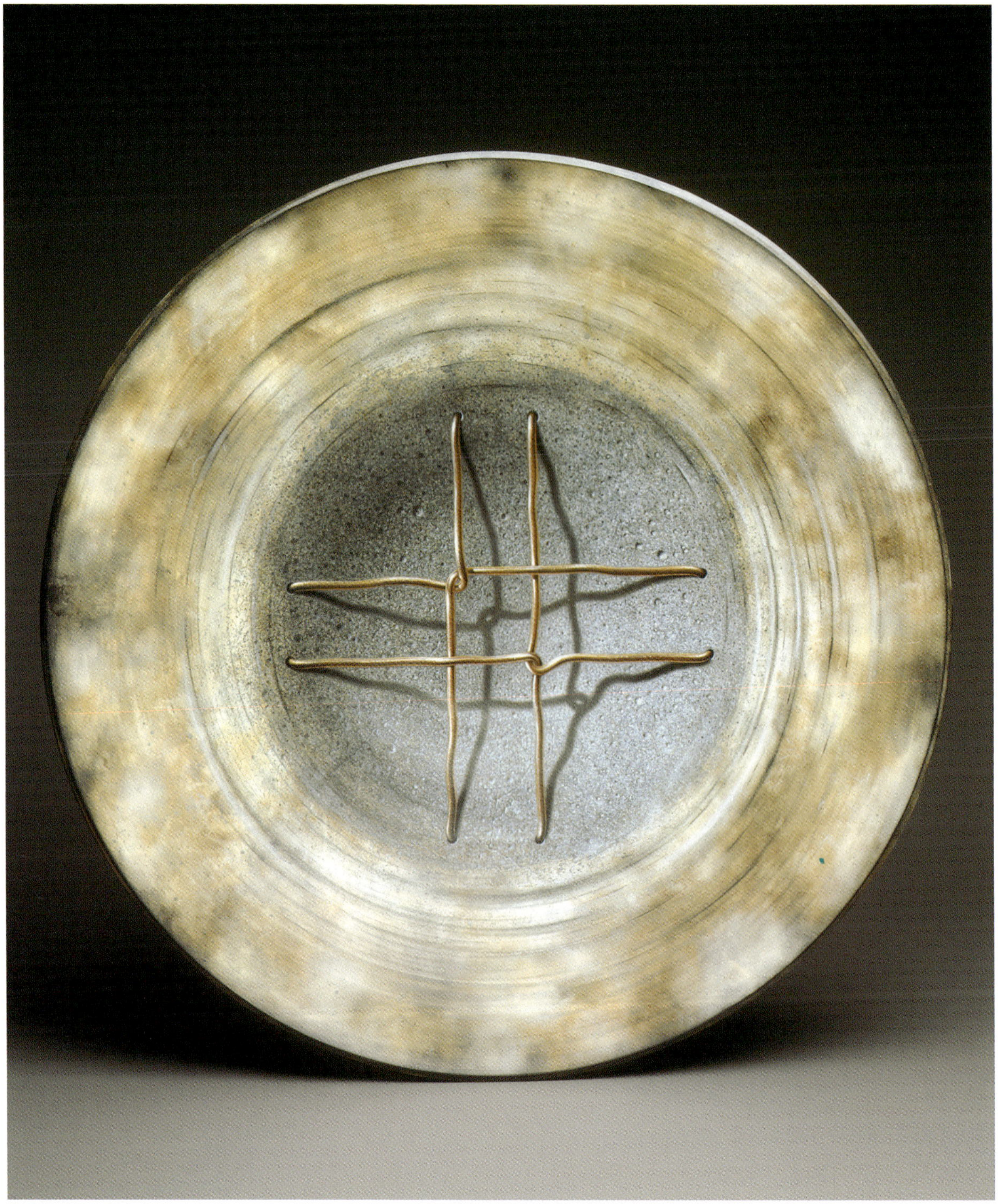

CROSSWIRED
OIL ON SMOKE-FIRED PORCELAIN, TROMPE L'ŒIL
25D INCHES

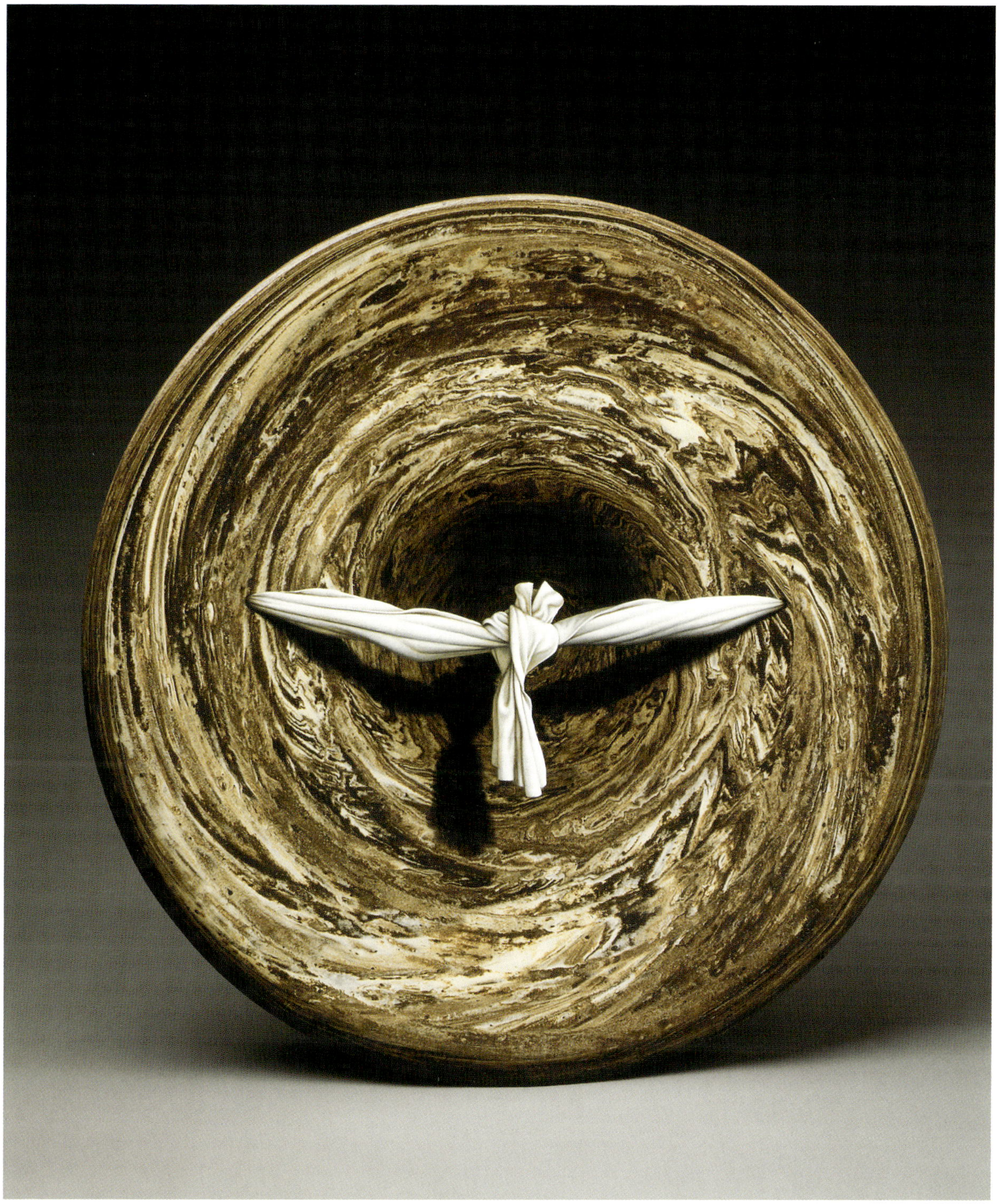

KNOTTED
OIL ON PORCELAIN, TROMPE L'ŒIL
22.5D INCHES

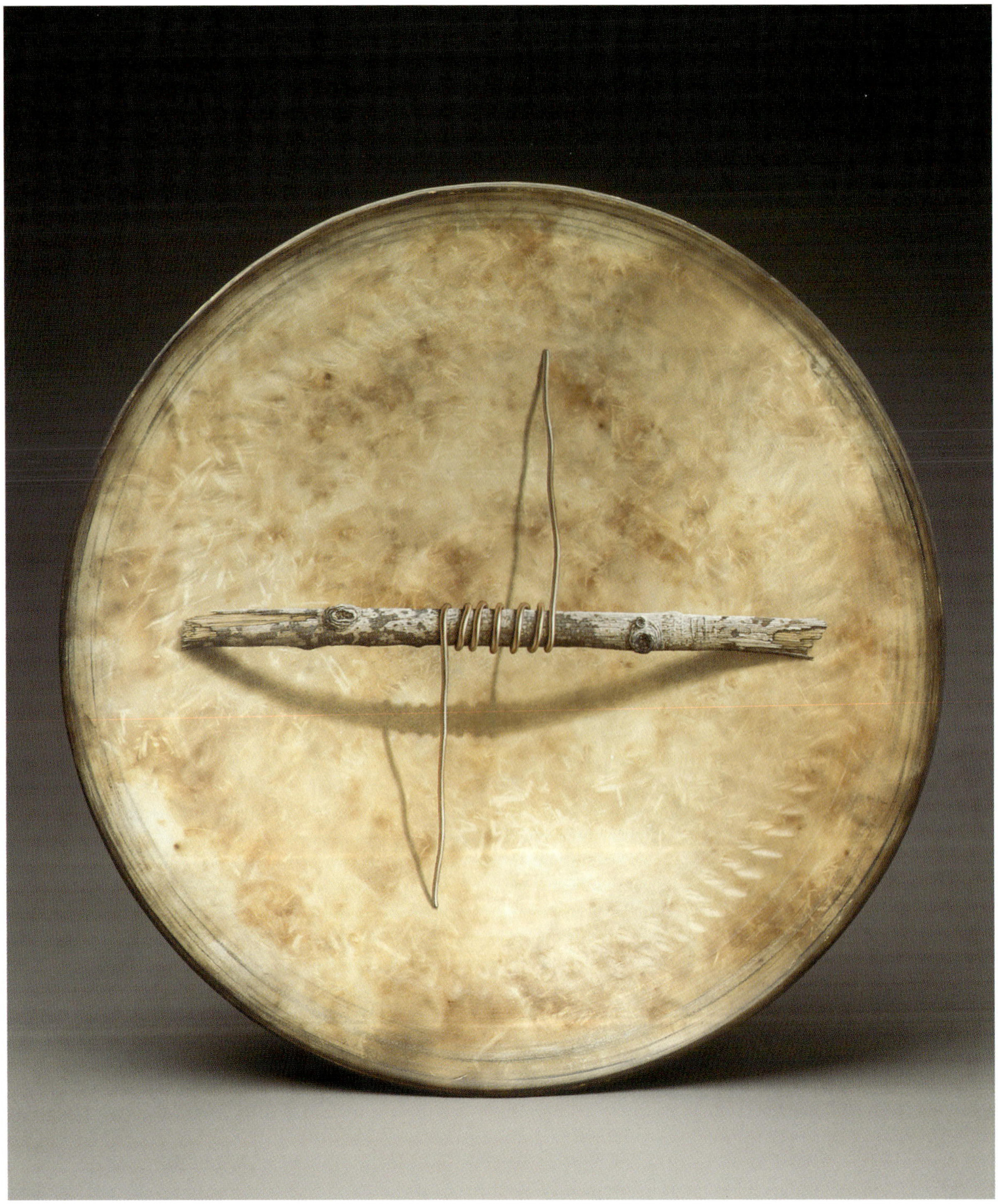

COILED
OIL ON SMOKE-FIRED PORCELAIN, TROMPE L'ŒIL
28D INCHES

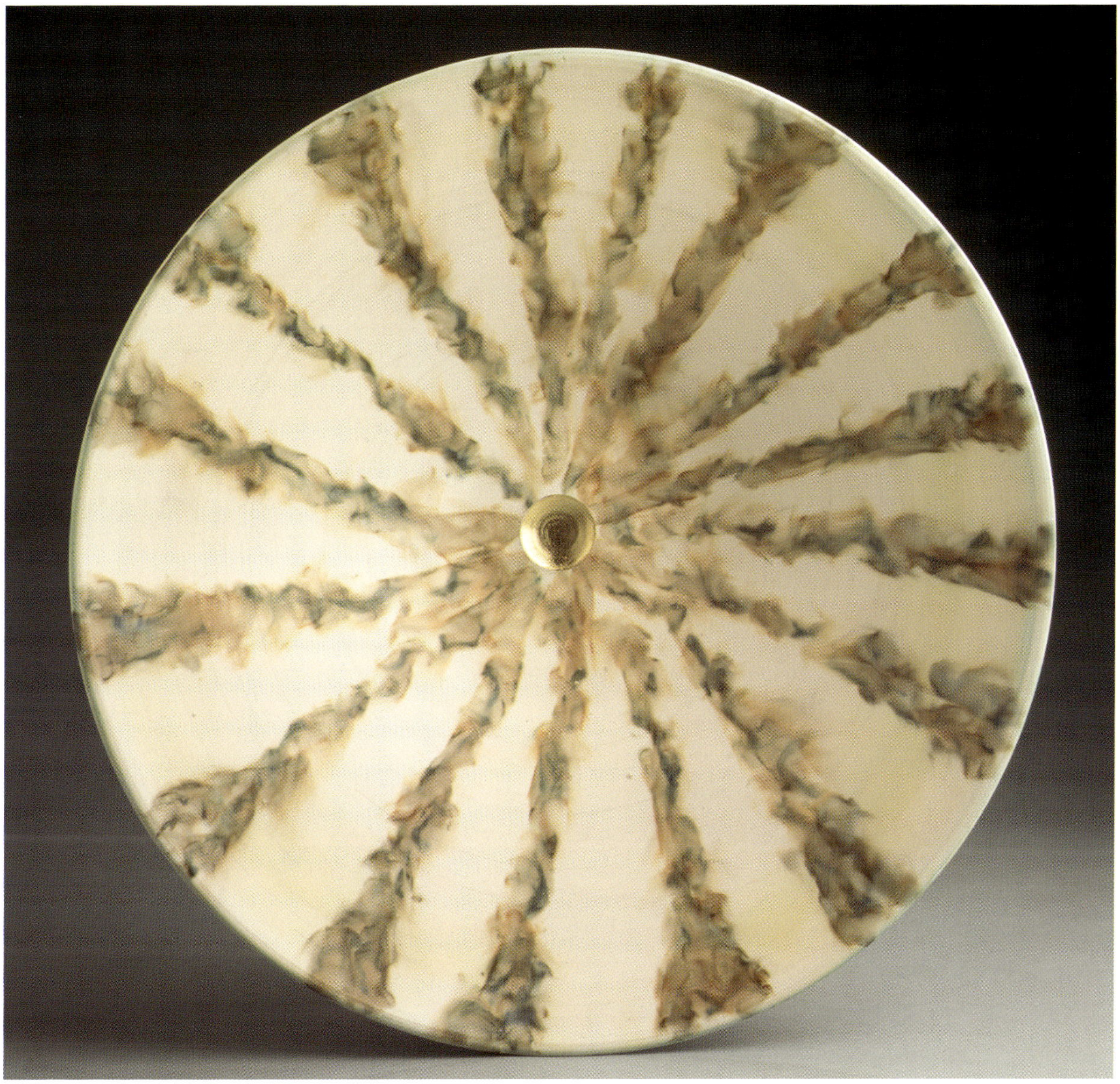

HEIDI LOEWEN b. 1956 Providence RI. *Ed:* BS Skidmore College, Saratoga Springs NY; Univ. Paris, Sorbonne, Paris; Radcliffe College, Cambridge MA; Haystack School of Crafts, Deere Isle ME. *Representation:* Heidi Loewen Porcelain, Santa Fe; Seven-O-Seven Contemporary, Santa Fe; Lumina Gallery, Taos; Human Arts, Ojai CA; Fenton Fine Arts, Fort Worth; Katie Gingrass Gallery, Milwaukee; Cynthia Drennon Fine Arts, Los Angeles; Memorial Art Gallery, Rochester; Lyon and Lyon Fine Art, New Orleans; C. Anthony Gallery, Beaver Creek CO.

BRALDT BRALDS b 1951 Hoghkirk, The Netherlands. *Ed:*.Self Taught. *Awards:* Clio Award for Best Illustration. *Coll:* The Rockefeller Foundation, New York; Der Speigel, Hamburg, Germany; Time Magazine, New York; Celestial Seasonings, Boulder. *Representation:* Heidi Loewen Porcelain, Santa Fe; Seven-O-Seven Contemporary, Santa Fe; Lyon and Lyon Fine Art, New Orleans; Greenwich Workshop Gallery, Shelton CT.

RADIANT
SMOKE-FIRED PORCELAIN, 22 KARAT GOLD LEAF
22D INCHES

MADELIN COIT

It is in her three-dimensional forms that Madelin Coit's process of assemblage can be described as the contextualization of text, putting text back into context. Her works are open-ended yet tightly crafted. They are also poignant and ring of truth. Some of the sculptures include her original writing, others may have quoted text.

There is pointed commentary and content in Madelin Coit's artwork, woven in with a seasoned aesthetic. The play of materials, scale, text and context concretizes the meanings she gives to form, fact and fiction.

The text on a timeworn baking sheet makes three ages in *Aunt Mackey's...* life real: 1952—a child's experience; 1967—emergent sexuality; and 2002—the humor and generosity of Mackey's fifties. Coit uses text and object to point up some of the depth we may overlook, providing that *frisson,* that little electric charge, that non-verbal understanding.

It is the mixing of the intimacy of handwriting (her own) with the generality of welded steel for the seventeen foot long *Line* that gives broader dimension to the text. This elegant length of steel gesturally casts a second shadow line when lit from above.

Coit transferred text from a damaged book to Dupioni silk for the *Floating World Footstool* from the series, *Footstools for Sex in the World's Religions*. The surface shimmer is reminiscent of the dresses of icons, and the contrapuntal textures of silk and wood are used for explication.

An oversized, kinetic, stainless steel pop-up book, coyly named *Promises IV*, combines cool sheet steel with responsive motion to welcome and rebuff and amuse. The piece awakes, responds to the viewer, and changes its shape.

In the case of *Shredder, an Autobiography*, Coit uses the deconstruction of extensive memorabilia including family photographs, exhibition invitations and reviews, all those things that mark her life. The small parts shift and mix, a kind of *pentimento*. This modern mechanical manipulation echoes the synthesis of life's moments, the shifting parts that create the whole. *Shredder, an Autobiography*, is made up of video, installation and performance.

There is a place between reason and unreason, a "green belt," that interstice where one's natural state is renewed even under the eye of culture and era. As evidenced by her beautifully polyvocal objects, Madelin Coit inhabits this "green belt" superiorly.

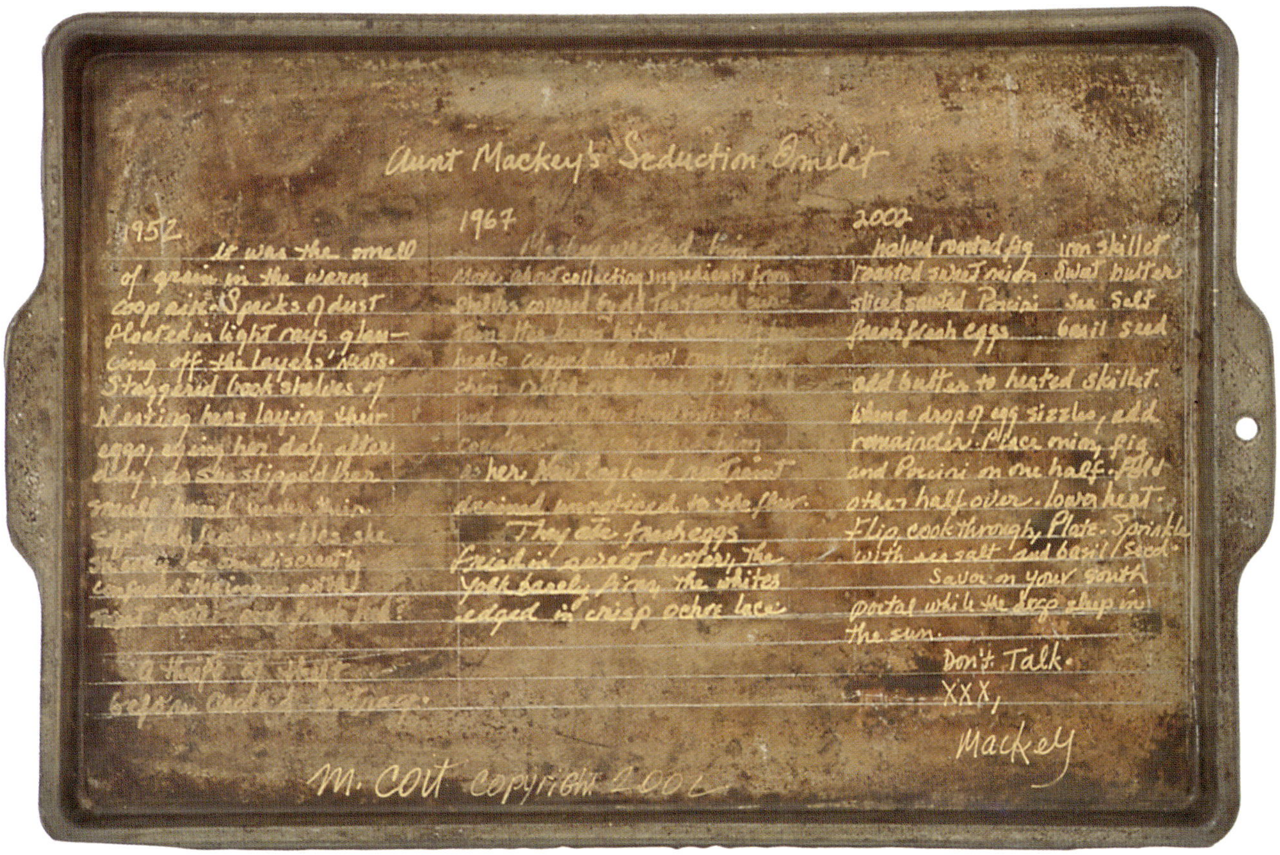

AUNT MACKEY'S SEDUCTION OMELET
METAL BAKING SHEET
12 X 18 INCHES
*Text on page 214

Collection of Barbara and Jerry Rosen, Santa Fe

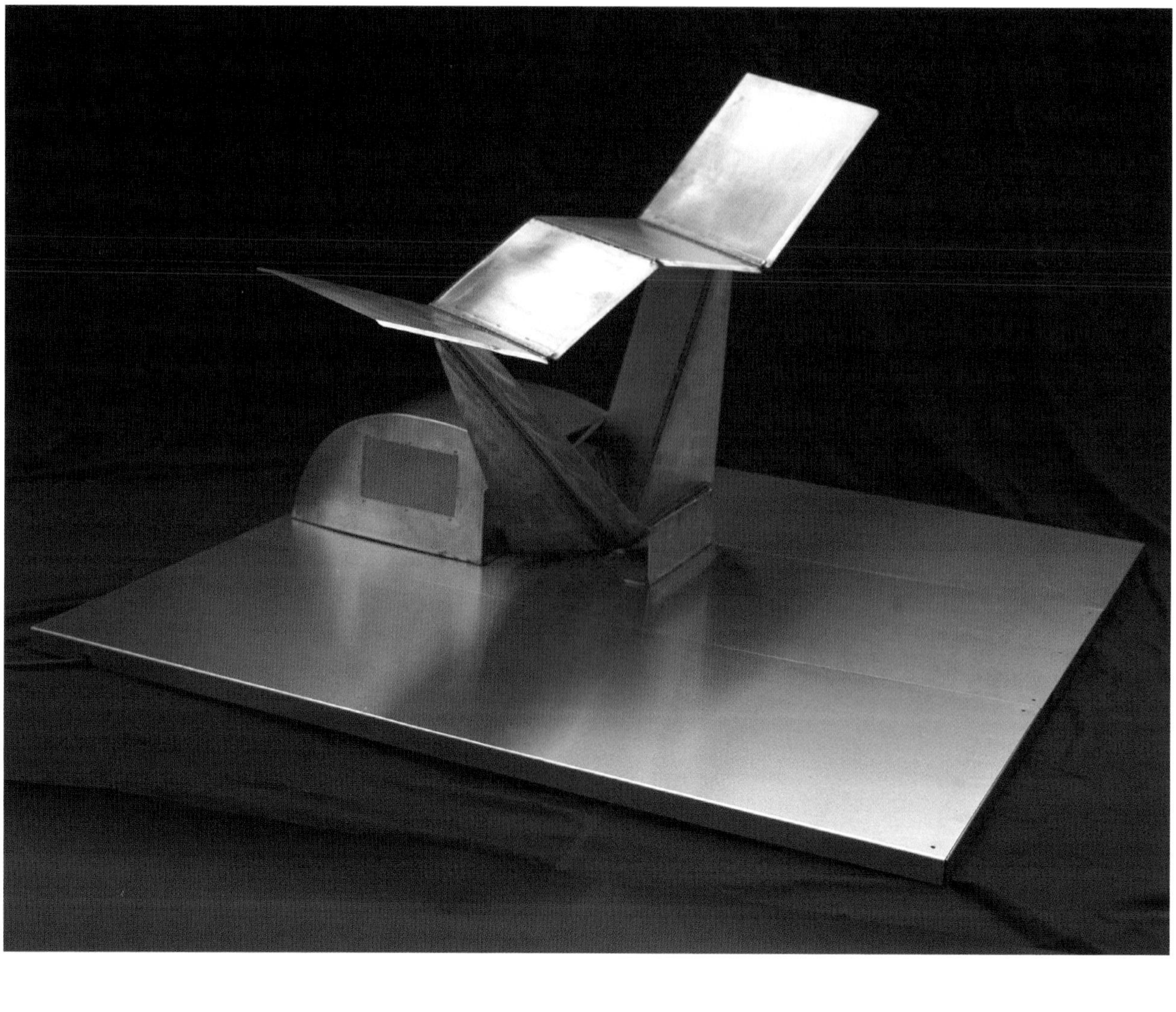

PROMISES IV
STAINLESS STEEL, MECHANICAL
36 X 60 X 60 INCHES

MADELIN COIT

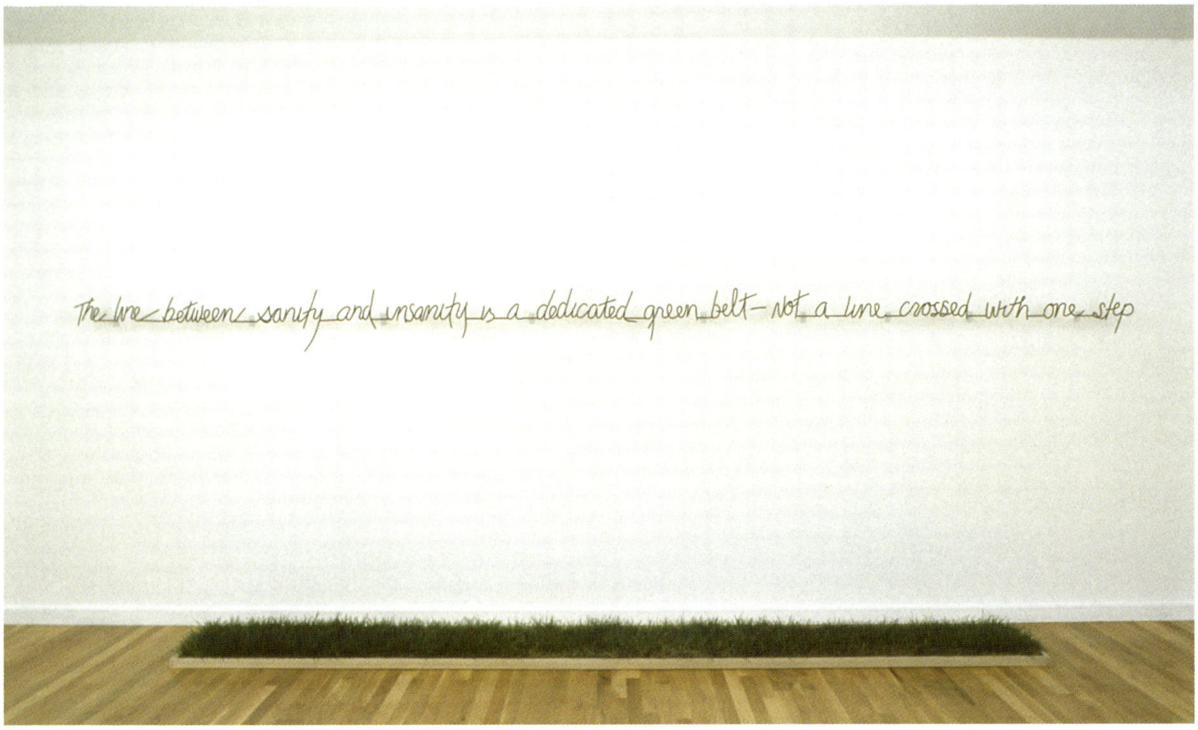

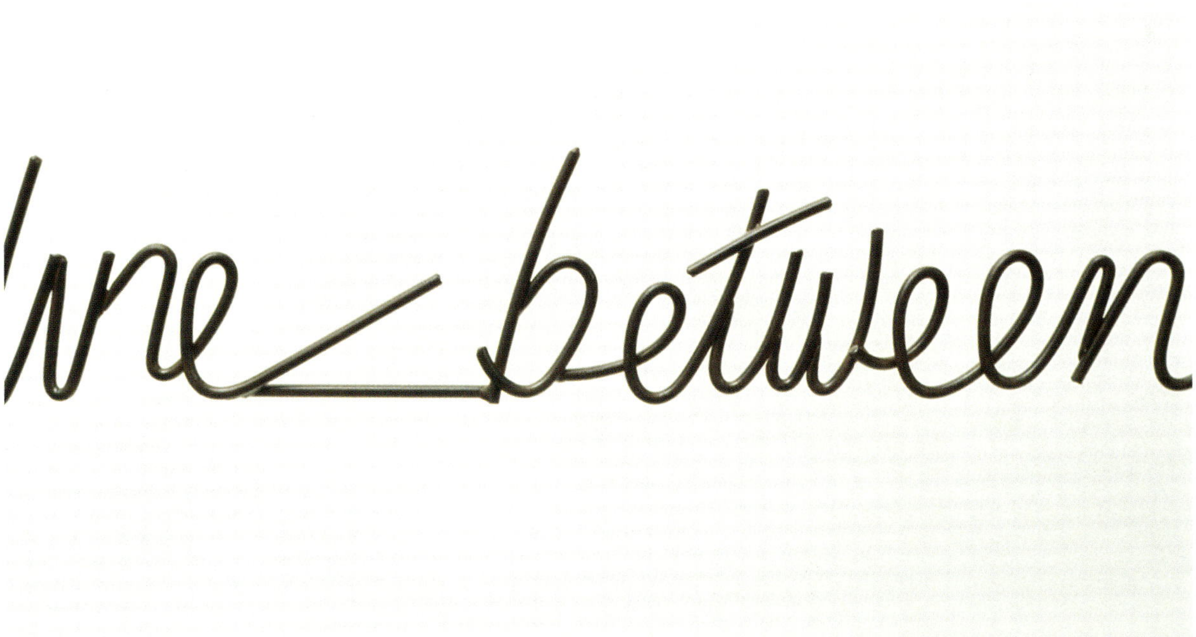

THE LINE, 2003
WELDED STEEL
17 FEET

THE LINE, 2003 (DETAIL)

MADELIN COIT

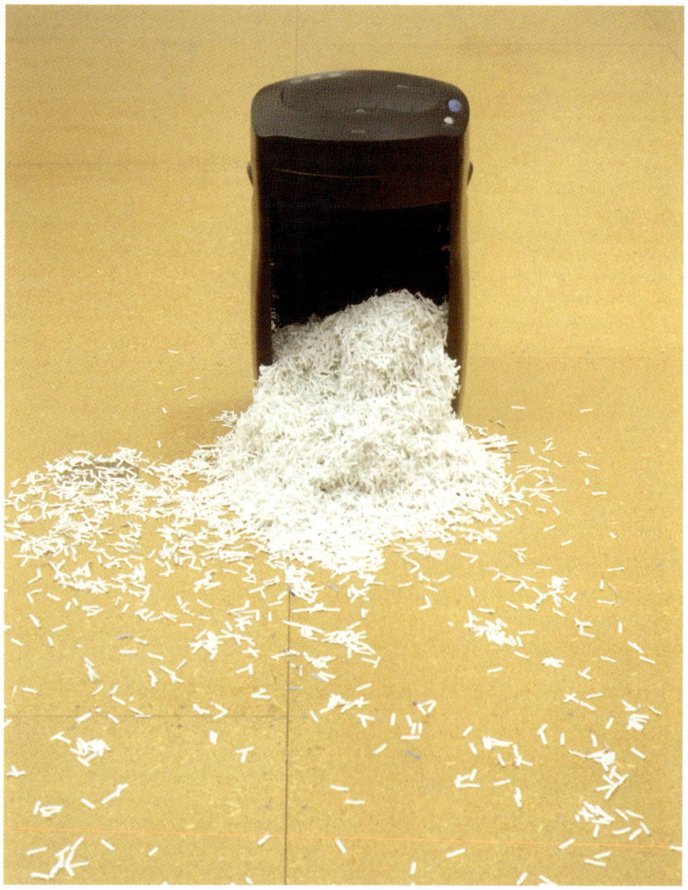

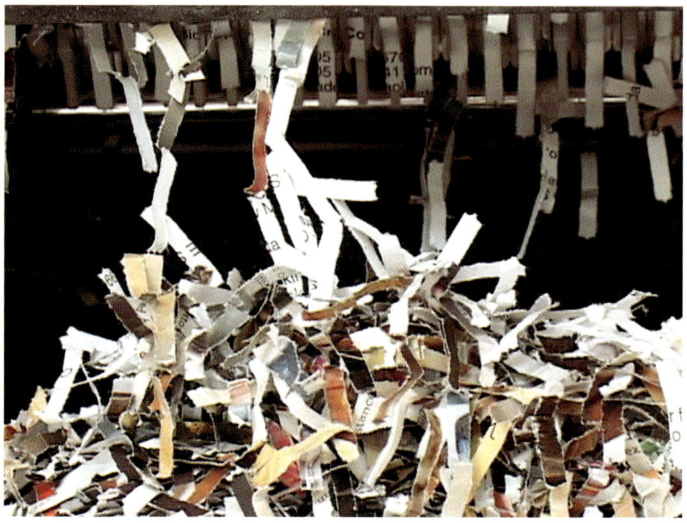

SHREDDER, AN AUTOBIOGRAPHY, 2004
INSTALLATION, VIDEO & MIXED MEDIA

SHREDDER, AN AUTOBIOGRAPHY, 2004 (DETAIL)
INSTALLATION & VIDEO

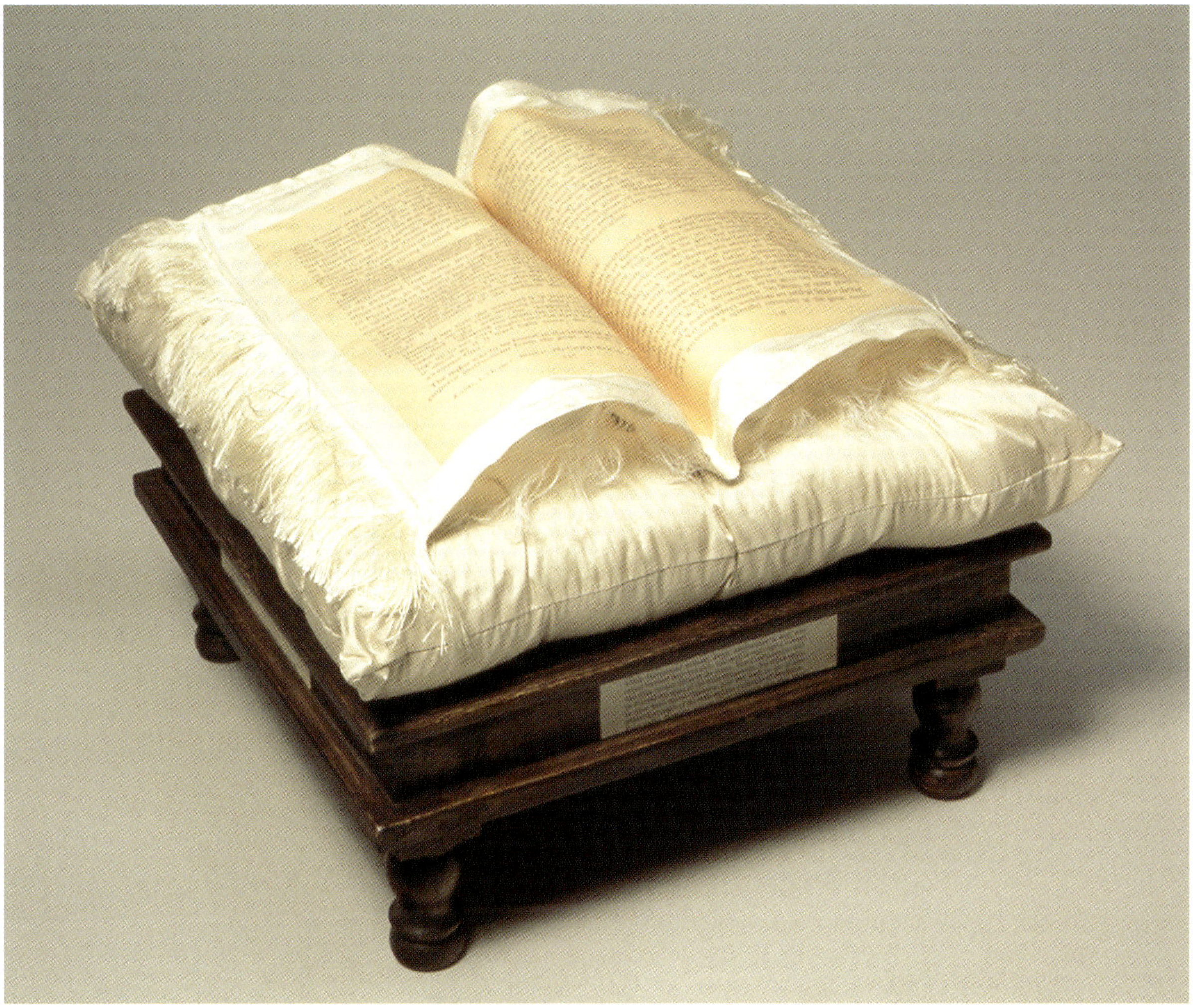

MADELIN COIT b. 1943 CT. *Ed:* BFA Univ. Connecticut. *Selected Exhibitions:* Institute of Contemporary Art, Boston; San Antonio Art Institute TX; Anchorage Museum AK; Los Angeles County Museum of Art CA; Museum of Fine Arts, Santa Fe. *Selected Public Collections:* Skirball Museum, Los Angeles; Museum of Fine Arts, Santa Fe; Executive Life Insurance, Los Angeles; Port Authority of New York and New Jersey DC; Mitsui Manufacturers Bank, Los Angeles; Security Pacific Bank, Los Angeles. *Representation:* EVO Gallery, Santa Fe.

FLOATING WORLD FOOT STOOL FOR
'SEX IN THE WORLD'S RELIGIONS'
MIXED MEDIA
9 X 16 X 16 INCHES

TIM JAG

Culture worker Tim Jag has gone off the wall. He's wearing day-glo orange coveralls and moving a load of brightly colored bricks from one side of the gallery to another during the opening. Something of the same slapstick pertains to his paintings and picture scatter-shots, drawn with a mellow Southwestern cartoon twang. Linked on the wall, they represent a wild variety of experimentation with materials, imagistic devices, and painterly procedure that is pure adventure. He calls them *Pop Groupings*.

Linkage is a signifying motif in Jag's wacky wondrous work. In *Haiku (3-D)*, the elements are literally connected, implying a kind of reciprocal energy flow. There is the suggestion of a surreal electrical line, pictorial plumbing, and conceptual conductivity. This is a three-dimensional diagram, mapping the construction of a benign art terrorist's time-bloom.

Industry Codes/California Fauna is, as the title implies, more Constructionist than Constructivist. This is some of the best stuff that can be done with materials from your local Suburban Home and Garden Center. If Wil E. Coyote got an art kit in the mail from Acme he might well end up with a Tim Jag type machine. The artist playfully captures a current of uneasy symbiosis with technology, posing oscillating questions. What is real and what is fake? What is true form? What is simulated form? Where exactly does the art reside in the artificial?

Jag joins colorful kitsch to hardware store paraphernalia to produce entities that verge on the biological, like a crazy uncle creating mechanico-genetic mutations under cover of the tuff-shed out back. His aesthetic is recombinant in the extreme, and his wild and domestic wonders take on a life of their own in ways that can unnerve the denial of even the staunchest anti-environmentalist. Even as he reworks the doubtful ductwork of topical thoughts about technology and its benefits, this faux-fur flaneur's refusal to stop having fun remains his greatest strength. Sprouting function, fashion, and fixtures, he giggles under goggles—as we subject nature, we subject ourselves—tee hee.

Like many of the artists in this book, Tim Jag's production is not limited to sculptural by-products. His rampant process is radioactive across modalities, from painting to performance. He comes with more than a dollop of Pop, but most of all he reminds me of the Robert DeNiro character in filmmaker Terry Gilliam's Orwellian epic, *Brazil*. Remember the unflappable duct and plumbing guy who appears outta nowhere?

DeNiro, Gilliam, Orwell—Tim Jag seems to have hired on with a damn good Company. It's hard work these days to subvert, replumb, and re-route the boundaries of conventional taste, and have a good time doing it. Still and all, it's gotta be done. For art with aplomb, call on Tim Jag, culture worker.

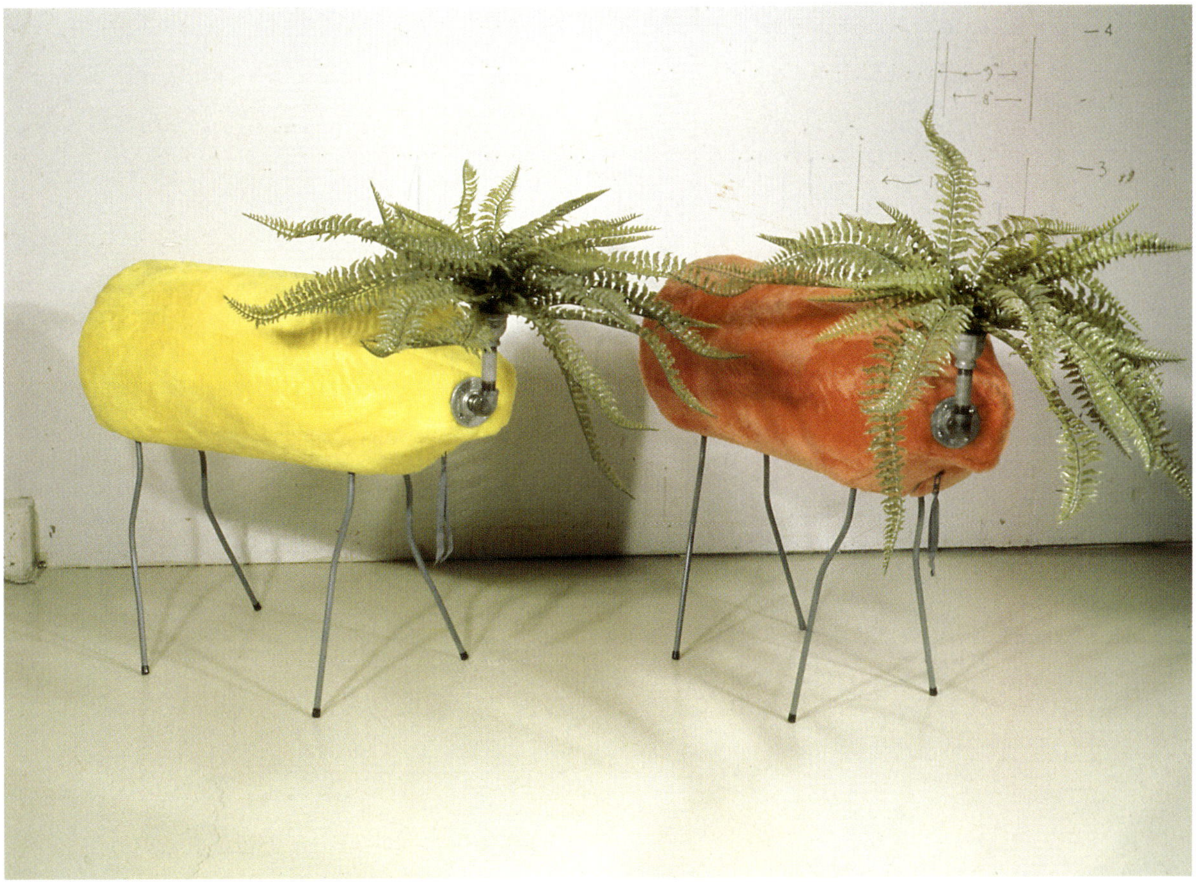

INDUSTRY CODES/BIO CODES
FAUX FUR, FAUX PLANTS, STEEL & PIPING
48 X 36 X 60 INCHES

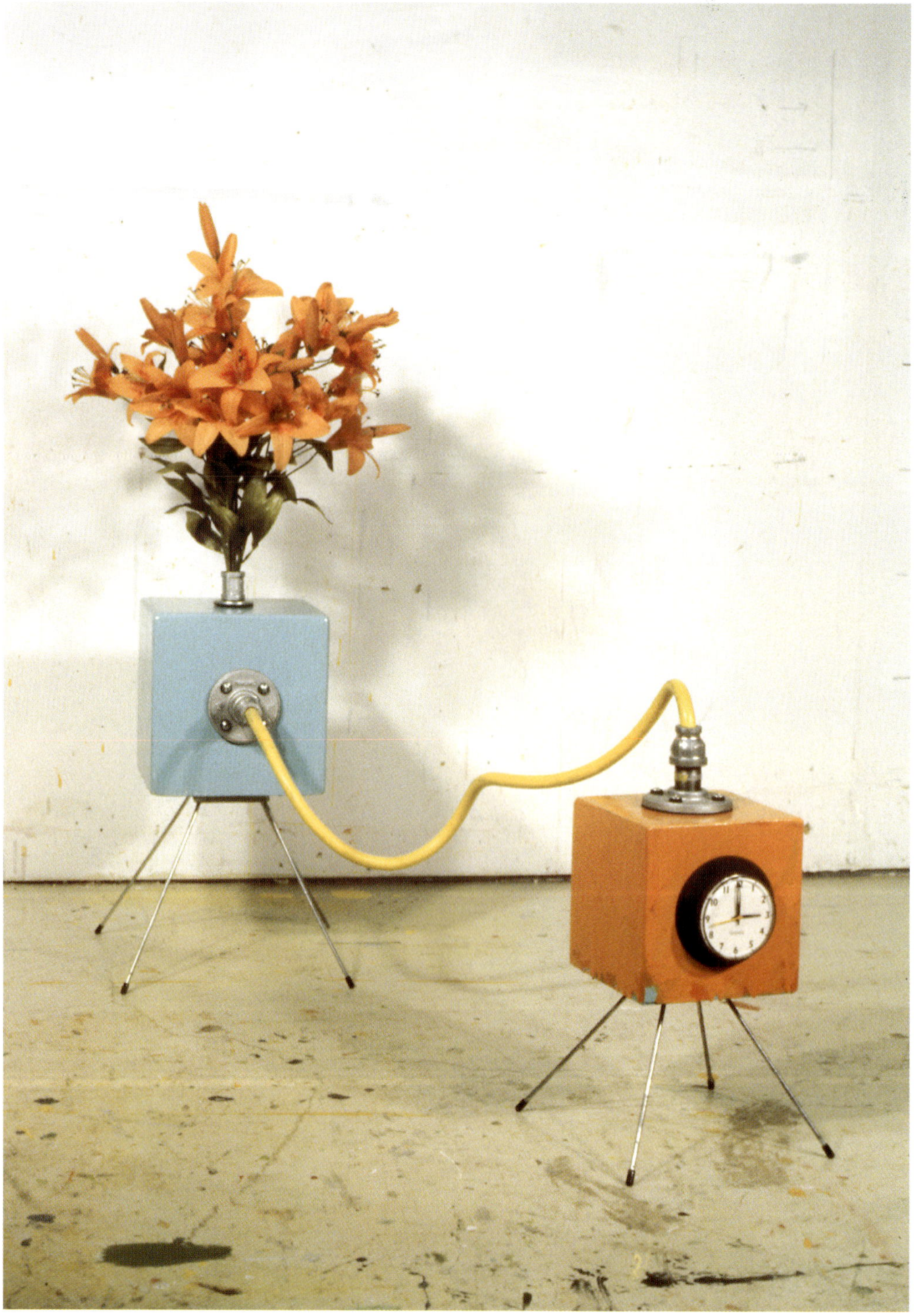

HAIKU (3-D), 2002
FAUX FLOWERS, WOOD, PIPING, HOSE, CLOCK & STEEL
36 X 48 X 36 INCHES

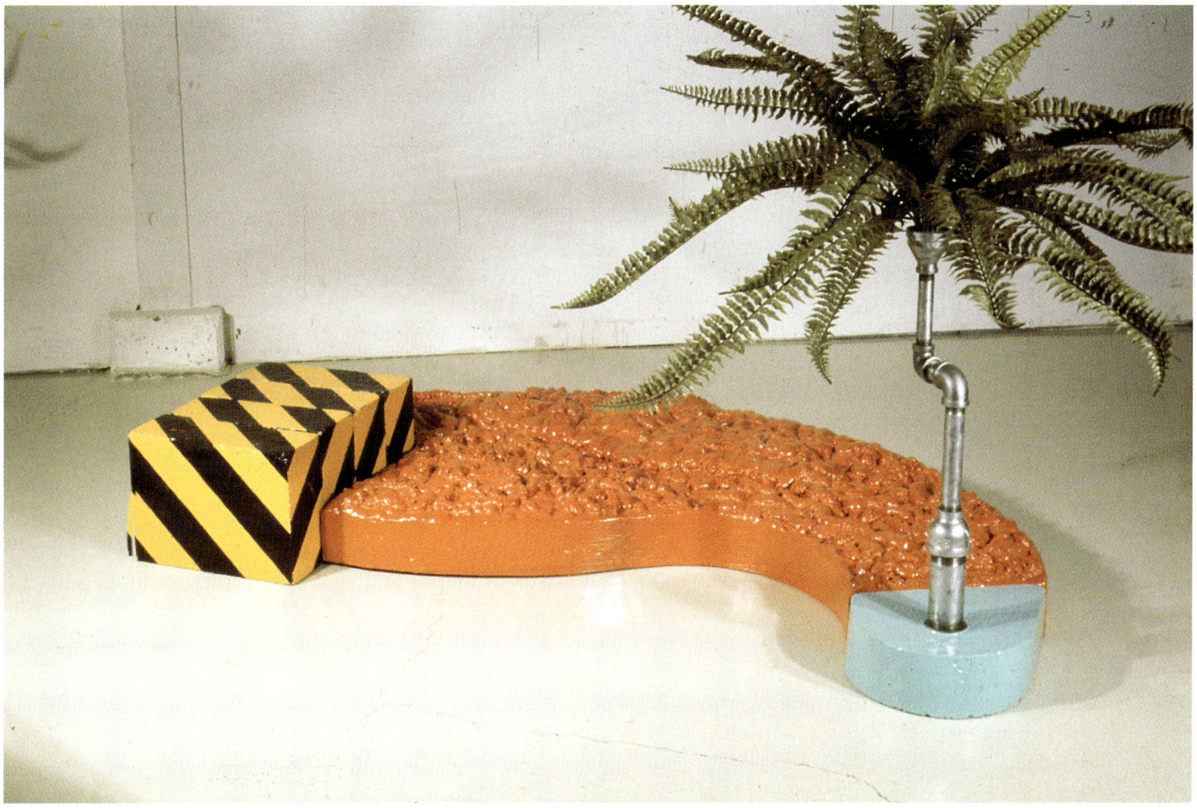

INDUSTRY CODES/CALIFORNIA FAUNA, 2000
FOAM, PIPE, CAST CEMENT & PLASTIC FERN
36 X 72 X 72 INCHES

TIM JAG

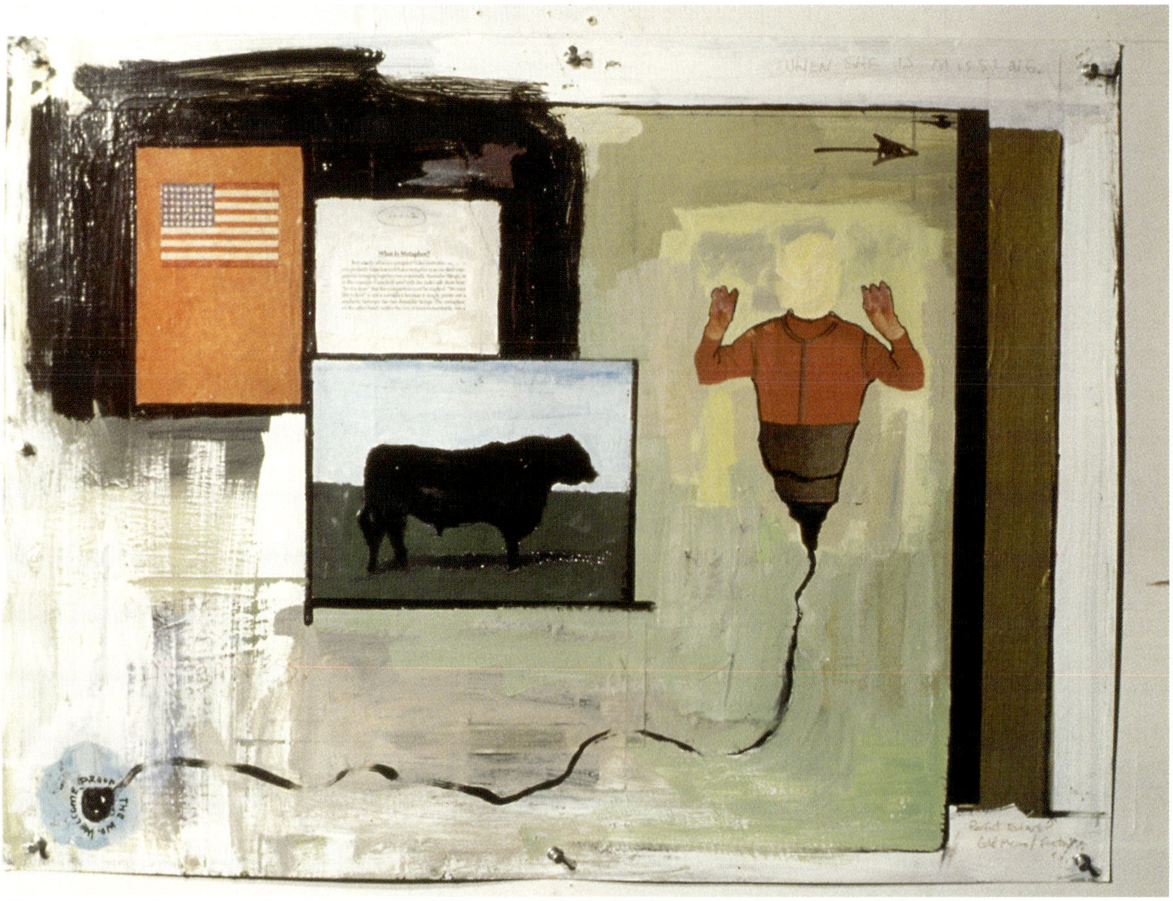

TRANSFORMER MACHINE/COLONY
MIXED MEDIA/ARCHIVAL PAPER
30 X 36 INCHES

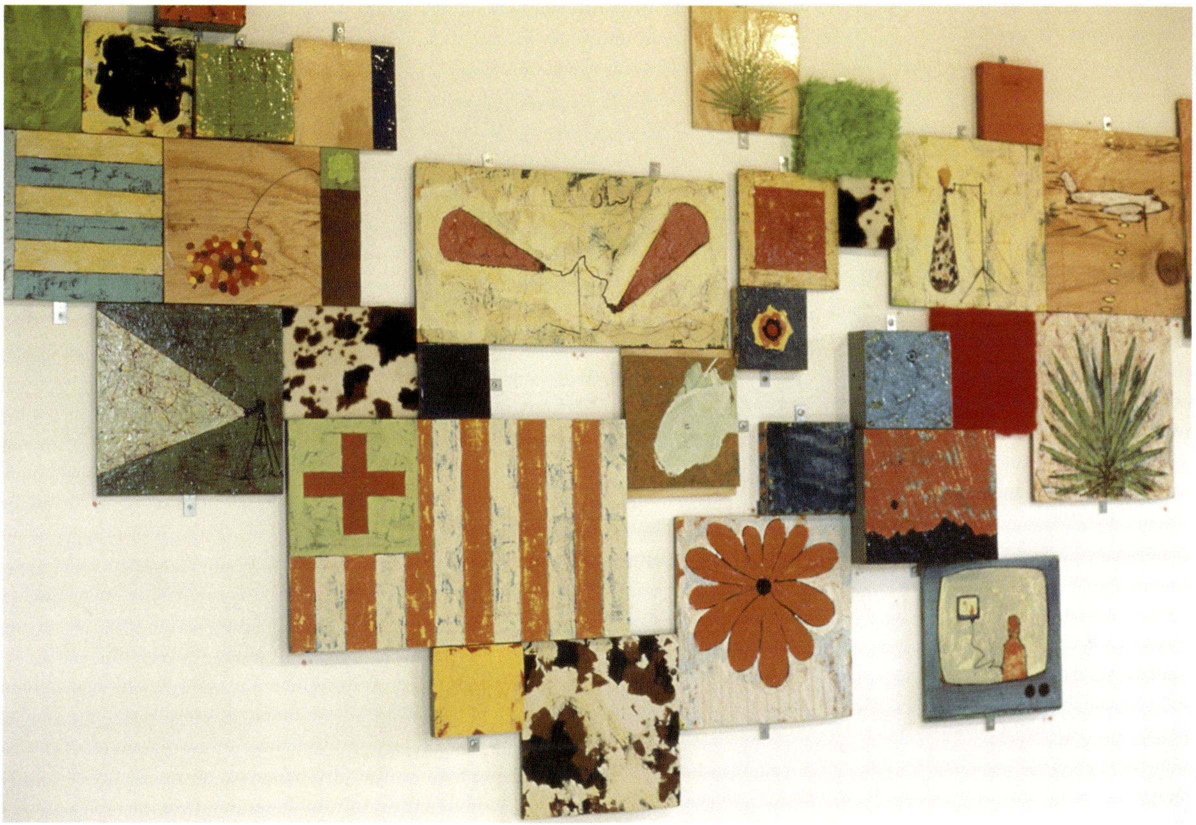

TIM JAG b. 1962 Coeur d'Alene ID. *Ed:* MFA Montana State Univ.; BFA Sonoma State Univ. CA; AA Santa Rosa Junior College CA. *Coll:* di Rosa Arts Foundation/Rene di Rosa, Napa CA; Chistian Klyabo/Pensione International, San Francisco CA.

POP GROUPING (64), 2003
MIXED MEDIA

SHIRLEY KLINGHOFFER

Your belly button is the center of your body and your body is at the center of what Shirley Klinghoffer does. In *Umbilicus Multitudinous* she turns the self-centeredness of navel gazing inside out. The sweet spot of her work is this expansive omphalo composed of hundreds of plaster casts lifted directly from the bodies of friends and volunteers. Encompassing perfectly the intimacy of individuality, this sculptural mandala swells to become the collective belly button of the world. Meditation before this generous post-conceptual icon nourishes the soul of possibility. Feed your world.

From your belly, up over your nipples, Shirley Klinghoffer runs her hands across your brain. A tumescent mind is perhaps her favorite anatomical feature and her art is, befittingly, intellectually tight. Like Louise Bourgeois she exhibits a scary, smart sense of play. In a bold act of parking lot guerrilla art during the opening festivities of the last SITE Santa Fe biennial, she staged an opening in her hatchback, showing a piece that belonged inside. Titled *What Was I Thinking?*, this massive mental apparatus, composed of hundreds of cast penises, marvelously mocks a certain male mentality. Amusingly, she gave this soft testosterone brain the pet name, George, as he spins on his own axis.

Her high concepts are carried out with a visceral sensuality. Changing direction, her work runs down between your legs, and while her overall *oeuvre* is polymorphously perverse, it is often genitally fixated, vulvically and phallically, in the best possible ways. This unity of body and mind allows her to slip nimbly though a variety of moods, from caustically humorous, to poignantly elegiac, to politically charged.

The nightmarish quality of her Duchampian installation, *Who Cares?*, is a cathartic comment on rape set aquiver within an atmosphere of fiesta gone wrong, juxtaposed with the gently curative power of flowers. Few and far between are the artists brave enough to deal with the abject horror of such subject matter, and fewer succeed so sublimely.

At the threshold of Klinghoffer's work is her feminist fetishist's sense of humor, her love of visual punning, wordplay, and the inside joke. Through a doorway of schoolboy laughter and irony, you find in the rooms of her sculptures a strong feminine force in full bloom. Her core is a human empathy that the bad boys of surrealism are rarely capable of divining. Her laughter is ultimately the joyous sound of angels, rather than the hiccup mockery of devils; or to escape such puritanical dualisms, call it the transformative laughter of Venus.

Shirley Klinghoffer has dealt earnestly and exquisitely with the serious issues of sexual abuse, breast cancer, body image, gender and unabashed intimacy in ways that often belie one's first take. Male or female, belly button focused or not, Shirley Klinghoffer shows us that our greatest strengths are nourished by transforming our vulnerabilities while reclaiming and recasting our bodies and minds.

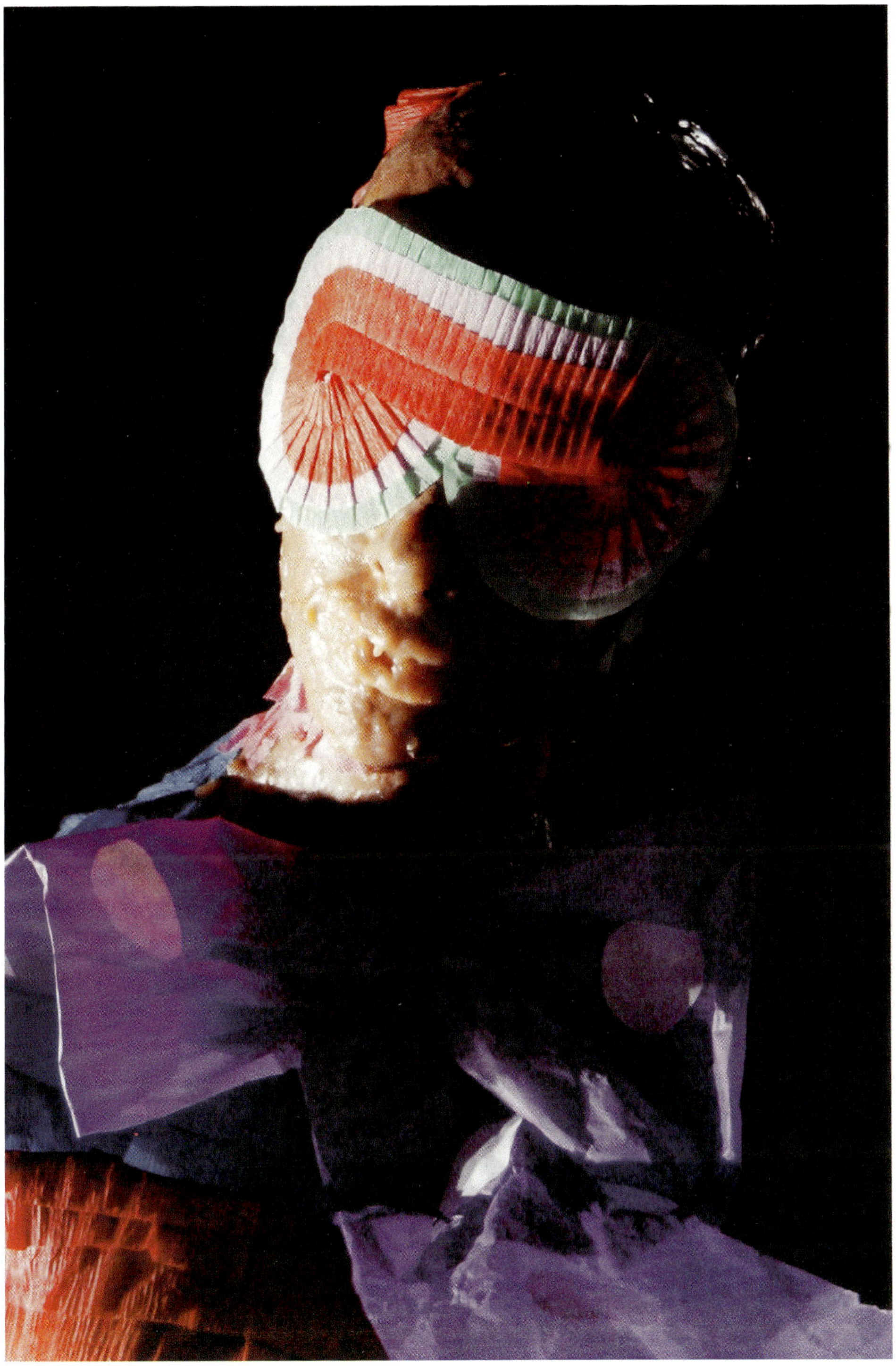

WHO CARES? NO.1 2004
DETAIL FROM MULTI-MEDIA INSTALLATION
GICLEÉ PRINT ON THIN FILM & PLEXIGLASS
40 X 28 INCHES

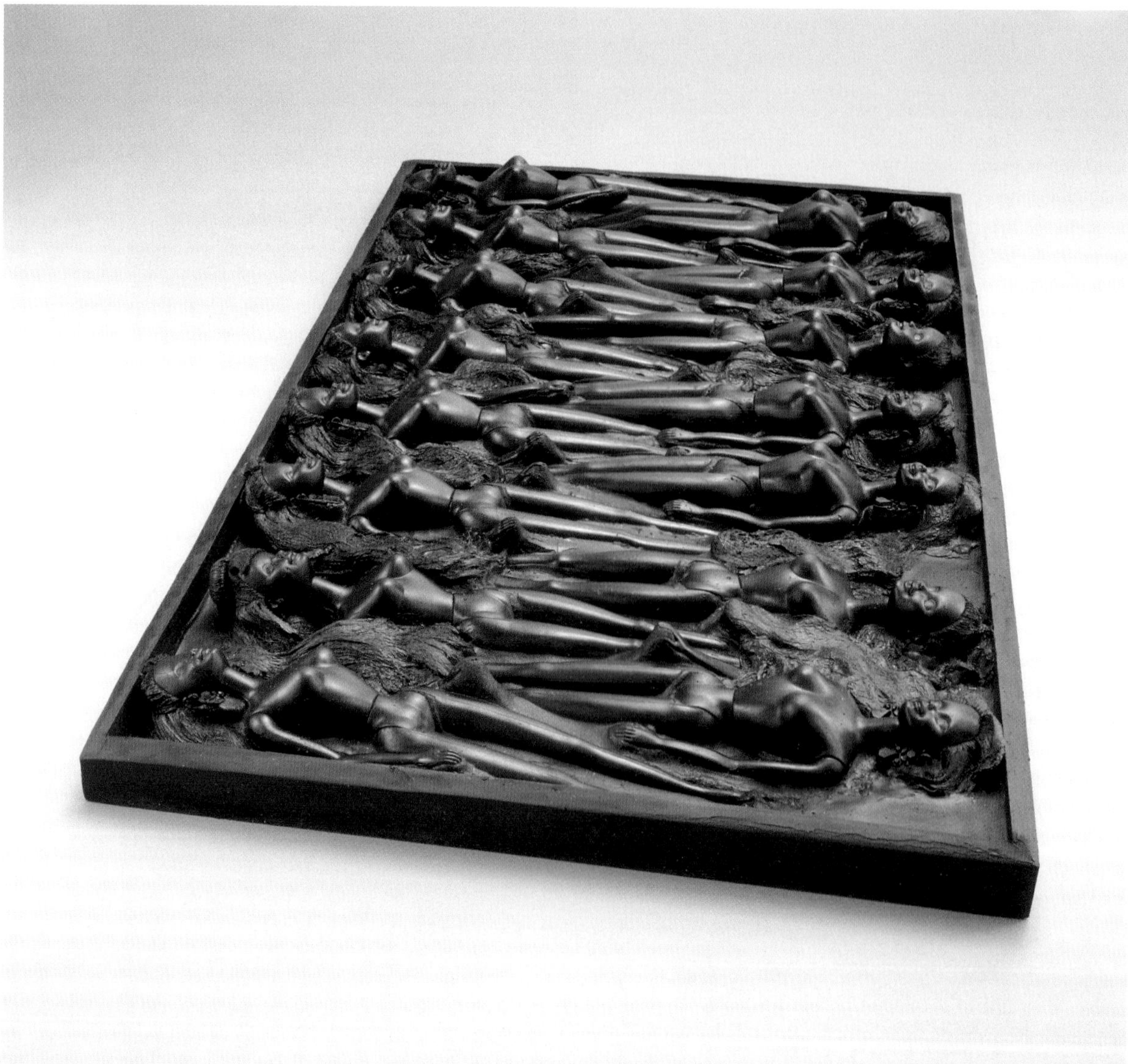

DOORMAT, 1996
CAST BLACK RUBBER
2 X 27 X 17 INCHES

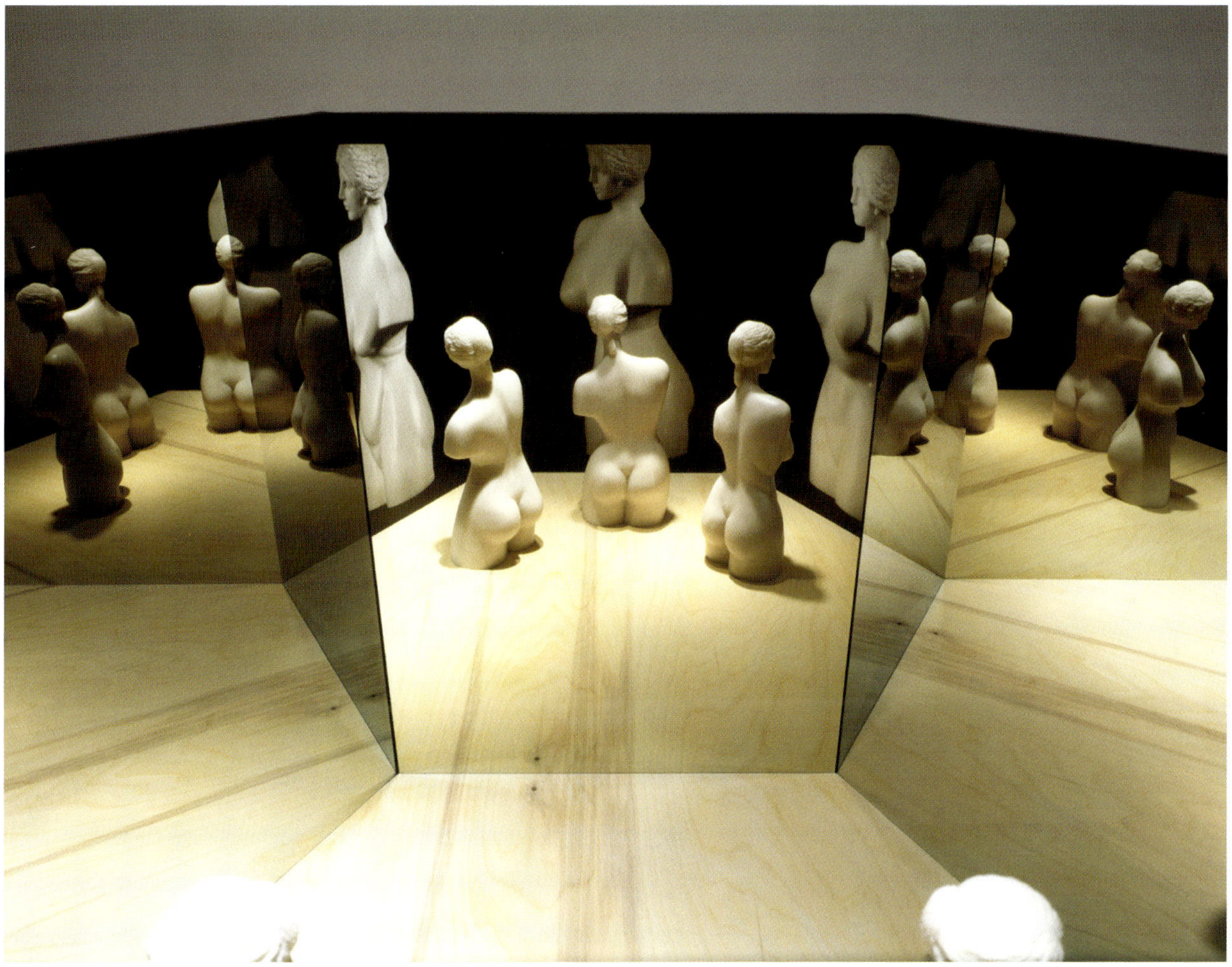

VENUS IN TIME - REFLECTIONS AND ILLUSIONS (DETAIL), 1995
CAST STONE, WOOD, STEEL, PHOTOGRAPHS
& ONE-WAY MIRRORED GLASS
53 X 28 X 28 INCHES

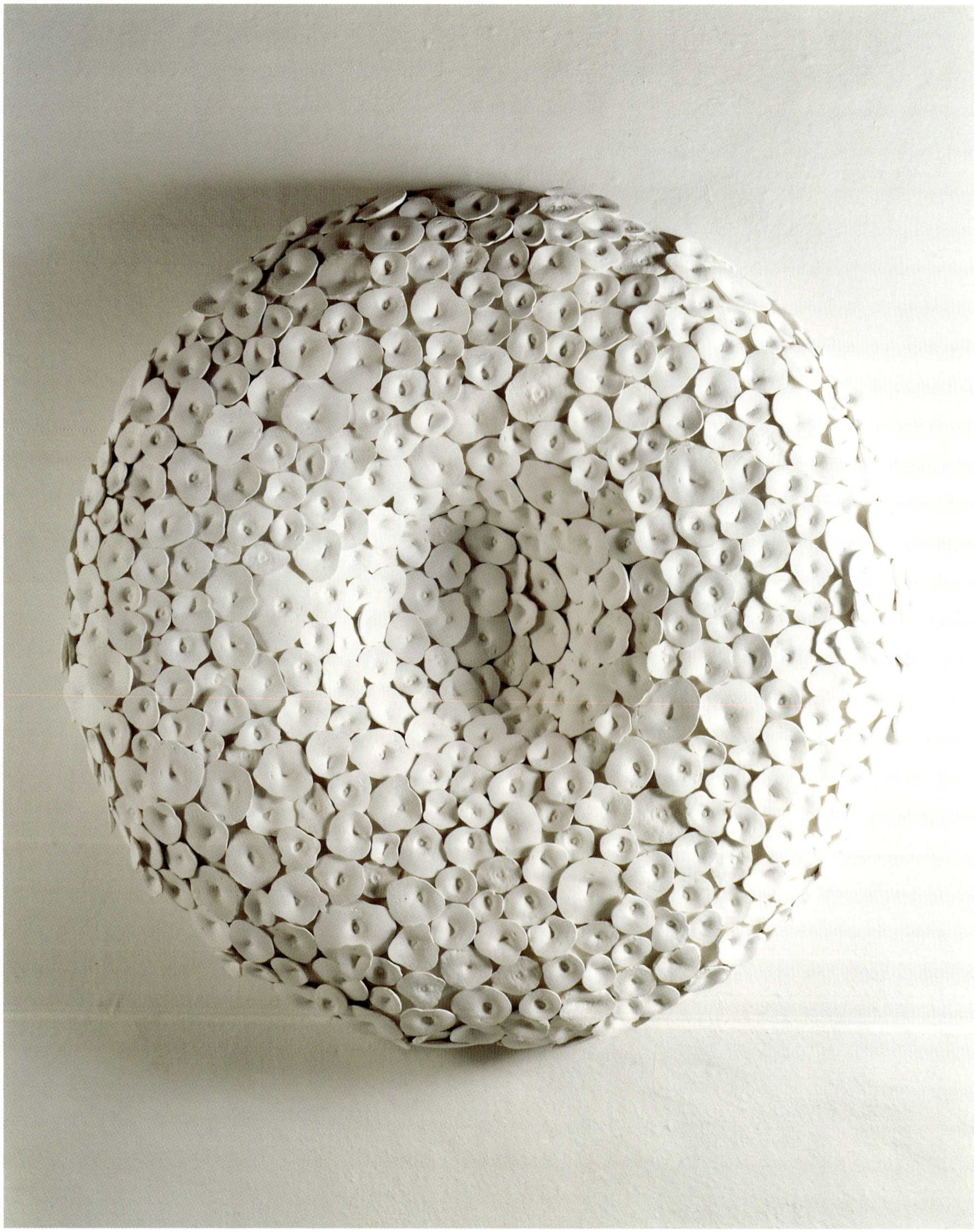

UMBILICUS MULTITUDINOUS, 2001
PLASTER, WOOD & METAL
40(D) X 8 INCHES

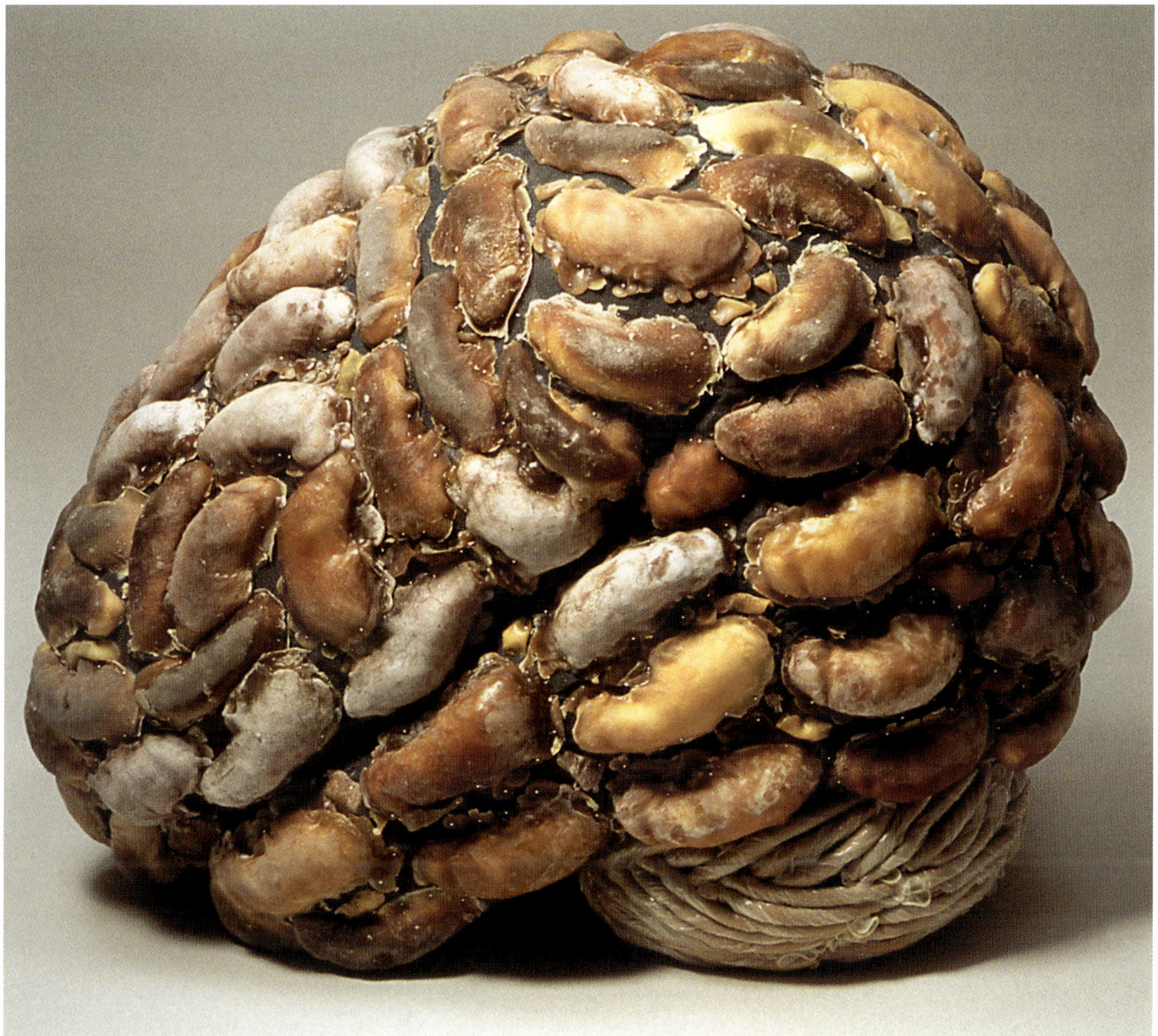

SHIRLEY KLINGHOFFER b. USA. *Ed:* B.Ed Magna Cum Laude, Univ. Miami; School of Visual Arts, New York; ISIA, Urbino, Italy; New York Univ.; Pilchuck Glass School, Seattle. *Exhib:* Museum of Modern Art, New York; New Museum of Contemporary Art, New York; Smithsonian Museum DC; Dali Museum, St. Petersburg FL. *Coll:* New Mexico State Univ., Alamagordo NM. *Representation:* Klaudia Marr Gallery, Santa Fe.

A TESTOSTERONE BRAIN
WHAT WAS I THINKING? 2004
RUBBER, FOAM, COTTON & STEEL PINS
32 X 34 X 32 INCHES

EVELYN ROSENBERG

It's hard to believe that the beautiful detail, remarkable depth and exquisite raised surfaces of Evelyn Rosenberg's large-scale metal sculptures and bas-reliefs literally are formed in chaotic explosions. Since 1985 she has pioneered an incredible artistic technique for shaping metal for which she has coined the term—Detonography or drawing by detonation. She sets off sheets of plastic explosives over a sandwich of carved images and a metal plate. The blast forces the metal to assume the image and the resultant bas-relief is what she calls a detonograph. Using destructive force to create beauty is a wonderful metaphor along Kali-esque "destroy to create" lines, and Rosenberg's results are stunningly unique, both as a result of her unusual approach to artmaking and because of her intense artistic abilities.

Her subject matter and sculptural forms are always site specific as most of her artmaking is dedicated to public and private commissions. Permanently installed indoors and outside in public spaces, she has completed 35 such commissions since 1986. This is a daunting number and makes Rosenberg unrivaled in this realm of achievement. She has received an NEA grant and been written up in the *Smithsonian Magazine*, the *New York Times*, *Sculpture Magazine* and fifty or so other publications. She has appeared for interviews on *Nightline*, the *Today Show*, and *National Public Radio's* "All Things Considered." From the Serengeti Visitor Center in Tanzania—where she created a mural sized relief titled *Mzanzo Mpya*, (Swahili for "continuously repeating") linking a herd of wildebeests to intricate chthonic realities—to the Sonoran Desert Museum in Tuscon, Arizona, to a *Clock of Dreams* for New Mexico State University in Las Cruces, Rosenberg has produced an outrageously impressive body of flowing sculptural forms. Her fantastic *Scales of Justice* fountain for the Albuquerque Courthouse is a remarkable monument to the vital importance of an empowered judiciary and the origins of law, providing the pleasures of kinetic function from a distance and awarding close attention with jewel-like surfaces interwoven with ancient imagery.

Her concerns are with the cycles of life, how the Phoenix of beauty continually rises from the ashes of destruction and decay, and how technology can be used to serve truth and righteousness rather than environmental destruction and war. Her artistic origins as a painter and printmaker are clear and her use of mythologies and adaptations of established iconographies are richly personal, yet universally accessible. The depth of her commitment to the integrity of human, plant and animal life is everywhere apparent, from the fossils of prehistory to the future interplanetary. The immense power of her imagery and her sculptural forms harnesses the big bang energy of the cosmos to explode with heartfelt homages in honor of hope for humanity.

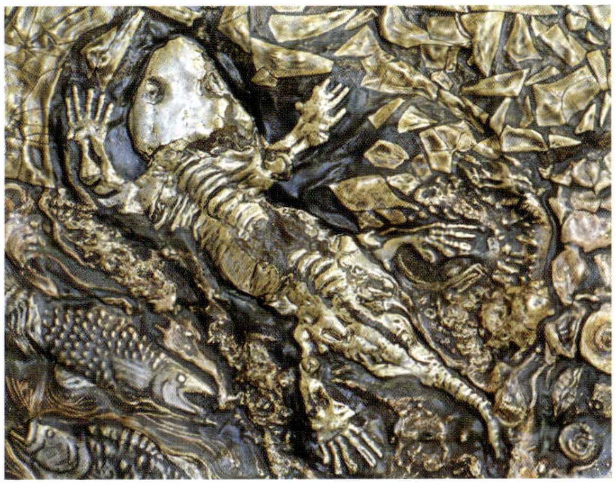

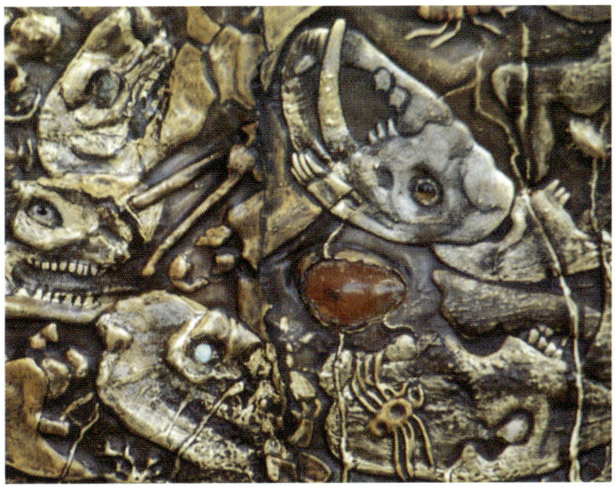

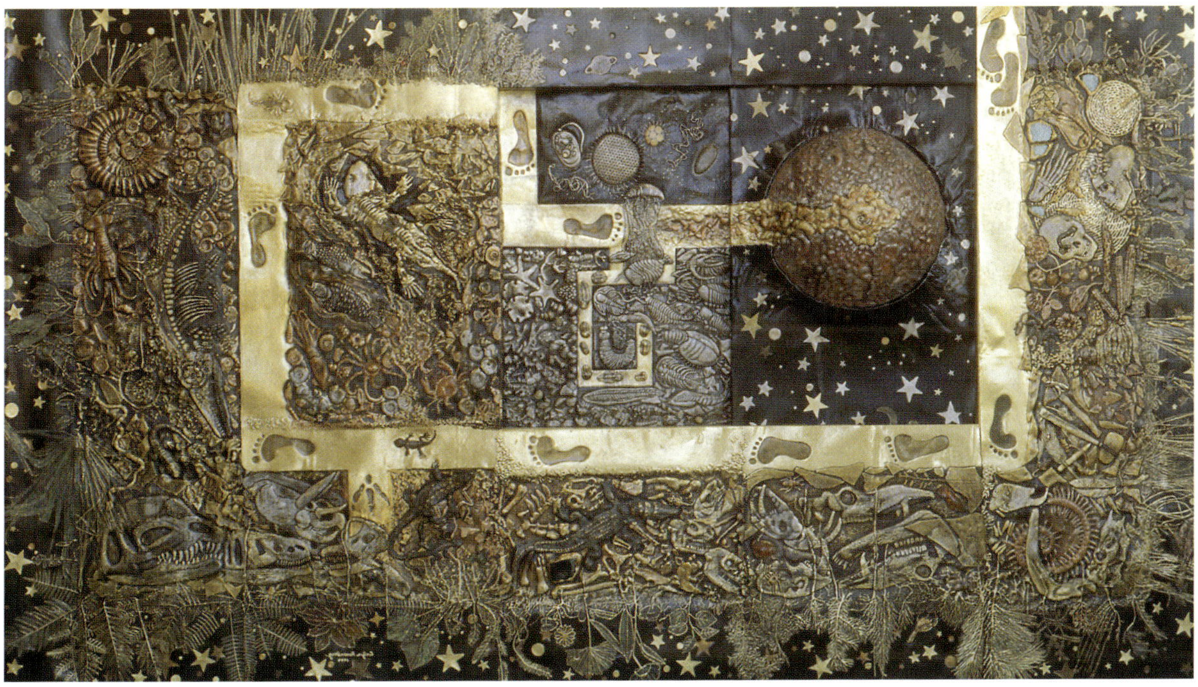

GAIA GENESIS, 1994
COPPER, BRASS, STAINLESS STEEL,
GEMSTONES & ACRYLIC CASTINGS
8 X 17 X 2 FEET
Sonoran Desert Museum, Tucson, AZ

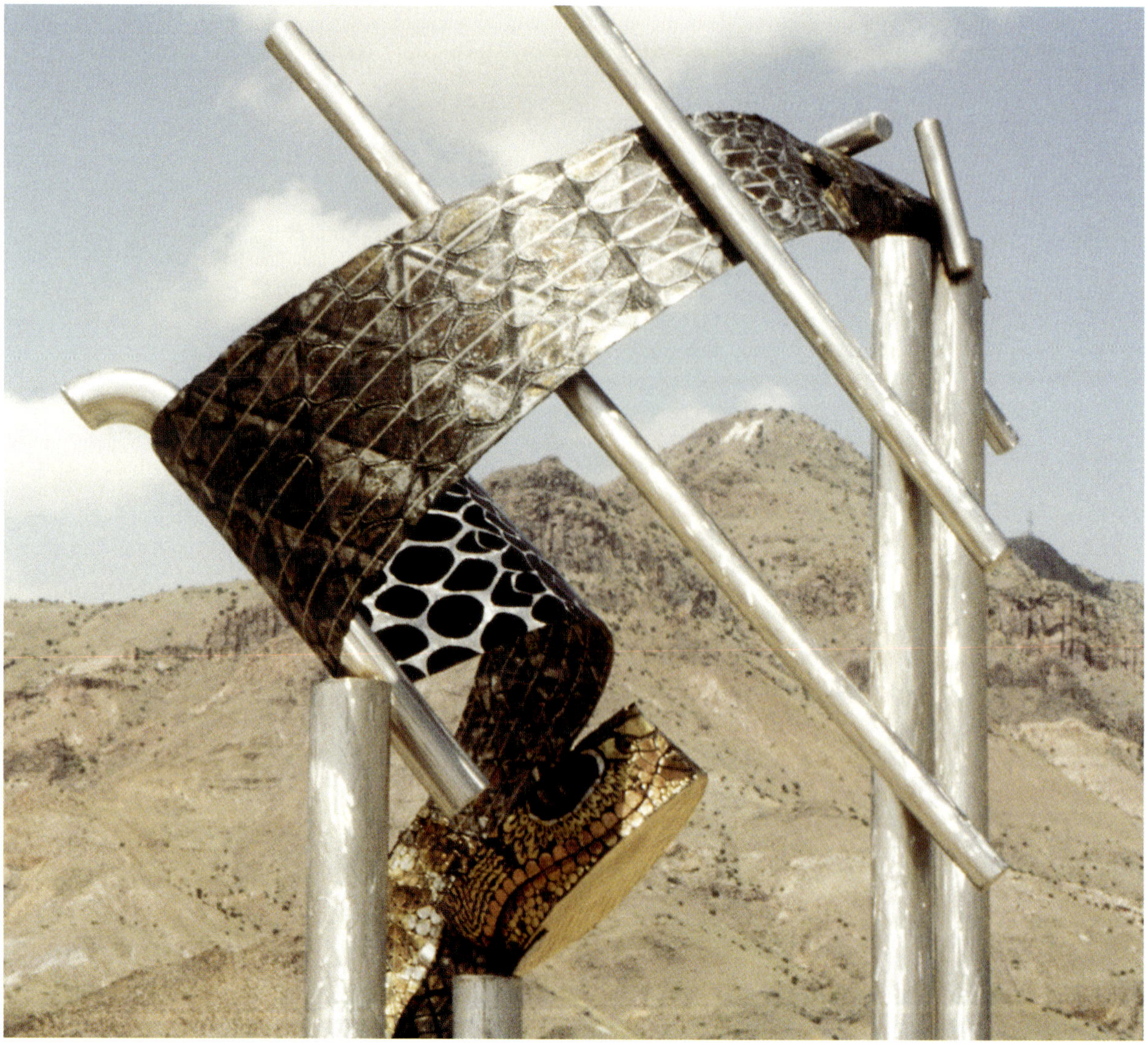

DREAM SNAKE, 1997
ALUMINUM, BRASS & COPPER
LENGTH OF SNAKE: 30 FEET

Energetic Materials Research Technology Center
Socorro, NM

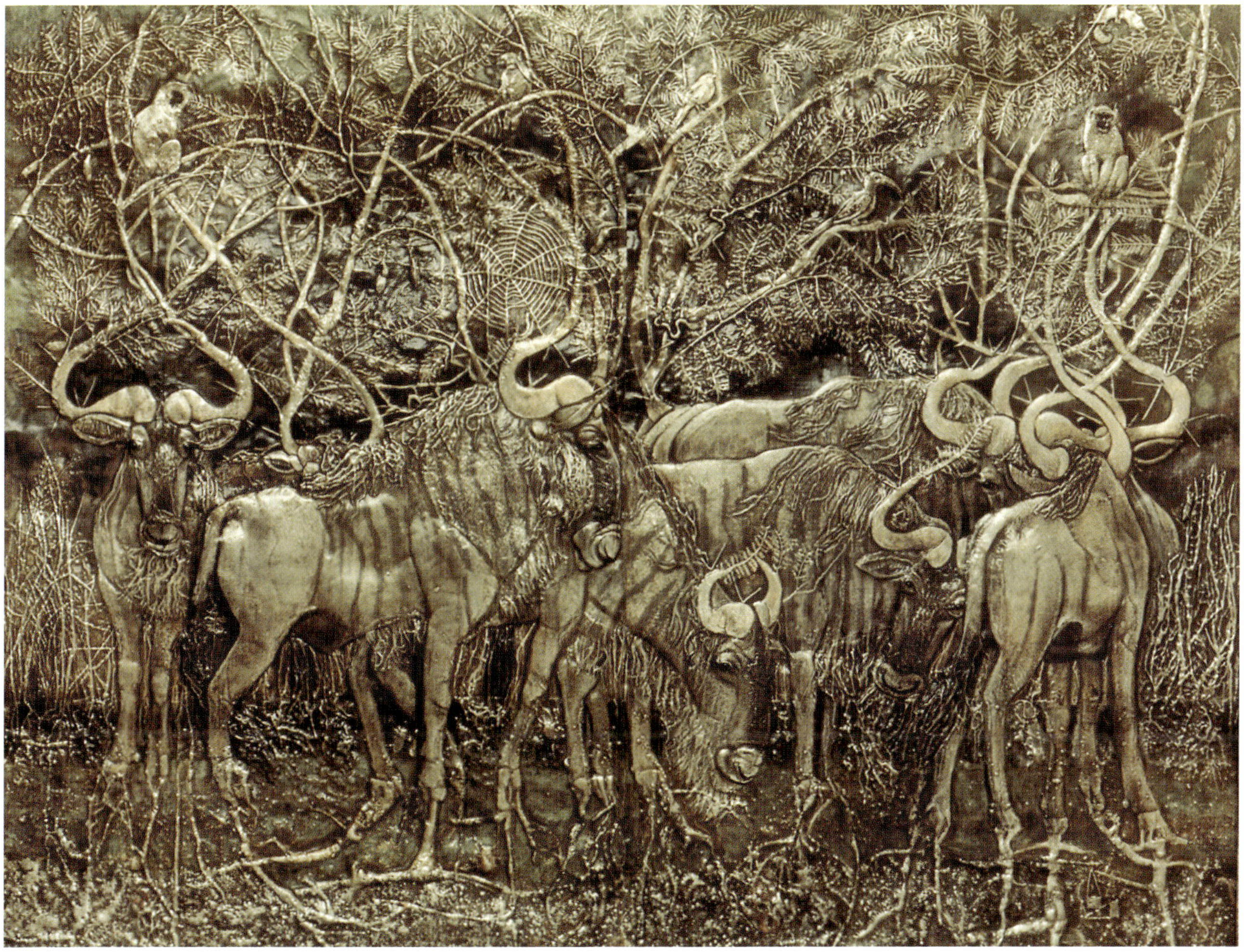

MZANZO MPYA, 1998
STAINLESS STEEL WITH BRASS & COPPER
10 X 8 FEET
Serengeti National Park, Tanzania, Africa

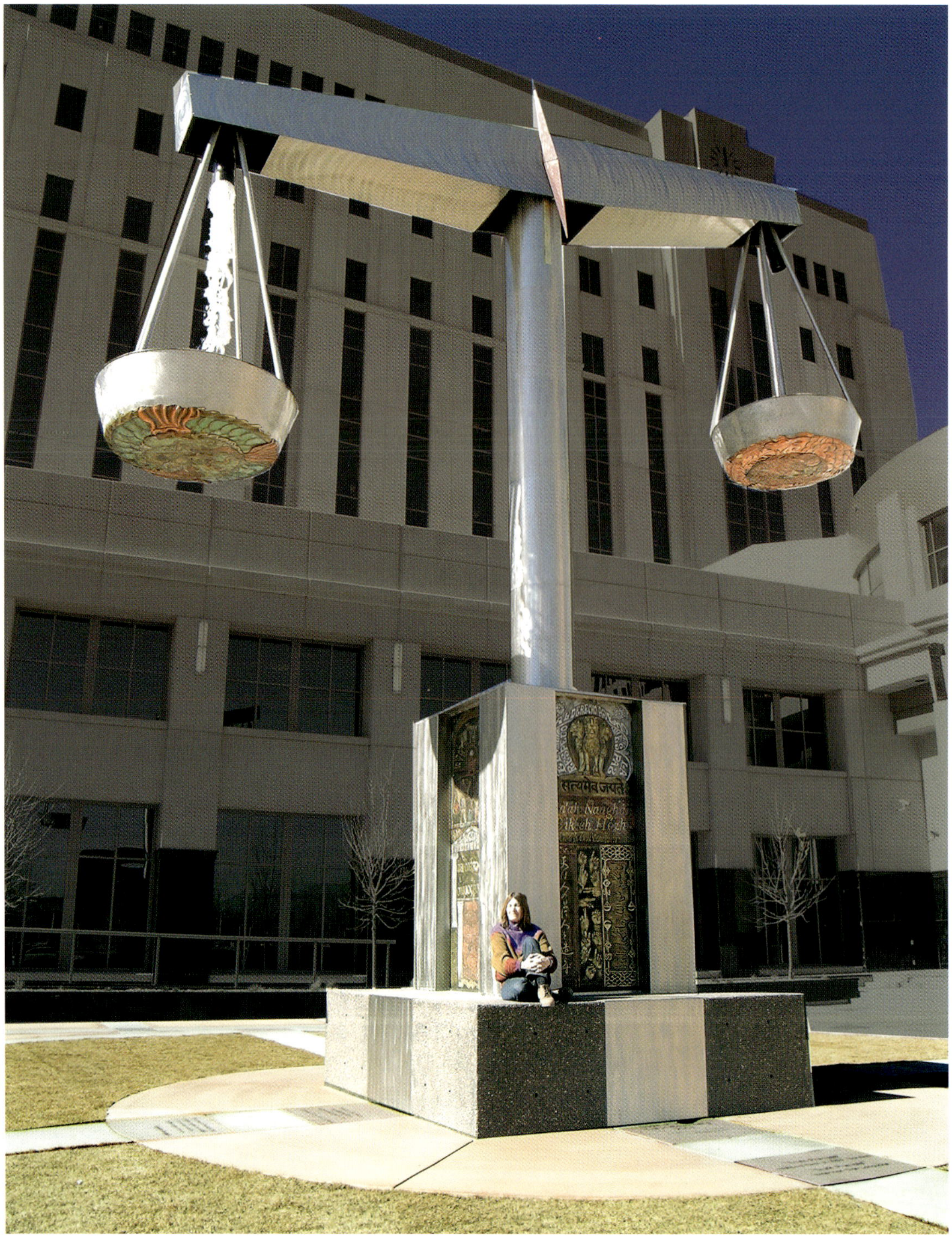

SCALES OF JUSTICE

COPPER, BRASS & STAINLESS STEEL

38 FEET TALL

Bernalillo County Courthouse
Albuquerque, NM

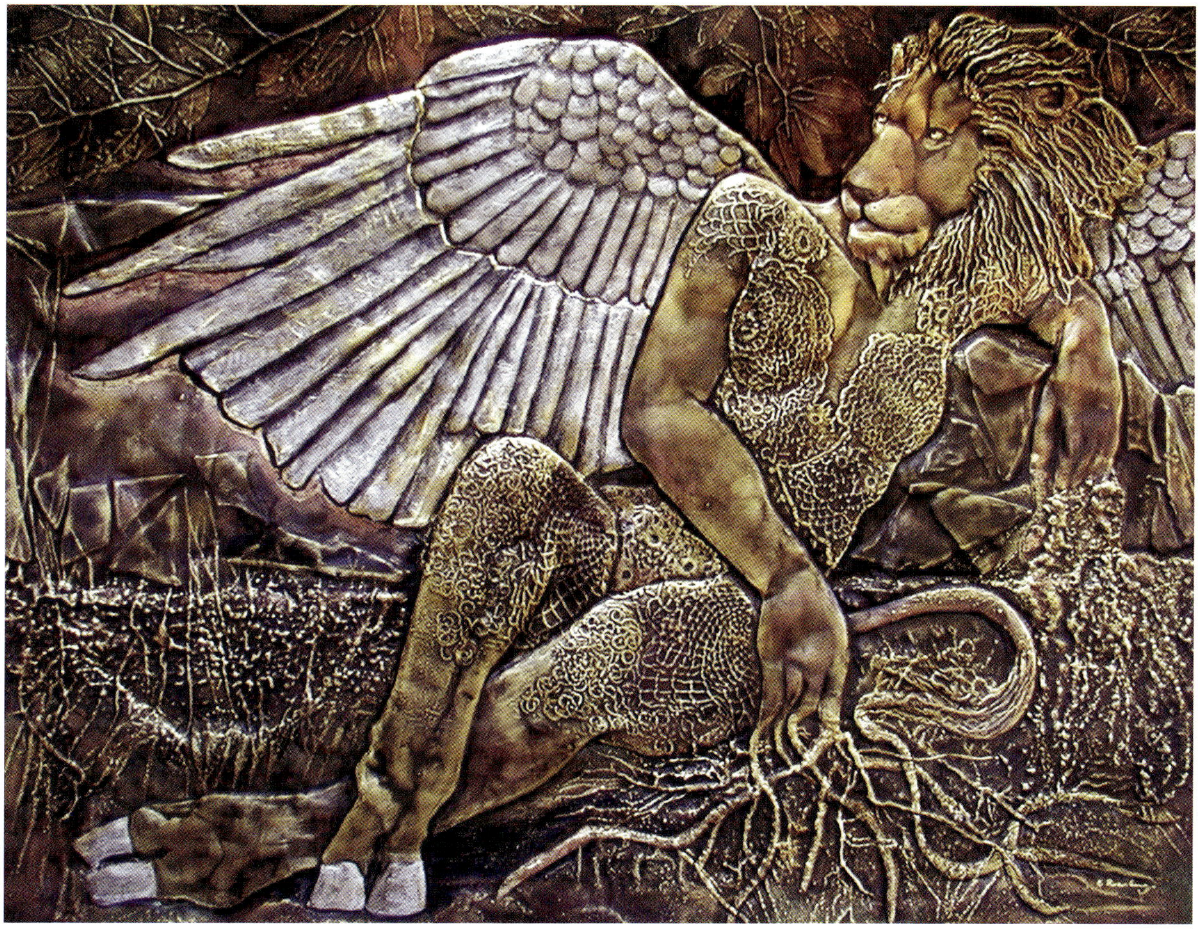

EVELYN ROSENBERG *Ed.* MA Fine Arts, Univ. New Mexico, Albuquerque; AAS Commercial Art, Rochester Institute of Technology; BA English and Philosophy, Univ. Maryland. *Public Commissions:* Univ. Central Florida; Univ. Minnesota; Serengeti Visitor Center, Tanzania; Sonoran Desert Museum, Tuscon; Albuquerque International Airport; Nebraska State Capital Building, Lincoln; BDM Corporation, McLean VA; Medical Complex, Chicago. *Awards:* New Horizon Prize, International Society of Arts, Science and Technology; National Endowment for the Arts Grant.

METAMORPHOSIS, 2002
COPPER & ALUMINUM ON BRASS
ONE OF FOUR PANELS: 3 X 4 FEET EACH

Eastern New Mexico University
Roswell, NM

HEIDI KUJAT

The invisible originating is everywhere omnipresent. Unseen ultraviolet light passes through your body in the sunshine; you can't live without it. Neither can the trees. It passes through them too, through the landscape, the mountain streams and the animals. The sun enlivens the Hamadryad to stretch her limbs in unceasing thanks to the sky, and the sun enlightens the spirits of the flowers. They step from their bright stems and petals to dance their brilliance in the eye of the wind of human vision.

Those that guarded the spirits of trees had such deep roots in the religion of nature, were so solidly earthbound in transcendence, that of all the ancient pagan mystos societies of ancient Greece, they alone never participated in the divine processions. The Oreads, Napaeae, Auloniads, Alsaeids, and Hylaeorae all attended the sacred parade but the Dryads, crowned in leaves of the mighty oak, stayed home. The tree creates her own unity of heaven and earth, encompassing the love of the light from her unchanging place in the nurturing firmament. She, the tree, is her own sanctified stability, alone in a forest of harmonious freestanding ritual.

The same might be said of Canadian born artist, Heidi Kujat. Her profound love of earth and sky find unique expression in her faceless bronze goddesses. Rather than depicting specific personalities, each arboreal nymph, expectant mother and offering angel here faces the unseeable as a particular aspect or quality of love, much in the same way a Hindu deity takes multiple forms. They are each, by turn, goddesses of joy, generosity, gratitude, compassion, bliss, peace, forgiveness, faith, hope, grace, etc. The endless list of names for love blooms eternally.

Love parts seas, moves mountains and sends prophets to heaven in chariots of fire. Love is a universal conflict solvent and the strongest of earthly transformational forces. Love is so simple, to coin a phrase. Love is so fearless that love will save the day. Life is another word for love, and it is Heidi Kujat's gift to give emotive presence and a sweet, subtly turned, living beauty to her sacred female figures.

Heidi Kujat's working process is one of rapture and beatific meditation as she carves with fire and caresses the beeswax that brings these figures into being beneath her gifted hands. From these lost wax originals, which melt back into the invisible, a mold is made and these inspiring bronzes are cast, passing on to the appreciative eye or the serious collector, her heartfelt love for all those who connect with her work.

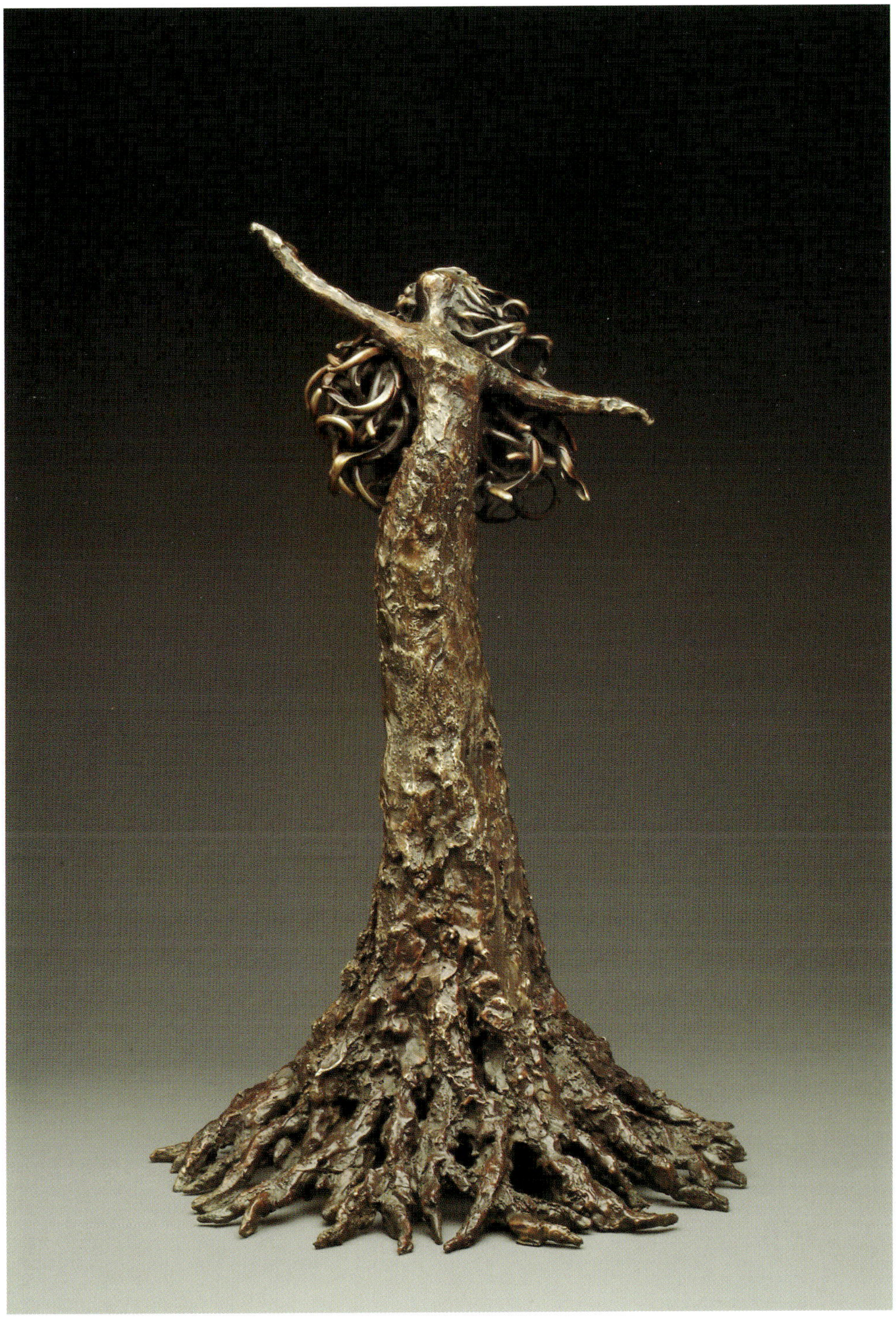

CELEBRATION
BRONZE
20.5 X 14 INCHES

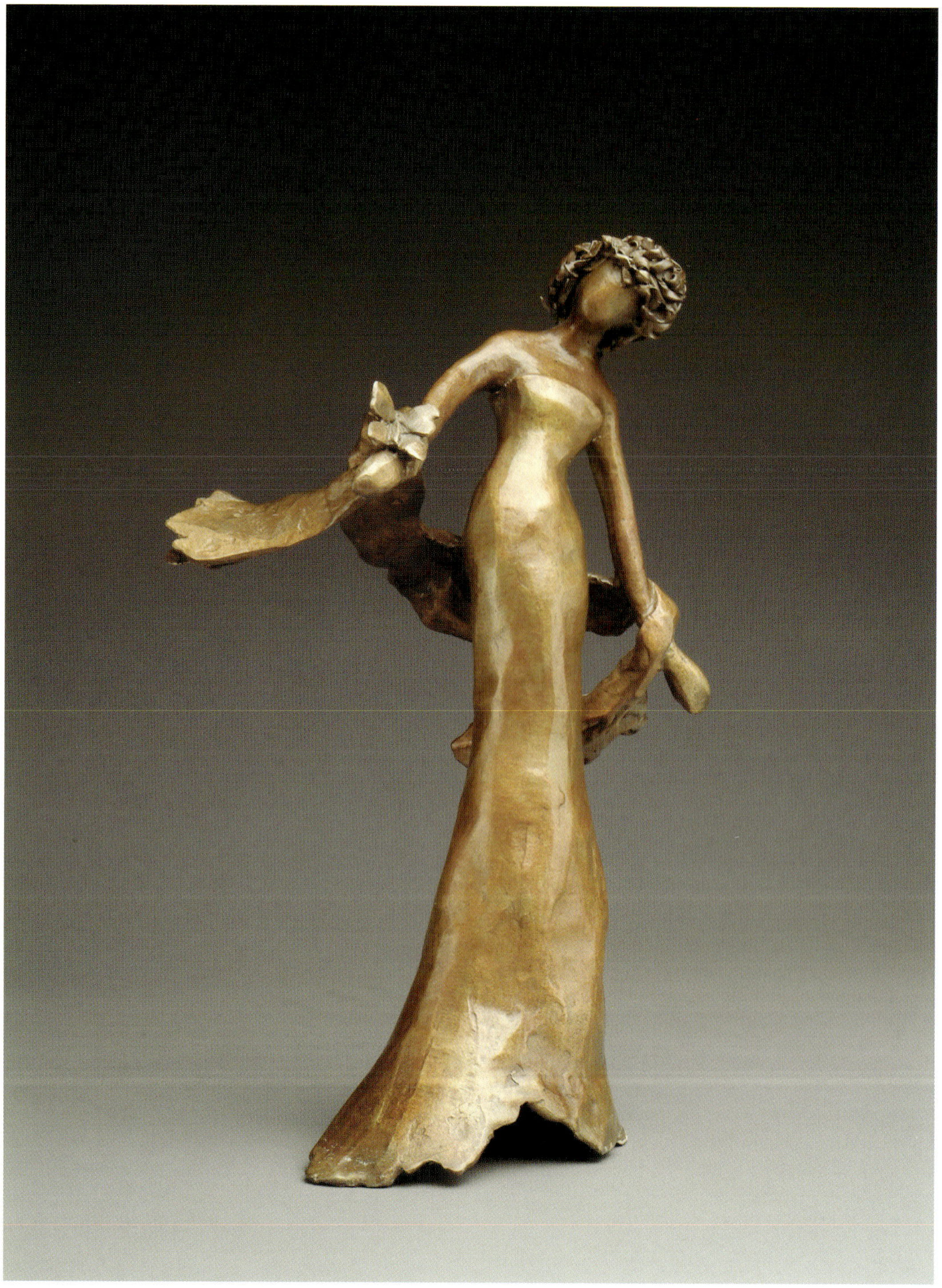

METAMORPHOSIS
BRONZE
13 X 8 INCHES

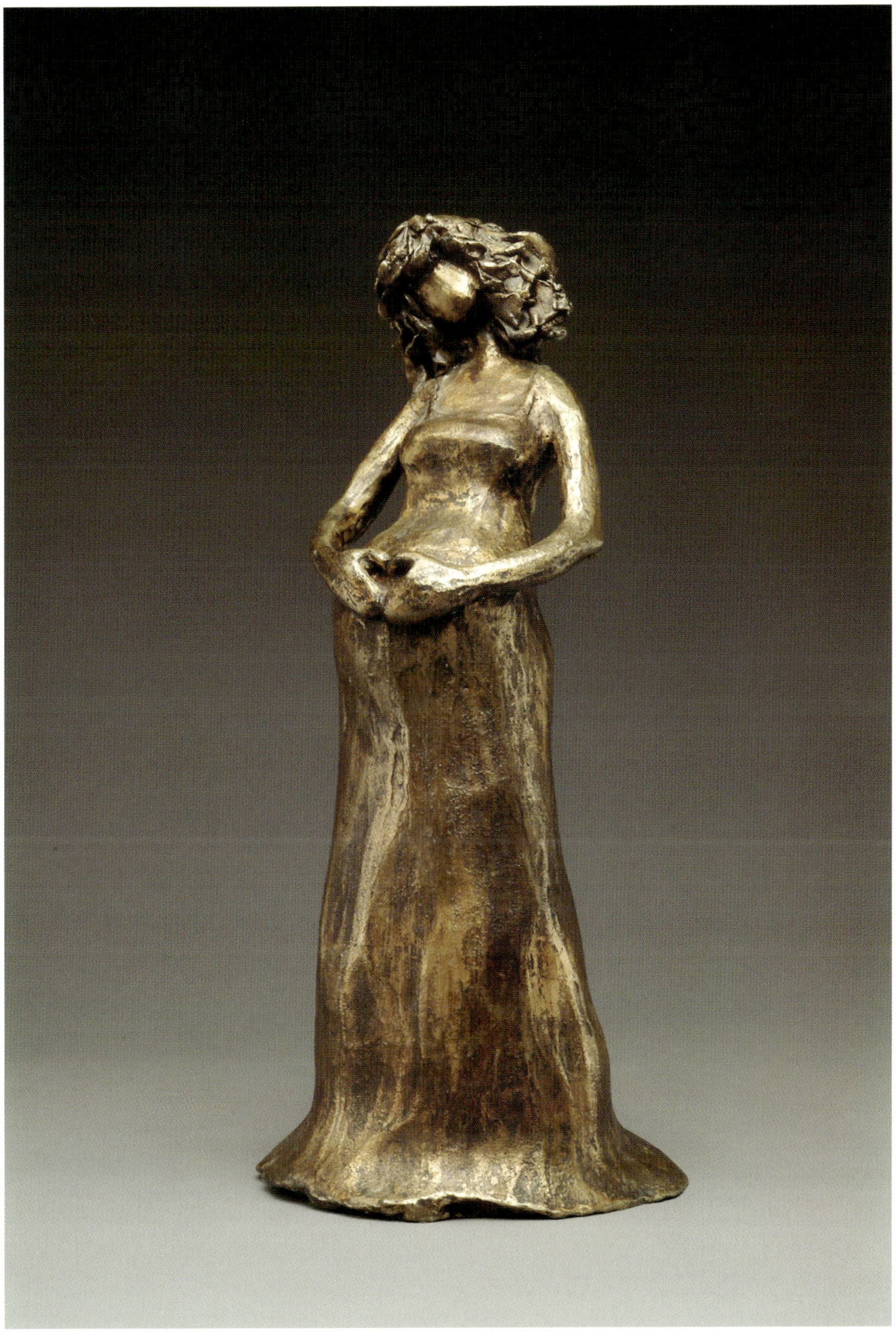

CREATION
BRONZE
15 X 8 INCHES

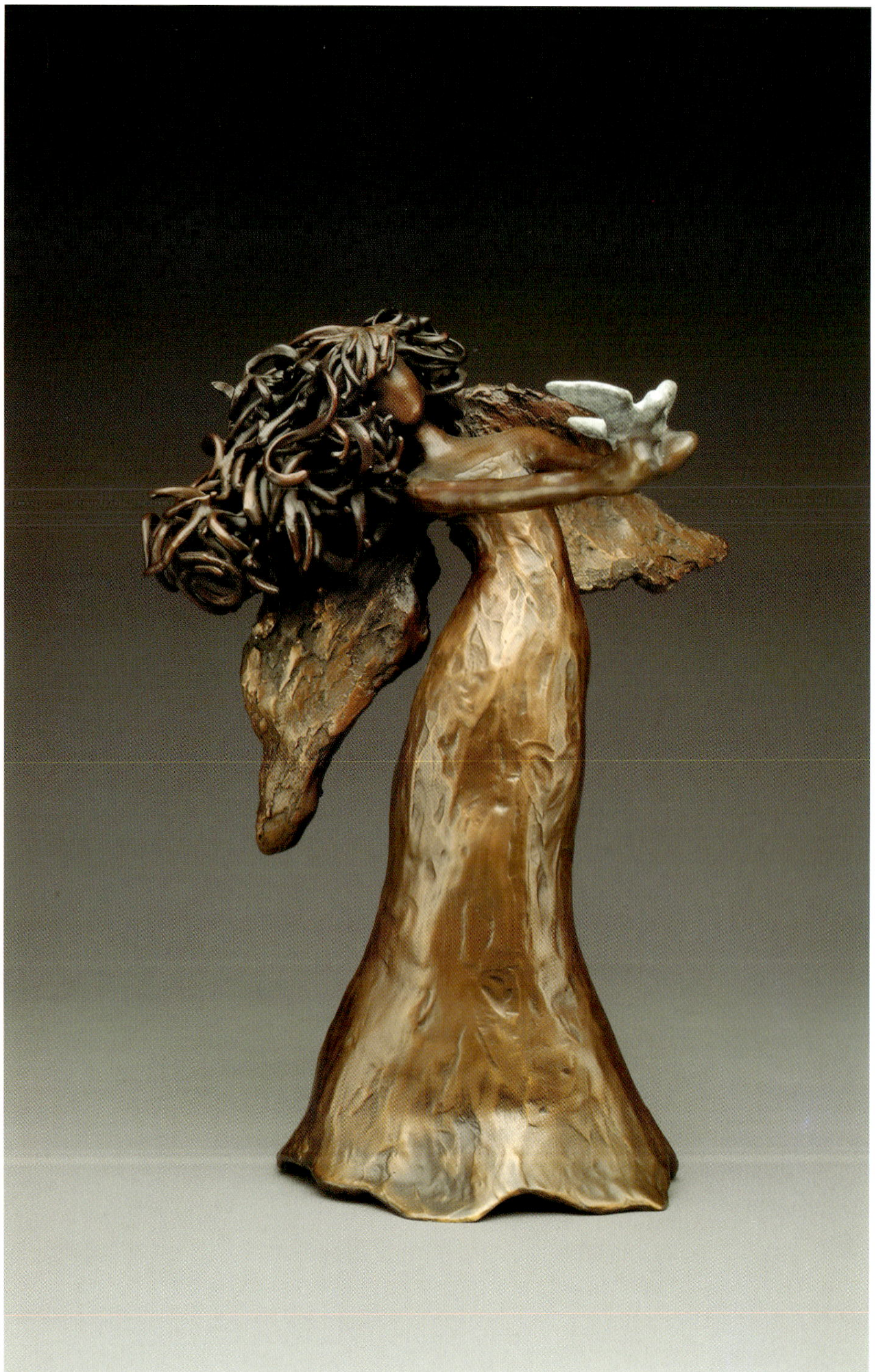

WATCHING THE PATH TO FREEDOM
BRONZE
11 X 7 INCHES

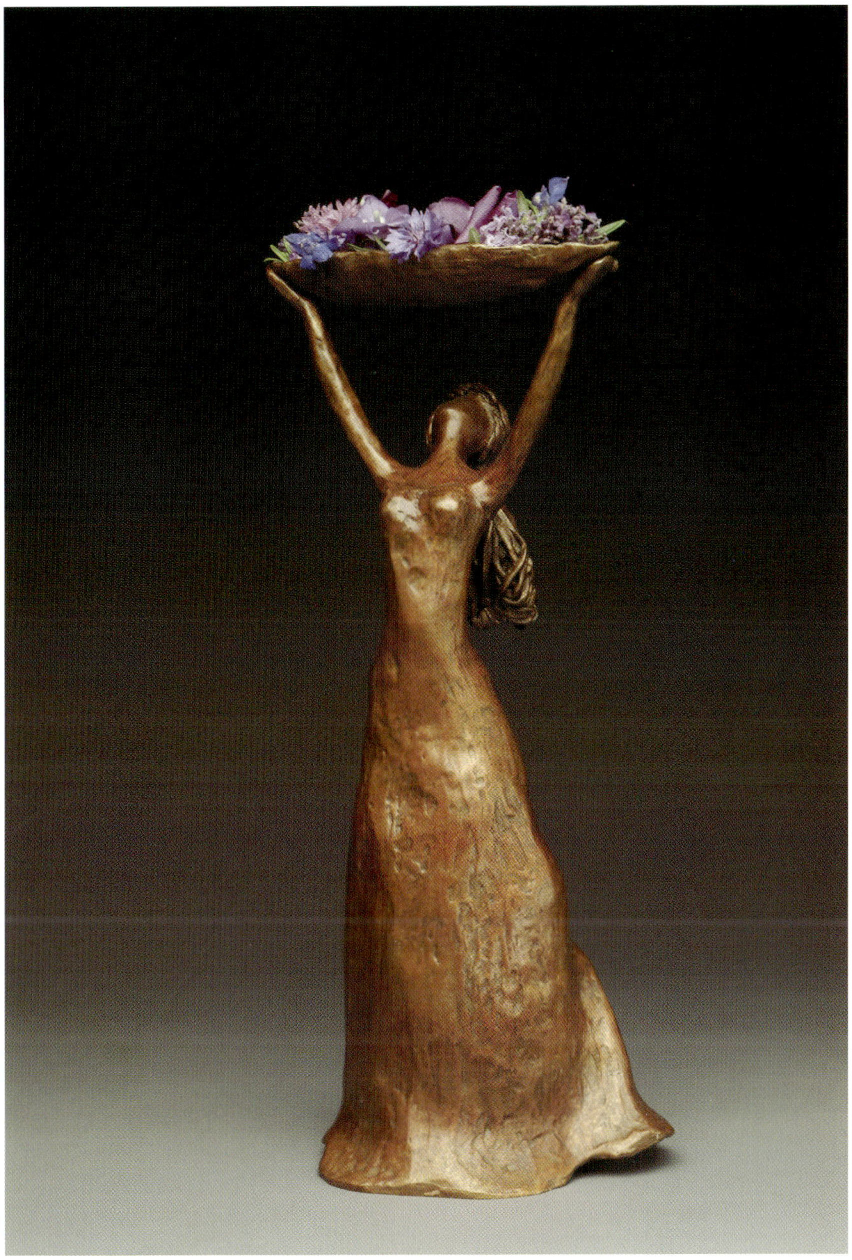

HEIDI KUJAT b. Calgary, Alberta, Canada. *Ed:* BA Honors, Communication, Culture & Society, Queen's Univ., Kingston, Ontario; Instituto de Allende, San Miguel, Mexico; Victoria College of Art. *Representation:* Studio Di Angeli, Santa Fe.

ABUNDANCE
BRONZE
15 X 7 INCHES

LISA FREEMAN

A river of harmony runs through the trees and cliffs, through slot canyons and ancient ossuaries, and quickens in the pulse beneath your skin. It is this current of harmony, this spiraling river of life that we recognize in the sincerely sensual bronzes of artist Lisa Freeman. Her curvilinear forms encapsulate the oneness of the world, and to respond to her bronzes is to find the refrain of natural affinity sounding in one's self.

Pantheistic religions, poetic metaphor, and modern genetics all hinge on the fact that the differences in the DNA of everything are imperceptibly slight. A horse's fetlock is just a twist away from a human torso. The living world pulses in splendid proliferation. The whole is spun from a series of expanding and expiring spirals inextricably linked. This is the heart of Freeman's exceptional expression of the nature of nature.

Lisa Freeman was born loving horses, and was drawn to move to the high desert of Northern New Mexico in 1994 to realize her dreams of living in nature and making art. Her passion for nature is apparent in the tactile surfaces of her bronzes, and more than a little of her intimate connection to the equine finds its way to the foundry. Her work has the sculptural push and pull of a Henry Moore, but is more grounded in the real. The other similarity with the British bronze-master lies in Freeman's incredible use of scale. The massive magnification that takes place in *Leg Bone* exposes the folds and roundnesses of the Southwest desert every bit as much as it precisely delineates the stolid structure that underlies bovine anatomy.

Her pieces in the *Bone Form* series take this expansion even further and swell to arrive at a place where bone rhymes with *Belvedere Torso*. The *Belvedere Torso* is a monumental fragment of Hellenistic sculpture that was excavated during Michelangelo's lifetime and had a profound effect upon his style. Later, Yeats was inspired by it and Rilke writes in *Archaic Torso of Apollo* that the stone spoke to him saying, "You must change your life." Freeman's masterful cast bronzes are the emanation of the energy of this old world tradition in interaction with real life on the ranch.

Modeled on the plenitude of found animal bones and plant forms on her 100-acre sanctuary near Abiquiu, her magnified forms begin as hand built clay sculptures. Working with large slabs of water-based clay and using the forces of her body, she becomes one with the pliable earth. A mold is made and a wax replica cast. The artist retouches the wax with her fingers, tools and heat. Now it is ready to be dipped into a ceramic slurry and a shell hardens around it. This second mold is heated. The wax burns away leaving an absence for the molten bronze. At about 2,000 degrees Fahrenheit, Lisa Freeman's consecration of the earth finds permanent form.

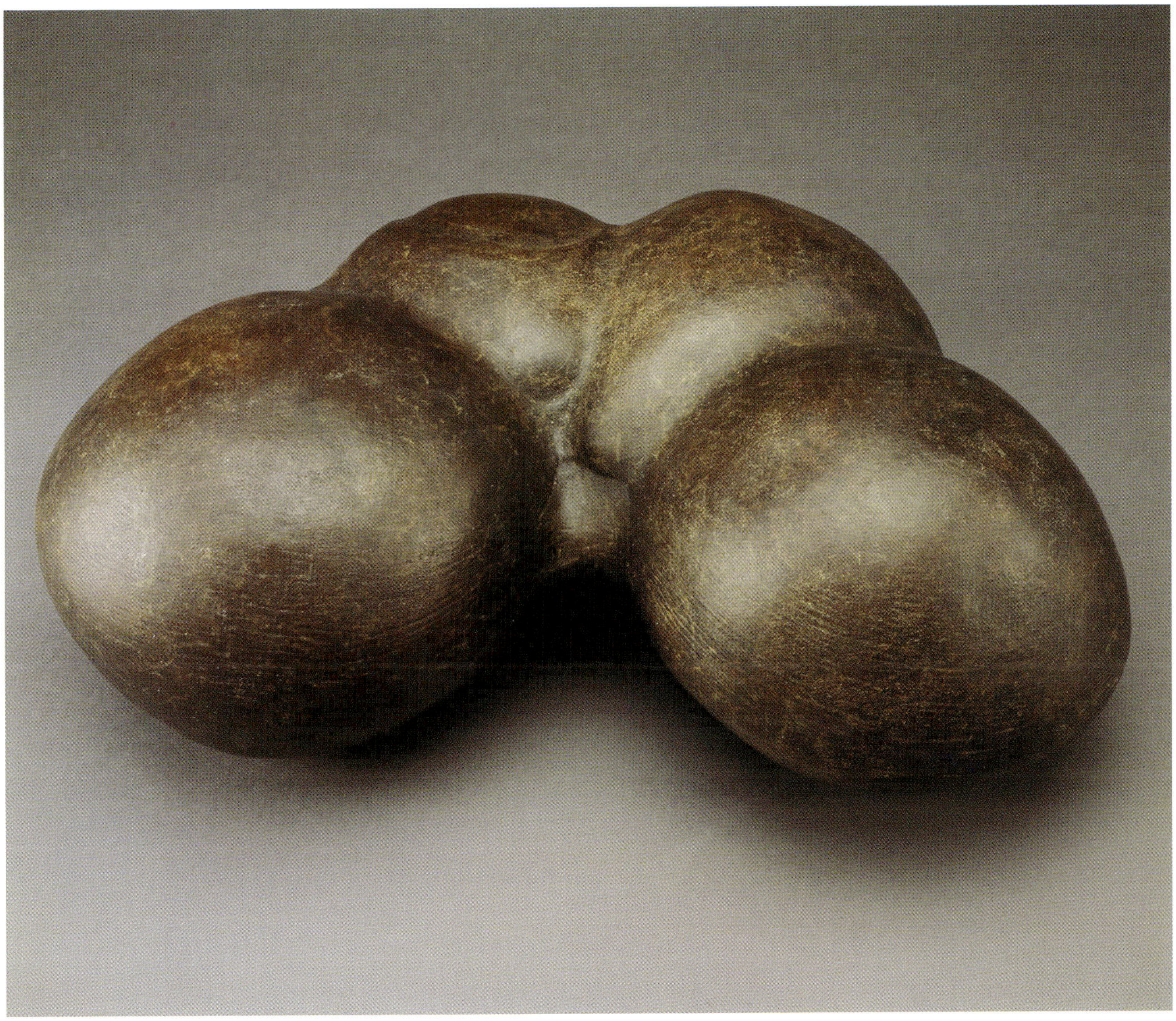

CONCRETION
CAST BRONZE
6 X 16 X 11 INCHES

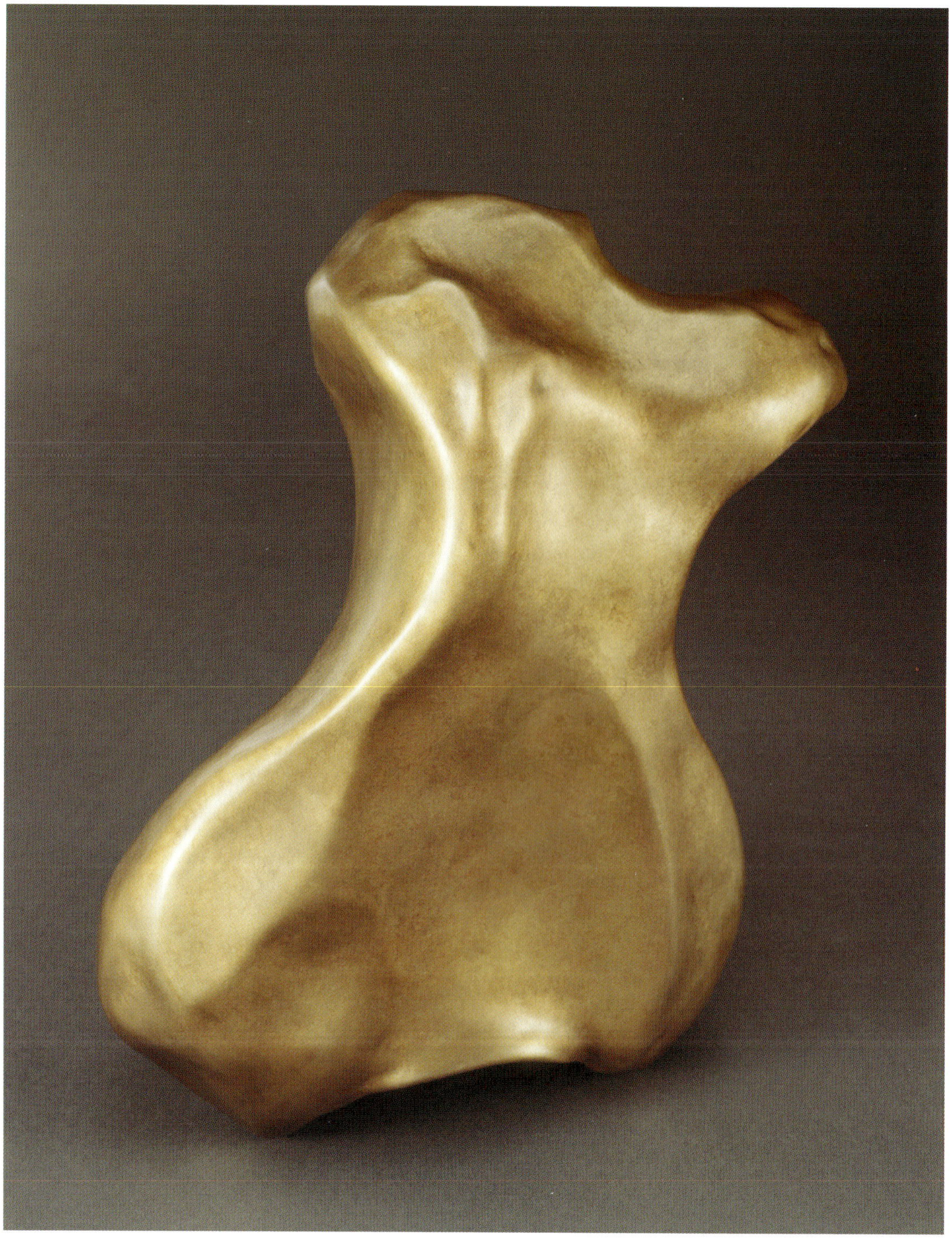

BONE FORM I
CAST BRONZE
15 X 10 X 5 INCHES

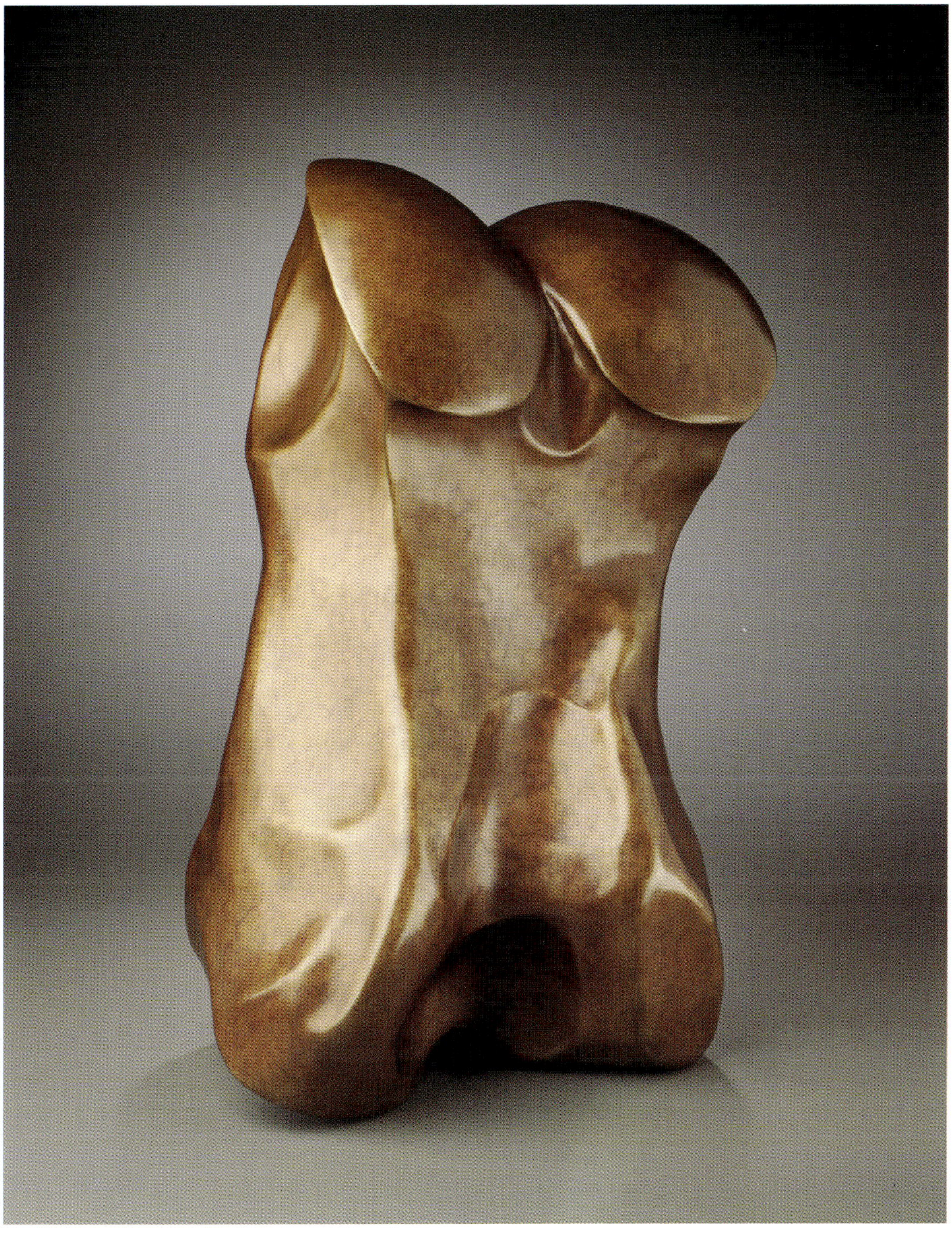

BONE FORM III
CAST BRONZE
20 X 8 X 11 INCHES

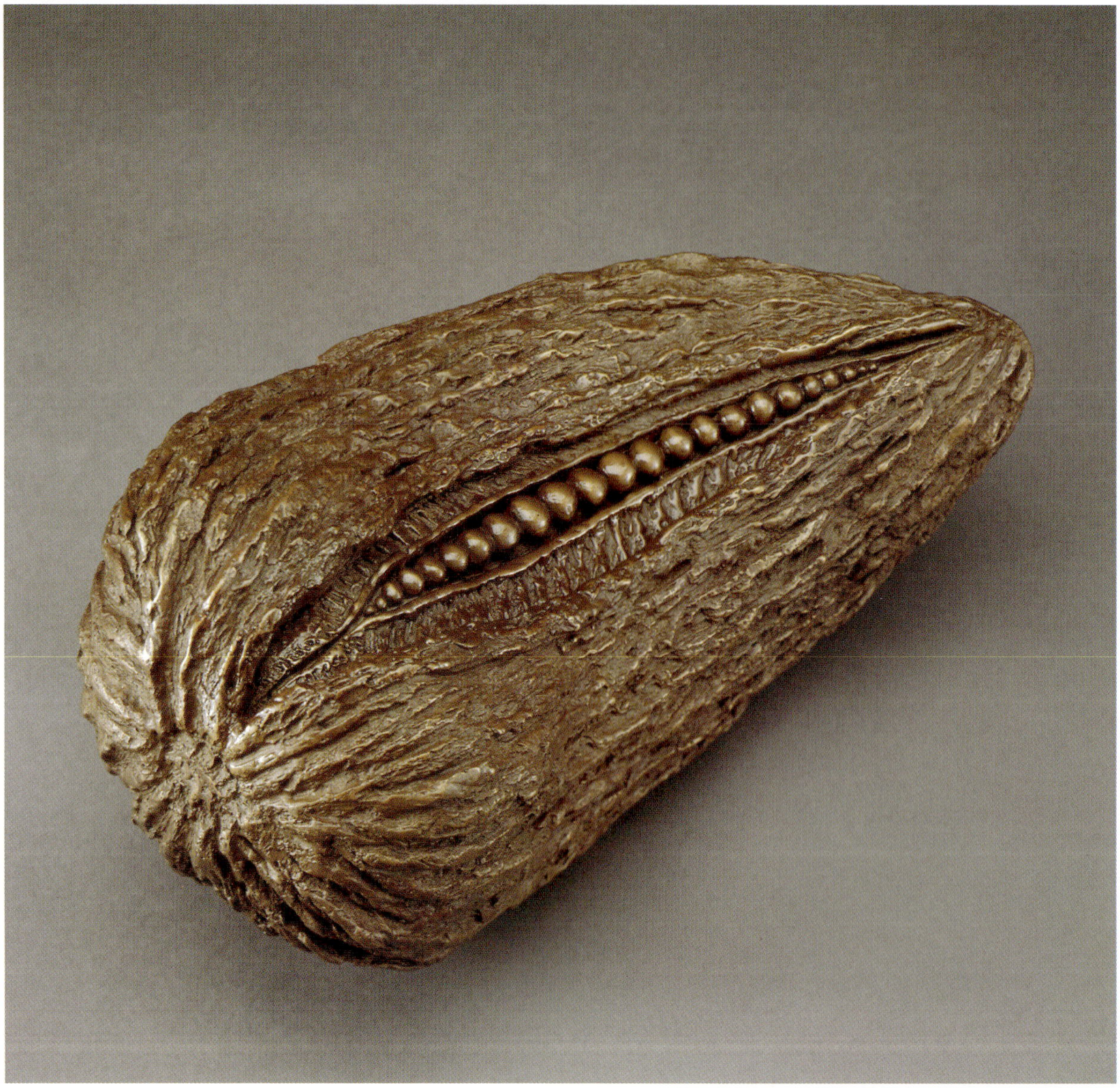

SEED POD
CAST BRONZE
6 X 11 X 6 INCHES

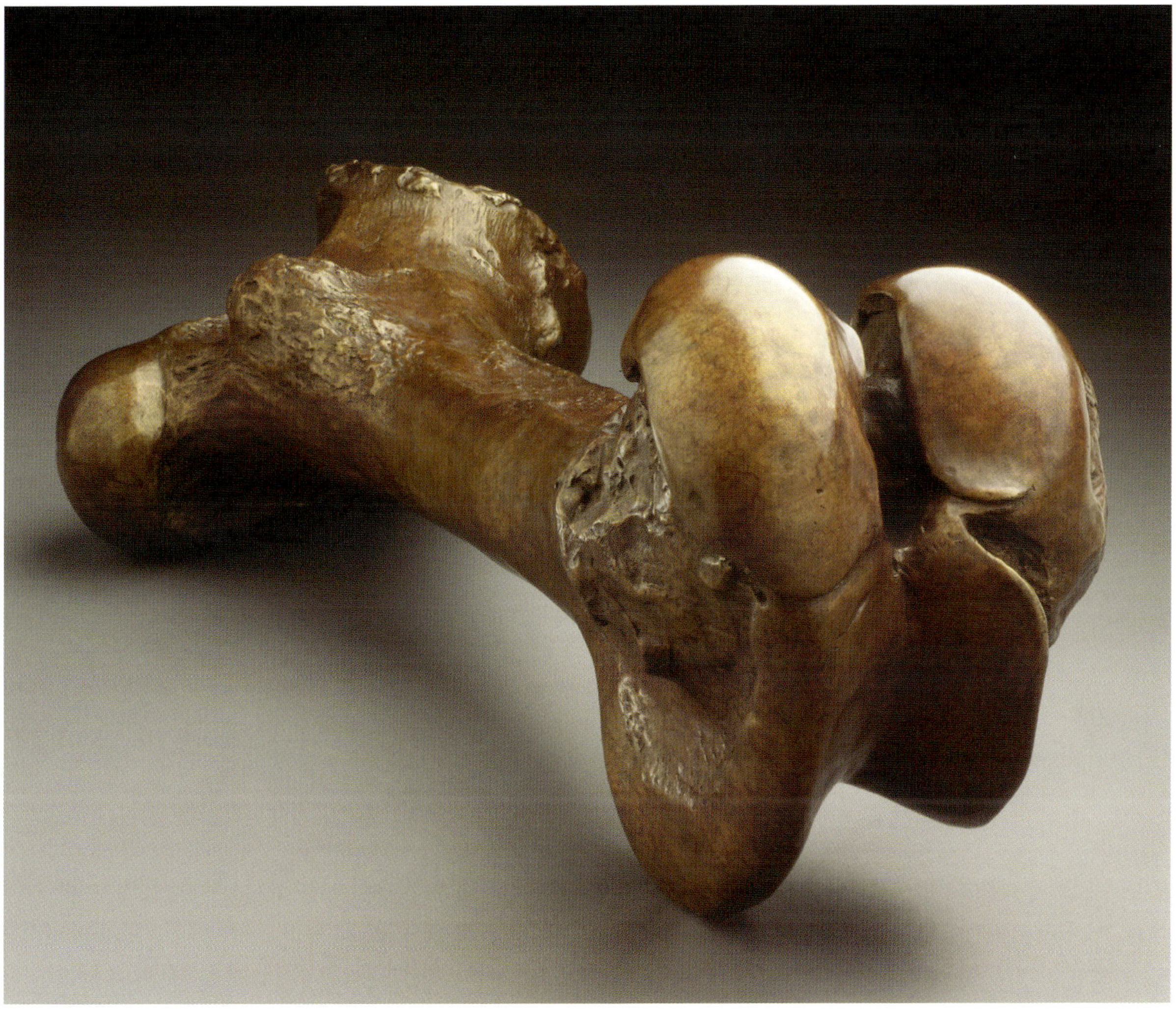

LISA FREEMAN b. 1946 Washington DC *Ed:* BFA in Sculpture, Univ. Chicago. *Additional studies:* Chicago Art Institute; Illinois Institute of Technology, Chicago; Corcoran School of Art DC. *Collections:* Longview Museum of Fine Art, Longview TX; The Capitol Art Foundation Collection, State Capitol Building, Santa Fe; The Robbins Center for Art and Science DC; Standard Oil Company, Chicago; College of Santa Fe NM. *Representation:* Hand Artes Gallery, Truchas NM; Gallery Zipp, Glorieta NM; Tadu Contemporary, Santa Fe.

LEG BONE (FEMUR)
CAST BRONZE
10 X 25 X 11 INCHES

SALLY ANDERSON

Sally Anderson lives in a zone of formal play and experimentation beyond elucidation. Living, after all is said and done many times over, is simply an experience given without explanation by an essentially ludic universe. In Sally Anderson's life and art, making work is serious play.

While Anderson claims that any resemblance between her work and anything else is purely accidental, she has absorbed the lessons of great formalists like Brancusi, El Lissitzky, and Miró, and distilled them to pure abstraction. Her ribbons of bronze and bonded mylar twist and curl through weightless space like three-dimensional versions of Paul Klee's "lines taking a walk."

Her wall reliefs become sculpture in a way that would make any Russian Constructivist breathy. *Pyramid* stacks up the wall, gaining greater dimensionality as it goes, like an emergent amplification of edge. As the title implies, there is a system of structure here that is fundamentally architectonic, commanding yet quiet. This steady building of form might well stand as a metaphor for Anderson's process of endless experimentation and ceaseless expansion of minimalist vocabularies. She easily achieves each next artistic plateau and is impressively prolific—the best measures of an artist's pleasure.

She has twice been awarded NEA grants. In Europe and the U.S., major home furnishings companies have licensed her designs for textiles, rugs, furniture, and wall coverings. Mondrian, with his concept of "total environment" would be envious. In a very real way she's a one woman Bauhaus.

Her work is stunningly crafted. Her subtle surfaces seduce and supply substance for endless inspection. At a distance her work can appear reserved, but up close you discover a rare artistic generosity that provides the pleasure of supporting infinite interpretation. A Sally Anderson construct gives the gift of a generative center.

Half Round with Sienna is just such a set of shaped volumes. Is it being between a half moon rock and a dark place or is it the edge of a wedge of night sky betwixt canyon walls? It suggests rites of passage and alignment, and again elicits issues of edge and register. There is a taut tension of suspension, an inarguable monumentality, and an excellent interplay of the organic curvilinear and the strictly straight. For all this the piece has the succinctly satisfying sense of a novel solution, and the power of Anderson's steady resolve.

Sally Anderson has been an established Santa Fe presence since the 1960s. Her elegant San Francisco Street gallery is an impeccable exhibition space, and her decision to become her own best dealer, after considerable success early on in other reputable spaces, may well make her admirably ahead of her time. Certainly, there is no better recipe for maintaining artistic autonomy. Artists and collectors alike ought rightly admire this move.

In the end, it is the pleasure of her choices and the subsequent solid strength of Sally Anderson's work that convinces.

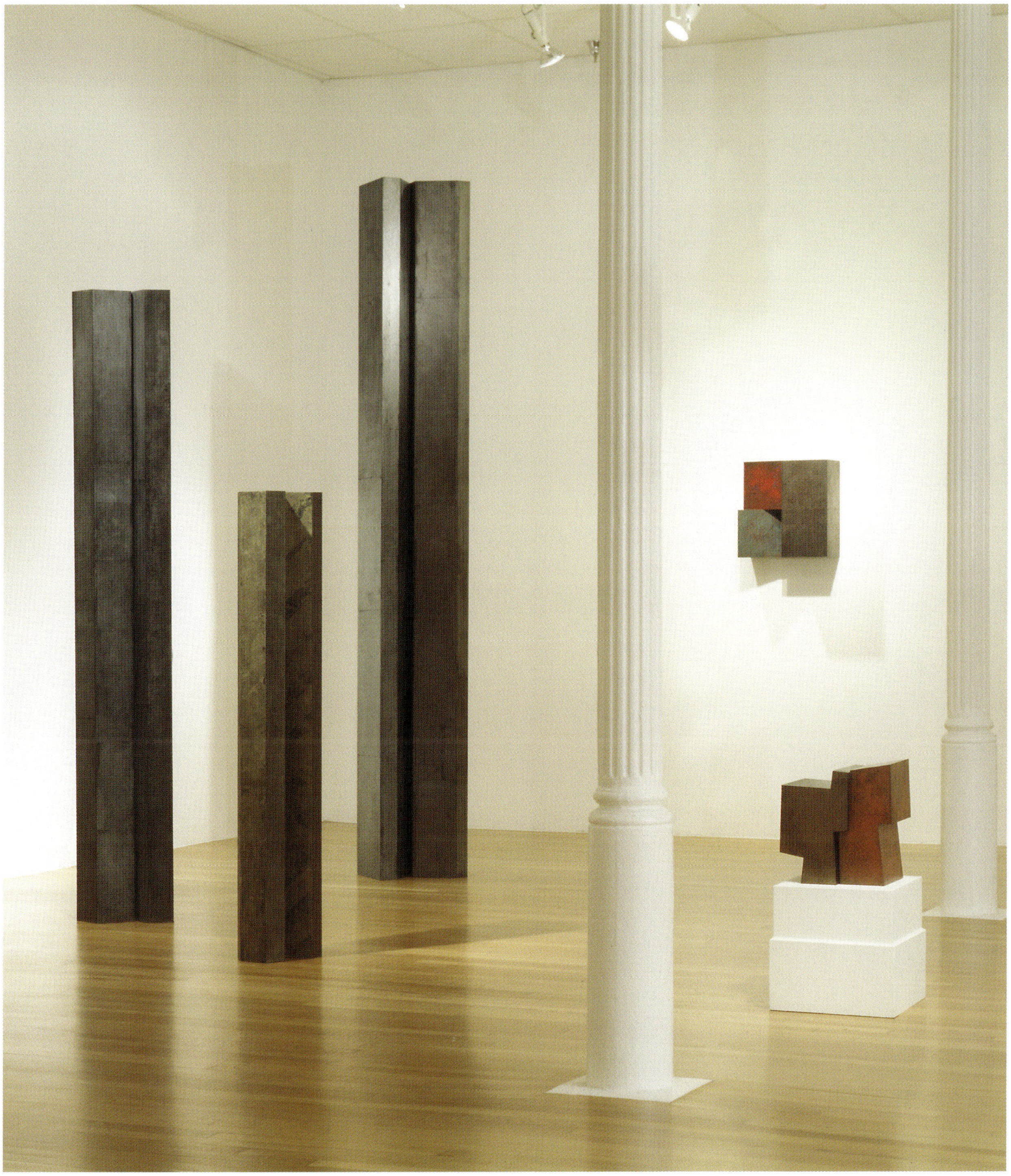

From left to right:
COLUMN, 90 X 14 X 11 INCHES
WHO WILL WATCH THE PARADE, 60 X 10 X 9.75 INCHES
BREAKING BOUNDARIES, 114 X 15 X 11 INCHES
IN AND OUT, 18 X 18 X 9 INCHES
LOOK ALIKE, 13.5 X 13 X 9.5 INCHES
ALL WORK WITHIN VIEW IS OIL, WAX, MYLAR & WOOD

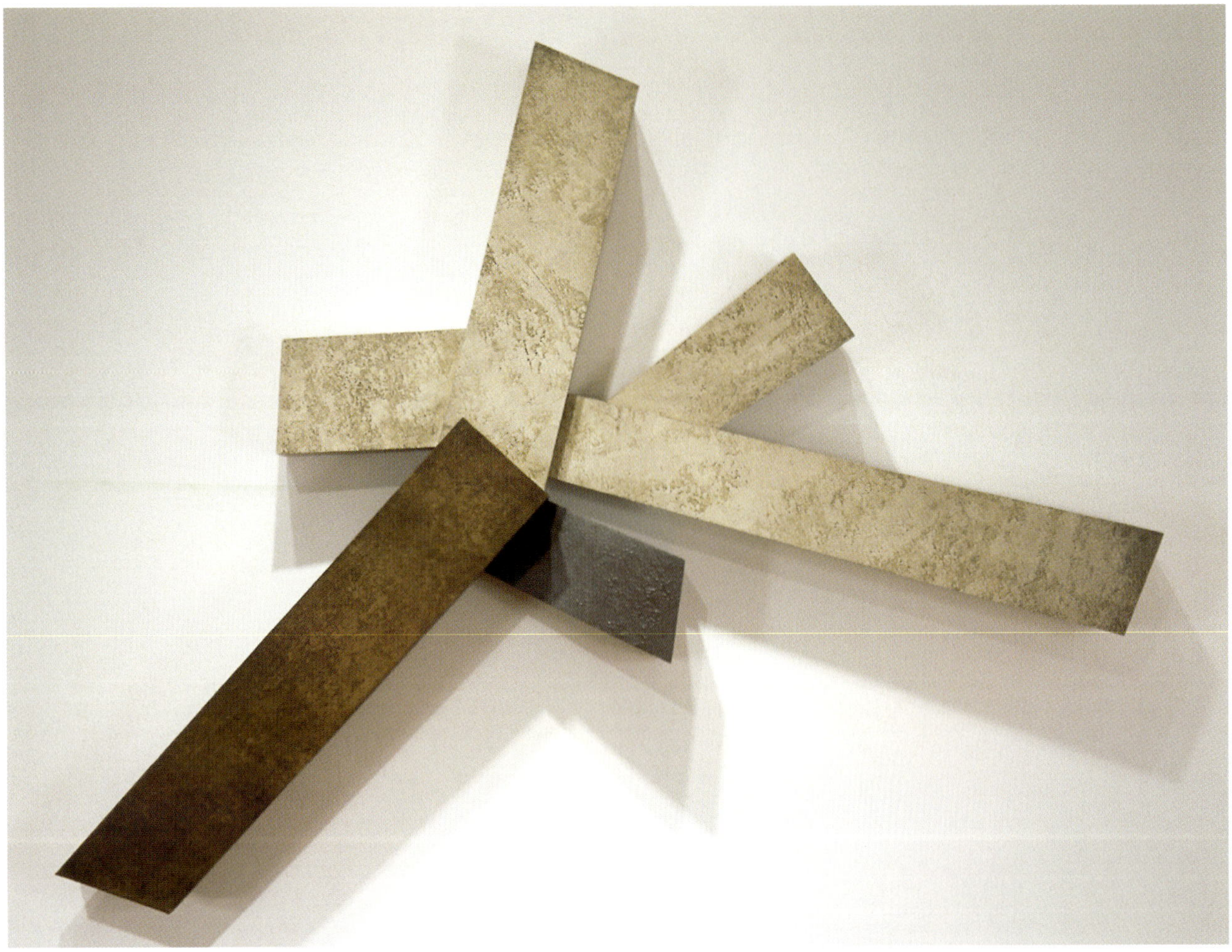

LONE STAR
MYLAR ON WOOD
40 X 51 X 5.5 INCHES

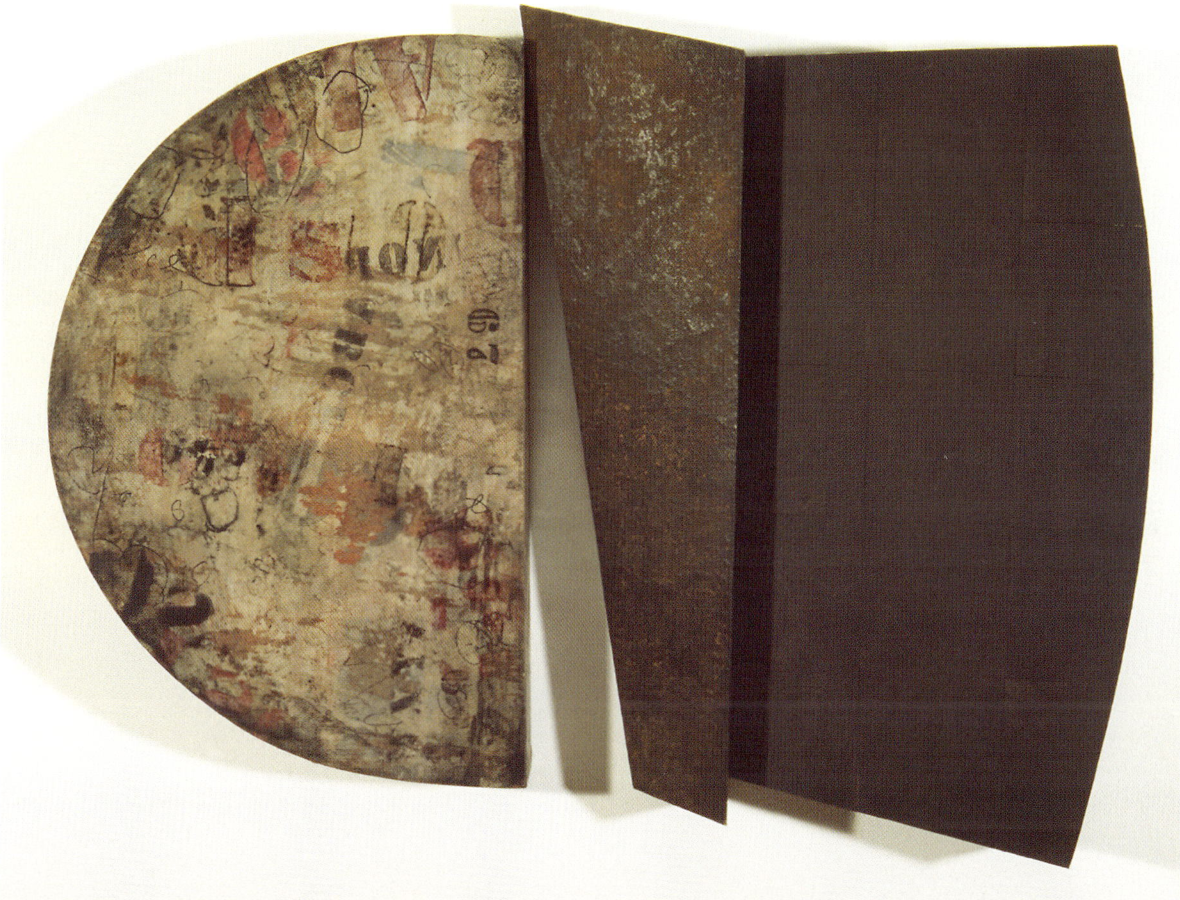

HALF ROUND WITH SIENNA
MIXED MEDIA
21.5 X 25.75 X 5 INCHES

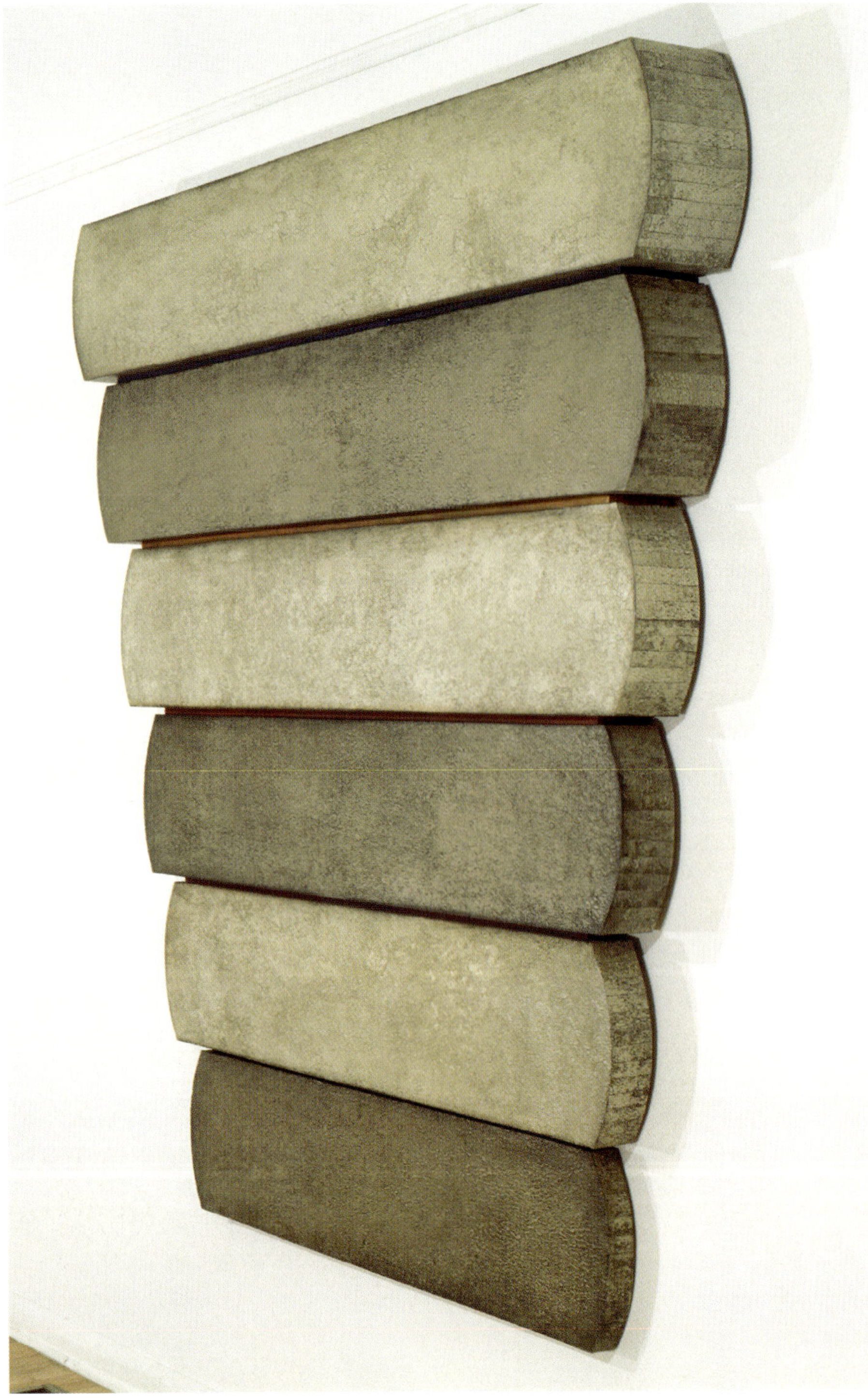

PYRAMID
MIXED MEDIA ON WOOD
76.5 X 72 X 7 INCHES

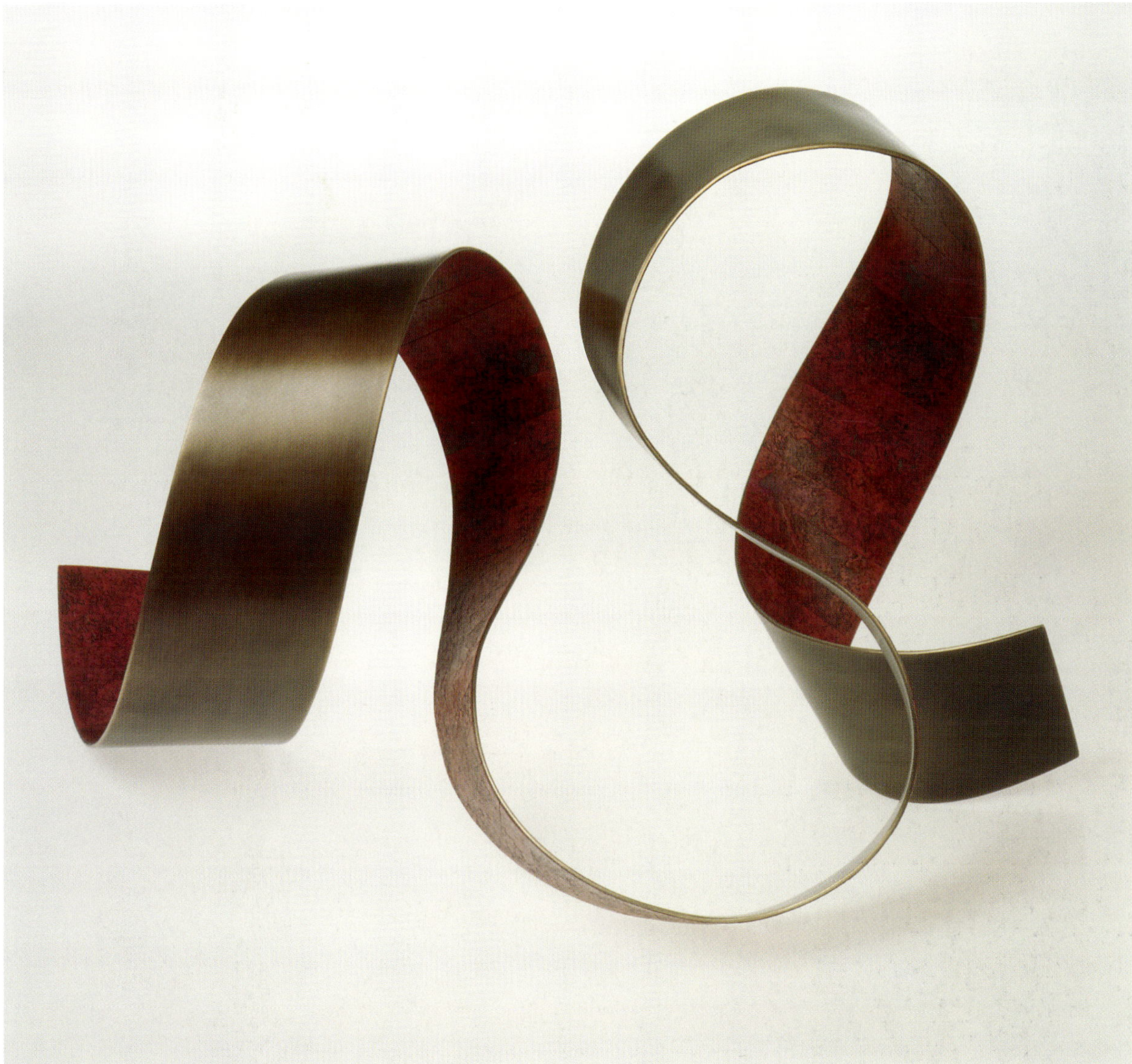

SALLY ANDERSON b. Rockford IL. *Ed:* BA in Art, Beloit College, Beloit WI; Instituto de Allende, San Miguel de Allende, Mexico; Univ. Wisconsin. *Invitational Exhibits:* Beloit College Art Museum WI; Phoenix Art Museum; El Paso Museum; Carnegie Institute Museum PA; Albuquerque Museum, Museum of Fine Arts, Santa Fe; International Folk Art Museum, Santa Fe; Tucson Museum of Art; New Mexico Artist Series, *Abstract Art*. Solo Exhibition: Roswell Art Museum NM. *Awards:* Two National Endowment for the Arts grants. *Representation:* Anderson Contemporary Art, Santa Fe.

RIBBON
BRONZE WITH MYLAR OVERLAY
18 X 9 X 2.5 INCHES

MARY BETH BLISS AND PETER VANDERLAAN

First there was drawing on cave walls, and chipping away at stones. Then there were experiments with fire and how it effected minerals. The discovery that silica could be melted for glass is lost in a time when the only writing was that writ in the sand by the tracks of the ibis. Way before any of this, even before oral history, came music.

In my perspective, the abstract concept of setting color to sound, making paintings of musical colors and shapes, has never been realized as clearly and cleanly as in the Optical Laminate and Dichroic Glass of sculptor Mary Beth Bliss. One definition of music's naturalness might attribute it to chance interacting with structure, or a series of perspectives varying across terrains of refrain. The main thing about music is that it happens, when it happens, in the here and now.

This is the experience when you're in the mix with a Mary Beth Bliss composition: As you move in relation to a large block of invisibly laminated optical glass (set to different refractive levels, the sharp edges beveled) a wild wealth of intricately patterned colors dance like fractals set in time to the random arrangements of your bi-optic eye-mind interface, circling the three-dimensional, then glimpsing a fourth, a fifth, a sixth... Bliss' sensibility is delicately attuned to the clear sound of what absolute beauty looks like.

Her husband Peter VanderLaan creates colorful curvaceous sculptures that are equally revelatory. Both VanderLaan and Bliss have been part of a vibrant Santa Fe glass scene since 1969, and their work still contains the best parts of psychedelia. Glass legend Dale Chihuly blew glass and tipped it molten into the snow in the seventies at their first Canyon Road studio, *Glory Hole Glassworks*. Its recent reincarnation, on the same legendary street, is an elegant exhibition space for a revolving compendium of Studio Glass artists as well as a working glass furnace and studio, hearkening back to when Canyon Road was basically all working artists.

Peter VanderLaan's sculptures are about making the unseen palpable. The urge to reach out and touch the negative spaces of his brilliantly hued forms is irresistible. Telling the difference between glass and not glass in the sublime spiral pockets of his blown works, shaved in places to micron thin edges with a mirror beveling tool, isn't easy. It is a great, strange sensation to see the invisible so clearly that you want to touch it.

The best thing would be to have a piece by either or both artists, appealing to all your senses from a place on your desk or coffee table where you and your family and friends could watch the colors change in all directions, like poetry in motion, while you listened to Mozart or some serious techno-funk.

Framed within the cutting-edge of an ancient technology, these glass and color crystals and rounds let you see into the future. I see Mary Beth Bliss and Peter VanderLaan changing the world with their brilliant light and color-transforming glass artworks.

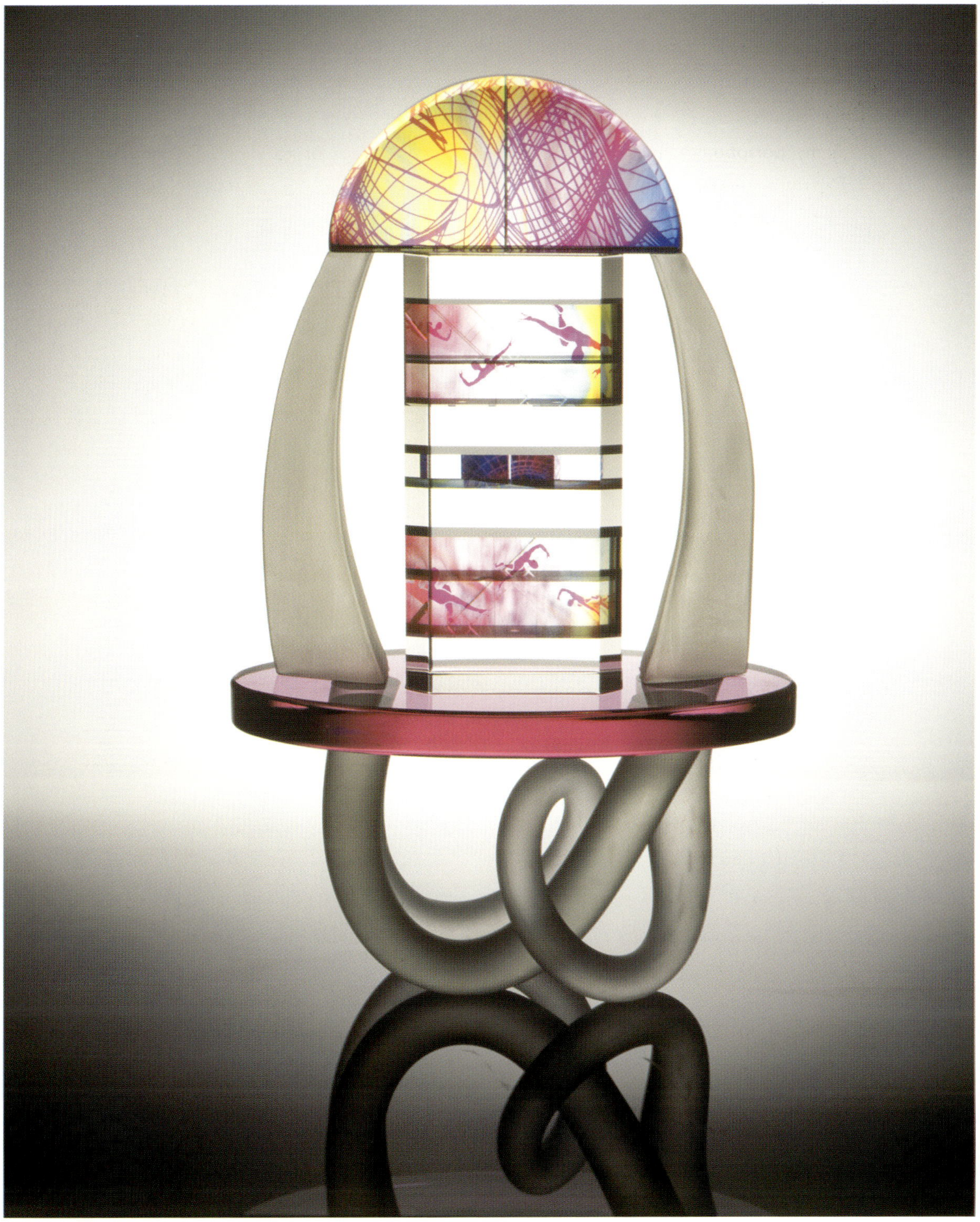

FALLING DREAMS #3, 2003
BLOWN, LAMINATED, ETCHED & CAST GLASS
16 X 8.5 X 31 INCHES

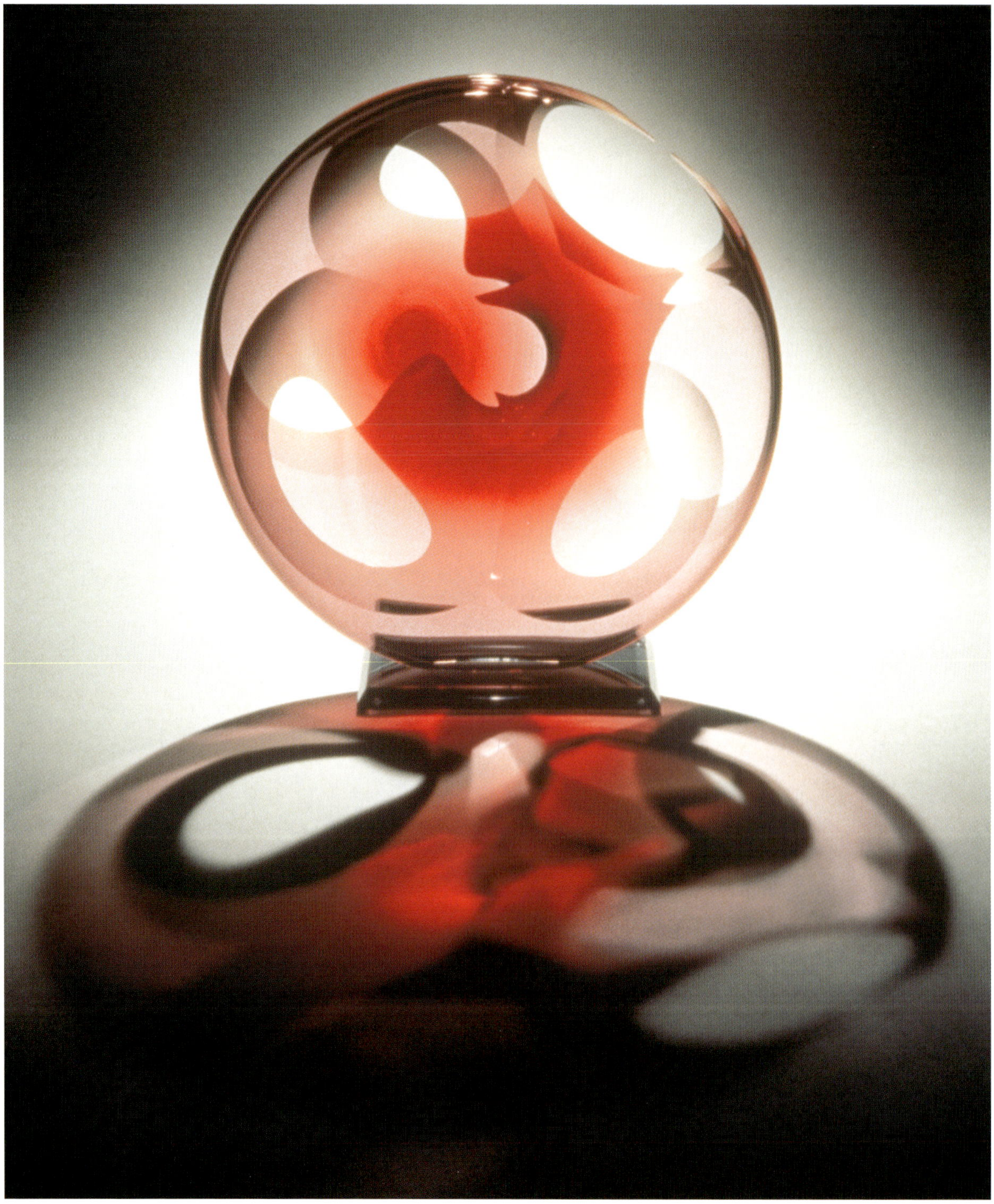

RED CUT FORM, 2003
BLOWN & BEVELED GLASS
13 X 13 X 3.5 INCHES

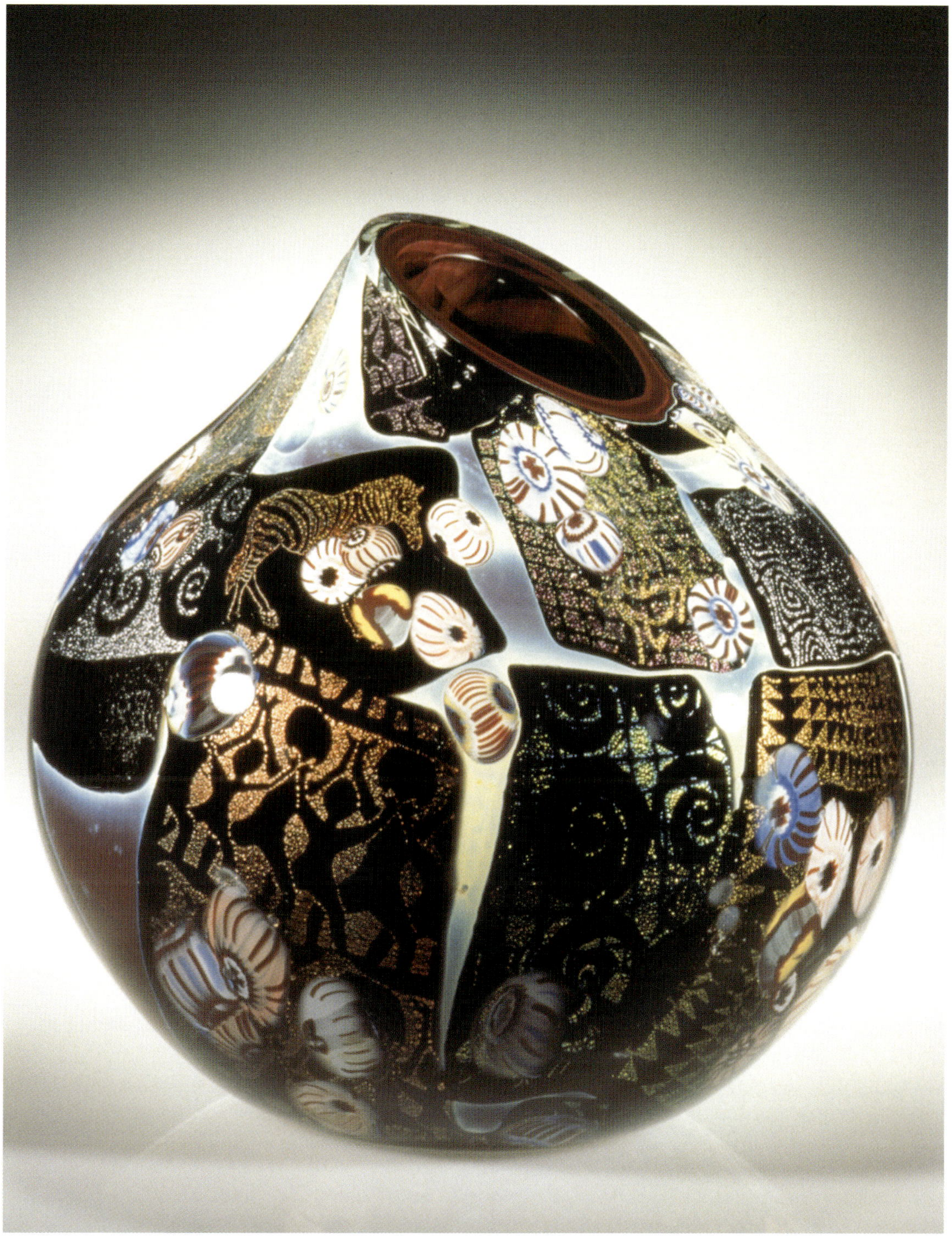

POT FORM, 2004
HANDBLOWN GLASS WITH ETCHED
DICHROIC ENTRAPMENTS
13 X 12 X 12 INCHES

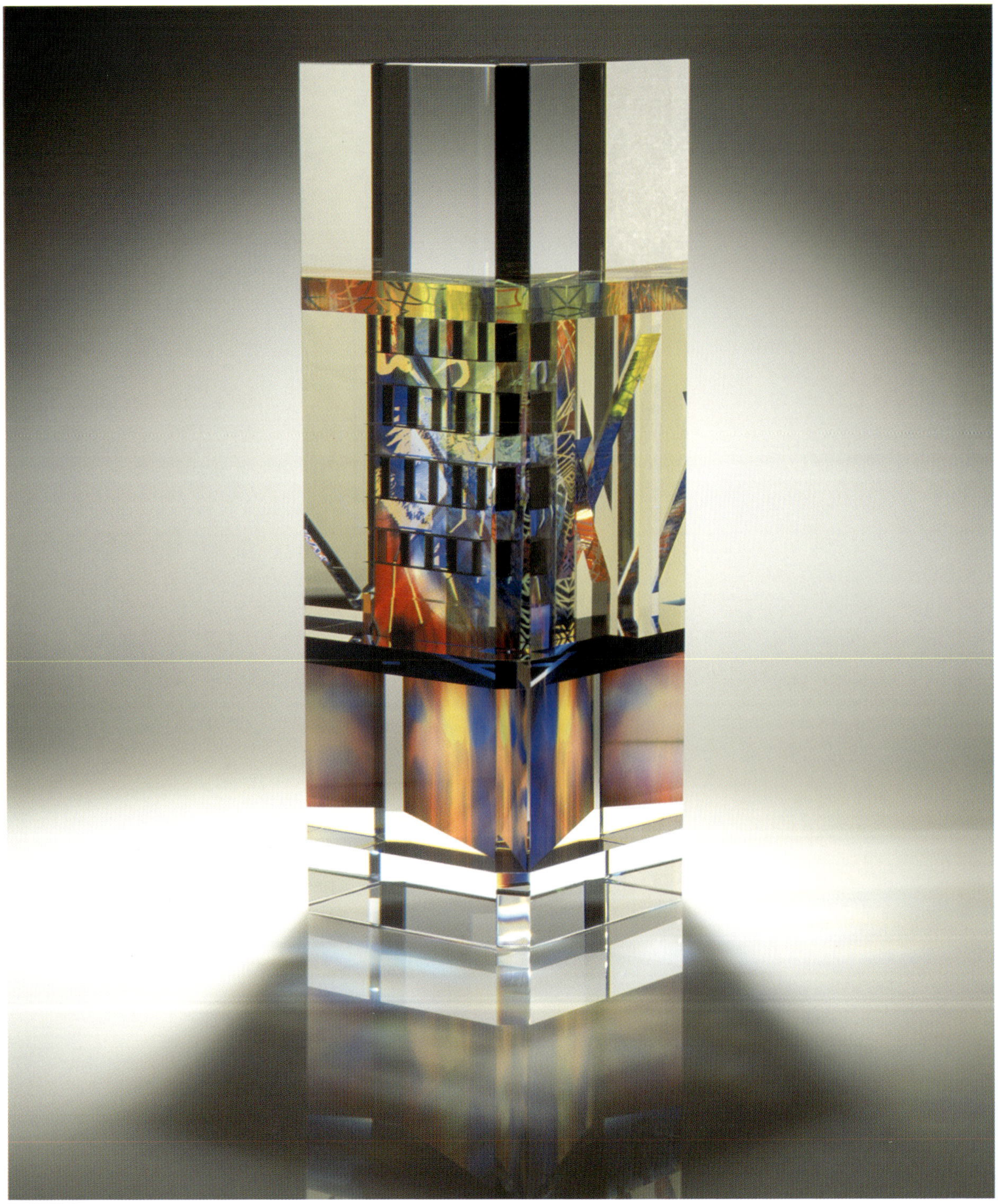

LA CIENEGA DREAMS, 2003
BEVELED GLASS, LAMINATED
WITH ETCHED INCLUSIONS
6 X 16 X 6 INCHES

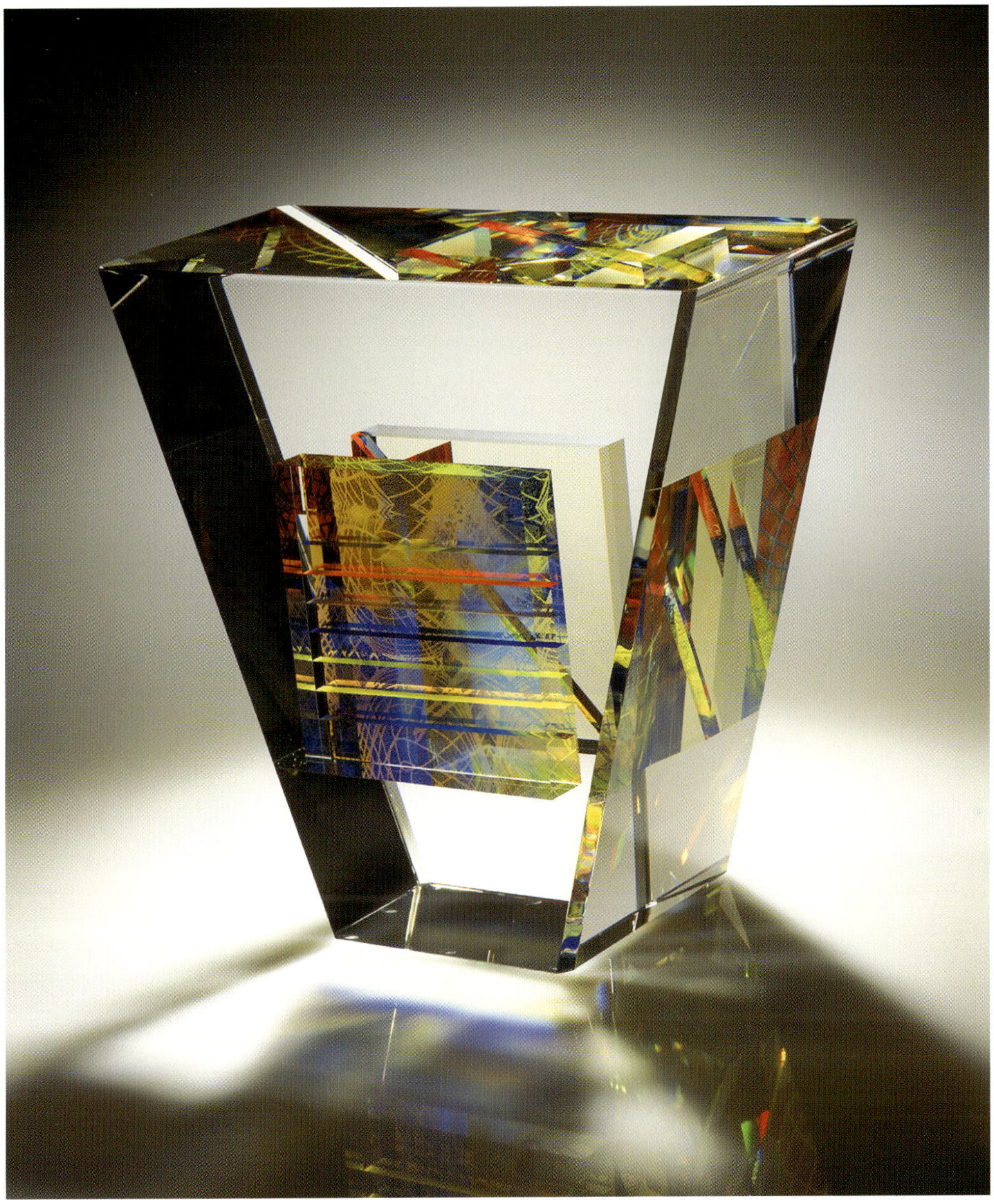

MARY BETH BLISS b. 1952 Tucson AZ. *Ed:* BA St. John's College, Santa Fe. *Coll:* Merck Sharpe & Dohme, Cointreau, Neiman Marcus. *Representation:* Glory Hole Glassworks, Santa Fe.

PETER VANDERLAAN b. 1950 Boston MA. *Ed:* St. John's College, Santa Fe. *Coll:* Albuquerque Museum, Greenville County Museum of Art, Greenville SC. *Representation:* Glory Hole Glassworks, Santa Fe.

LA CIENEGA DAYBREAK, 2003
BEVELED & LAMINATED GLASS
13.5 X 14 X 6.5 INCHES

SUSAN MARGIN

The outside holds the inside in. The inside holds the outside out. What is between the inside and the outside? What is beyond them? Of all the dualities the human mind makes of the seamless oneness of the world, perhaps the most profound, most continually implicit, is the notion of inside and out.

Your first big experience was coming into this outside called living from the inside of a woman's womb. The only thing comparable to that (that you can count on) will be that rarest of days when you go outside yet again, from this inside of being alive; the day your old outside is mixed back into the mud.

Susan Margin makes large ceramic vessels that—inside and out—defy time and confound duality. The work exhibits a meticulous attention to detail and a sense of the expanded moment that was all but lost with the arts of the ancients. She engages in an intense working process. Time falls away in an infinite search for perfection through intricately woven clay surfaces. For Margin, weaving is a metaphor for the fragile, tenuous, connections between living things. Each vessel is a sacred space, sheltering and sustaining the web of life.

What aligns these anti-temporal objects with post-modernism is fourfold. One is the sheer perversity of painstakingly immortalizing in clay, objects typically made of far more temporary materials, and two is when she lets these basket-forms slump like fragile eco-systems during firing. Three is her humble respect for the oneness of humanity found in the elevation of these a-historical constructs. And four is the fact that her archetypal forms exist as much in a viewer's internal image reservoir as they do in the external world of perception. One of the strangest things about experiencing her work is the initial misapprehension that you've seen and held these objects before. You haven't.

Her pieces are rubbed by hand with inks, dyes, and metallic pigments after firing, giving them the look of patinated bronze or hard darkened leather at first glance. Their outer surfaces invite tactile inspection, while gazing into their smooth depth defying interiors mirrors glimpses of unconscious collective substrata. Lightly ping one with your finger and it synesthetically rings with a tone in total harmonic accord with its visual beauty.

For millennia the reeds grew inside the earth and water, visited mainly by the ibis, like a yogi on one foot. Then one day the first people, worshiping the birds still, gathered the reeds and carefully wove them into usable nests; containing them in grids of order and function, giving them an inside and an out. Hominid, Susan Margin, creates paradoxical memorials to these long lost vessels, granting them new imaginary lives and simultaneously committing them—by the artist's hands and purifying fire—back to earth.

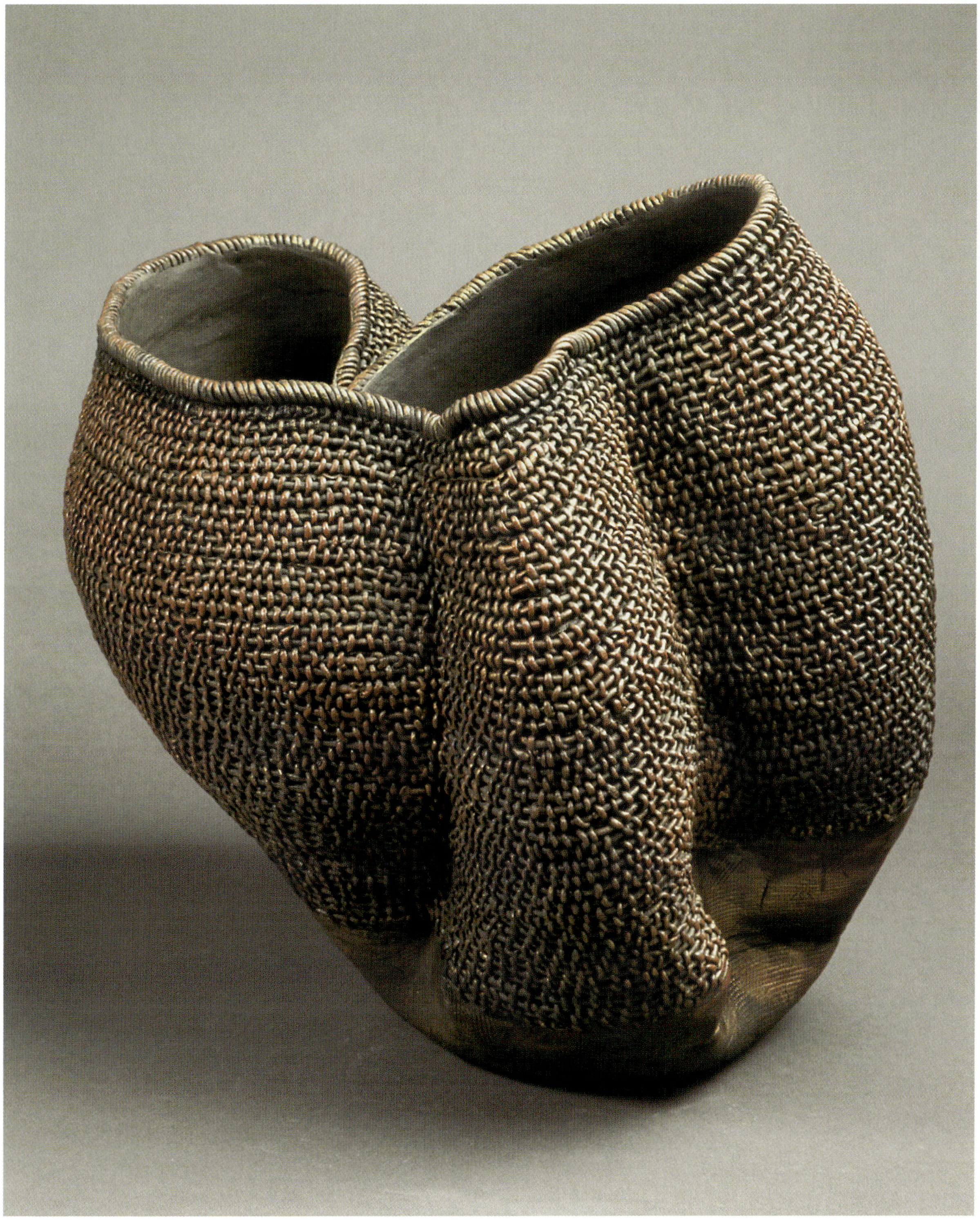

CONVERSATION 1, 2003
CERAMIC STONEWARE WITH METALLIC PATINA
WITH INKS & DYES
14 X 12 INCHES

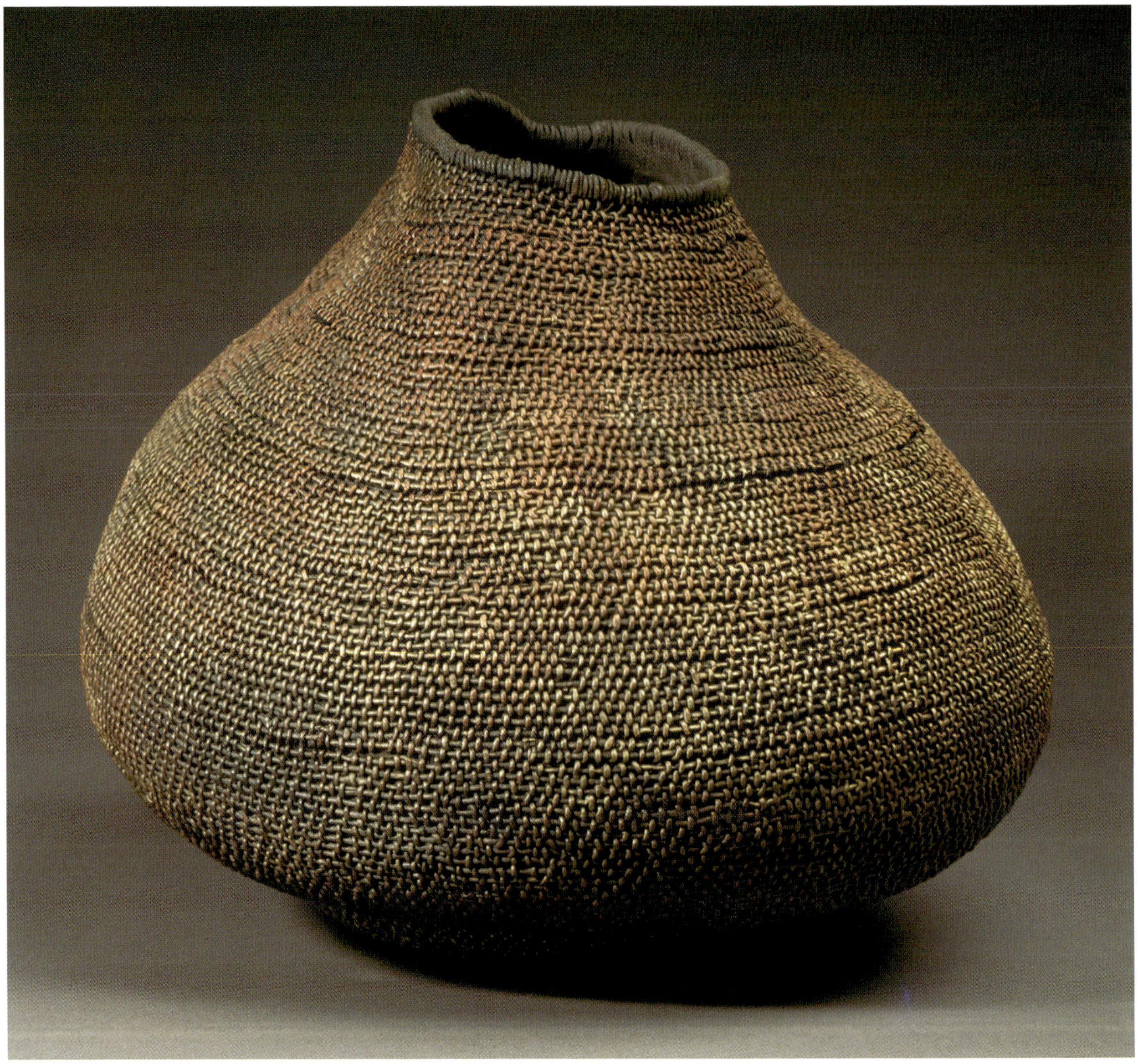

HABITAT 2, 2003
CERAMIC STONEWARE WITH METALLIC PATINA
WITH INKS & DYES
16 X 20 INCHES

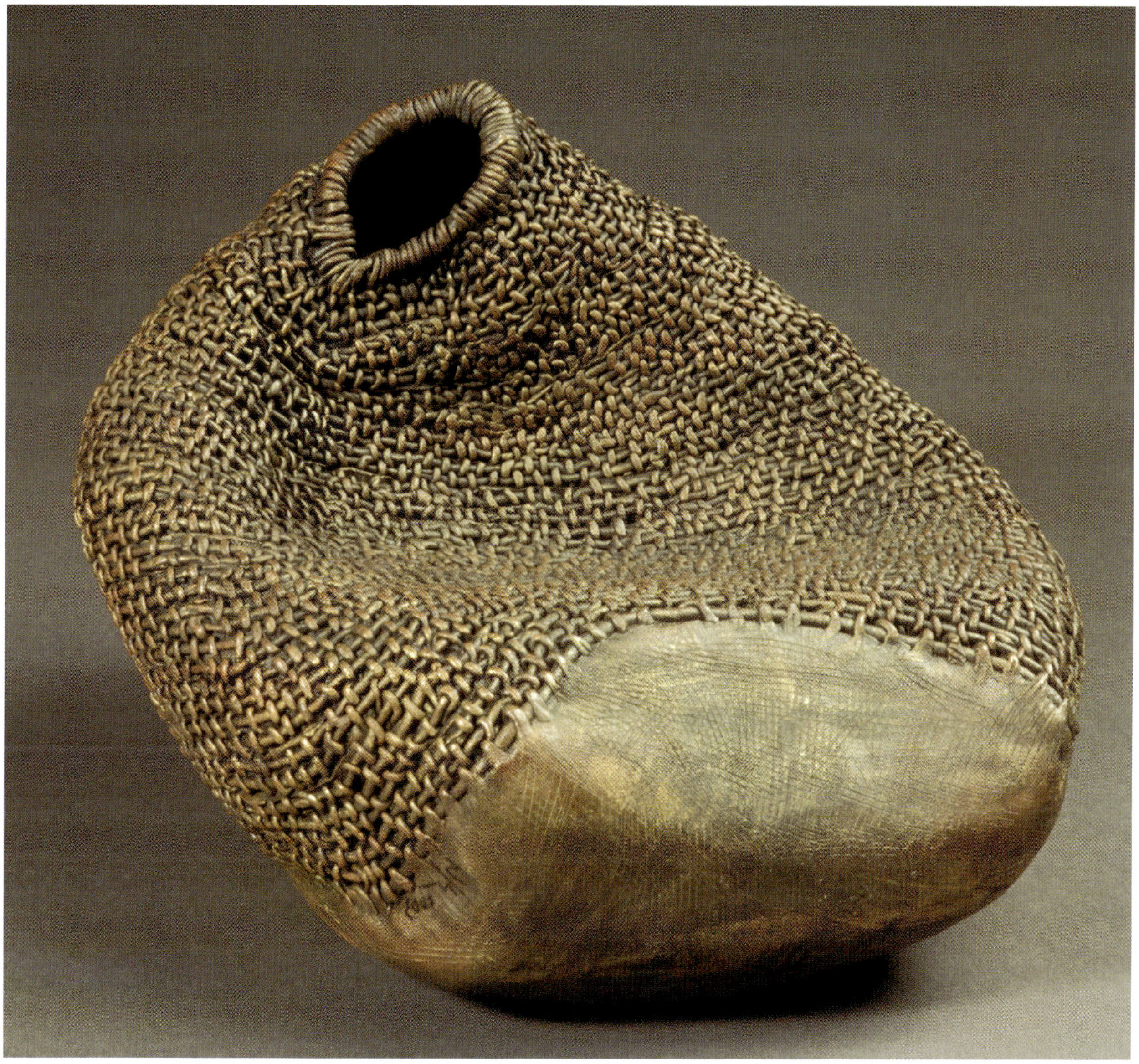

HABITAT ABANDONED, 2003
CERAMIC STONEWARE WITH METALLIC PATINA
WITH INKS & DYES
5 X 10 INCHES

SUSAN MARGIN

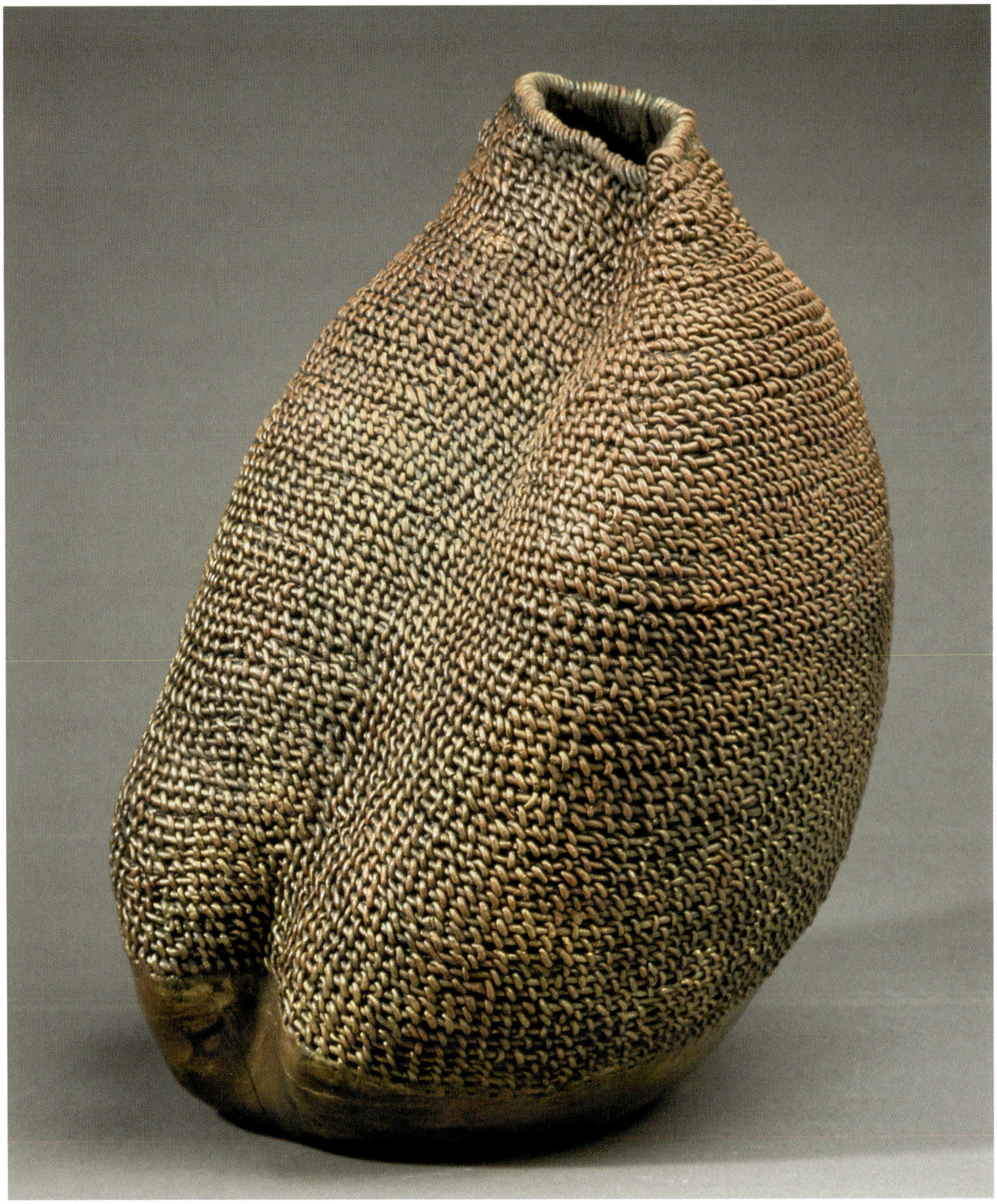

CONVERSATION 2, 2003
CERAMIC STONEWARE WITH METALLIC PATINA
WITH INKS & DYES
15.25 X 12 INCHES

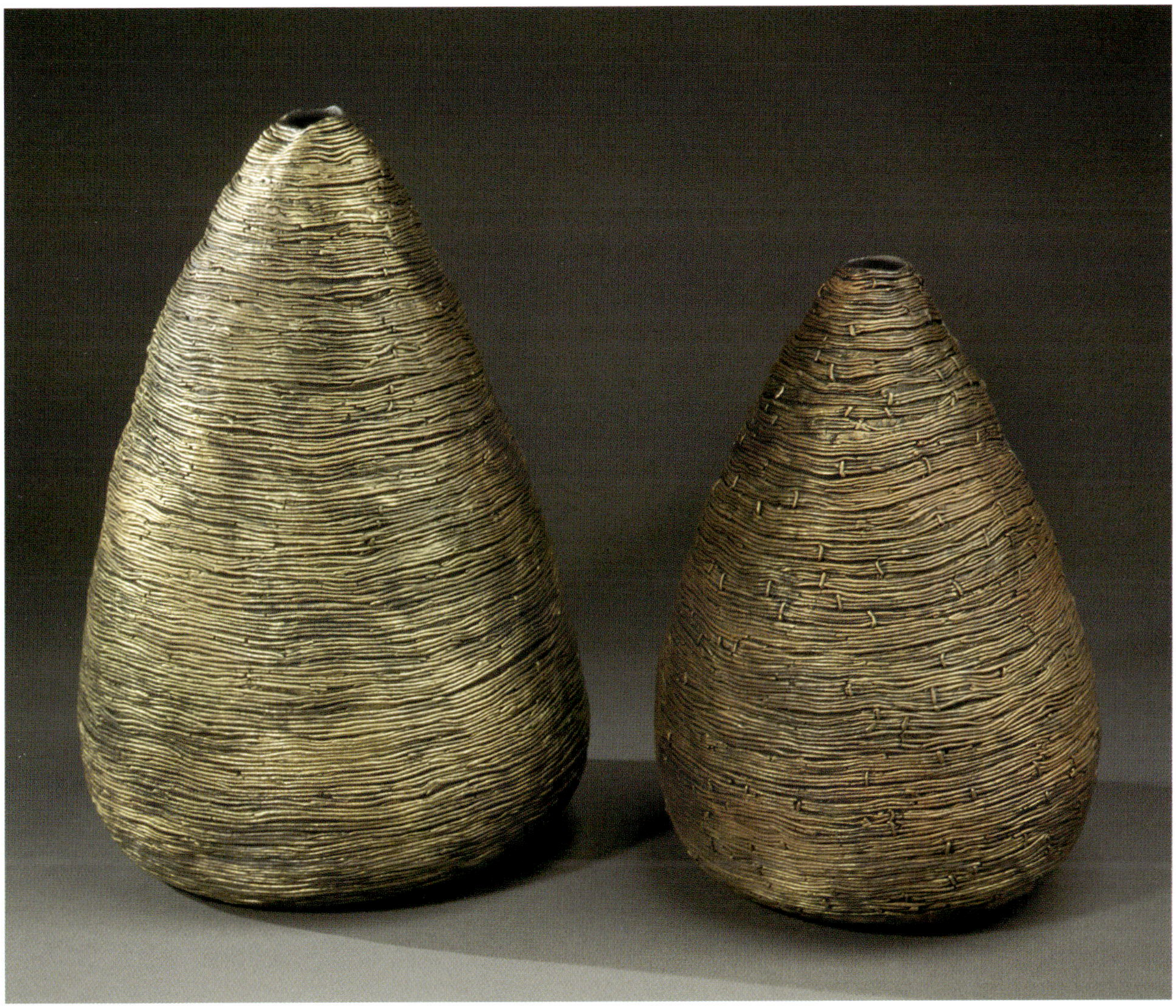

SUSAN MARGIN b.1943 New York NY. *Ed:* BA New York Univ., New York; Art Students League, New York; Boston Univ.; Long Island Univ., Greenvale NY; Paul Margin Workshop, Long Island NY. *Selected Exhib:* Friends of Contemporary Art annual group show, Santa Fe; American Women Artists, Santa Fe; Museum of Fine Art, "The Show," Santa Fe. *Awards:* American Women Arts, Award of Merit. *Representation:* The Meyer-Munson Gallery, Santa Fe; Andora Gallery, Carefree AZ.

LOVING COUPLE, 2003
CERAMIC STONEWARE WITH METALLIC PATINA
WITH INKS & DYES
10.875 X 7.5 INCHES

GEORGE ALEXANDER

Inspired by his boyhood experience of the lush vegetation of the Southern United States and his extensive European travels, unabashed Romantic, George Alexander, has applied his skilled hands to forming wondrous clay earth into a luminous pageant of fantastic flora and fauna. Although his influences vary from Flemish tapestries, to French and Spanish *Majolica*, the Italian *Capadimonte* especially inspires his passion.

His flowers are vehicles of discovery and expansion upon the nature of clay's possibilities; they are three-dimensional canvasses through which he can explore form, color and texture. He belongs to an extremely small group of artists worldwide who have the technical skill and vision to produce such rich complex color and form.

The cult of nature roots in the soil of prehistory, and flowers in fabulous expression throughout epochs and today as during the first recorded days. George Alexander's work is a post-modern *pastiche* of riotous garden and early civilization that bespeaks an intense human-natural harmonic as well as a tendency towards time travel. The blue glaze and architectonic forms he uses in *Poppies and Doves*, recall the *Ishtar Gate* of ancient Babylon, circa 575 BC. *Audrey's Cousins*, the utterly fantastic red poppy fount sprays like Pompeii in her heyday, and brings to mind India at the time of the Vedas. These giant water poppies are sirens luring sustenance. *Dancing Corn* is an upside down Tempietto, a joyous dance of abandon celebrating a promised future. Bejeweled by golden drops of dew, the spirits of the blue corn hold husks and circle dance along the rim of bowl, like caryatids in a nourishing architecture that from the time of the ancestors has sustained.

George Alexander's ceramics have the delicacy and absorbed attention to fine detail that is so oft admired in the artistry of antiquity. He shares also their sincere celebration of the abundance of life. His creativity is cornucopial! His flowers spill out beyond the bounds of their architectural frames and vessels, or sit simply expanding in scale as if the gallery wall had decided to pop open and bloom. A deliberate wit and tongue in cheek sense of humor infuse the artist's work.

Inspired by the splendid profusion of nature, yet eschewing botanical accuracy, the images of George Alexander's remarkable art are fantastical. They are removed from the everyday real world, allowing curious examination and exploration, even as he references nature's cycle. As all things come to a full "flowering" they begin to deteriorate and decay, to produce the nutrients for future growth and fulfillment. His individual pieces explore this in different ways, but their timeless beauty and delicate strength spring from one source. What they all have in common is George Alexander's fearless grasp of life affirming exuberance.

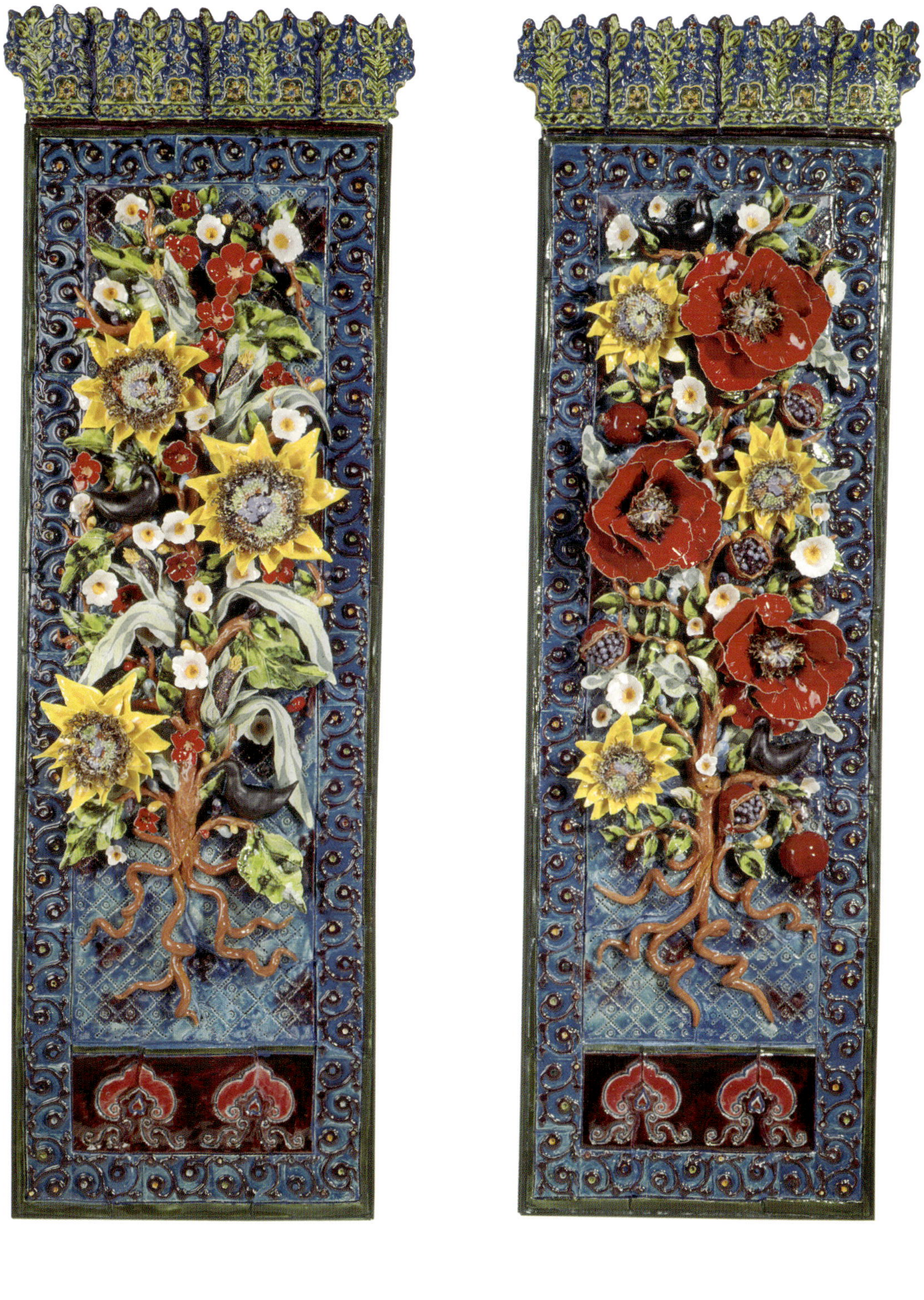

TAPESTRY SERIES
SUNFLOWERS, POPPIES & DOVES
CERAMIC
60 X 20 X 6 INCHES

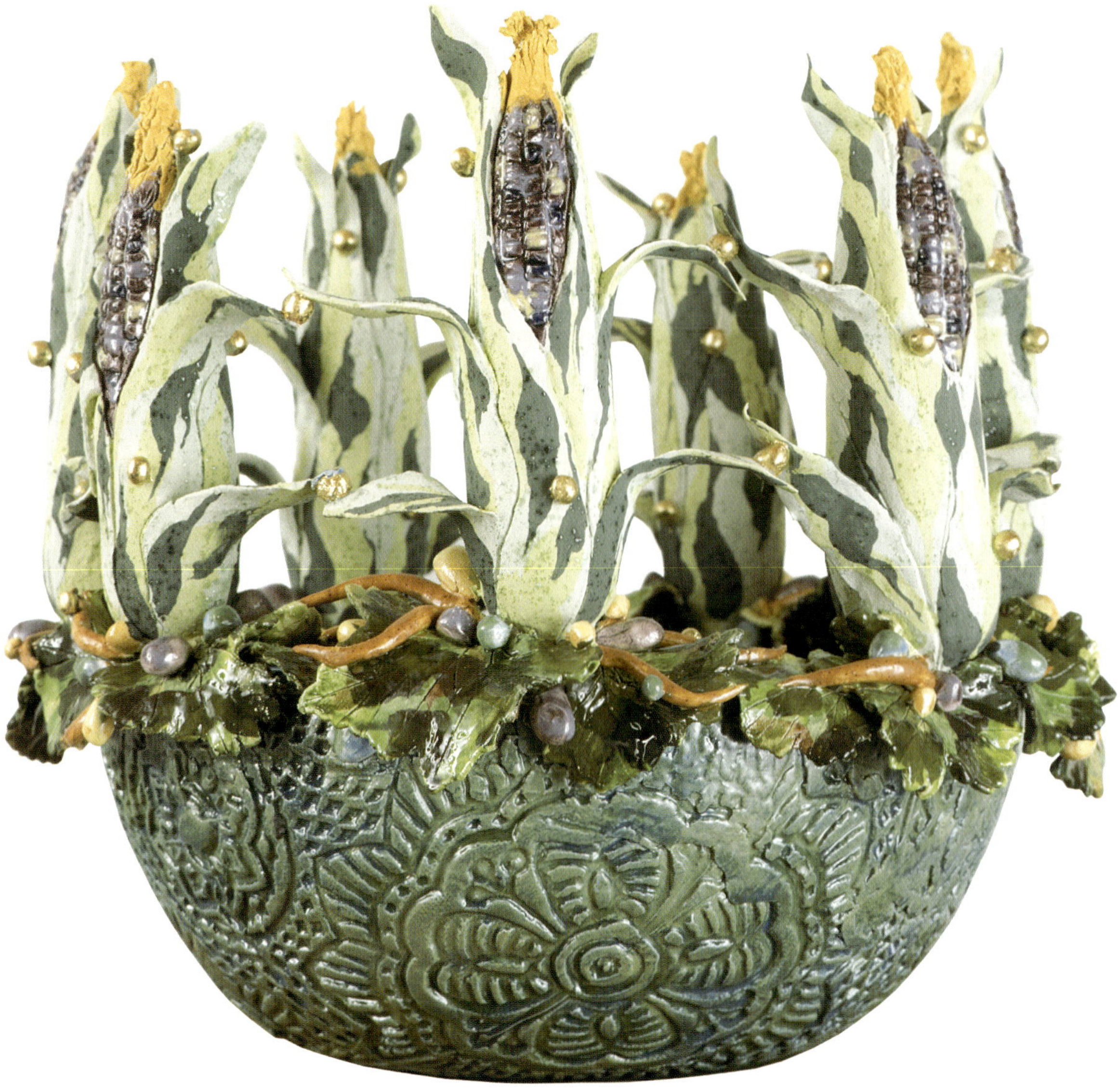

DANCING CORN
CERAMIC
14(D) X 15 INCHES

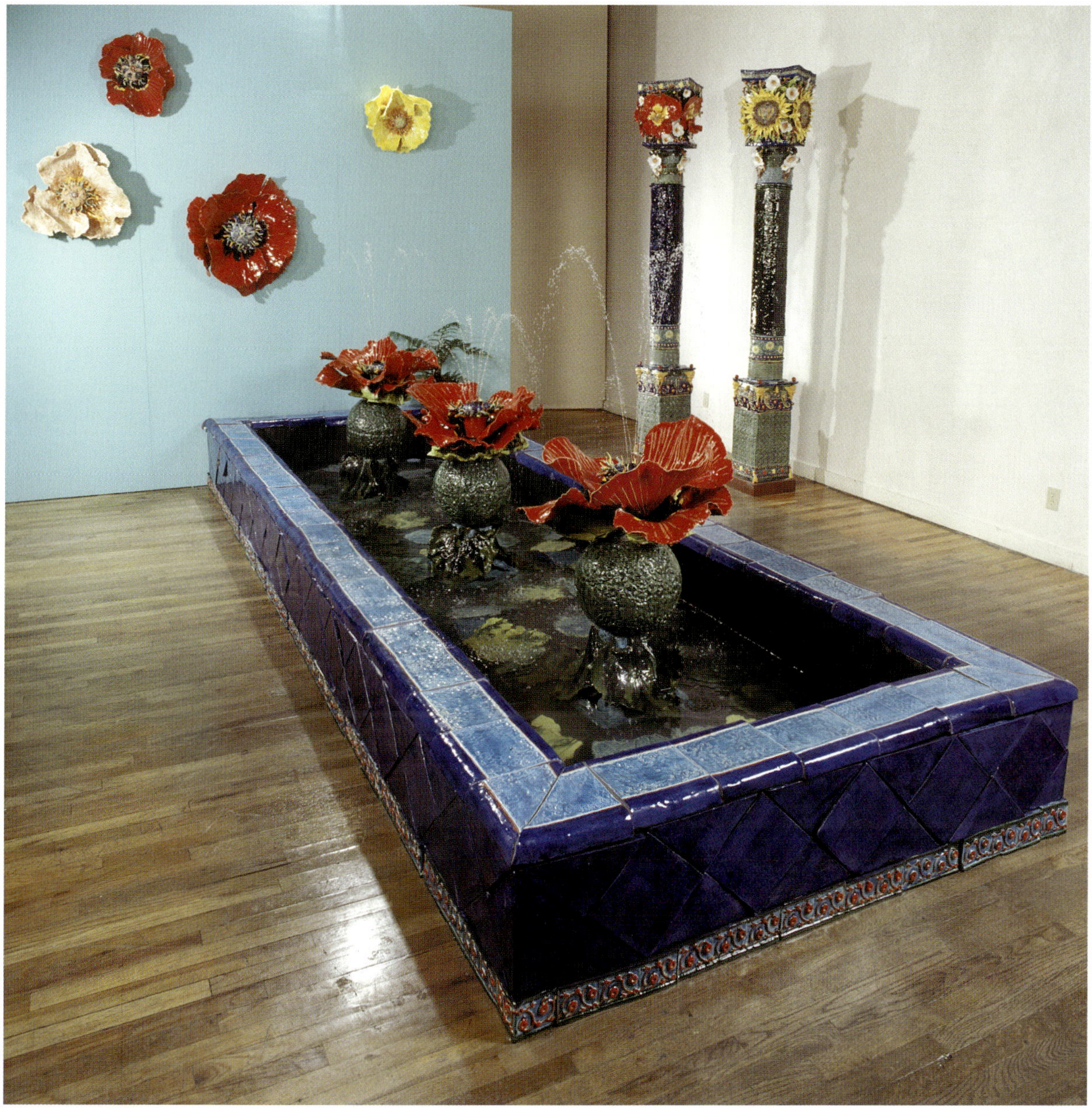

FANTASTIC GARDEN SERIES INSTALLATION

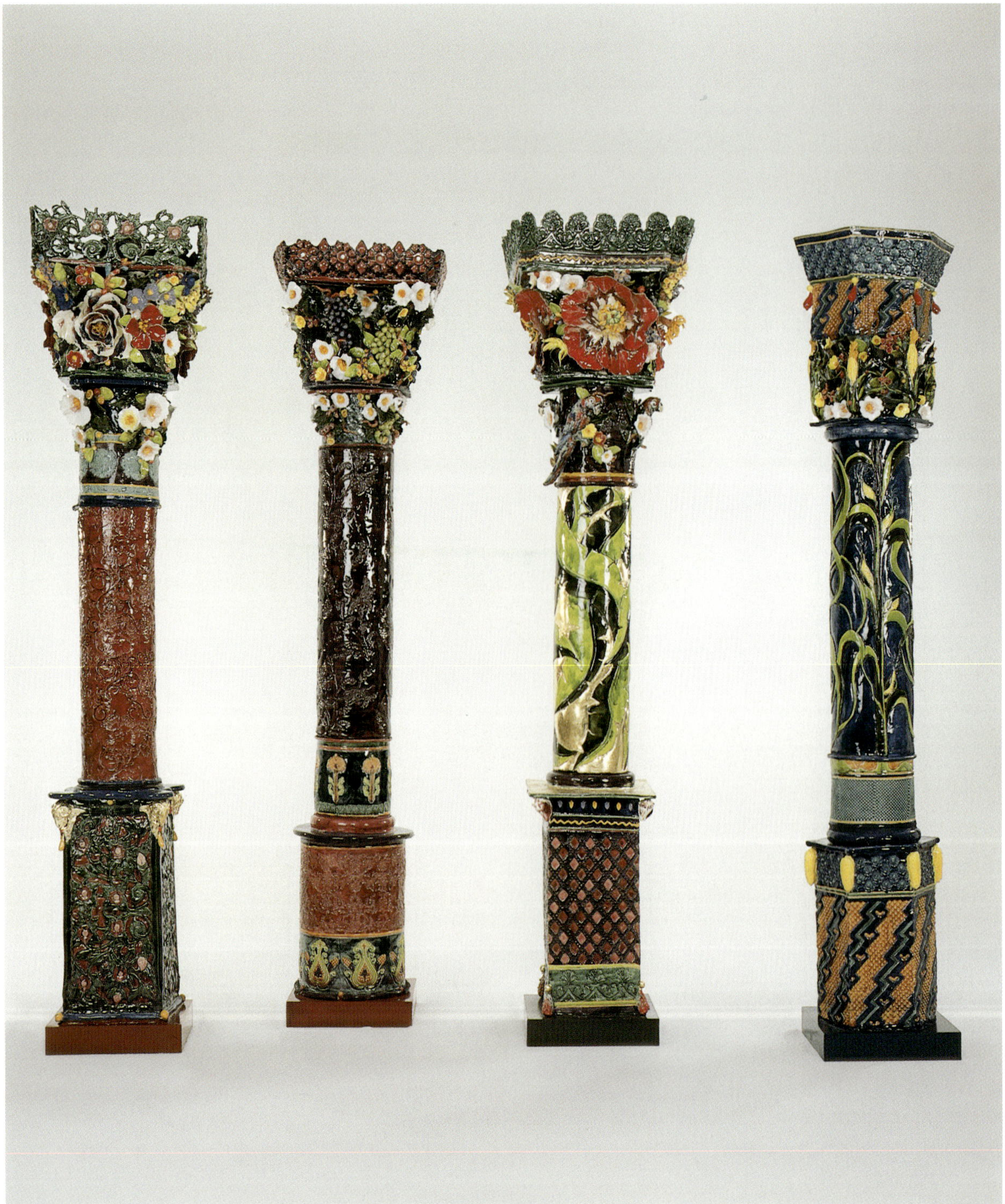

FANTASTIC GARDEN SERIES
COLUMNS
CERAMIC
96 X 16 X 16 INCHES

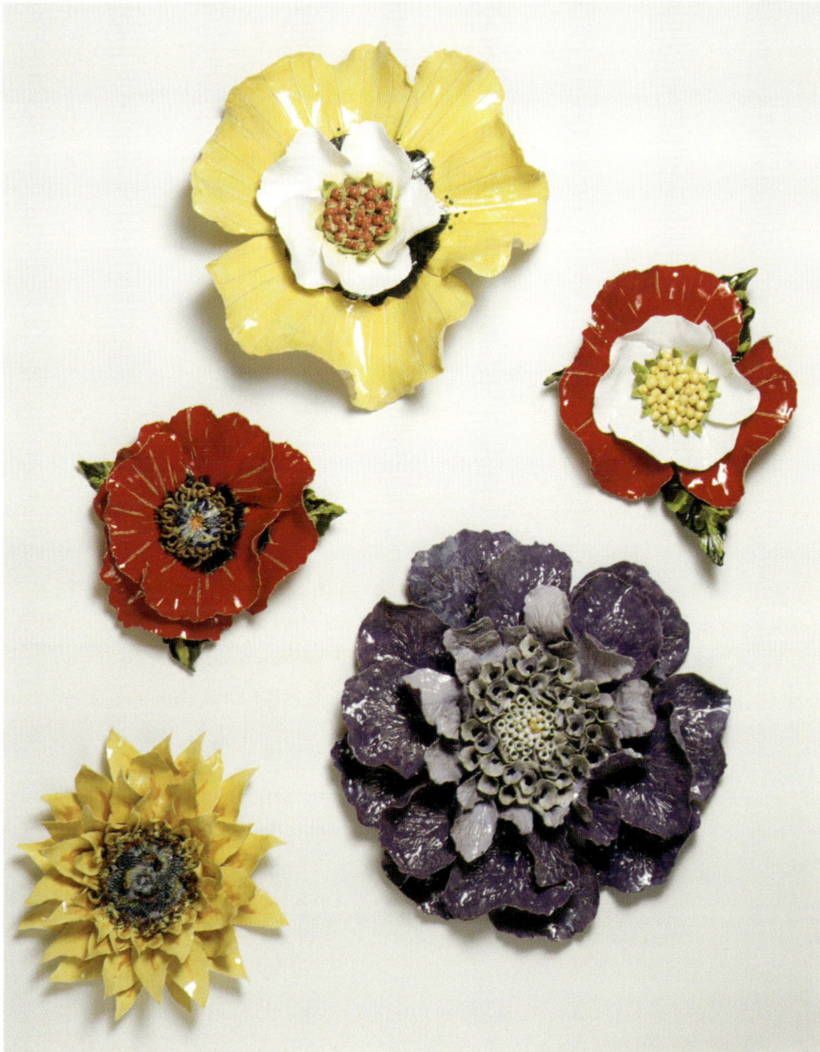

GEORGE ALEXANDER b. 1940 *Ed.* BFA and MFA Univ. Mississippi, Oxford; Univ. San Francisco Foreign Study Program: Estudio General Luliano, Palma de Mallorca, Spain. *Coll:* Mr. and Mrs. Max Baril, Beverly Hills; Mr. and Mrs. Steve Wynn, Las Vegas; Mr. Jim Caradine, New York; Mr. and Mrs. Jeffery Cole, Hunting Valley OH; Mr. Edgar Daniels, Santa Fe; Mr. and Mrs. Reginald Haines, Winston-Salem; Mr. and Mrs. Kerry Hoggard, Auckland, New Zealand; Mr. and Mrs. John Hushon DC; Milliken & Company, La Grange GA; Mr. and Mrs. David Salmon, Santa Fe; Mr. Udal Tettenborn, Oestrich- Winkel, Germany; The Semler Foundation, Portland; Tavern on The Green, New York; The Alladin Hotel, Las Vegas; The Healing Center, Phoenix; The Valley Hospital NJ. *Representation:* Handsel Gallery, Hudson NY.

FANTASTIC GARDEN SERIES
WALL FLOWERS
CERAMIC
18-30 X 7 INCHES

JACK SLENTZ

The strange, raw sculptures of Jack Slentz exist beyond the arbitrary stoppage of words. Inspired by the quotidian and domestic, (as is most speech) they achieve a simple state of metaphorical, even moral ambiguity tantamount to that of language.

3 Into 1, 1 Into 3—in red oak and rubber, recalls Richard Tuttle in it's questioning of form and surface on the seemingly simplest of levels, but then branches (actually and metaphorically) in at least six or eight directions. As the title makes clear, the piece poses issues of enumeration. How does the one become two, and the two become three? And how does the three go back into the one? This is the duct and plumbing aspect of language. Verbal, visual, mathematic; they are all one in this way. There is a point in every linguistic construct where authoritarian *logos* is subvertible, where stoppages may be removed or reconfigured, where appendages formed from other coding sources may be affixed, and generally, where the flow of understanding resumes.

3 Into 1, 1 Into 3 makes the simple suggestion of encasement enticing. Are these two versions of the same thing, in different materials, or is one the holder for the other? Issues of containment figure prominently in Jack Slentz's *art brut* approach to woodworking. His sometimes chainsaw-scarred shapes assert themselves in space while housing signature soot-blackened voids. A sculpture like *Distortion* expands externally into the white box of the gallery while, like a paradox, it also progresses inwardly with the light-swallowing gravity of a black hole. It exists as a connector (linguistically, a conjunction) between multiple spaces, as it simultaneously segments, maps, re-routes and distorts them. *Distortion* is a transgressive duality-devastating adapter providing contiguous continuity. If space is the medium through which sculpture speaks, Jack Slentz has plenty to say.

If these rough and ready pieces seem like the work of a man simply focused on getting his ideas into form, *Target* shows him equally capable of polish and polite society. This wall work is akin to painting of the iconic sort that occupied Jasper Johns early on. The piece can be read in any number of directions for any length of time, but it invariably results in an awkward asymmetry and gives the feeling that you need to keep reading, reading differently. *Target* invokes a visual text of triplicities over dichotomies, a disruption of duality, a generous return of responsibility to the reader/viewer.

Speaking of the returning of subjectivity to the individual subject—if Jack Slentz' *Family Portrait* has a moral, and all family tales do, it is this: we all carry resonating centers in contact at the unconscious core with the vast spaces of being in ways that are ours alone. Carved from such different woods, society (which begins at home) requests that we strive to contrive absurdly similar exteriors. Absurd because we are, in our onenesses, one to begin with—one family, animals included.

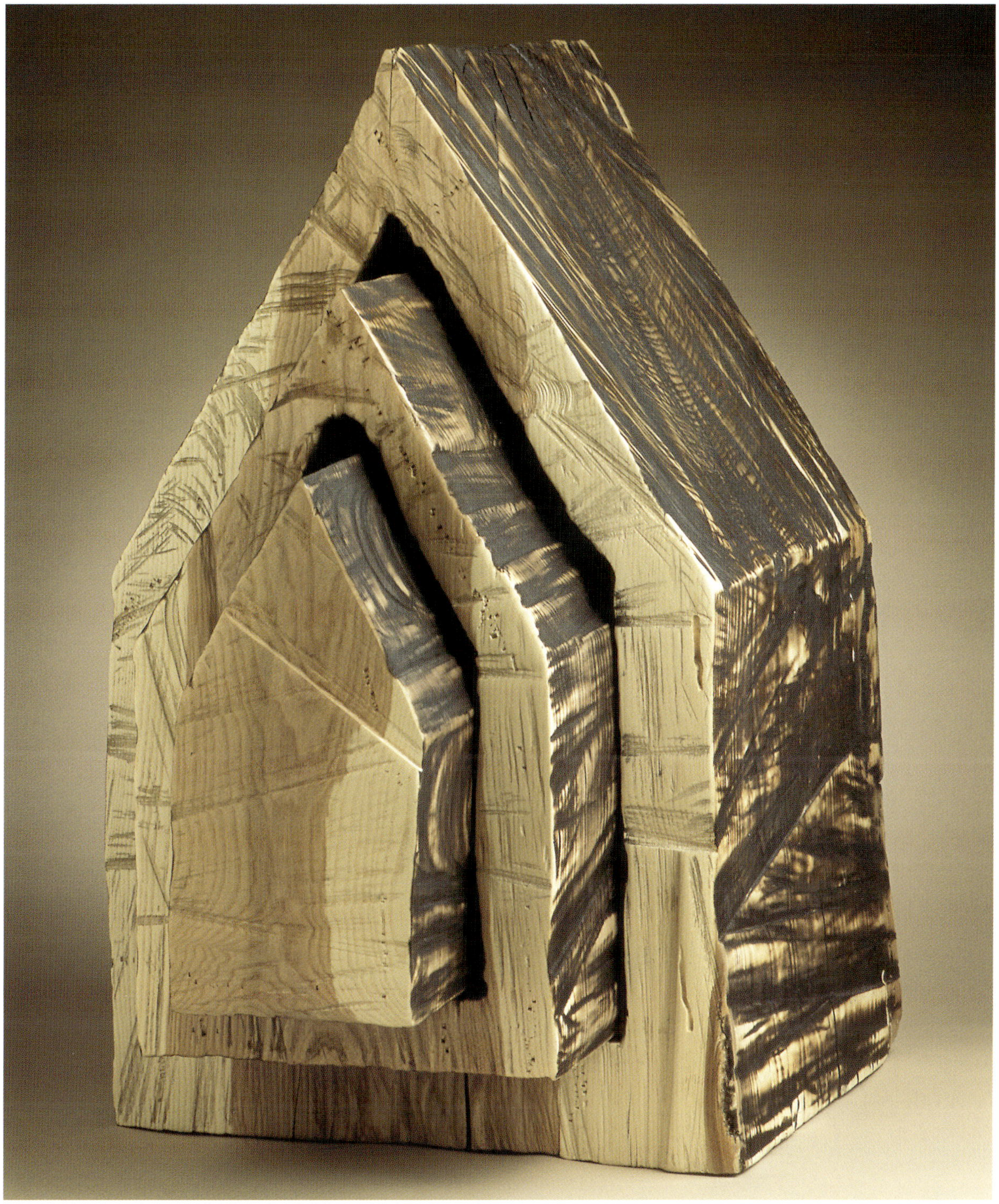

VENCINDARIO, 2004
ASH
26 X 16 X 21 INCHES

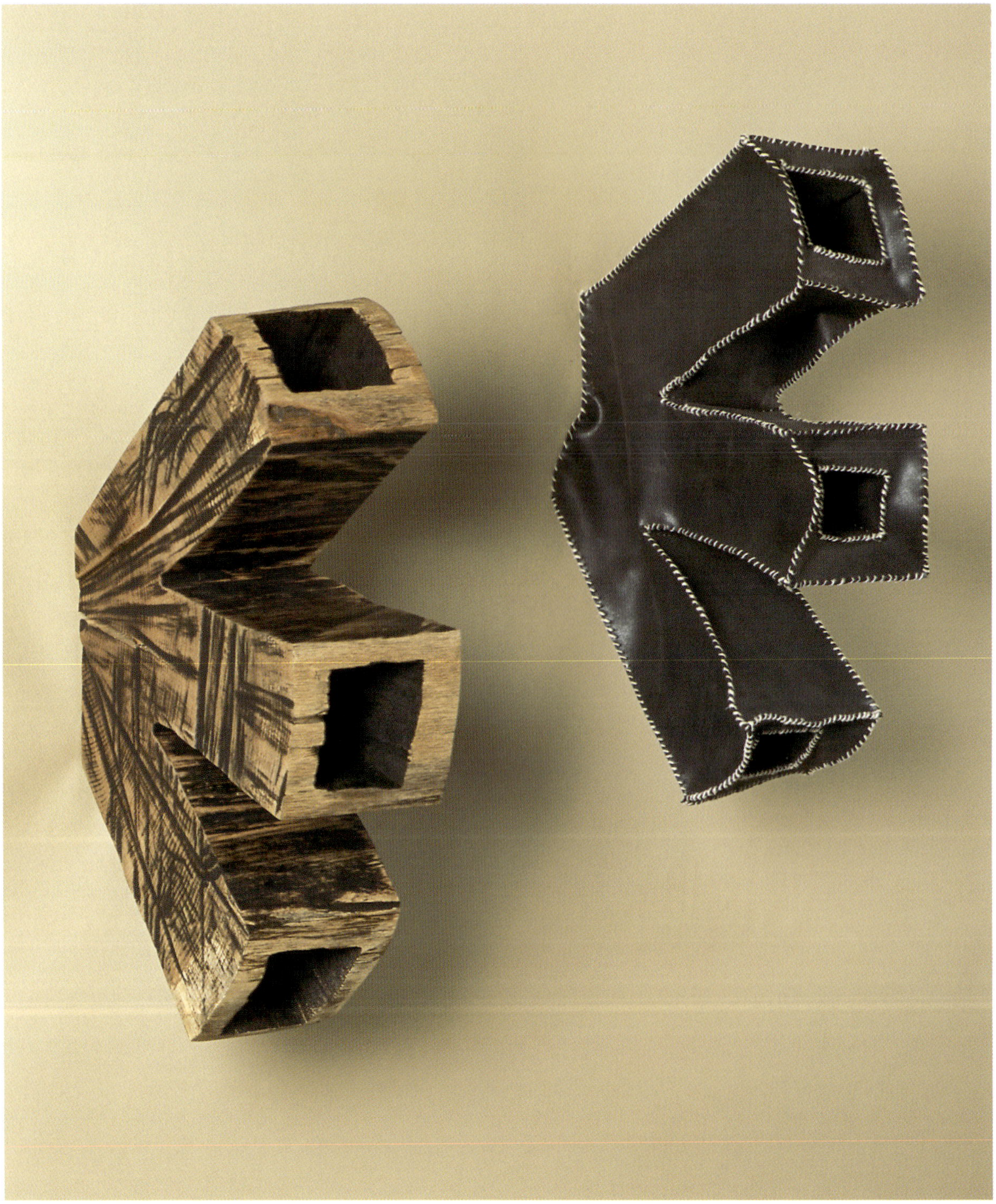

3 INTO 1, 1 INTO 3, 2003
RED OAK & RUBBER
33 X 31 X 14 INCHES

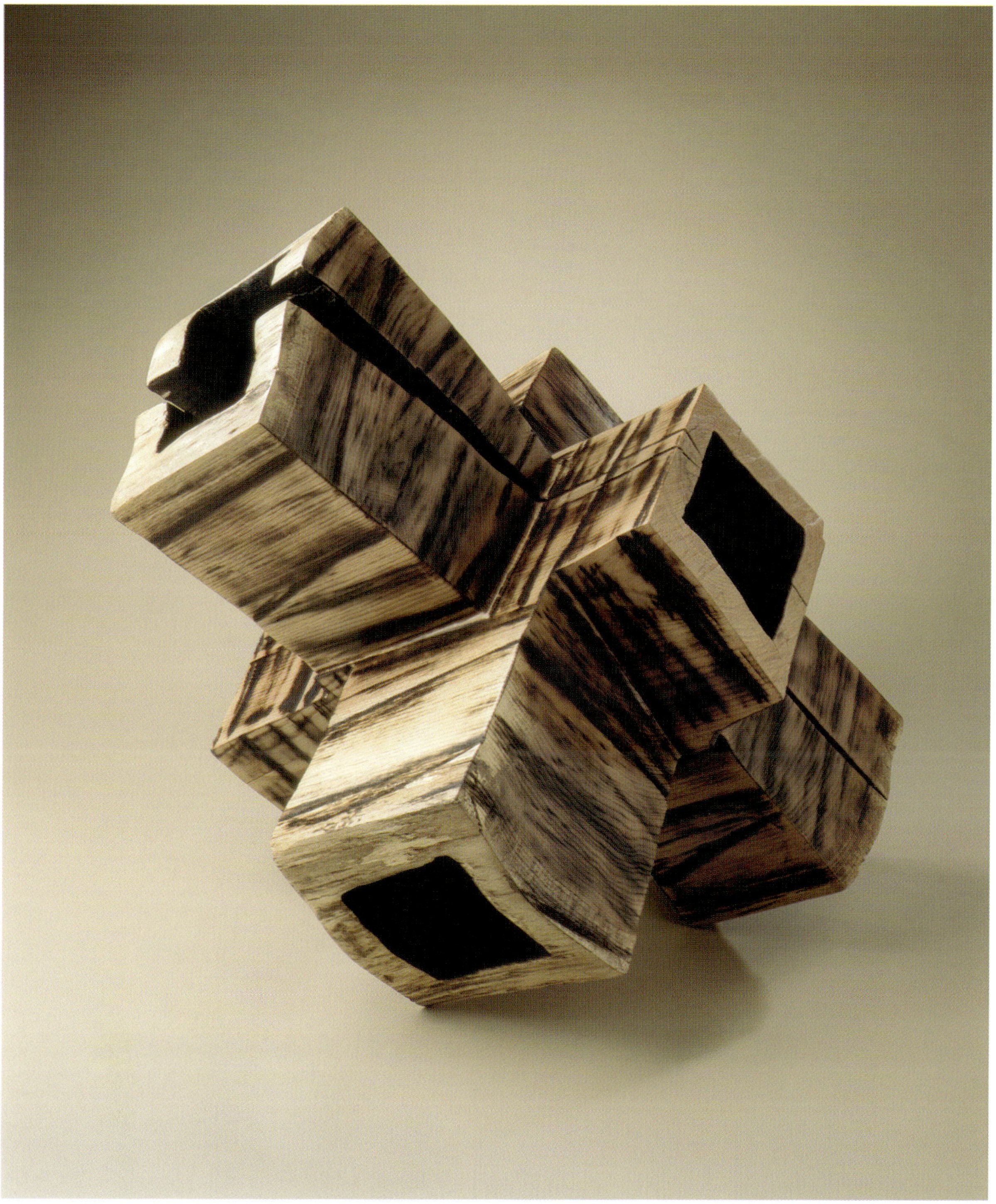

DISTORTION
RED OAK
27 X 36 X 33 INCHES

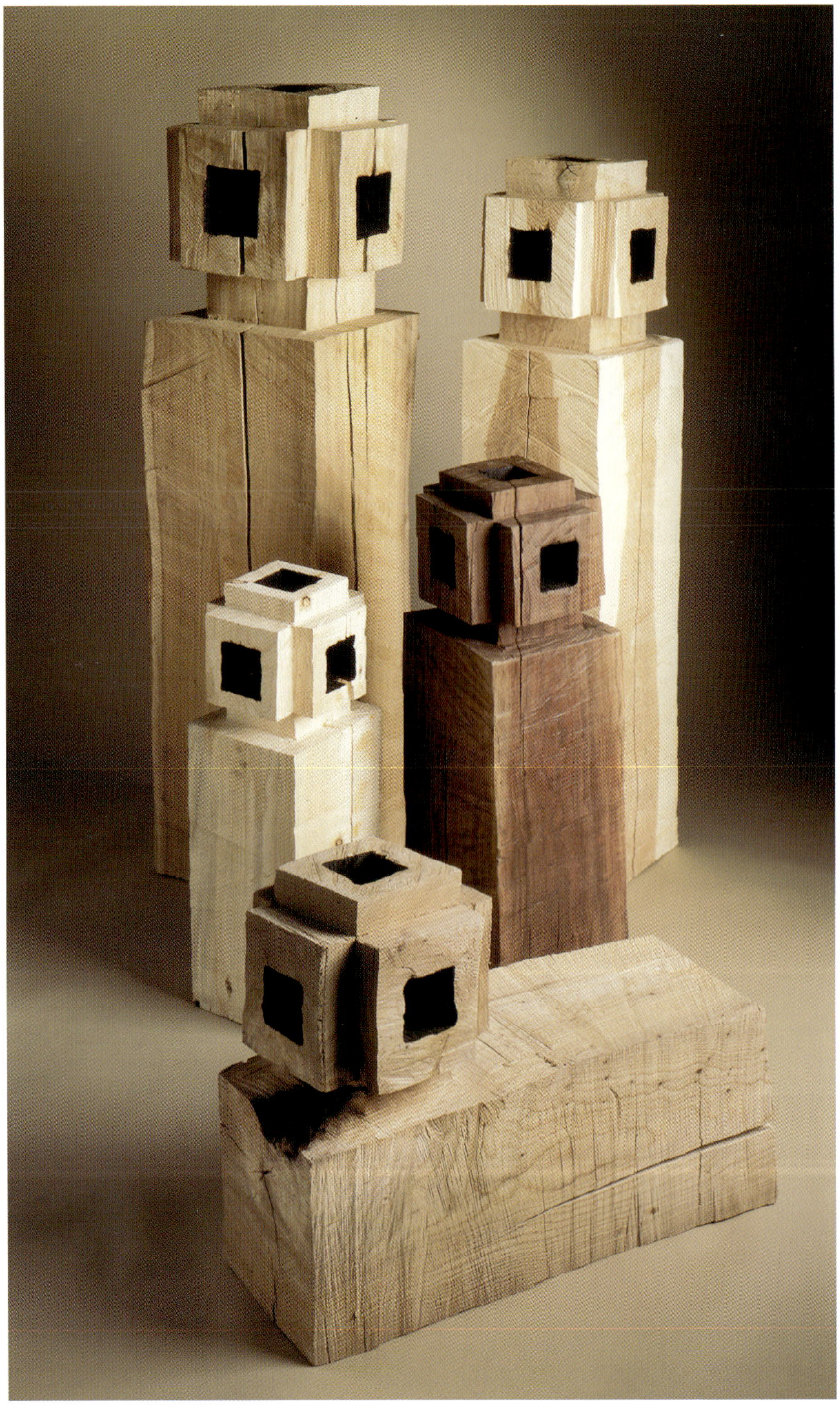

THE FAMILY UNIT, 2004
ELM, ASH & WALNUT
65 X 60 X 60 INCHES

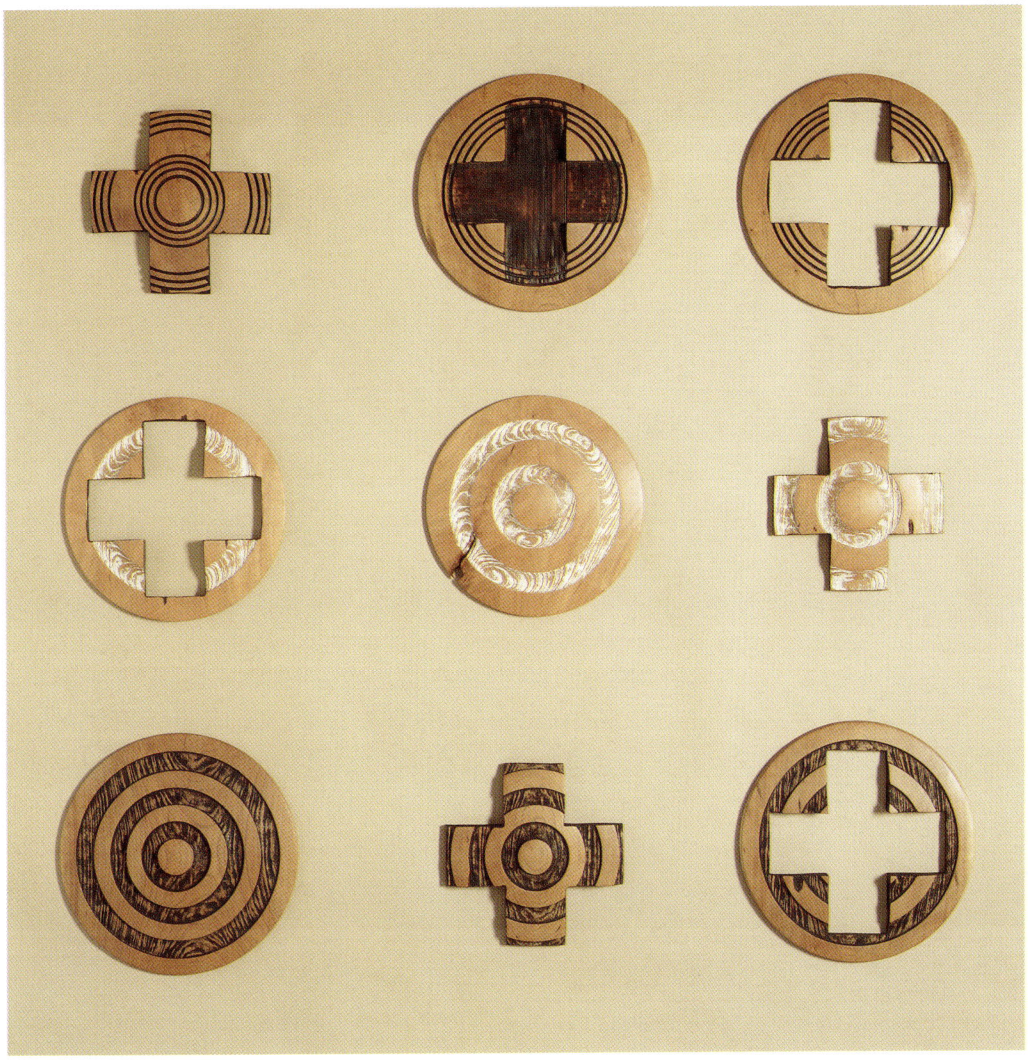

JACK R. SLENTZ b. 1963 Oklahoma City OK. *Ed.* MFA Univ. Memphis TN; MA Univ. Arkansas, Little Rock; B General Studies, Univ. Ozarks, Clarksville AR. *Coll:* Renwick Gallery of the National Museum of American Art, Smithsonian Institution DC; Minneapolis Institute of the Arts; Mint Museum of Craft and Design, Charlotte NC; Ogden Museum of Southern Art, New Orleans; Long Beach Museum of Art CA; Mobile Museum of Art AL; Museum of Art and Design, NY; Yale Univ. Art Gallery, New Haven CT; Arkansas Arts Center, Little Rock; Arizona State Univ. Art Museum, Tempe; Univ. Arkansas, Little Rock; Wood Turning Center, Philadelphia; John and Robyn Horn, Little Rock; Ron and Anita Wornick, Hillsboro CA; Sanford Besser, Santa Fe; Bob and Carol Warren, Santa Fe; Arthur and Jane Mason, DC; David and Ruth Waterbury, Minneapolis. *Representation:* Patina Gallery, Santa Fe.

TARGET, 2004
CHERRY
61 X 60 X 2 INCHES

GRETCHEN WACHS

Some are grounded. Some are in the air. Some move from where they are with the materials that come to hand. Earth is the first art medium. Imagine a whole art history of lost likenesses, abstract forms and functional entities made of mud, and long ago returned to mud. The discovery that fire and water, in conjunction with air, could transform clay into more durable forms is an early technological revolution.

In archaic Greece the word, techné, the root of technique, stood for both art and technology, meaning simply how things are done. Gretchen Wachs' clay work seems to originate from this kind of primacy, from an ontological respect for the human hand that makes, builds and discovers. Her process arises from an inner compulsion in tacto-visual connectivity with the earthly harmonics of color and form.

Her earliest art experiences happened in the realm of photography and printmaking. The latter remains an abiding passion. Wachs often exhibits prints alongside her spatial abstractions and enjoys printmaking workshops on her studio press with her son and his classmates. A largely unseen aspect of her abstract art are the ceramic cylinders she designs to stamp and pattern the clay slabs that go into her sculptures, after the manner of Mesopotamian messengers.

Yet, her towers resemble steles or signposts from a people whose native language is cubism. They have the presence of artifacts—objects that have endured the rugged past and survived—yet they engage space in a way that is quintessentially modern. Her forms assert themselves as simple sculptural volumes while their skins create a highly complex, pictorial space. These charged surfaces here reassert the sculptural presence of their support while there again denying it. This interplay of solid ceramic form with a Hoffmanesque shifting of planes, imagistic elements, and textural change produces the tension upon which the fine artwork of Gretchen Wachs hinges.

Her abiding obsession with the imaginary, multi-dimensional spaces of color, texture, figure, ground, light and dark, has in the past threatened to overwhelm her three-dimensional concerns, so her recent move towards paintings and collages as an investigation of purely artificial space is, like the rest of her work, paradoxically natural. It is as if the juxtaposition of earthbound structure and surface effects of color, light and texture have taught Gretchen Wachs their true differences in a way that few of us have known them. Her paintings represent the freedom that comes from hard won knowledge. Gretchen Wachs has moved in steady steps (art is long and life is short) and is now sprouting new wings. Where her flight beyond earthbound solidity will take her is anyone's guess. The pleasure for the viewer will be in watching how she inhabits the transcendent weightlessness of her new technology as she takes to the air.

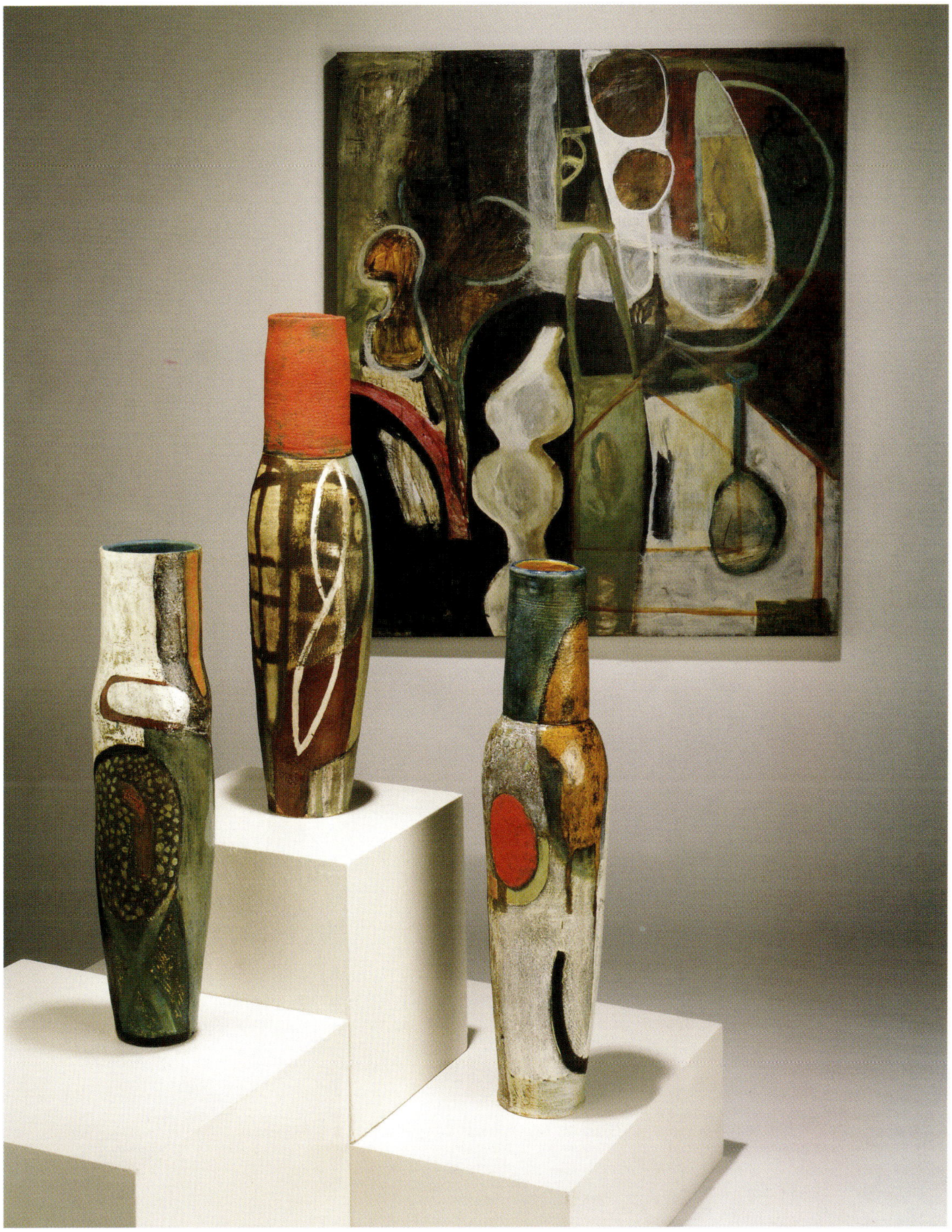

INSTALLATION
GLAZED CERAMIC VESSELS
7 X 27; 6.5 X 27; 6 X 24 INCHES

UNTITLED
ACRYLIC ON BOARD
42 X 48 INCHES

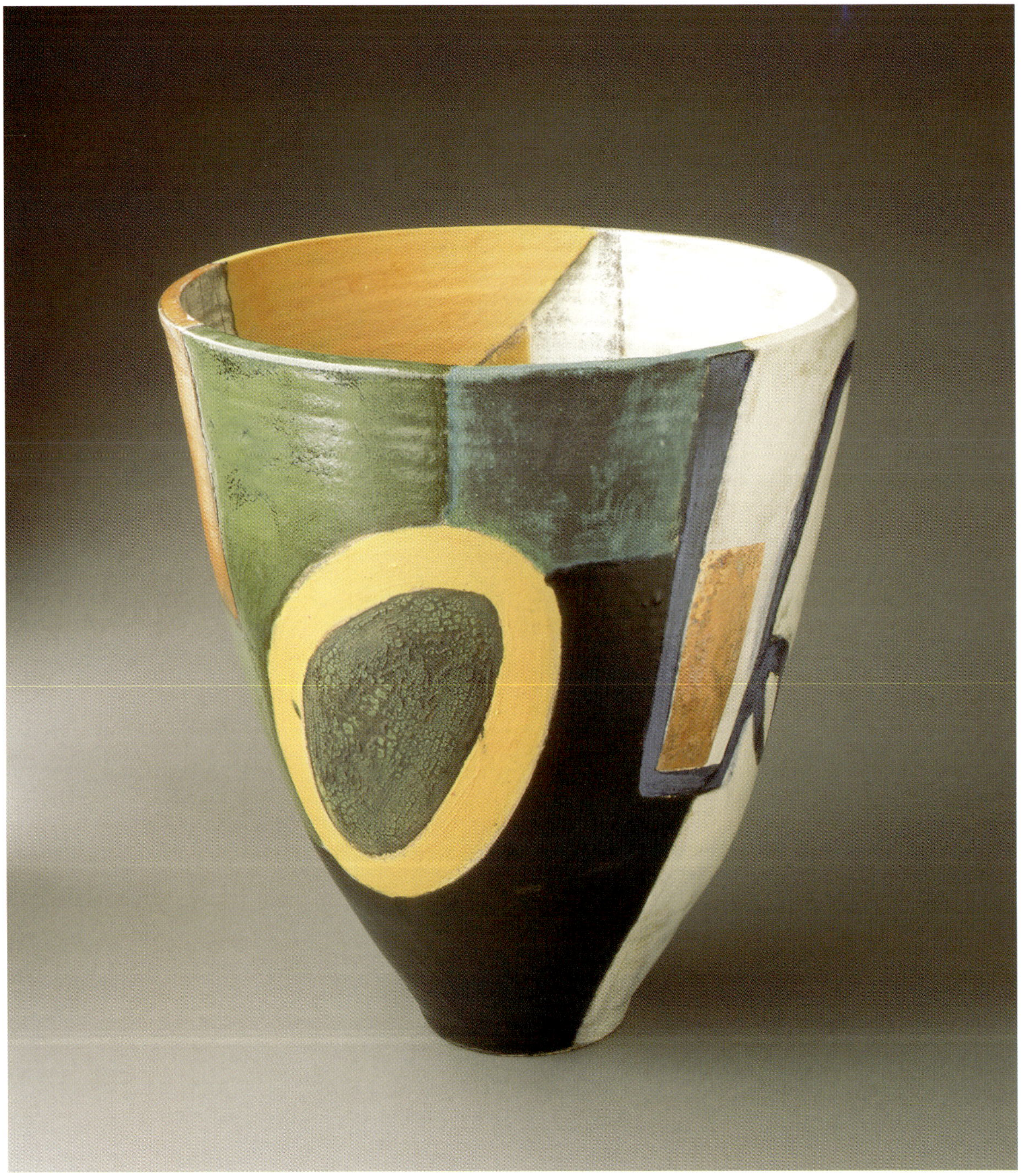

BOWL
GLAZED CERAMIC VESSEL
16 X 15 INCHES

GRETCHEN WACHS

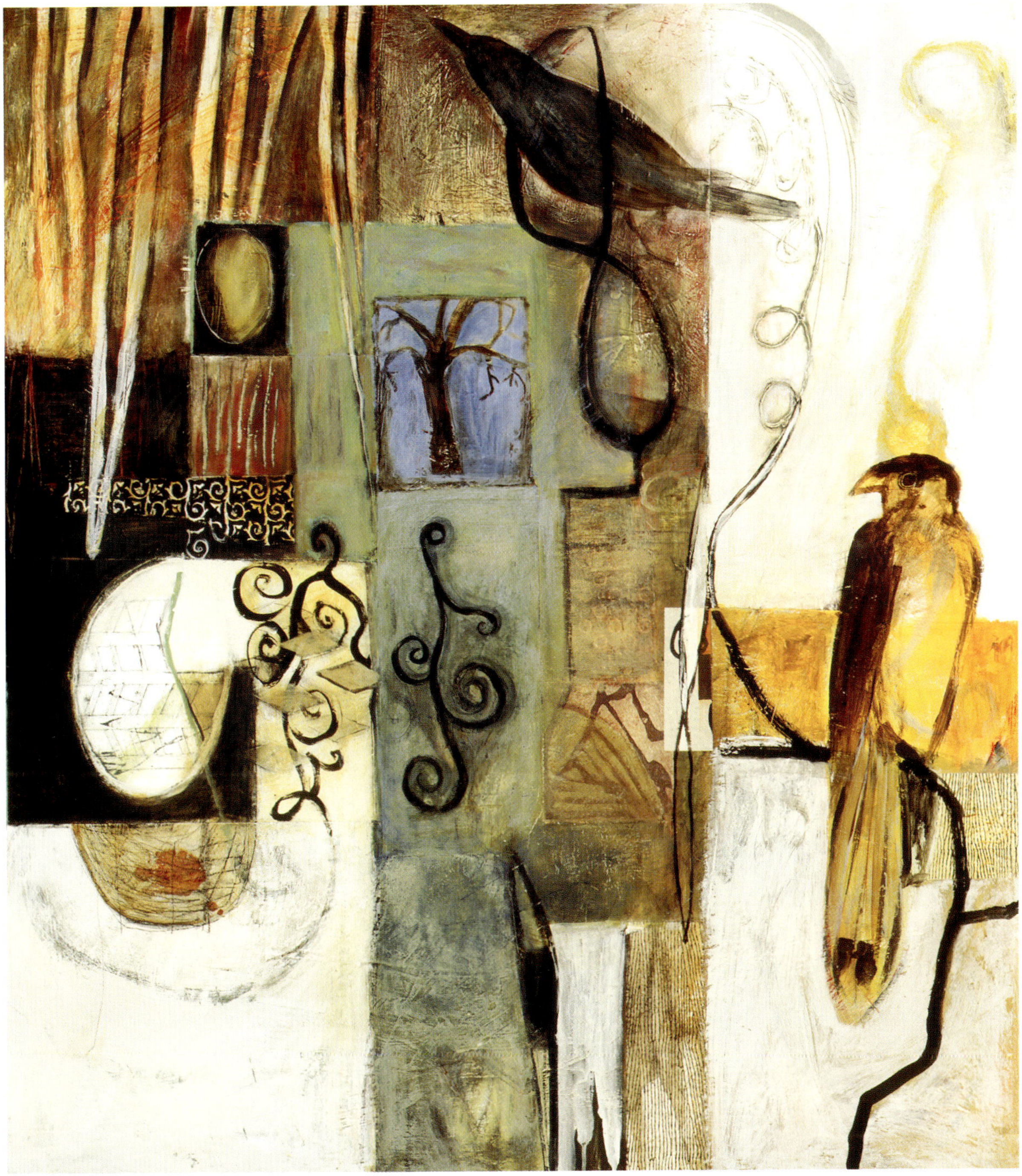

HOME
ACRYLIC ON BOARD
42 X 48 INCHES

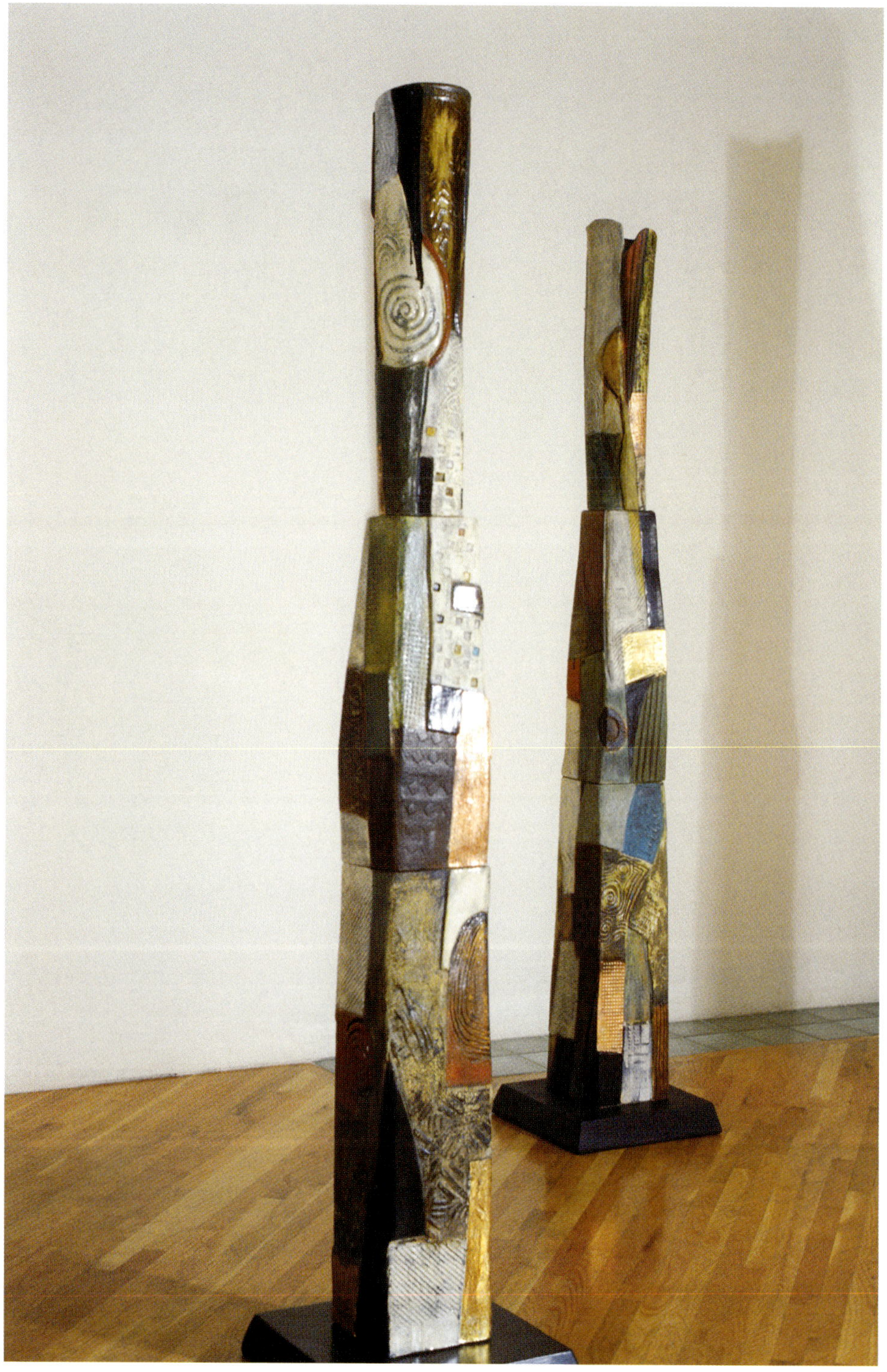

COLUMNS, 2001
GLAZED CERAMIC
92 X 18 X 17; 89 X 18 X 17 INCHES

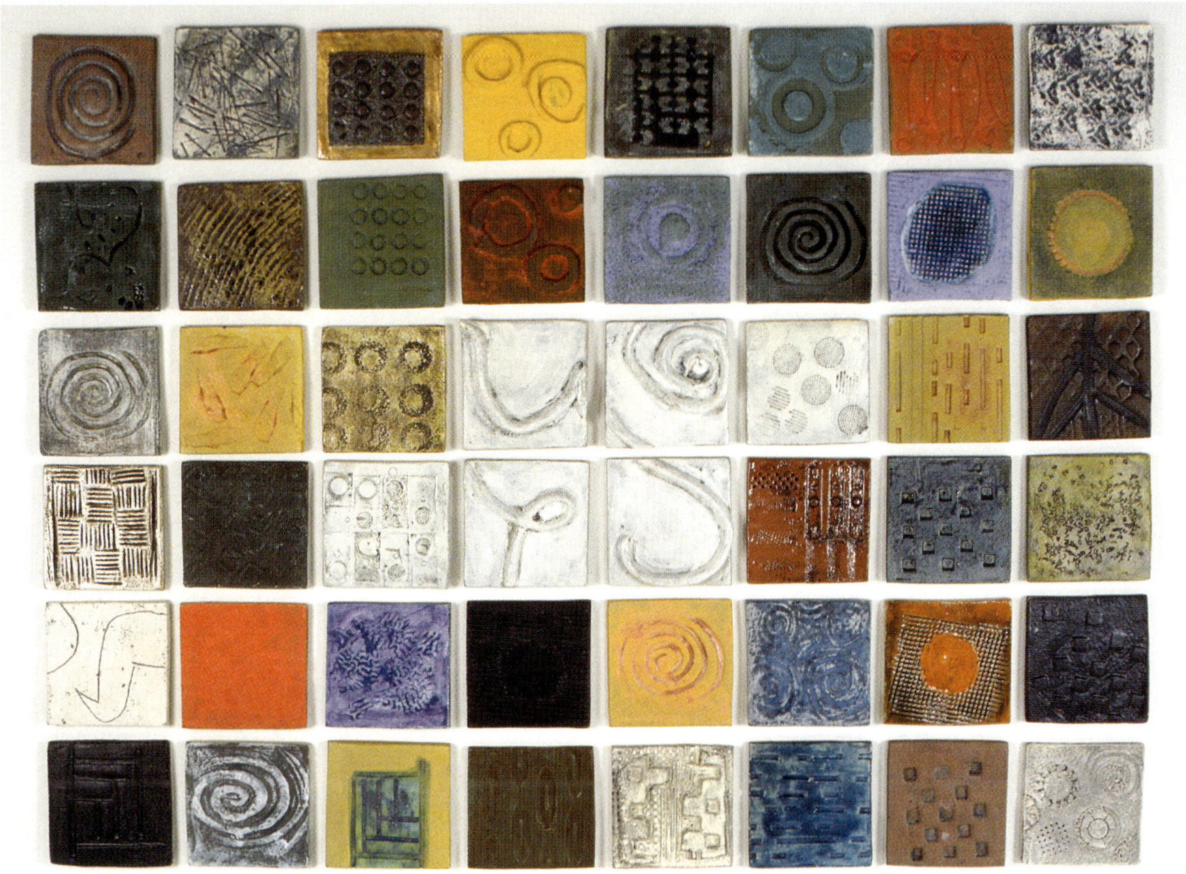

GRETCHEN WACHS b.1952 Hagerstown MD. *Ed.* MA Art Therapy, Southwestern College, Santa Fe; Santa Fe Art Institute; BFA Alfred Univ., Alfred NY; Maryland Institute of Art, Baltimore. *Coll:* Governor's Gallery, Santa Fe; Hallmark Cards, Kansas City MO; Glen Gate Co., Wilton CN; Stonehill Investment, New York; Santa Fe Community College; Canton Art Institute, Canton OH; Great Western Life, Denver; Synergen, Denver; COHBO, Denver; Texas Instruments, Denver; Kaiser Permanente, Denver; Littleton Hospital, Denver; Bixby Ranch, Los Angeles; Delta Airlines, Atlanta; Sky Tokyo, Japan; New Mexico Museum of Fine Art, Santa Fe; Consulate General of Japan, Denver. *Representation:* LewAllen Contemporary, Santa Fe; Anderson O'Brien Fine Art, Omaha NE.

TILES
GLAZED CERAMIC
38 X 52 INCHES

SABRA MOORE

We ride all in the same boat on a cosmic sea of multi-spiral intentionalities, which is our fate and our destiny. We are more void, more universal anti-matter, more time, than anything else—more nothing than something. We are multiplied atomic galaxies of whizzing electrons born on oceans of ever-shifting magnetic waves. Sabra Moore's boats are our bodies, our skeletons stretched with skin. We board them at birth for the journey home to the sea of the unseeable.

A palm reader searches your palm for points on the line of your fate. Your skin holds your history, your geography, your genetic code. Sabra Moore's history zigzags from Texarkana to a two-year stay in N'Zerekore, Guinea, to Birmingham, England as a Fulbright Scholar in West African studies to twenty plus years as an art worker and feminist activist in NYC. In the early 90s she and her husband built an adobe house amidst the colorful cliffs and *barrancas* of Abiquiu, New Mexico, where she currently lives and works.

Her mode of artistry derives from the reiteration she found in the work of the artists of West Africa of her grandmothers' Acworth, Texas quilting traditions. Both artistic realities encode personal stories in abstract patterning and both cultures practice hands-on communal artmaking. In neither is artmaking limited to a special class of artists, nor is any distinction made between arts and crafts.

Primarily, Sabra Moore is a maker. Working with juniper wood and other materials she finds around her Abiquiu home, she constructs a sophisticated art that defies categorization. There is no high or low art here; there is just the making of truthful objects. Many of her wooden surfaces are burned with text and images recording her personal experiences, interwoven with pointed questions about the fate of us all, and our teetering society. *We Are All In The Same Boat*, made of found rusted metal, bailing wire, wood branches, and oil paint, probably most easily encapsulates Sabra Moore's recent concerns, yet her artistic range is far more expansive than this implies.

What Sabra Moore offers the viewer is an honesty about materials and an earnestness of expression that is lacking in much contemporary art. Her visual, textual, and sculptural explorations of metaphor verge on allegory, and her message of respect for our individual histories, our environment, and all life are hard won and well earned in her powerful drawings, sculptures, and installations.

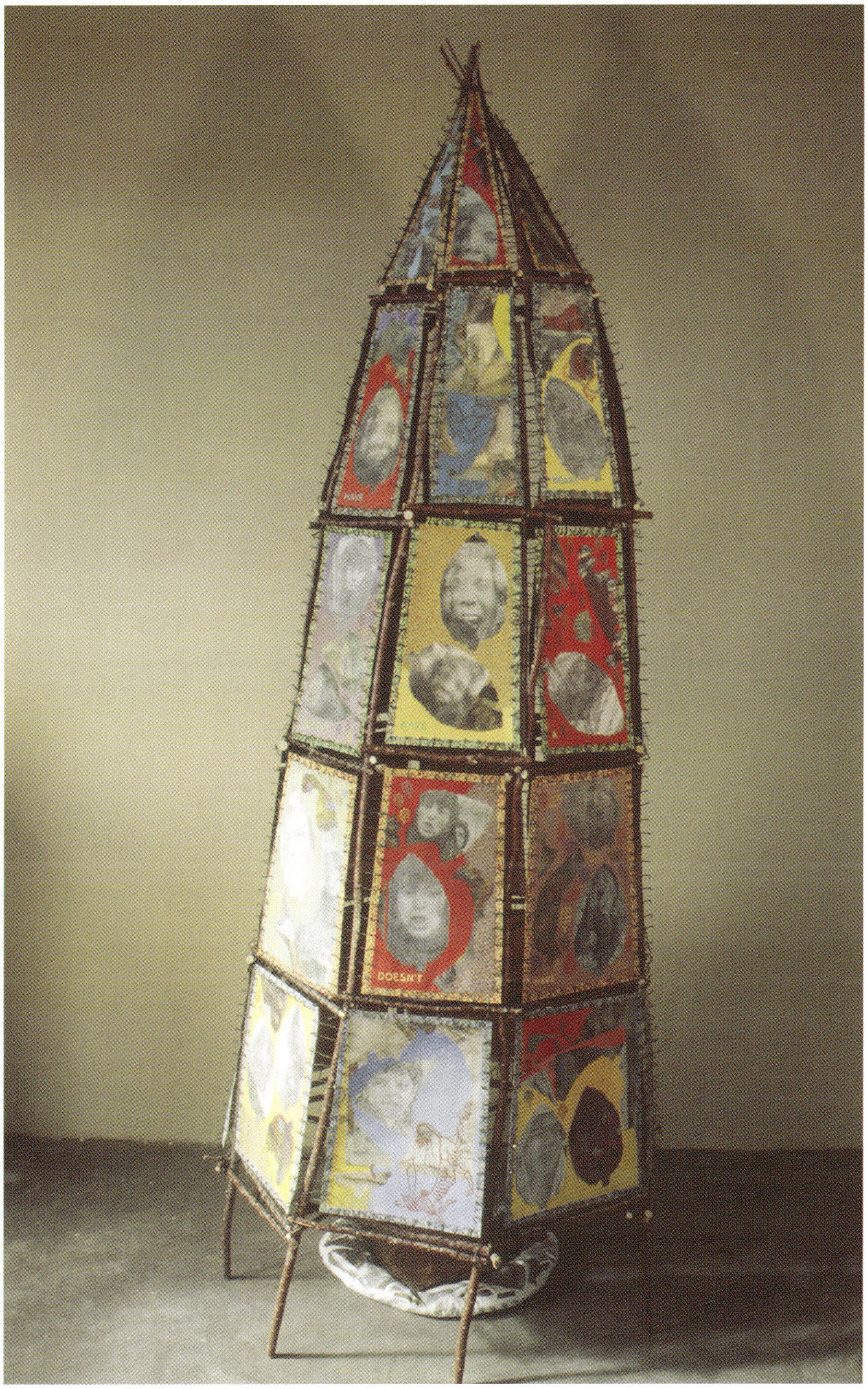

A WARHEAD DOESN'T HAVE A HEART, 2003
OIL ON GESSOED PAPER, TAMARISK
(SALT CEDAR) BRANCHES & WIRE
LASER TRANSFER PRINT
94 X 36 X 31 INCHES

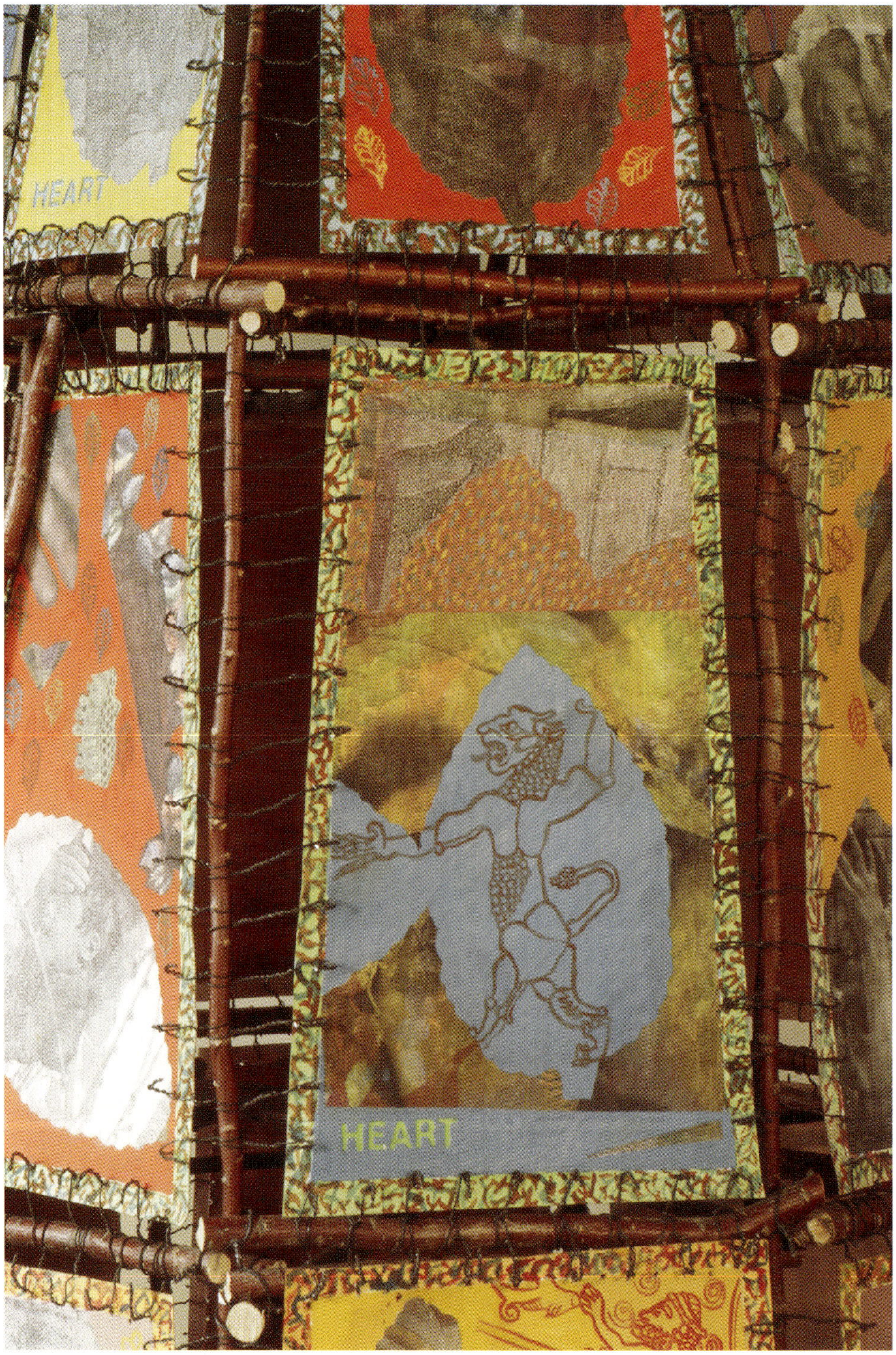

A WARHEAD DOESN'T HAVE A HEART, 2003 (DETAIL)
OIL ON GESSOED PAPER, TAMARISK
(SALT CEDAR) BRANCHES & WIRE
LASER TRANSFER PRINT
94 X 36 X 31 INCHES

SABRA MOORE

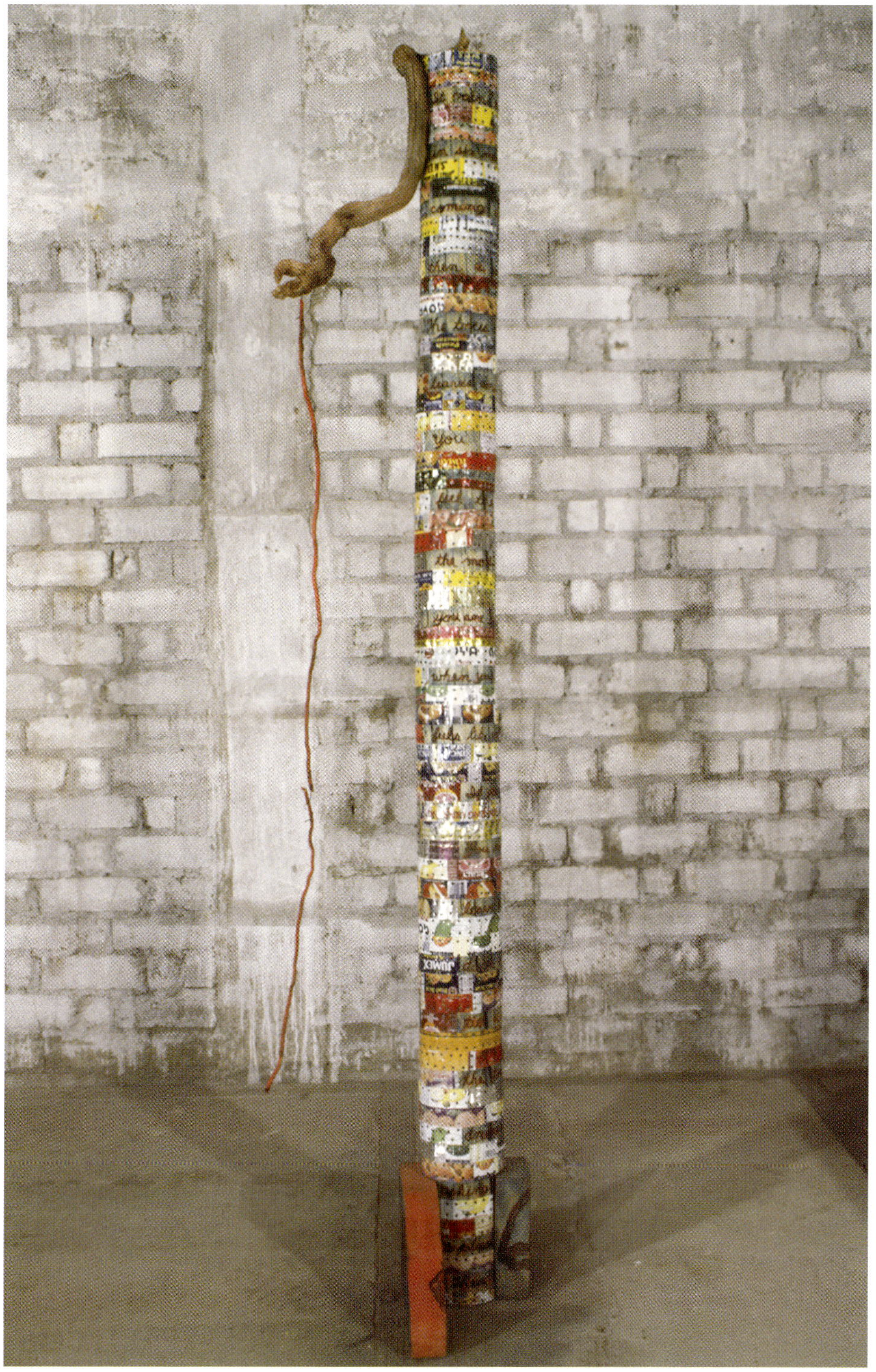

STRING TREE, 2000
81 X 244 X 6.5 INCHES
WOOD, METAL, OIL & TWIG

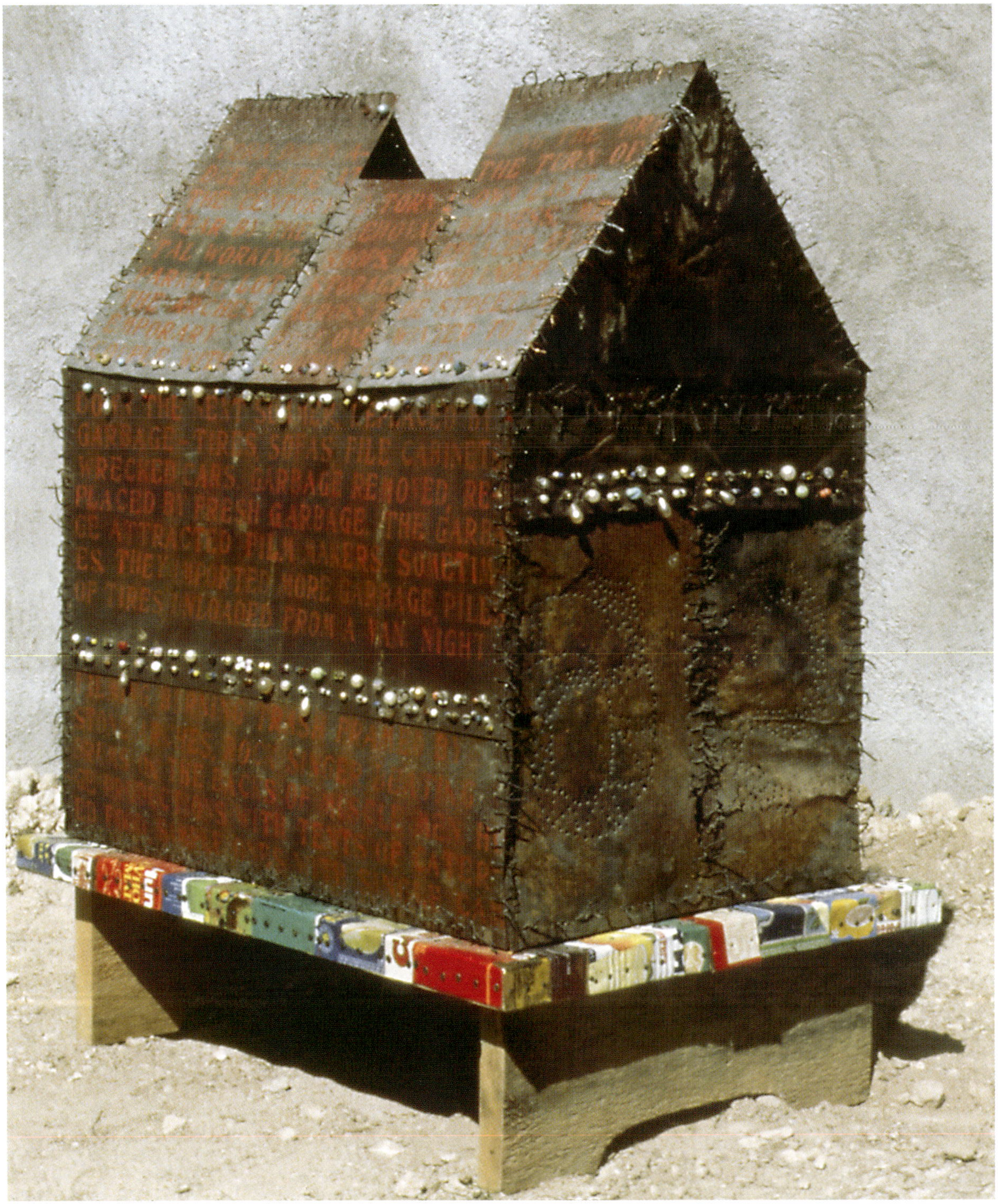

BRIDGE LOT HOUSE, 1994
FOUND METAL, WIRE, BEADS, OIL, WOOD
34 X 19.5 X 27 INCHES

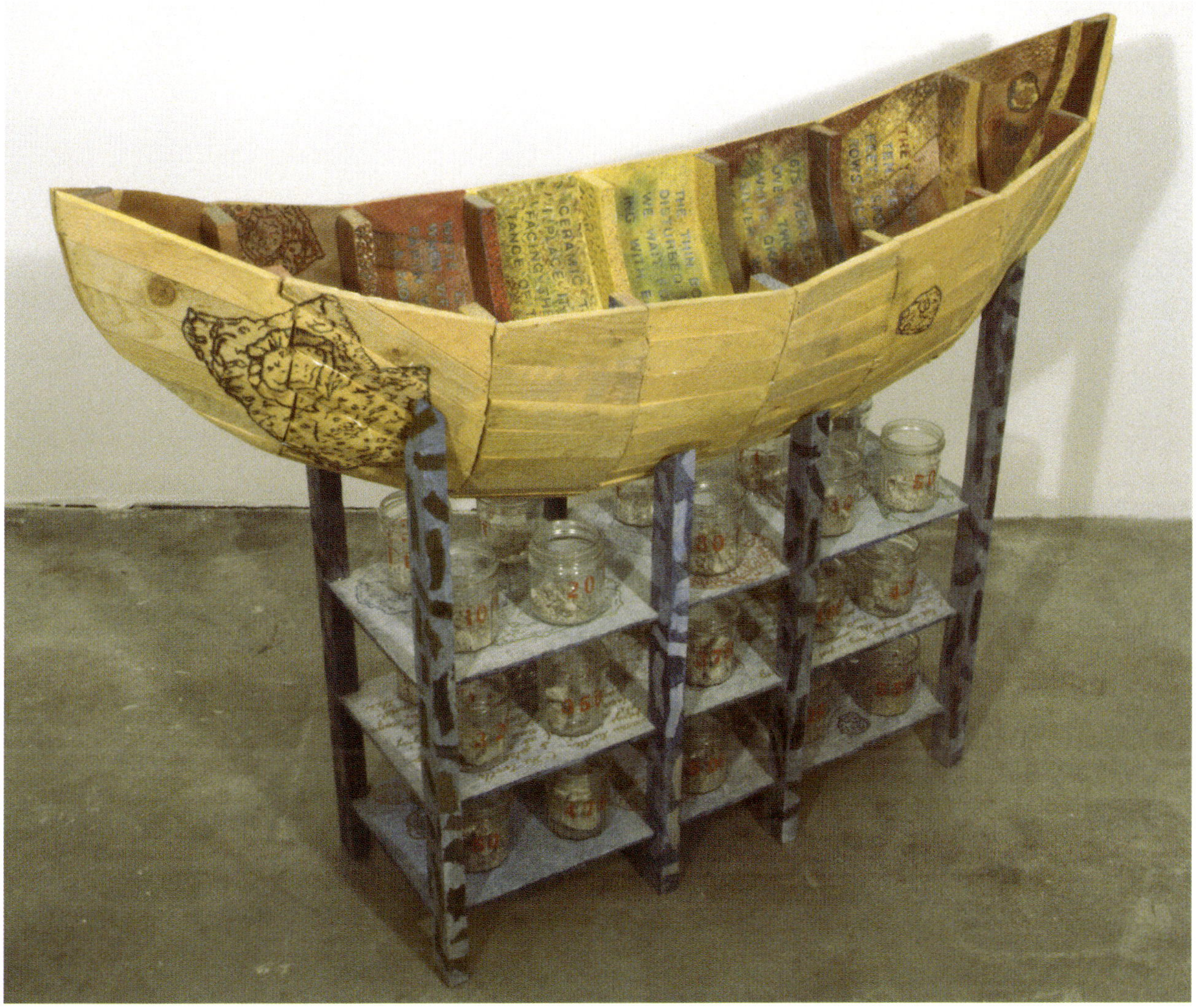

SABRA MOORE b. 1943 Texarkana TX. *Ed:* BA Cum Laude, The Univ. Texas at Austin; Brooklyn Museum Art School NY; Centre for West African Studies; The Univ. Birmingham, England. *Coll:* New Museum, New York; Brooklyn Museum of Art; California Institute of Art; Fine Arts Academy, New Delhi, India; Guggenheim Museum; Israel Museum, Jerusalem; Museum of Modern Art; National Museum of Women DC; Whitney Museum of Art.

RED RIVER BOAT, 1996
OIL ON GESSOED WOOD, GLASSES, DIRT
50.5 X 36 X 11 INCHES

INDEX

George Alexander
Handsel Gallery, Hudson, NY
www.handselgallery.com

Malcolm Alexander
Ventana Fine Art, Santa Fe
www.ventanafineart.com

Sally Anderson
Anderson Contemporary Art, Santa Fe
www.anderson-contemporary.com

Mary Bennett
EVO Gallery, Santa Fe
www.evogallery.org

Michael Bergt
Turner Carroll Gallery, Santa Fe
www.turnercarrollgallery.com

Mary Beth Bliss
Glory Hole Glassworks, Santa Fe
www.guadalupeglass.com

Braldt Bralds
Heidi Loewen Porcelain, Santa Fe
Seven-O-Seven Contemporary, Santa Fe
Lyon and Lyon Fine Art, New Orleans
Greenwich Workshop Gallery, Shelton CT
www.heidiloewen.com
www.seven-o-seven.com

Madelin Coit
EVO Gallery, Santa Fe
www.evogallery.org

Linda Fleming
Linda Durham Contemporary Art, Santa Fe
www.lindadurham.com

Lisa Freeman
Tadu, Santa Fe
Hand Artes Gallery, Truchas
Gallery Zipp, Glorieta
www.taducontemporary.com
www.LisaFreemanArt.com
handartes@la-tierra.com

John Geldersma
LewAllen Contemporary, Santa Fe
Jean Albano Gallery, Chicago
Marguerite Oestreicher Fine Art, New Orleans
Galerie R. Treger, Paris
www.lewallencontemporary.com

Doug Gray
Gallery 234, York, PA
717 854-7028

Sydney K. Hamburger
Von Schlegell Fine Arts
sydney@skhsculpture.com

Munson Hunt
Chiaroscuro Gallery, Santa Fe
www.chiaroscurosantafe.com

Tim Jag
www.timjagart.com

Jennifer Joseph
EVO Gallery, Santa Fe
www.evogallery.org

Tom Joyce
EVO Gallery, Santa Fe
www.evogallery.org

Shirley Klinghoffer
Klaudia Marr Gallery, Santa Fe
klaudiamarrgallery.com

Tracy Krumm
Linda Durham Contemporary Art, Santa Fe
www.lindadurham.com

Heidi Kujat
Studio Di Angeli, Santa Fe
www.heidikujat.com

Heidi Loewen
Heidi Loewen Porcelain, Santa Fe
Seven-O-Seven Contemporary, Santa Fe
Lumina Gallery, Taos; Human Arts, Ojai, CA
Fenton Fine Arts, Fort Worth Katie Gingrass
Gallery, Milwauke
Cynthia Drennon Fine Arts, Los Angeles
Memorial Art Gallery, Rochester
Lyon and Lyon Fine Art, New Orleans
C. Anthony Gallery, Beaver Creek, CO
www.heidiloewen.com
www.seven-o-seven.com

Susan Margin
Meyer-Munson Gallery, Santa Fe
Andora Gallery, Carefree, AZ
www.munsongallery.com
www.andoragallery.com

Sabra Moore
mandmarts@cybermesa.com

Priscilla Robinson
New Directions Gallery, Taos
Wally Workman Gallery, Austin
National Art, Houston
www.newdirectionsgallery.com
www.priscillarobinson.com

Gail Rieke
riekestudios@aol.com

Evelyn Rosenberg
evelynrosenberg@comcast.net

Andrea Senutovitch
Andrea Senutovitch Studio
Winterowd Fine Arts, Santa Fe
Barristers Gallery, New Orleans
www.Andrea-Volkoff.com
karlawinterowd@yahoo.com

Jack Slentz
Patina Gallery
Andora Gallery, Carefree, AZ
The Signature Shop and Gallery, Atlanta
www.patina-gallery.com
www.jackslentz.com

Peter VanderLaan
Glory Hole Glassworks, Santa Fe
www.guadalupeglass.com

Gretchen Wachs
LewAllen Contemporary, Santa Fe
Anderson O'Brien Fine Art Gallery, Omaha
Friesen Gallery, Sun Valley, ID
Robischon Gallery, Denver
Tercera Gallery, Los Gatos, CA
Trinity Gallery, Atlanta
www.lewallencontemporary.com
www.aobfineart.com

Tom Waldron
Linda Durham Contemporary Art, Santa Fe
www.lindadurham.com

Erika Wanenmacher
Linda Durham Contemporary Art, Santa Fe
www.lindadurham.com

James Westwater
James Kelly Contemporary, Santa Fe
Klaudia Marr Gallery, Santa Fe
Rule Gallery, Denver
Santa Fe Editions, Santa Fe
www.jameskelly.com
www.klaudiamarrgallery.com
www.santafeeditions.com
www.jameswestwater.com

Barbara Zusman
Linda Durham Contemporary Art, Santa Fe
www.lindadurham.com

PHOTOGRAPHY: CREDITS

23,25,26,27 Nick Merrick/Hedrick Blessing
24 John Michael Kohler Art Center
41-45 Eric Swanson
53,55 James Hart Photography
53,55 David Alfaya Photography
54,56,57 Daniel Barsotti Photography
65-69 Wendy McEahern
137 J. Schlesinger
138 Michael Garland
139,140,141,153 Herb Lotz
140 Erik Zipf: Video Still
149 Shirley Klinghoffer
150 Cathy Carver
151 Malcolm Varon
152 Kim Kurian

Aunt Mackey's Seduction Omelet
Madelin Coit
Page 137

Part I, Colloquial

To egg on
To have all of one's eggs in one basket
To tread upon eggs
To be a good egg
Egg head
Egg shaped
To have egg on one's face

The portion of life produced
by the females of a species

To form
To conceive
To beget
To begin

Part II, 1952

It was the smell of grain in the warm coop air. Specks of dust floated in light rays glancing off the layers' nests. Staggered bookshelves of nesting hens laying their eggs, eying her day after day, as she slipped her small hand under their soft belly feathers. Was she sneaky as she discreetly confused the issue with sweet water and fresh feed?
A thrift of theft before cackled outrage.

Part III, 1967

Mackey watched him move about collecting ingredients from shelves covered by old tea towel curtains. Her knees hit the cabinet; her heels cupped the stool rung. Her chin rested on the back of her hand and ground her elbow
into the counter. She watched him as her New England restraint drained unnoticed to the floor.

They ate fresh eggs fried in sweet butter, the yolk barely firm, the whites edged in crisp ochre lace.

Part IV, 2002

halved roasted fig	iron skillet
roasted sweet onion	sweet butter
sliced sauted porcini	sea salt
fresh fresh eggs	basil seed

Add butter to heated skillet. When a drop of egg sizzles, add remainder. Do not brown. Place onion, fig and porcini on one half. Fold other half over. Lower heat. Flip, Cook through, Plate. Sprinkle with sea salt and basil seed.

Savor on your south portal while the dogs sleep in the sun.

Don't talk.

XXX,

Mackey